ALTAI-HIMALAYA

A TRAVEL DIARY

Portrait of Nicholas Roerich by Svetoslav Roerich

ALTAI–HIMALAYA

NICHOLAS ROERICH

A TRAVEL DIARY

NICHOLAS ROERICH MUSEUM

NEW YORK   MMXVII

Nicholas Roerich Museum
319 West 107th Street
New York NY 10025
www.roerich.org

© 1929 by Corona Mundi, International Art Center, Inc.
© 1957 copyright renewed by Svetoslav Roerich.
© 2017 by Nicholas Roerich Museum.
First edition published 1929. Second edition 2017.

Cover illustration: Nicholas Roerich. *Stronghold of the Spirit.* 1932.

ISBN-10: 1-947016-21-0
ISBN-13: 978-1-947016-21-7

CONTENTS

INTRODUCTION *BY CLAUDE BRAGDON*   vi

I.   INDIA (1924)   15

II.   SIKHIM (1924)   45

III.   PIR-PANZAL (1925)   84

IV.   LADAK (1925)   98

V.   LAMAYURU–HEMIS (1925)   115

VI.   LEH–KARAKORUM–KHOTAN (1925)   140

VII.   KHOTAN (1925-1926)   173

VIII. TAKLA MAKAN–KARASHAHR (1926)   206

IX.   KARASHAHR–DZUNGARIA (1926)   266

X.   ALTAI (1926)   343

XI.   MONGOLIA (1926-1927)   360

XII.   TIBET (1927-1928)   375

GLOSSARY   404

INTRODUCTION TO THE FIRST EDITION

ON May 8, 1923, Nicholas Roerich left America for India, and he has been wandering about in remote, dangerous and seldom- visited parts of Asia ever since. "Altai-Himalaya" is the record of his mission, just as his series of pictures "Tibetan Paths," "Banners of the East," "His Country," are records in terms of paint. But "Altai-Himalaya," though penned on horseback and in the tent, under conditions the most difficult, is as much more, and as much richer than the ordinary diary of travel, as his paintings of the Himalayas are more than a literal transcription of some of the earth's most magnificent scenery. For in whatever medium Roerich works, or in whatever he is expressing, there shines forth not only the artist, but the embodied intelligence— *the man*, the whole character of the man. Though sincere and simple, it is a character compounded of such unusual elements as to be on its esoteric side uncomprehended.

Now, "esoteric" is to most ears either a meaningless or a hateful word: what do I mean by it in this connection? I should perform for Roerich an ill service if I failed to answer such a question, because it would be to avoid mentioning what seems to me the very *raison d'etre* of his journey, his art, his life. And yet how is it possible to make intelligible or even plausible what I have in mind? Without attempting to elucidate, explain or justify it, therefore, I shall simply say that there is a tenable point of view from which one may regard Roerich as an envoy of those powers which preside over the life and evolution of humanity in the same sense that gardeners preside over a garden: that he journeys into desolate and forbidden lands for the fulfillment of a mission the purpose of which will increasingly reveal itself. Whether one believes this or not, it would be hard to imagine a better ambassador of good will from the West to the East, for the reason that although he represents the summit of European accomplishment and culture, Roerich is deeply Oriental in his temperament, sympathies and point of view.

One has only to look at him to see—or, if you must have it so, imagine—the reincarnated Eastern sage. Certain it is that in India, in Tibet, in Ladak (Little Tibet), and in the white fastnesses of Siberia he was received with an honor, accorded a confidence and even an affection, quite different from the ordinary attitude of these peoples toward strangers, which has the reputation of being covertly or openly hostile. Roerich and his caravan encountered frustration and hostility, too, and in full measure, but it is interesting to note how exactly in proportion to the spiritual development of the various peoples he encountered was their response to his unique quality, and their recognition of the unprecedented nature of his mission among them.

This book was written "in the saddle," more literally than figuratively. There is a certain vividness, immediacy, authenticity about it for this reason, giving the reader a sense of actual participation perhaps impossible to be imparted in any other way, together with intimate glimpses of the workings of the author's mind in the presence of sublime scenery, new human types, strange manners and customs, and under the assaults of hardship, danger, and the stresses and strains of exploration in almost untrodden lands. Roerich is a man of original, strong and definite personality, of which everything he does bears the stamp. His expressions are themselves revealing, eloquent—not only of himself, but of the thing he is attempting to describe. The one-, two- and three-word sentences, the subjects without predicates—they have been suffered to remain just as he wrote them because they have so much the merit of the sketch, the jotting, put down in the moment of that "first fine careless rapture" which in a more premeditated form of art is likely to leak away.

This is a book whose surface exists for the sake of its depth, and even for concealing from all but the most penetrating, what that depth contains, as surfaces sometimes do. But in order to give you every possible advantage, and for your further enlightenment upon Roerich's antecedent accomplishments and life, I shall devote the remainder of this essay to what I have learned and know of Roerich, and what I think of him.

In the history of the fine arts, certain individuals have appeared from time to time whose work has a unique, profound and indeed a mystical quality which differentiates them from their contemporaries, making it impossible to classify them in any known category or to ally them with any school, because they resemble themselves only—and one another, like some spaceless and timeless order of initiates. Such were Leonardo, Rembrandt, Dürer, Blake, and, in other fields, Beethoven and Balzac; such also, in our own times and in a lesser way, were Rodin, Ryder and Burne-Jones, for their work shows flashes of that daemonic and eerie beauty which is the sign whereby they may be identified as belonging to that mythical mystic brotherhood.

Roerich, in his life, in his character and in his art reveals himself as a member of this fraternity. For thirty-five years—since the time of his first exhibition in Russia—he has been going up and down the world—Europe, America, Asia—absorbing the auras of diverse peoples, making pilgrimages to remote places, and always and everywhere scattering wisdom, planting seeds of beauty, some of which have sprung up, flowered, and scattered seeds of their own.

In Russia, as secretary of the Society for the Encouragement of Arts, and later as director of the school of that society, he was an important agent in organizing and coordinating that native, new and powerful impulse which in painting, in music, in the drama and in the dance later spread throughout the civilized world: for it is not too much to say that everything which now goes by the name of modernism had Russia for its cradle. It is significant in this connection that Stanislavsky enlisted Roerich's aid in the Moscow Art Theatre, that Stravinsky, dedicated to him the *Sacre du Printemps*, for which Roerich designed the original *mise-en-scène*, and that Andriev, Gorky, Mestrovic, Zuloaga, Tagore and others throughout the world who represent *the newness*, have paid him the tribute of their homage and their praise.

Coming to America with an exhibition of his paintings, at the invitation of the Chicago Art Institute, Roerich immediately took steps to resume and repeat the work he had inaugurated in Russia, that of uniting the arts, and thus uniting men through beauty, for he believed, as many others are coming to believe, that beauty is the universal and true solvent whereby racial and national animosities may be dissolved. To this end he founded, with the help of friends, a school in which all of the fine arts were to be taught, under the title of Master Institute of United Arts, and a year later he established Corona Mundi, an International Art Center. The school passed through those vicissitudes which usually beset enterprises of this character in a civilization such as ours, the best image of which would be a rush-light in a wind-swept darkness—but it survived, and has to-day a permanent home on Riverside Drive, New York. Other vast outlines, sketched by Roerich at this time, have not been filled in: they include Cor Ardens, an affiliation of the creators of beauty everywhere throughout the world, and Alatas, an international, non-commercial publishing association for the interchange and dissemination of new and constructive ideas through the mediumship of the "art preservative."

I mention these enterprises to show the vast sweep of Roerich's vision, to indicate his function as a prophet and a pioneer, clearly foreseeing and quietly planning a better order in a world still in the grip of its so recent terrible nightmare, not yet risen from a bed drenched with blood and stained by tears.

Should his prophecies come true, and should his dreams of binding humanity into a brotherhood through beauty materialize, it is for this that he will doubtless be most honored and longest remembered, but to us, his contemporaries, he is naturally best known as a painter of hauntingly beautiful pictures. These are of all kinds and on a vast variety of subjects, but in general they represent nature strained through a mystical consciousness —the light that is on sea and land translated, by some potent magic, into the light that never was on sea or land. Roerich satisfies the idealist without affronting the realist. Mukerji, the Hindu novelist and poet, remarked to a friend that if he wanted to know how the Himalayas impressed a beholder, he should see Roerich's paintings of them, because along with a true rendering of their form and color, something of their spirit was communicated too.

After a brief sojourn in America he forsook the ordered and easy life of cities, and unappalled by the rigors, dangers and difficulties of such a quest, he set out for Asia, "trailing clouds of glory" as he went, so to speak, in the shape of paintings of the Grand Canyon, the Santa Fe country, the Pacific, India and the Far East. The culmination of his life work, up to the present, is in those groups of paintings named by him "The Tibetan Path," "Himalaya," and "Banners of the East." These are freighted with mystical meanings which, even though unintelligible to all save the initiated, yet act upon the unenlightened consciousness as does perfume upon the senses, or as music upon the emotions. It is not that Roerich attempts to be deliberately cryptic—on the contrary, a great deal of his symbolism is almost naive in its simplicity—but the average mind so resents the very idea of esotericism, that it closes itself to a certain extent.

Roerich's symbolism, as I say, requires no glossary, possessing the characteristics of directness and universality. An example of his general method is seen in that painting of what he names the Messiah series, entitled, "The Miracle." It represents a titanic valley, not unlike the Grand Canyon, a world primeval, stark, rock-strewn, without visible flora or fauna. Prominent in the foreground is a natural bridge, and over this bridge passes a road. On the near side of the bridge are a few human figures, prostrate before the miracle of a great radiance coming from behind the bridge, the aura of some supernatural presence whose figure is not yet visible. Here is a simple, natural symbology subject perhaps to different interpretations, but none of them contradictory. Considered objectively, the picture is simply a dramatization of that expectancy of a messiah which is so general nowadays, and it holds forth the healing promise, that though his presence is not seen, his aura brightens the darkness, his influence is already felt. Considered from the standpoint of subjectivity, the denuded valley might symbolize the condition of the soul after trials and purgations; the road, the "small old path" to freedom and perfection; the bridge, that stage on that path where the transit is effected between the lower and the higher consciousness; the prostrate figures, those "qualities" which must be redeemed and "carried over," awe-struck at the miracle of the felt approach of the "golden person" bringing release from bondage through the shining of the inward light.

But the great merit of this picture, freighted as it is with meaning (and that of others of its class), lies in its beauty of color and composition. The mystic and metaphysician in Roerich never submerge the artist, with the result that when he permits himself the use of symbols he is still lyrical and not literary: his pictures are not sermons, but songs. "The Miracle," despite the fact that it conveys a message, is not a morality so much as a delight to the visual sense, abounding in spatial rhythms and color harmonies as line and subtle as those of some priceless old yellow Chinese rug. The "story" is there, but the final indelible impression is one of beauty, and this is as it should be, for in the hierarchy of trades and talents the creative artist is nearest to the throne of God.

Of Roerich's archaeological pictures I shall not speak, nor of his pioneer work in the theatre, important as that has been, because I feel that these things, which at one time absorbed his mind and dominated his consciousness have since become far less important to him than what I shall call his *mystical quest.* One has the feeling that in everything he does he is seeking the hidden truth, the unrevealed beauty, the Lost Word, in point of fact. Like some mighty indefatigable hunter, armed not with a gun, but with his pen and brushes, he stalks his quarry across oceans, rivers, mountains, though knowing all the while that the thing he is seeking is in himself. Both in his writing and in his painting he permits us to participate in this adventure, and thus draw nearer to that truth which is beauty, and that beauty which is truth.

CLAUDE BRAGDON

ALTAI–HIMALAYA

A Travel Diary

PART I

INDIA

(1924)

SINAI glides by. Here are the Wells of Abraham. Here are the "Twelve Apostles"—fantastic little islands. Here is Jeddah, the gateway to Mecca. The Moslems on the steamer are praying toward the East, where, behind the pink sands, is hidden their center. To the right the boundaries of Nubia are lying like an ancient cornice. The hulks of wrecked vessels cleave to the reefs. The Red Sea can be merciless as can the Arabian sandstorms. Not in vain does the fiery finger of the Stromboli Volcano threaten and warn by night. But now in the winter the Red Sea is blue, not hot, and the dolphins leap in mad merriment. In a fairylike design lie the Arabian Bays—Korya Morya.

. . . . .

The Japanese do not lose an opportunity to visit the Pyramids. This nation does not waste time. One should see how quickly and sharply their field-glasses move about. And how persistently practical are their questions. Nothing superfluous. This is not the vacant touring of tired Europe. "Well, now finally we will come to an understanding," says the Japanese in a businesslike way without any sentimentality. And may this businesslike attitude be the guarantee of cooperation!

. . . . .

In Cairo in the mosque sat a boy of seven or eight and chantingly read the lines of the Koran. One could not pass by without noting his penetrating striving. And in the walls of that same mosque was boldly imbedded the cannon-ball of Napoleon. And that same conqueror of empires broke the image of the Great Sphinx.

But if the sphinx of Egypt is mutilated, the sphinx of Asia remains safeguarded by the great deserts. The treasures of the heart of Asia are preserved and its hour has come.

. . . . .

Ancient Ceylon—the Lanka of the Ramayana. But where are the palaces and pagodas? It is strange. In Colombo we are met by the Swiss Consul. The policeman is Irish. A French peddler. A Greek with post-cards. Dutch tea-peddlers. An Italian chauffeur. But where are the Singhalese? Have they all emigrated to Europe?

. . . . .

The first aspects of Buddha and Maitreya reveal themselves in the Kelaniya Temple near Colombo. The powerful images are guarded in the dusk of the temple. Hinayana prides itself before many-varied Mahayana on the refinement and purity of its philosophy. The great restored stupa near the temple reminds one of the ancient foundation of this place. But, after all, only in fragments do Colombo and Ceylon recall the ancient Lanka of Hanuman, Rama, Ravana and other giants. And for Buddhism, Ceylon is an important site. Many temples and palaces guard the fragments of one of the best periods of the Teaching. Outside of the ruins which are known, numerous unsuspected treasures are buried under the roots of powerful jungles. That which has remained above the soil gives an idea of the past splendor of the former mighty city. You do not need to search for the places. They proclaim themselves. But exploration can only give results if it is carried on in a broad measure. One must approach such ruins fully fortified, as one palace alone has nine hundred chambers. Ceylon is an important site.

. . . . .

The public baths near the bitter-sweet mountain, Lavinia, do not suggest the domain of ancient giants. Slender palms shame-facedly bend down to the spray of the tide. Like skeletons stand the fragments of Anuradhapura; consider that Anuradhapura is not entirely explored. And Adam's Peak is not enticing. By the remains of Anuradhapura one may judge how powerful was Borobodur in Java.

. . . . .

And again, ceaselessly, are gliding by the faces of our fellow travelers: the Japanese, with whom we wept over the remains of the Cairo Pyramids, which have passed from a valiant history to become the curio-museum of a greedy guide.

. . . . .

Is it really India? A thin shore line. Meager little trees. Crevices of dessicated soil. So does India hide its face from the south. And the black Dravidians as yet do not remind us of the Vedas and Mahabharata.

. . . . .

Multicolored is Madura with the remains of Dravidian strata. All the life, all the nerve of the exchange, was near the temple. In the passages of the temple are the bazaar, the court, the sermon, the reciter of the Ramayana, the gossip, and the sacred elephant who wanders in freedom; and the camels of the religious processions. The ingenious stone carving of the temple is colored with the present-day crude colors. Sarma, the artist, sorrows over it. But the city council did not listen to him and colored the temple according to their own plan. Sarma is saddened that so much of fine understanding is gone and has as yet been replaced only by indifference.

He warns us not to go far in our European attire because some elements of the population may be hostile. After all, Madura is a city of one million. Sarma inquires about the condition of artists in Europe and America. He is genuinely surprised that the artists of Europe and America can live by the labor of their hands. It is incomprehensible to him that art can provide a means of livelihood. With them, the occupation of artist is the most profitless one. There are almost no collectors. Sarma himself, tall, in white garments, with sad, calm speech, awaits something better, and knows all the burden of the present.

. . . . .

There was no possibility of a meeting with Tagore. Strangely such things happen in life. In London, the poet found us. Then in America we succeeded in meeting him in New York; and he also met George in Boston. But in India itself we did not meet! We could not go to Bolpur and Tagore could not be in Calcutta. He already was preparing for his tour in China.

There were many curious occurrences. In Calcutta we tried to find Tagore. We thought that in his native city his name would be known on every corner. We took a motor and requested to be taken straight to the poet Tagore, and in vain we rode for three hours through the city. First we were taken to the Maharajah Tagore. Then a hundred policemen and peddlers and passing *Babus* sent us into the most varied alleys. Finally six volunteer guides were hanging on our motor. And so we ourselves, in this bushy manner, finally remembered the name of Dwarkanath Tagore Street where the house of Tagore was situated.

It is said that when Tagore received the Nobel prize, a deputation from Calcutta came to him, but the poet severely asked them: "Where were you before? I remain the same person, and the prize has not added anything to me." Greetings to Tagore!

. . . . .

We met the relations of our friend Tagore—Abanindranath Tagore, brother of Rabindranath, artist head of the Bengal School. Gogonendranath Tagore, nephew of the poet, also an artist, secretary of the Bengal Society of Artists. Now he imitates the modernists. A splendid artist is Kumar Haldar, present Director of the School in Lucknow. Hard is the life of the Hindu artist. Much resolution is needed in order not to abandon this thorny path. Greetings to the artists of India! Why is it that in all countries of the world the condition of scientists and artists is so precarious?

· · · · ·

Thorny also is the way of the Hindu scientists. Here, before us is an example, in a struggling young scientist Bose Sen, a biologist and pupil of Sir Jagadis Bose. He began his laboratory in the name of Vivekananda. In his peaceful little house above the laboratory is a room dedicated to the relics of Ramakrishna, Vivekananda and other teachers of this group. This young man, pupil of the closest pupil of Vivekananda, carries into life the principles of this master, who fearlessly proclaimed his evocation to action and knowledge. In this little top chamber he formulates his thoughts, surrounded by the things which belonged to his beloved leaders. One remembers vividly the portraits of Ramakrishna and his wife. Both faces impress one with their purity and striving. We sat in complete silence near this memorial hearth. Greetings!

· · · · ·

Who can explain why the path of knowledge and beauty is the most difficult? Why does humanity accept with such hesitation all that is predestined? It is therefore the greater joy, to see in India, the signs of an ascent of knowledge and art. It is joyful to see that in India the number of schools is increasing and that legions of new enlightened workers for science and beauty are ready to serve in the victory of evolution.

· · · · ·

In Calcutta, not far behind the city, are two monuments to Ramakrishna. On one shore, Dakshineswar, the Temple where long lived Ramakrishna. Almost opposite, across the river, is the Mission of Ramakrishna, the mausoleum of the teacher himself, of his wife, of Vivekananda, and a collection of many memorable objects. Vivekananda dreamt that here should be a real Hindu University.

Vivekananda took care of this place. There is a great peace here and it is with difficulty that one realizes oneself so near to Calcutta with all the terror of its bazaars and confusion.

We met Sister Christine, almost the only living pupil of Vivekananda. Her useful work was broken up by the war. And now, after the lapse of many years, Sister Christine has returned again to the old site. The people are changed. The consciousness is consumed with local problems. And it is not easy for Sister Christine to find contact with the new waves of Hindu life.

On the memorial day of Ramakrishna, as many as half a million of his admirers gather.

. . . . .

From the purest to the most hideous. In special streets of Bombay, behind bars, sit the women prostitutes. In this living merchandise which clings close to the bars, in these outstretched hands, in their calls, is contained the whole terror of bodily desecration. And a Hindu Sadhu passes through with his burning incense in order to purify the spot!

. . . . .

When we entered the Chartered Bank of India— the sacred cow came out of the door to meet us; and how strikingly amusing was this correlation of bank and sacred cow!

. . . . .

The tigers roar in Jaipur. The Maharajah has forbidden any one to shoot them. In Golta Pass two tribes of monkeys are at war. The guide arranges a battle for a most reasonable fee. Nowadays all battles may be arranged thus easily!

The Fakirs are seated, "charming" the old, half-living toothless cobras. The pitiful Hatha-yogi is whirling in the bazaar, performing his gymnastic contortions for the purification of his spirit. "The spiritualist" offers to make the carriage move without horses, but to do this it is necessary "that there should not be one cloud in the sky."

. . . . .

And along with this is a fantastic and romantic fragment of old Rajputana—Amber where the princesses looked down from their balconies upon the tournaments of their suitors; where every gate, every little door, astonishes one by the correlations of its beauty. Near here is the penetrating and fantastic Golta Pass which could not be imagined in any fantasy—only the "play" of life can accumulate such unexpected creations. And here also is Jaipur with its fairylike astrological observatory and with the charm of an unspoiled Hindu Moslem city. Fatehpur-Sikri, Agra—rare chips of a departed culture. And the frescoes of Ajanta are already unsafe.

. . . . .

All the remains of the constructions of Akbar have a veil of seeming sadness. Here the great Unifier of his country buried his best visions so misunderstood by his contemporaries. In Fatehpur-Sikri, he conversed with his wise Birbal, and with the few who had attained his level. Here he built the temple of universal knowledge. Here he lost his few friends and foresaw that the welfare of the State created by him, would not be preserved. And Agra and Fatehpur-Sikri are full of a kind of limitless sorrow. Akbar knew how the well-being which he bestowed on his people would be pillaged. Perhaps he already knew how the last emperor of India would live to the middle of the nineteenth century, peddling the furniture of his palace and chipping from the walls of his palace in Delhi the fragments of mosaics.

. . . . .

With all the dustiness gathered by time, the architecture of Benares still retains its charm. All the mixture of form of the old Hindu, Dravidian and Moslem, can give new solutions to the unprejudiced architect. One can easily imagine a combination of the many-storied Tibetan structure, with the comforts of an American sky-scraper. One can draw a parallel from the palaces of Benares to the palaces of Venice and to a livable private dwelling. One can develop the style of American pueblos, with the newest understanding, as is being done in Santa Fe.

. . . . .

A Hindu complained to me of the lack of Hindu architects. I said to him, "If there are no architects, let an artist develop an idea, but let him proceed from out of the harmony of the folk consciousness combined with the character of its nature." The whole world must not be defiled with some generic bungalow. One cannot make out of Java a Swedish Stockzund. And one cannot visualize Comanches and Apaches in the houses of Boston. Commensurability must be observed.

. . . . .

On the shores of the Ganges, a gray-bearded man, cupping his palms like a chalice, offers his entire possessions to the rising sun. A woman counting quick rhythm performs her morning pranayama on the shore. In the evening she may again be there, sending upon the stream of the sacred river a garland of lights as prayers for the welfare of her children. And these fireflies of the woman's soul, prayer-inspired, travel long upon the dark watery surface. Beholding these offerings of the spirit one can even forget the stout priests of the golden temples. We are minded of other things. We recall those Yogis who send into space their thoughts, thus constructing the coming evolution. Not the usual priests these, but active hermits; they are bringing our thought near to the energy which will be revealed by scientists in the very near future.

. . . . .

Gigantic stupas of Buddhism—burial mounds surrounded by a fence. The same Kurgans of all centuries and nations. The Kurgans of Upsala in Sweden; Russian

Kurgans of Volhov on the way to Novgorod; the Steppe Kurgans of Scythians, surrounded by stones; all tell the legends of the same solemn cremations which have been described by the skillful Arabian traveler, Ibn Fadlan. Everywhere, the same purifying conflagrations.

.   .   .   .   .

Everywhere, much incense, rose water and fragrant sandalwood. Hence the smoke from the bodies in the Burning Ghats of Benares is not turbid. And in Tibet, also, cremation is used.

.   .   .   .   .

Regard the gentle child games of the Orient—and listen to the complicated rhythms of the chants and soft music. There are not evident the profanities of the West.

.   .   .   .   .

The Maharajah of Mysore is awakened with special songs—songs of beginning and of end.

.   .   .   .   .

In Madura in a crowded alley, an old man models the forms of the "sacred images." He is the last old man—with him dies this knowledge. Thus is dying the past. So is approaching the future.

.   .   .   .   .

On the fields are standing, in circles, the figures of white ceramic horses. Whence are these resplendent mounts? Upon them, the subtle bodies of women are said to go galloping through the nights. Backs, which are doubled during the day in household tasks, at night are made erect in flight. Shall one say it is a goat's leap to the gathering of witches? No, rather is it the flight of the Valkyries—the virgins of the air—the leap toward a wondrous future.

Each day a woman's hand molds the sand at the entrance of the house into a special design. This is the

symbol that within the house all is well, and there is neither sickness, death nor discord. If there be no happiness
in the house then the hand of the woman becomes stilled.
A seeming shield of beauty is placed before the house by
the hand of the woman at the benevolent hour. And little
girls in schools early are being taught a variety of designs
for the signs of happiness. An inexplicable beauty lives in
this custom of India.

. . . . .

Vivekananda called the women of India to work and to
freedom. He also asked the so-called Christians, "If you
so love the teaching of Jesus why do you not follow it?"
So spoke the pupil of Ramakrishna who passed through
the substance of all teachings and learned through life
"not to deny." Vivekananda was not merely an industrious
"Swami"—something lion-like rings in his letters. How he
is needed now!

. . . . .

"Buddhism is the most scientific and most cooperative
teaching," says the Hindu biologist, Bose. It is a joy to hear
how this truly great savant who found his way to the mysteries of plant life speaks about the Vedanta, Mahabharata,
and about the poetry of the legends of the Himalaya. Only
true knowledge can find the merited place for all existing
things.

And accompanying the voice of the savant, simple and
comprehensive, the silvery tones of an electric apparatus
tinkle out the pulse of the life of the plants, reopening
pages of the world's knowledge, long since sealed.

Bose's mother in her day sold all her jewels in order
to give her son an education. The scientist, in demonstrating "His kingdom," says: "Here are the children of the
rich in luxurious conditions. See how they become puffed
and baggy. They need a good storm to bring them back to
healthy normalcy." Knowing the pulse of the plant world,
the scientist approaches wholesomely all the manifesta-

tions of life. He values highly Timiryaseff's review of his works. One of Bose's best books was written on the heights of the Punjab in Mayavati—in the shrine of Vivekananda. Vivekananda departed too soon.

Bose and Tagore—noble images of India!

. . . . .

The frescoes of Ajanta, the powerful Trimurti of Elephanta, and the gigantic stupa in Sarnath, all speak of other ancient times. And this former beauty also glimmers in the fine and slender silhouette of a woman who carries her eternal water—water which feeds the hearth. And the well, as in biblical times, remains the central spot of the whole population.

. . . . .

In the very backyard, in a tiny bed of meager flowers, rests a homely image of Ganeshi, elephant of happiness. The family of Hindu coolies living in the shanty offers to him its last grains of rice. Not much happiness has this image brought to them.

. . . . .

Against the evidence of such refined values as are seen in Ramakrishna, Rabindranath Tagore, Sir Jagadis Bose, one cannot become reconciled to that which still constitutes the contents of the temples. Here is a phallic cult—Lingam in Elephanta. Up to now in the sanctuaries of this cult are seen the traces of fresh offerings. From the ancient wisdom we know that "Linga is the vessel of knowledge" and we know the scientific explanation from times immemorial of this wise distribution of energy. But now the basis of this worship is forgotten and it has degraded into superstition.

Another ugly spectacle! In a golden temple of Benares, before us, was led a white little goat. She was led into the sanctuary. There evidently she was approved of because in a little while, frantically protesting, she was hurriedly dragged before us. In a minute, she was stretched out on the threshold of the temple and the broad knife cut off her head. It was difficult to believe that a sacred action had taken place! The meat of the goat evidently went for food, because priests do not partake of any meat except that of offered sacrificial animals. And such animals the population evidently brings each day. The teaching which sanctioned the priests, evidently pictured them as quite different. Even their appearance is undecorative and they cannot guard the beauty of the symbols of knowledge. As long as the rule of castes is not comprehended properly the country cannot develop.

During our stay we read of several difficult family dramas founded on this ground of an evidently surviving prejudice. At the same time, the Vedanta and Advaita clearly establish the principle of unity. Some of the most cosmogonic parts of the Vedas are written by women, and now in India has arrived the epoch of the woman. Greetings to the women of India!

. . . . .

In spite of a superabundance of tourists they seem to know America very little. One can understand this. The whole mass of tourists quickly flows through the sheet-iron channels of tourist companies, and never enters into a real and active contact with the life of the country. In the north of India, Americans are called "nomads" because the agencies give to these hurrying, breathless groups a special character, completely outside of the people's understanding.

Out of the windows of the car glide by huddled little villages, those original producers of all utilities and the makers of the nation. But who cares for these primary sources?

. . . . .

Ramakrishna says: "In Atman there is no distinction of male or female, of Brahmin or Kshatriya and the like."

Ramakrishna executed the work of the sweeper to show, personally, that there were no distinctions.

.　.　.　.　.

In December, we want to go into the Himalayas. We are regarded with astonishment: "But now there is snow!" Snow is feared. Whereas the only time for the Himalayas is from November to February. Already in March the curtain of fog rises. From May to August only rarely and for brief periods can one see the entire glimmering range of snow; and truly such grandeur is nowhere paralleled.

.　.　.　.　.

Just as when you are approaching the Grand Canyon of Arizona, when you approach the foothills of the Himalayas you go through the most uninteresting landscape.

And only for a moment, at dawn in Siliguri, do the white giants appear before you as the first messengers. And again they are hidden in the curly jungles. And again tea plantations. And again barrack-like structures and factories. And only sometimes does a typical habitation appear and conceal itself again as a vision from another world. There are tales about the attacks of tigers and leopards. There are mountains of cases of tea with the mark, Orange Pekoe. There is a Belgian missionary from Kurseong.

It becomes cool. Crowds of small coolies are repairing the cave-ins from the last monsoon. In the frosty air one cannot imagine the pressure of the summer monsoon downpour from which all nature becomes moldy. There are few birds. Eagles are seen.

.　.　.　.　.

Mountains are densely covered. The view of Darjeeling itself disappoints you. Is it necessary to seek the Himalayas in order to find merely a corner of Switzerland? The colorful types of the bazaar are not apparent at once, and the regular barracks and bungalows already strike one's eye.

Wesearch for a house. The first information is not encouraging. We are assured there are no good houses. Some are shown to us, lacking outlook and grounds, some immersed in the little streets of wooden country houses and fences. This is not suitable. We want something, beyond—there before the image of all the Himalayas, where the city orchestra does not play its conventional tunes. "You will find nothing there!" But we are persistent. We go ourselves, and we find an excellent house. And calmness and solitude, and the entire chain of Himalayas before us. And still another surprise. Just here lived the Dalai Lama during his long flight from Lhasa. For us, this house is just what is needed.

Not on one occasion only were we awakened by the chanting and the rhythmic beats around the house. These are the lamas who, bowing to the ground many times, marched around our dwelling.

Somewhere the people are babbling that in this house lives a devil which appears as a black pig. A haunted house, as we were told. But we are not afraid of devils, and in the neighboring village, Bhutia Basti, there are many black pigs which resemble boars. Did not our dear monkeys who came into the bathroom and ate the peas and flowers around the house play the part of the devil?

There is the tiresome need of having many servants—and the reason always the same: castes. It reaches absurdity. The porter does not clean the path. Why? It appears that according to caste, he is a blacksmith and has no right to take a broom into his hand. Otherwise he will become defiled and become a sweeper. He decides the problem in a very original fashion. He begins to brush around the garden with five fingers, creeping along the ground. The groom is from the high Kshatriya caste and hints at his descent from a king, which did not hinder him from mysterious operations with the horse feed. Sometimes in the kitchen religious meetings are arranged. And the cook, chairman of the local Arya Samaj, persistently persuades his listeners to something. Buddhists are not limited by caste and are free to perform all kinds of work. They work fast, are merry, are quick to understand and easy to adapt themselves.

There are many tales about Tibetans, the warrior-like tribe of Kham and about the wild Goloks, who call themselves wild "dogs." They bring one back again even to the times of Siegfried. They cement their brotherly oaths by mixing and drinking brotherly blood. They never part with their weapons.

"His Country" begins to unfold, as the series "Banners of the East" is begun. In June, after the first rains, all the tempera begins to be covered with white spots of mold. One has to heat up the place considerably in order that the mold should dry and come off.

· · · · ·

"His Country." In Sikhim, itself, was one of the Ashrams of the Mahatmas. To Sikhim, Mahatmas came on mountain horses. Their physical presence communicates a solemn importance to these parts. Of course now the Ashram has been transferred from Sikhim. Of course now the Mahatmas have left Sikhim. But they were here, and therefore the silver peaks of the chain glimmer still more beautifully. . . .

· · · · ·

Accompanied by pupils, artists and a sculptor, comes the majestic Rinpoche from Chumbi. He walks throughout the whole country erecting new images of Maitreya. All is being hastened. In a long talk, the lama points out that all may be attained only through Shambhala. For those who imagine Shambhala as a legendary invention, this indication is a superstitious myth. But there are also others, fortified by more practical knowledge.

· · · · ·

The noble Atisha, the Pillar of the teaching, walked from India to Tibet for the purification of the teaching.

The teacher passed by the retreat of Milarepa. The great hermit became conscious of the passing procession and wishing to test the forces of the Pillar of the teaching, appeared sitting on the end of a blade of grass. The noble Atisha seeing this manifestation of the hermit, came down from the porte-chaise and also rose upon the end of the next blade of grass. And when the teachers exchanged brotherly greetings, Milarepa said: "Our knowledge is equal, but why is the blade of grass under me slightly bent, while under thee, it has retained its tension?" The noble Atisha smiled: "Verily, equal is our knowledge; but I come from the country where the Blessed Tathagata himself lived and taught, and this consciousness raises me."

. . . . .

What magnets are laid in India? Indescribable is the charm of the children's round dance near Madras, with its tiny Gopis and miniature Krishna, Lel and Kupava. The greatest imagery is bestrewn in unperceived abundance. India knows the all-penetrating power of the magnet.

. . . . .

And how about miracles in India, friends of the west will ask? We will say that we have not seen "miracles," but we have encountered every manifestation of psychic energy. If one wants to speak about the manifestations of a "higher miraculous" power—then it is useless to talk altogether. But to comprehend the materially-attained development of psycho-physical energy, then India gives even now the most remarkable manifestations. The celebrated "evil eye" of the east exists, and the people die submissively at the ordained date, if they are not able to counteract it by a still more greatly trained will. The transmission of the command of will from a distance does exist. Suggestion in any form exists in highly complicated correlations. Some manifestations are being performed consciously and a greater part subconsciously through natural ability and beneficial atmospheric conditions. And that which is unusual for a civilized European, that very thing for the cultured Hindu, or rather Asiatic, will be an almost daily material occurrence.

. . . . .

Observe how remarkable are the physiological comparisons traced by the Hindus between cosmic manifestations and the human organism. The womb, the navel, the phallus and the heart, all these long since have been included in the fine system of development of the universal cell. Only it is difficult to entice the people into a discussion of this. Again is necessary that confidence which cannot be established at the dining table.

During the period of Inquisition people were burned for invoking the teraphim. But in India even now this means of influence is practiced. Even now, in the Malabar Hills, dark persons may come and because of an unfulfilled request will try to touch you, while they say to you: "Sahib will be sick" or "You will live only ten days." If the organism at that moment is fatigued or if the will is weak, the command is fulfilled, and one can remedy this only by a counter-suggestion. But often the counteraction is less powerful or not applied in time.

The cases related about the "evil eye" provide a remarkable, and as yet unstudied, problem for the psychiatrists and criminologists. The person who has received this stroke of the will, on the appointed day begins to lose his life energy and his power of resistance and finally the apparatus stops. The doctors who do not apply suggestion in time are at loss for a cure, and begin to poison the paralyzed nervous system still more. Incipient anaemia, a stroke of the heart or spleen, or gall bladder, nervous spasms and choking are often the visible effects of the command of the invading will. It is difficult to ascertain just how the nature of the attack on the particular organs occurs; one may rather imagine that the most feeble organ succumbs to a nervous attack. In a lesser and more crude manner the same practice is apparent in Shamanism, but the gradations of the will and its applications are entirely incomparable. It is justly pointed out that such murder or harm by will power is far more dangerous than a physical one. And where can one seek the limits of such suggestions? In the East one sometimes hears a significant sentence: "He shall not live." It means one has sensed the spark of the will-stroke.

. . . . .

Two qualities must be conceded to the English: steadfastness and precision. For the East, both qualities are remarkable. Precision according to the ordained dates of course is absolutely necessary because "the worst theft is the theft of someone else's time." Do not be late if you wish to be respected.

. . . . .

It all began with the strange footprints found by the Everest Expedition. Then in the *Statesman,* an English Major related how during one of the expeditions into the region of the Himalayas, he encountered a strange mountain inhabitant. At sunrise, amidst the frosty snows, the Major walked away from the camp and climbed the neighboring rocks. Glancing at the near-by rocks, the Major to his astonishment beheld a tall man almost naked, standing, leaning on a high bow. The mountain inhabitant did not look at the Major, his attention being completely attracted by something unseen behind the curve of the slope. And suddenly the man bent, strained himself, and by madly dangerous leaps rushed from the rocks and disappeared. When the Major told his people about the meeting they smiled and said: "Sahib has seen a 'snow' man. They are watching the guarded places."

. . . . .

They tell of a recent case in Bengal. A Sadhu was traveling in a train without a ticket. At the first station he was put out of the train. The bells rang. The locomotive whistled and did not move. So it continued for some time. The passengers remembered the Sadhu who had been put off and demanded that he be put back in his place. Then the train moved. Some serious mass impact!

. . . . .

A European lady living in India entered a dense part of her garden and became lost in a reverie as to why the garden walks were not laid out in that place. Three days later she went there again and saw a freshly traced path, but the end of the path was somewhat lost. She called the old gardener:

"Who has made the path?"

"Mem-Sahib wanted to have the garden path but I did not know how to end it!"

Then the woman remembered that the completion of her thought about the garden path was not clear.

. . . . .

Sir Jagadis Bose affirms that the sensitiveness of plants is completely astonishing. As the plants feel the formation of a cloud long before it is visible to the eye, so the East feels the thought at its inception.

. . . . .

In the close interrelation between the visible and the invisible, and in the epic simplicity of their interplay, lies the charm of India.

. . . . .

The Tibetan tailor is making *kaftans*. He takes all measurements with his eye, but most astonishing is it that the *kaftan* comes out well-fitting. And all this is not done without care! The quality of gold for the trimming, the color of the lining and the length—all this is thought out. The local homespun is very narrow and one is astonished how evenly they can smooth the many seams.

. . . . .

If we take the accredited historical data of the last century it is astonishing how definitely the folk-consciousness was freed from the obvious survivals of the middle ages. Those who defend such survivals should examine these historic paths and convince themselves and realize that what is occurring now is not accidental but under rational guidance and control. He who fails to recognize this rationality, cannot understand evolution.

. . . . .

In sudden support of fundamental Buddhism, the realist of realists, Huxley says, "No one but a superficial thinker rejects the teaching of reincarnation as nonsense. Like the teaching of evolution itself, reincarnation has its roots in the world of reality and is entitled to the same support commanded by every consideration which evolves from analogies."

. . . . .

Two beautiful characterizations of Buddhism: "As a lion unfrightened by noises. As a wind, not to be captured by a net. As a lotus leaf impervious to water. As a rhinoceros treading in solitude!"—"The study and manifestation of energy in all its forms. Energy of armament. Energy of application in action. Energy of dissatisfaction giving birth to the eternal striving which brings man into the cosmic rhythm." So said Asanga.

Where, then, is the inactive pessimism? Where is the philosophy of despair, as Buddhism is sometimes called by persons of small comprehension. How many books have been written under the false romanticism of the nineteenth century? How many scientists, not versed in the languages, have fed their minds with these vague sour conclusions? But at last we now have a different Buddha—with a sword, with leonine daring, armed with all energies amidst universal activity, in cosmic aspiration.

· · · · ·

"Watch the movement of the stars, as one who participates in them, and constantly consider the transmutation
of one element into another, because such a process purifies one from the grime of earthly life." So reflects Marcus
Aurelius. So also says an educated Hindu from out the
Himalayas.

· · · · ·

L. Horn writes: "With the acceptance of the teachings
of evolution, the old forms of thought everywhere are
crumbling. New ideas arise in the place of outlived dogmas and we have before us the spectacle of a general
intellectual movement in a direction becoming ever more
strange—parallel with eastern philosophy.

"The unheard-of speed and variety of the scientific progress current in the last fifty years cannot but call forth an
equally unprecedented hastening of thought in the broad
non-scientific circles of society. That the highest and most
complete organisms develop out of the simplest organisms;
that upon one physical basis of life stands the whole living
world; that there cannot be traced a line which divides
animal and vegetable kingdoms; that the difference
between life and non-life is a difference in gradation and
not substance—all this already has become commonplace
in the new philosophy. After the recognition of physical
evolution it is not difficult to say that the acknowledgment
of psychic evolution is only a question of time."

· · · · ·

The observation of the East astonishes and rejoices one.
And not the obvious power of observation which leads to a
dead stereotype; but observation, fine and silent in its substance. One remembers how the teacher asked the newly
arriving pupil to describe a room, but the room was empty
and in a vessel was swimming only a tiny fish. In three
hours the pupil wrote three pages, but the teacher rejected
him saying that about this one little fish he could have

written all his life. In technical imitation is revealed the same sharp observation. In the adaptation of the meter of a song, in the character of a call, in movements, you see an all-powerful culture. Somewhere the Hindus, enveloped in their mantles, were compared to Roman senators. This is an inane comparison. Rather liken them to the philosophers of Greece, and still better, call them the creators of the Upanishads, Bhagavad-Gita, Mahabharata. For neither Rome nor Greece existed when India was flourishing. And the latest excavations begin to support this indubitable deduction.

. . . . .

In the Tao Te Ching are drawn the following subdivisions of the types of scientists: "Scientists of the highest class, on hearing about Tao, seriously bring their knowledge into life. Scientists of the middle grade, on hearing about Tao, sometimes observe it, sometimes lose it again. The scientists of the lowest class on hearing about Tao, only laugh loudly at it." Lao Tze knew.

. . . . .

Hindus regard objects of art with fine understanding. From a Hindu, you naturally expect an interesting approach and unusual remarks, and so it is. Therefore to show paintings to a Hindu is a real joy. How captivatingly they approach art! Do not think that they are occupied only in its contemplation. You will be astonished by their remarks about tonality, about technique, and about the expressiveness of the line. If the observer be long silent, do not think that he has become tired. On the contrary this is a good sign. It means he has entered into a mood, and one can expect from him especially interesting deductions. Sometimes he will tell you a whole parable. And there will be nothing vulgar or crude in it. It is astonishing how transformed are the people of the East before the creations of art. Indeed it is more difficult for a European to enter into the current of creation and as a rule he is less able to synthesize his impression.

· · · · ·

In the epic designs of India all can be coordinated. If in the crowd, your next neighbor should be a skeleton, pale with leprosy, you are not frightened. Next to you will lean a Sadhu, colored with blue stripes and with a head-dress made of cow dung. You are not surprised. A Fakir with toothless cobras will cheat you. You are smiling. The chariot of Jagernath crushes the crowd—you are not aston-ished. There is a procession of fearful Nagis of Rajputana with blades like curved fangs. You are calm. And where are those for whose sake you have come to India? They do not sit in the bazaars and they do not walk in processions. And you will not enter their dwellings without their consent. But do they really exist? Are not leisurely authors writing about them only for the sake of being unique? Yes, they do exist. Their knowledge and their skill do exist. And in this sharpening of human qualities is being exalted all human substance. And no leprosy will turn you away from India.

· · · · ·

All that takes place at the metapsychical institute in Paris—the experiments of Nötzing and Richet in ecto-plasm; the experiments of Baraduque in the photography of physical emanations, the works of Kotik in the exterior-ization of sensitiveness and the attempts of Beckhterev in thought-transmission at a distance—all this is familiar to India. Only, not as unbelievable novelties, but as laws long since known. They speak little on these themes, because of the dearth of scientifically enlightened fellow-conver-sationalists. The ancient method of Hinduism and Bud-dhism is to open the doors to him who knocks, but not to call any one and not to coerce any one. But the quality of the knock also must be powerful. In the practical teaching of Buddhism, independence of consciousness is sharply emphasized, and as its consequence, an unconquerable forbearing and all-conquering patience. The greatest patience will win a victory. So let the ignorant deniers immerse themselves in the true East to learn to absorb the power of containment.

. . . . .

Two characteristic episodes are related about the Tashi Lama. When he was in India, he was asked whether he possessed any psychic powers. The Tashi Lama silently smiled. In a short time, though closely surrounded by guards and officers, he suddenly disappeared. All search was in vain. Finally, after a considerable period of time, the officers saw him calmly sitting in the same garden and around him were running, in fruitless search, the guards. This incident reminds me of Gorki, who many years ago told me that he himself saw vivid images of Indian cities upon the blank metallic leaves of an album, which was shown to him once in Caucasia by a Hindu. With all his realism, Gorki absolutely affirms that he saw in vivid colors that which the Hindu pointed out to him. Greetings to Alexei Maximovitch!

. . . . .

Attraction by thought is astonishing. The desire was expressed to have an old Tibetan Buddha, but this is already difficult. We spoke and thought among ourselves how to get it. In a few days came a lama and brought an excellent Buddha: "The lady wanted to have a Buddha and I am told to give the Buddha from my house altar. I cannot sell the sacred image—accept it as a gift."

"But how did you know of our desire to have a Buddha?

"The White Tara came in a dream and told me to bring to you."

And so it happens.

. . . . .

Recently we read in the *Statesman* that the lowest castes of India begin willingly to accept Buddhism. Rabindranath Tagore, in a talk with Gandhi, spoke against castes. Out of the mouth of a Brahmin this avowal is significant. Many significant and beautiful signs.

. . . . .

Special attention must be given to the Puranas—therein are many most valuable indications: "When the sun and the moon, and Tishya and the planet Jupiter are in one mansion, then the Krita (Satya) age will begin." So does the Vishnu Purana point out the age of Maitreya.

. . . . .

Lamas are constantly coming to us. They spread paintings on the lawn; and chantingly pointing with a little stick, they relate a whole epic. The vivid colors of the paintings merge with the natural colors of nature. The visual reactions have been valued since long ago. A nun comes. She sits at the threshold and throwing back her handsome head she chants her prayers. We can only distinguish "Tra shi sho!" Altogether the question of language is very difficult. All these mountain dialects somewhat resemble Tibetan. But still the difference is very great and the number of dialects of the small tribes is also great. Finally from Lhasa comes Kung Kusho of Doring to salute the house of the Dalai Lama. The Kung (this is a title like a duke; remarkable is the coincidence of Conung, Kung, King) is an important old man with a wife and daughter, round of face like a Ukrainian; with numerous servants; on big black mules shod with silver are high saddles and many-colored horse blankets. On their foreheads they wear vivid red caps with the image of Chintamani. In 1912 the Kung was attacked by Chinese soldiers. They almost wounded him. They killed his secretary. This led to a revolt in Tibet. The Kung is astonished and rejoices at our Buddhist objects. We are breakfasting. We are making Tibetan dishes. We speak of the movement of Buddhism. He is a very ceremonious old man.

Interesting are the tales about the attacks of the cavalry of Kham and Golok. Wild riders do not need reins.

Their horses, as in ancient narratives, take part in the battle with teeth and hoof. During battle, the riders take off their *khalats* up to the waist. Helmeted, with swords, lances and guns, this avalanche is borne onward. Sometimes they disappear under the stomachs of the horses. If all means of attack are exhausted the riders take stones from the ground and fight with screams resembling laughter. There is one sign which at once quiets this avalanche. Of course every tribe has its particularities in battle and by not knowing them one can weaken the best force. Tibetan women in songs and in life sometimes are not behindhand in manifestations of courage. They throw hot water on the enemy; they meet the temporary conquerors with derision.

. . . . .

Near Ghum stands a high rock. It is said that on its peak is lying a significant prophecy. In each stupa are enclosed significant objects. It is wrong to think that the bookshelves displayed in temples to some travelers comprise the entire book treasures of the monastery. Besides these official volumes of teachings everywhere in the secret recesses of the abbot there are manuscripts of unusual interest. One thing is dangerous. Often these hidden places are harmed by dampness, or mice, or are simply forgotten during some hasty evacuation. Often a lama will tell you: "I have written down the prophecies but I do not carry them with me. They are lying under a stone." Then some unexpected event happens; the lama hastens to put his sack on his back and departs; and the invaluable manuscripts are lost.

Some idiomatic commands are characteristic: "To put on trousers" means to get ready for a march. Idiomatic terms often bring difficulties into negotiations. Once an ambassador spoke in very high terms about "the hair of Brahma." Nobody under stood him and the negotiations had to stop. However, he had nothing else in mind than the river Brahmaputra. Often the languages taught in universities do not help in the local places.

. . . . .

A Chinese book, "Wei Tsang T'u-Shih," thus describes the Potala: "The mountain palaces are glowing in a purple sheen. The luster of the mountain peaks is equal unto emerald. Verily the beauty and perfection of all objects make this place incomparable."

We are reading of the builder of the Potala, the fifth Dalai Lama, named "Ruler of conjurations, eloquent, holy ocean of fearlessness." It is he, who on becoming His Worthiness the Dalai Lama in 1642, built Potala, the red palace, Pho Brang dMarpo, on the red mountain Marpo ri. He also built the remarkable monasteries Mo-ru, Labrang Garmakhiya, and many others. He also erected on the rock the colossal relief of Buddha and the saints of Buddhism. During his rule Mongols entered Tibet the second time. Gruber, the Jesuit, dislikes very much this strong leader, although he finds that he was cautious in his methods, assiduous and devoted to art and knowledge.

Unusual is the end of this Dalai Lama. According to one version the Dalai Lama died in the eighties and his death was hidden for a few years in order to give opportunity for various political matters to be adjusted. According to another version the Dalai Lama voluntarily abandoned his rule and hid himself for many years in that very same seclusion in the Himalayas.

History is paralleled by the following ancient legend: "Every century the Arhats make an effort to enlighten the world. But until now not one of these efforts has been successful. Failure has followed failure. It is said that until the day when a lama will be born in a western body and appear as a spiritual conqueror for the destruction of the century-old ignorance, until then there will be little success in dissolving the snares of the West."

. . . . .

The Chinese emperors lived according to the astronomical seasons of the year. For each season of the year there was a special colored garment. Each period of the year used to be spent in a special part of the palace.

. . . . .

The method of Buddhist teaching reminds one of the method of the Kabala, that of not imposing, but attracting, and pointing out the best way. They speak about a remarkable monastery, Mo-ru, and about the special learning of the lamas of that monastery. For the three summer months the lamas go away to the west for meditation.

During the "hearings" the lamas often cover their heads with cloth. This recalls "biblical" ceremony. It recalls the statement of Damis, the pupil of Appolonius of Tyana, of how Appolonius, when he heard a "soft voice," always wrapped himself completely, from head to foot, in a long scarf of woolen texture. This scarf was kept only for this purpose. From altogether other times, the very same details reach us. Contemporaries were astonished how strangely Saint Germain sometimes "wrapped himself up." Let us remember also the warm shawl of Blavatsky. Lamas carefully observe a certain condition of temperature which is favorable to the induction of different manifestations.

. . . . .

Lady Lytton came to see the pictures. In the Lytton family splendid traditions remain from their celebrated grandfather Bulwer-Lytton. Then came Colonel Bailey. Then came the whole Everest Expedition. By the way, they persistently wanted to find out whether we did not ascend Everest. In the painting, "Burning of Darkness," they recognized the exact image of the glacier near Everest, and they did not understand how this characteristic view, seen only by them, could have come into the picture.

. . . . .

A page of the true East: "Again they will come with the question, 'How shall one deal with obstacles?' One person is hindered by the family; one by a distasteful occupation; one by poverty; one by the attacks of the enemies. A good rider likes to show his skill on untrained horses and prefers obstacles to a smooth path. Every obstacle must be the birth of possibilities. When difficulties appear in the face of obstacles, they result precisely from fear. No matter in what attire a coward would garb himself we must find the page about fear. Friends, so long as obstacles do not seem as the birth of possibility, so long do we not understand the teaching. Success lies in the enlarging of the consciousness. It is impossible to come near in the presence of fear. The ray of courage shall lead above the manifestations of obstacles, because now, when the world knows where to go—the seed of blood is growing. If the path is strewn by bones one can go courageously. If peoples speak in unknown languages—it means we can open the soul. If one has to hasten—it means that somewhere a new enemy is ready. Be blessed, obstacles, through you we grow."

. . . . .

India, I know thy sorrows, but I shall remember thee with the same joyous tremor as the first flower on the spring meadow. From thy Brahmins we shall select the greatest who understood the Vedic wisdom. We shall select the Rajah who strove for the finding of the path of truth. We shall notice Vaishya and Shudra who have exalted their craft and labor for the upliftment of the world. A boiling kettle is the forge of India. The dagger of faith over a white goat. The phantom flame of a bonfire over a widow. Conjurations and sorcery. Complicated are the folds of thy garments, India. Menacing are thy vestures blown by the whirlwind. And deadly burning are thy inclement rocks, India. But we know thy fragrant essences. India, we know the depths and finesse of thy thoughts. We know the great

[43]

Aum, which leads to the Inexpressible Heights. We know thy great Guiding Spirit. India, we know thy ancient wisdom! Thy sacred scriptures in which is outlined the past, the present, the future. And we shall remember thee with the same tremor as the most precious first flower on the spring meadow.

PART II

SIKHIM

(1924)

EVOKINGLY and sharply the arrows whistle across the gulley, from out the bamboo grove. The Sikhimese remember their favorite ancient pastimes. One says: "The arrow is better than a bullet. It sings as it strikes while the bullet screeches as it flies outward."

. . . . .

In the morning a red leaf was brought to us: "In the evening *Senge* will arrive." After sunset upon the zigzag of the path, the fires began to flash out and the trumpets to resound. And finally it came rolling on—motley, noisy, trumpeting, drumming; with a dragon, with handmade horses, with paper yaks. With popguns and many-colored fires the dance proceeded, the motley crowd receding into the violet enamel of the night amid the explosions of the flaming spark. . . . These are Polovetsky dances! And the banners upon the staffs—these are the standards of Jenghiz Khan!

. . . . .

If you understand, then you will be understood. Touching are some of the gifts of the lamas. Knowledge is needed in order to understand all the finesse of intention in these gifts. To whom an image, and just which image; to whom, a bearskin; to whom, a leopard skin; to whom, a fur coat; to whom, a *khalat*; to whom, a *khatik*; and if so, whether one with designs or a white one. By the hieroglyphs of these objects one can read their entire relationship with you. Are you recognized as a great scientist? Or are you left within the limits of conventional politeness? Or are you left without attention? Often the non-understood "ceremony" is simply a short subtle code of gesture and conduct.

. . . . .

Two worlds find expression in the Himalayas. One is the world of the soil—full of the enchantment of these parts. Deep ravines and grotesque hills rear up to the cloud-line, into which melts the smoke of villages and monasteries. Upon the heights gleam banners, suburgans or stupas. The ascending mountain passes curve with sharp turns. Eagles vie in their flight with the colorful kites flown by the villagers. In the bamboo-stalks and amid the fern the sleek body of a tiger or a leopard adds a glimmer of rich supplementary color. On the branches skulk the dwarfed bears; and a horde of bearded monkeys often escorts the solitary pilgrim.

An earthly world this, full of diversities! A stately larch stands beside a blooming rhododendron. All is entangled. And all this earthly wealth shades into the blue mist of the rolling distances. A chain of clouds crowns the lowering mist.

Above this synthetic picture, it is strange, unexpectedly startling, to behold new ramparts mounting the clouds. Above the nebulous waves, above the twilight, glimmer the sparkling snows. Erect, infinitely beauteous, stand these dazzling, impassable peaks. Two distinct worlds, intersected by a mist!

. . . . .

Besides Mount Everest, fifteen peaks of the Himalayan chain surpass in height Mont Blanc. If from the great river Rangith we survey all the approaches to the snowy border and all the white domes of the peaks, nowhere, to one's recollection, is there such an open barricade of elevations. From this superb prospect one obtains an especially enthralling impression of the grandeur of the Himalayas—"Dwelling of snows."

[46]

. . . . .

To the side of the ascent, the summits merge into one implacable wall—the jagged, unending ridge of the Sacred Lizard. It is difficult to discern that just at that point are hidden the snowy summits of Jelep-la and Nathu-la on the way to Shigatse and Lhasa—the fog seems especially often to envelop this road.

. . . . .

The upper portion of the Buddhist banners bears the cross-shaped spear, disk, crescent and lotus-petals. Are not the emblems of all teachings intertwined upon one flag-staff? In these reminders of the symbols of the elements of Nature everyone will find an image near to him.

. . . . .

Upon the ikons and ornaments of Tibet often is found, glowing with precious stones, the image of the fish—that happy sign—the same found upon the walls of the Roman catacombs. In one conception is united the Buddha's "Wheel of life," the Circle of the "Elements forming the mystery" of the Christian church and the "Wheel of Eze-kiel." The many-eyed seraphim and multiple eyes of the Luminous Mother of the World penetrate equally into the recesses of the soul.

. . . . .

In the cults of Zoroaster there is represented the chal-ice with a flame. The same flaming chalice is engraved upon the ancient Hebrew silver shekels of the time of Solomon and of an even remoter antiquity. In the Hindu excavations of the periods from Chandragupta Maurya, we observe the same powerfully stylized image. Sergius of Radonega, laboring over the enlightenment of Russia, administered from the flaming chalice. Upon Tibetan images, the Bodhisattvas are holding the chalice blossom-ing with tongues of flame. One may also remember the Druid chalice of life. Aflame, too, was the Holy Grail. Not in imagination; verily by deeds are being interwoven the great teachings of all ages, the language of pure fire!

. . . . .

It has long since been said, "Faith without deeds is dead." Buddha pronounced three paths: the long way of knowledge, the shorter way of faith, and the shortest way—through action. David and Solomon also glorify the strivings of labor. The Vedanta extols the manifestation of works. Verily, in the foundation of all covenants, action is placed foremost. This is the creative fire of the Spirit.

. . . . .

Are the symbols of the Hindu Trimurti alien to the Trinity? Does the Buddhist *Tree of Wishes*, hung with the objects of all desires, not respond to our conception of the Christmas Tree? What of the details of the arrangement of the temple altars? What of the ascetics and hermits, who buried themselves in their stone coffins? What of the image-lamps and the fires of conjurations; the wreaths and candles of heartfelt prayer, flung upon the bosom of the Ganges? And the birch of Trinity, the musk and incense? And the wrought gem-bedecked vestments? And the stones, thrown at Buddha by his close relative, are they not the same as the stones hurled at Stephen? Verily, not by accident have Buddhist legends been carved upon the frescoes of the Campo Santo in Pisa. Profound in its significance too is the Moslem legend telling of the visitation of the mother of Jesus to the mother of Mohammed before the birth of the Prophet. And Ladakian castles are towering, in the very same flight, as the eagles' nests of Faienza or Montefalcone.

. . . . .

In Jeddah, this gateway to Mecca, the Mohammedans especially venerate and guard the so-called Tomb of Eve. And it is the same Archangel Gabriel—he of the Old and

New Testaments—who upon Mount Hira bade Mohammed commence his preaching—the same one!

. . . . .

Mogul queens bore the revered title of Miriam. Miriam, Mary, Mother of the World. From times immemorial
have the most ancient forgotten temples extolled the antic-
ipation of the new epochs.

. . . . .

In the ancient city, Kish, the Temple of the Mother of
the World has recently been discovered.

. . . . .

Sarnath and Gaya, the scenes of Buddha's personal
achievements, are fallen in ruins, now only the goal of
pilgrims. So too, Jerusalem. "Because Jesus himself witnessed that the prophet is without honor in his own country."

. . . . .

According to the legend, Buddha's initiation was performed in the presence of the High Ones. The site of initiation is called "the holiest stupa" but its location is not
disclosed. The sites of Buddha's achievements on the Ganges are known, as well as the scenes of the birth and death
of the teacher—in Nepal. According to some indications
the initiation was performed farther north—beyond the
Himalayas, because Buddha came down from the north
for the performance of his works.

But where was Jesus until his thirtieth year? Who
knows those haloed retreats? Whither lies Korya-Morya?
Shall they be revealed?

. . . . .

The legendary mountain Meru, according to the
Mahabharata, and the equally legendary height Shambhala in Buddhist teaching, both lay in the north and
served as the summit for initiations. And not everywhere

until the appointed date, can the details of these places of high knowledge be told.

. . . . .

Wise intercourses—one sees clearer from above. Instead of petty quarrels of denunciation, history recalls to us truly international ties. It is pointed out as a historical fact that a Mongolian Bogdo-Khan was saved from illness by the "appearance of Nicholas." This is averred by the Mongolian Khutukhtus, whose knowledge is considered very high. All is full of signs, only do not overlook them, Observe keenly and joyously, and flexibly.

. . . . .

Upon the wrist of a Tibetan woman we observed a strange blue sign, which on closer inspection showed the appearance of a tattooed blue cross of equal ends. When she was asked the explanation of this sign, the woman revealed that a Tibetan physician had applied the sign during "a very dangerous cough"—evidently pneumonia. Tibetan physicians generally inject medicines under such signs. This sign was made by the personal physician of the Dalai Lama during his three years' stay in Darjeeling. Swastika is a symbol of the conception of fire and life.

. . . . .

According to the prophecy of Lama Tsa-rinpoche, the present attempt to conquer Everest will end only in losses. Let us see whether the old lama is right[1].

. . . . .

The lama seemed astonished at the desire of foreigners to ascend the summit of Everest, at any risk. "Why expend such efforts in the physical body? Is it not simpler to be there in spirit?" For with ease do lamas project their astral bodies, for which, of course, no height is an obstacle.

---

[1] The Lama proved to be right

. . . . .

From this very window[2] the high priest sent prayers to Tibet which was troubled by the Chinese. For three years, facing the wall of the Himalaya, he kept vigil.

. . . . .

In the time of the old Jesuit mission, about three hundred years ago, in Lhasa, there was a Christian chapel. Great lamas visited it. Now no one even remembers the approximate site of it.

. . . . .

The lama here bewails the visiting hunters—they came and killed many stags! And now when the lama strolls into the forest, few are the stags that come to him. And he loves the animals to approach him! Not savagery but deep culture rings in his complaint. We are reminded of the tale of old Avramy, who was a shepherd beyond the Ural, and when he prayed to the East, all the sheep in silence turned also toward the sunrise.

. . . . .

In Buddhist monasteries it was the custom to confine in the library him who was defeated during a scientific argument. Let him learn more! An excellent custom!

. . . . .

"A Chinese Amban (governor), an evil and dissolute man, was desirous of visiting a venerated holy abbot of the local monastery in Tibet. By persistence and force he demanded an audience, but when he entered the reception room of the abbot, he saw on the throne, instead of the holy man, the image of a hideous pig, and in fright he rushed from the presence. Thus the dissolute man, making his way by force, found an image worthy of him!

---

[2]   The author lived in the so-called Talai-Pho-Brang where the Dalai Lama stayed about three years during his flight from Tibet.

A fine reminder to all despots. 'With what measure ye mete, it shall be measured to you again.' "

. . . . .

A legend of Central Asia tells of the mysterious nation, underground dwellers—the Agharti. Approaching the gates into this blessed kingdom, all living beings become silent, reverently pausing in their course. Recall, now, the Russian legend about the mysterious "Chud" which went underground to escape the persecution of the evil forces. To this secreted place also leads the sacred legend of the subterranean Kitege. Everything comes from the North.

. . . . .

The whole world tells its tales of underground cities, treasure troves, temples merging under water! The Russian and Norman peasant relates about this with equal surety. So, too, does the inhabitant of the desert know of the treasures which sometimes glimmer from under the sand waves and then—until the ordained time—recede again under the earth. Around one beacon-fire are gathering those who remember the predestined dates. We do not speak of superstitions but of knowledge—knowledge revealed in beautiful symbols. Why invent, when truth is so manifold? In La Manche even now is seen the city which has been "submerged" under water.

. . . . .

Many sources tell of the subterranean dwellings in the district of Lhasa and Koko-Nor. A lama from Mongolia recalls the following legend: When the foundations of the monastery Genden were built during the time of the Teacher Tsong-kha-pa, in the fourteenth century, it was noticed that through the gaps of the rocks there arose the smoke of incense. A passage was broken through and there was found a cave in which, motionless, was seated an old man. Tsong-kha-pa aroused him from his ecstasy and the old man asked for a cup of milk. Then he asked what teaching now existed upon earth. After which he disappeared. It is also pointed out that the Potala, the palace of the Dalai Lama, has hidden recesses of the greatest antiquity. By the facial expressions of the high lamas one will not discover anything. One must seek through other paths.

. . . . .

If so much lies underground—how much more lies under the veil of silence. It is naïve to insist, after the first cautious response. An authoritative astrologer assures us that he knows nothing—has only heard rumors. Another who is versed in the ways of antiquity just now insists he has not even heard of such things. And why should they answer otherwise? They must not betray. Most heinous is treason—and there are many traitors. We discern the true devotion and behind it the structure of the future.

. . . . .

It is said that Solomon manifested such devotion toward the Temple that even when breathing his last, lest he interrupt or harm the work of construction, he remained upright in prayer until an ant bored through his staff. The example of perseverance and devotion!

. . . . .

Unexplained have remained the strivings of Solomon toward the One Beginning, sheltering all forms of knowledge. Abandoned Fatehpur-Sikri (near Agra) is full of the signs of this unity which was understood by Akbar the Great who preached the spirit of One Temple. In the center of the palace-court is still standing the temple of united religion. Superficial writers wonder why the walls of this mysterious structure bear the remains of such varied signs—the traces of Buddhism mingled with Hindu and Christian fragments. This united torch was already manifested in life!

"Wise in heart and mighty in strength; who hath resisted Him and hath had peace, Who spreadeth out the heavens and treadeth upon the waves of the sea—Who maketh Arcturus and Orion and the Pleiades and the inner part of the south—Who doeth things great and incomprehensible and wonderful of which there is no number"—exclaims Job about the One. And are not the mysterious signs of Watan and Senzar received by great lamas pointing toward it? We asked the Lama, "Is it true that the Festival of Community is approaching?" He looked closely at us, then answered, "Such are the prophecies."

. . . . .

In 1924, according to Tibetan calculations, the new era began, for here a century is not calculated as a hundred years but as sixty.

. . . . .

You listen to the reading of the Bhagavad-Gita; you hear the exclamation of the Buddhist servers of the temples. You listen to the singing of the choir. Does there not appear before you the One Image—the One common Will toward happiness and joy, to the unity of consciousness, embracing and conquering, to the exalting and enlightening Aum?

. . . . .

Should we not reflect why all Covenants tell of the same active beginning? Why is the manifestation of phenomena always accompanied not only by the same unexplainable words, but always by a vivid action of spirit? The writings say, "He revolted." And without the wondrous "uprising," without this invisible action, nothing is decisive. He realized and became enlightened; became filled with invincible courage!

. . . . .

The formulas themselves often astonish by their universality. In them are united the summons of the mysteries with the prayers of the most unexpected cults separated by whole epochs and whole continents. The language of the Mother of the World is the same for all cradles.

. . . . .

"Hallelujah, Hallelujah, Hallelujah," or "Halelu, Halelu, Halelu" is a conjuration of ancient rites. From the Chaldeans, Babylonians, through the Israelites it reached our era. It is also known by several tribes of India.

. . . . .

In this region the simple guide will suddenly turn around on his path and proclaim: "But men must finally realize that all is one and all are equal! But will That soon come, Which will unite men?" So thinks and ponders the simple, poor man, among the blue hills of Sikhim. In the hope of the guide you discern the powerful proclamation of Vivekananda; without depreciation, only in all powerful unity and righteous understanding, he walked. One wishes that our priests of the West valued Buddha in the same way as the enlightened lamas speak of us. Only in such benevolent understanding lies the guarantee of the future structure. All creators of Community must be recognized.

. . . . .

Principally let us have less of ignorant denials.

. . . . .

With difficulty one succeeds in getting plants which nurture the musk-deer. But how to bring this mountain pine to the laboratory? Below the altitude of six thousand feet, the plants perish.

. . . . .

Most often from Bhutan the ragged, deep blue furling waves of fog crawl upward. Not only the snowy ridges but also the steps to the mountain paths are wrapped in the dense mist. It is difficult to believe there is a hidden glimmer. Shall we not begin denying the very existence of the Himalayas? If they are invisible, that means they are non-existent! Whenever something is invisible to

us we presume it does not exist. Such is the decision of
ignorance.

. . . . .

Intricate are the mountain paths with their many turns.
How many are the earth-covered pits under the horse's
hoofs! Many are the intercrossing currents and streams,
with the torpid dampness under the green-blue foliage.
Truly many are the serpents beneath the flowers. And the
language of the murmuring foliage is incomprehensible.

. . . . .

Early are the stars aglow here. Toward the East, undi-
minished, flames the triple-constellation of Orion, this
astonishing constellation which finds its way through
all teachings. In the archives of the old observatories,
undoubtedly much remarkable data could be found about
it. The cults which surround some constellations such as
the Bear and Orion amaze you by their widespread pop-
ularity.

The wisdom of the Shamans designates them for worship. Nor did Job accidentally point to them alone as the
supreme act of achievement. The glimmer spreads everywhere. In the latest number of the Journal of the London
Asiatic Society is this very important item: "The Emperor
Baber near the beginning of his memoirs says: 'On the
outskirts of Barakoh is a mosque called the Jawza Madjid.
The real meaning of the word is House of Orion. Jawza
is a name of Orion.' " With what ancient cult was the
mosque pointed out by Baber identified? It is now most
likely effaced by the sands of the great desert. Thus we see
how unceasingly does Orion attract the eye of men. Again
are the astronomic bulletins telling of the inexplicable
pink rays, which have suddenly flashed from this constellation. The constellation of Orion contains the signs of the
"Three Magi." The significance of Orion, too, in ancient
teaching was compared to the significance of Atlas, sup-

porting the weight of the world. Verily, the Star of the East!

. . . . .

Only in the East do you feel the vital sense of astrology and astro-chemistry in its scientific import. The observatories in Jaipur and in Delhi overwhelm one with their fantastic conviction.

. . . . .

The air is pure. The small Lepchas, coolies of Sikhim, bear huge stones up to the mountain on their backs. It is for the unknown structure. Their heads are bent so low that one cannot distinguish their faces, because of the shawl and metal rings and chains. Will they be able to bear it safely? How is it possible to overload a body four feet high with such an immeasurable burden of stones! Yet instead of groans you hear laughter from under the bent back. Much laughter is heard in Sikhim. The further one goes toward Tibet the more communicative are the people. And the more often one hears singing accompanied by a pleasantry. The air is clearer here.

. . . . .

The chief of the caravan is called Sardar. In his purple kaftan, he is mounted firmly on the white mountain pony. Many are the white horses here.

The caves of Kinchenjunga, where were guarded the treasures, are still far off. In one of the caves is the statue of Padma Sambhava (teacher of Tibet) and behind it is seen a stone door—never yet opened by man. And yet they say: "Nothing remains hidden!"

. . . . .

The human consciousness often is "like a dog's tail. If it has curled itself—no matter how you straighten it out, it still persists in curling back." Thus it was told by the ancient Chinese.

. . . . .

But it is also known how completely the consciousness has been transformed by a mere touch.

. . . . .

"Why do you not tell us all you know, as if you were strewing pearls or setting landmarks?" By these sign-posts you yourself will pass the entire way. You alone—by human feet. According to your growth shall you yourself gather pearls. By your own hands shall you match them. By your own hands will you develop dynamic power. "You will return" and project your will.

Otherwise matter will again not flow out in the "song of ceaseless labor." In this way, superficial curiosity will be divided from true striving. They tell of one "modern sage" who offered to found an institute where anyone coming from the street could at once be convinced of phenomena. But this "sage" forgot to offer these strange comers from the street at least the wherewithal to wash their hands for the tests. There are ways which we must approach only with pure hands and with our own will.

. . . . .

And if through the shell of the objects of every day you will be enabled to behold the summits of the cosmos— what a new wondrous and undiminishing outlook shall the world have for the unsheathed eye. The medical lore of the ancients acclaimed laughter as useful for the purifi- cation of the glands. How useful then must a smile be for the brain! Thus shall the trembling conjuries of fear be transformed into the valiant call of joy.

TASHIDING

The motley figures of hell are being trampled down by the powerful feet of the White Guards. Red and green "guardians of the entrances," many-armed and with horri- ble grins, are threatening the violators. In explosive gasps flare up the gold tongues of the primeval flame. The misty aureoles of lights are glowing. . . .

With cold respect or else with a clerical sense of the scientific, do we examine the Tibetan and Nepal banner-paintings in the British Museum, the Musée Guimet in Paris, or the Field Museum in Chicago. But in a completely different attitude do we approach the same paintings on this site, and they speak to you quite differently. Every gesture of Buddha's hand is of vital meaning for the local world. The good and evil entities with their endless symbols are transformed from ornaments into a living epos. The images are enfolded in a stirring harmony of tones. The finest of these are of ancient work although the new paintings are also at times excellent.

Let us predict for these images a great future—just as twenty years ago the future importance of the old Russian ikons was predicted. Merited attention has been given to the Chinese and Japanese art. An elaborate literature has expressed this free art concisely. But after a study of classic Egypt, after the subtlety of Japan, after the romance of China and after the arabesque of the Persian and Mogul miniature, now appears a new object for study and admiration. The art of Central Asia is coming to the fore. In the fiery fantasy; in the dignity of the fine form; in the intense and complex gradation of tones is manifested this completely unique and striking art. But in its quiescent expression this art responds to the mystery of the cradle of humanity. In itself it forms Asia, to which in time shall be directed inquiries and researches.

Only, it is necessary to knock upon the doors of this beauty without threats, without weapons, without pillage. With full readiness must we gather the pearls of profound and anonymous achievements; without superficial scientific hypocrisy and without bribed treachery.

To study the life of a nightingale by first killing it—is it not barbaric?

. . . . .

One remembers keenly some objects discovered by Kozloff in Kara-khoto in Mongolia. Especially does one recall the wondrous image of the woman's head. If such a people lived in the silenced cities of the deserts—how far were these places from being a wilderness!

Wisely, wisely did the deserts succeed in guarding for posterity new treasures, and not only material treasures. . .

. . . . .

One must recall not only the swords of the Tartar in measuring the life of Central Asia. There are also the tents of all travelers and searchers. Even to the Khan's camps were summoned the finest of artists.

. . . . .

I remember how badly fared one young doctor who was sent to Urga in Mongolia for service. Poor soul, he knew not what and how to search. If the young generation could realize what treasures were prepared for it, and lie at the edge of the road—unlifted. Sometimes it is only a question of lifting up the treasures.

A little shepherd boy found 120 pounds of gold in Scythian objects, because he was attracted by the glimmer of metal which sparkled on the slope of the hill, washed off by the rain. How many such sparks are glimmering! But often our eyes are dulled by laziness.

. . . . .

The blessed Maitreya is always represented crowned by a wreath, in a great image. Three years ago, a gigantic image of Maitreya, bearer of the new age of universal Unity, was placed in Tashi-Lunpo, the monastery of the Tashi Lama. This idea has been invoked with the new approaching era of Tibetan chronology.

. . . . .

During the service in the temples smoking Tibetan tea is passed around. Therein is the idea of the Grail in this filling of the vessels before the Blessed Image. One must never leave the vessel empty—this is contrary to the custom of the East. Then the gigantic trumpets are sounded, like the voices of storm and thunder, with their summons to the future. Backs adorned with their purple mantles are bent low, thinking of the future. And like a fiery field, under the image of the Dream of the World, one hundred and eight fires are glimmering.

.   .   .   .   .

In a special compartment are guarded the masks of the keepers. Is it possible that these frightful visages can symbolize the way of benevolence? However, these are not symbols of benevolence but symbols of earthly elemental forces. For there is the heaven and the earth.

Even the physical world of Tantrik teaching, which has been so degraded in modern understanding, must be conceived sublimely. The teacher, Padma Sambhava, would not have proclaimed only a physical teaching.

.   .   .   .   .

I look upon an ancient painting of the Monastery Daling. Here are the acts of the teacher, Padma Sambhava. All his forces are represented in action. Here is the teacher as a black-hatted lama with Solomon's Star upon his headdress, striking a dragon. Here is the teacher summoning the rain. Here he saves a drowning one; he charms small evil spirits; weaponless, he conquers beasts and by a magic weapon he smites a tiger, first covering his head with the sacred triangle. Here he makes the serpents harmless; here he conjures the stormy current; and he sends rain. Now he fearlessly converses with the gigantic mountain spirit. Here the teacher flies above all mountains. Now out of the shelter of the cave he hastens to comfort the world. And finally in the circle of a poor family, he prays for a benign sea voyage for the absent master of the house. No matter how clouded is his teaching now, its foundation stills gleams through.

·   ·   ·   ·   ·

Or again, another ancient painting: "The Paradise of Padma Sambhava." The teacher sits in the Temple surrounded by the Righteous Ones. The Temple stands upon a mountain separated from the earthly world by a blue river. Across the river are stretched white *hatiks* (scarfs) and upon them the self-denying voyagers are crossing to the temple. A clear picture of the illuminated ascent! Of course, his commentators have besmirched even this manifestation. How encrusted with false dogmas are also all religions.

·   ·   ·   ·   ·

Of course, the teacher, Tsong-kha-pa, is still nearer. He rose beyond the confines of magic. He forbade the monks to have recourse to magic powers. His teaching— that of the Yellow Lamas—seems less spoiled.

·   ·   ·   ·   ·

On New Year's Eve, February 4, after sunset, the fires in the monasteries upon the hill dart up. And the ringing gongs and the far-away drums reverberate. . . . In the morning are held the dances.

·   ·   ·   ·   ·

Before the New Year, the evil entities are destroyed by conjurations and dances. In the Dance of the Stags, the effigy of the evil entity is hacked and its parts strewn around. In the midst of the circle proudly walks the Guardian of the Teaching, brandishing his sword—while black-headed lamas whirl around, swirling the wings of their broad sleeves. Musicians in high yellow hats are coming to the fore, like Berendeys in "Snowmaiden." And above the ornamented cornices of the temple the eagles wheel, while from the turrets of the hill the assembled crowds stand out in colorful relief.

The dances themselves on the New Year's day acquire significance, with their frightful symbols of evil entities. How far removed is the impression made by these awe-inspiring masks, against the sunny background of the Himalayas, from the oppressive dark corners of Museums where these examples are so often collected, frightening the visitor by the apparition of a conventional hell! Of course, this hell is invoked only for the terrifying of the weakly developed souls, and much fantasy is devoted to the intensifying of these hellish countenances.

．　．　．　．　．

In the monastery of the Red Caps the impression is not so luminous. In the Red Monasteries of Padma Sambhava this symbolization is more physically conventional. The play starts with a simple "mystery" of the judgment over the dead. The chief lord of hell approaches with his assistants. The beastlike servitors drag forward the black soul of a dead murderer. They weigh out his crimes. The chalice of his sins weighs down the balance, and the murderer is thereupon thrust into a seething caldron. The same occurs to the soul of a female sinner.

But then there is summoned forth a saint in the vestments of a lama. He is adorned in a white scarf. Of course, the court must be just, so three messengers of joy lead the exalted one into paradise!

．　．　．　．　．

Fifteen years ago there died a remarkable lama who came from Mongolia. We saw his image—resembling the type of Russian ascetic. A powerful visage, unconquerably bold are the cheek bones; the eyes are piercing. "During the departure of this strong spirit, a rainbow shone over the monastery founded by him."

The lama possessed rare books—and it is very difficult to obtain rare books. One must send a trusted person into remote districts. Remarkable books exist; there is the book of one Tashi Lama, concerning his visit to sacred Shambhala. There are collections of symbolic parables. There is a treatise on the transmigration of souls. They are not translated.

. . . . .

The teachings brought from Shambhala often find their way into the works of European scientists. For instance, in the cemetery of Darjeeling is buried an enigmatic man, Hungarian by birth, who lived at the end of the eighteenth century. He came walking from Hungary to Tibet, remaining many years in unknown monasteries. In the thirties of the last century, Csoma de Koros, as he was called, died. In his works he pointed out the teachings from Shambhala, designating the next hierarchy to succeed Buddha. It is very characteristic that this savant came here from Hungary. His activity was entirely enigmatic.

. . . . .

One more spark about Shambhala. A very well known Tashi Lama often fell into an ecstasy during his talks with his pupils. Sometimes he seemed to disappear altogether, being transported into the sanctuary, Shambhala. These ecstasies vividly transport one to the discourses of the time of Saint John de la Croix with Saint Theresa when both blessed conversationalists in exultation were raised to the ceiling of the room.

. . . . .

Remembering exalted occurrences, one also recalls the sparks of indignation. "A slanderer once approached Buddha, but the Blessed One was so indignant, that a spark of lightning struck the offender. Of course, the Blessed One arrested the counterblow and revived the defamer, but the latter had been so shocked that he forgot his plan of attack. The sparks of the counterblow!"

. . . . .

"The case is also told that Sengchen Lama, before his execution in Lhasa, pointed out that he would soon reincarnate again on earth. And truly very soon in Chinese

Turkestan a boy was born with the same rare and characteristic physical defect on his knee, which distinguished the late Lama. Now this Mongolian prince is more than twenty years of age. At present in our service is the son of the servant of the late Lama, and he was wont to travel on the errands of his father to the young prince."

. . . . .

Whoever is acquainted with riding horseback in Caucasia or in the Arizona and Colorado canyons, will know how to climb the steeps of the hills of Sikhim. Only, instead of the colorful tragedy of American wonders, here you behold an ascending garden cultivated by the mysterious rise of exalted teaching. And in its unknown caves sit hermits, who upon the strings of earth are composing the legend of celestial life.

He who has known the approaches to the old monasteries and ancient town sites in Russia with their blossoming hills and fragrant pine groves, will understand the feeling on the approach to the monasteries of Sikhim. I always repeat that if you want to see a beautiful spot, ask the inhabitants of a town to point out the most ancient site. These people of times immemorial knew how to select the most beautiful places.

Every mountain summit is crowned by a beautiful *mendong,* with its wheels of life, its prayers carved in relief and with its niches for seats from which you behold the image of the far-off distances. Here lamas and travelers are meditating. Here banners are fluttering. Here each rider will slow down his horse.

. . . . .

From the mountain summit you plunge again into the receding hills. The ribs of the checkered hillocks also disappear, like the backs of panthers, tigers and wolves.

After the hills, again the fairy-tales of the forest. Green gnomes and monsters impede the way. The verdant webs intertwine. The snakes wind themselves around the trunks. The moss-like tigers and leopards here are lurking. An enchanted world this!

The most fantastic hills and rocks form themselves into a seeming Sacred Chalice—a vast valley. In the center of the valley unapproachably stands the mountain of the *White Stone,* girded by two rivers. It is crowned by the Monastery Tashiding, which means "Valley open to heaven." An ancient place this. Try to search the endless wrinkles and cavities of its rocks. Try to unearth the treasures collected by the monastery—the miraculous stone, fulfillment of all wishes; the immortal Amritha and a hundred images of Buddha; as well as all the sacred books temporarily hidden; and all else spoken of in the ancient manuscript, "The Voyage through Sikhim."

. . . . .

The approaches to Tashiding are very difficult. Only recently have the impossible trails been transformed into steep footpaths. Verily, the path of the spirit must be traversed by human feet!

One crossing on the suspended bamboo bridge is especially hazardous. Below, the mountain river rushes and roars, bearing down the icy current from Kinchenjunga. And above the bridge on the steep slope, you pause many times. Shall I at last arrive? One must hold one's breath to conquer this age-old mountain.

Upon the upper slope an honorary reception is arranged for us by the land owners. Ale, sugar-cane and tangerines await us, under the canopy of rushes adorned with their yellow garlands. Farther off resound the reverberant drums and silver gongs. The reception of the monastery. On the last slope we are met by the pipers and trumpeters.

Amidst the rows of a colorful crowd you reach the ancient place. Behind the gates of the monastery, the lamas receive you in purple garments. In the front row a venerable old man, head lama of the monastery, stands like a delicately carved image of the fifteenth century. Thus you walk up to the spreading turquoise tents in the

midst of a forest of stupas and amidst many-colored banners, amidst the sparkling rows of fires.

．　．　．　．　．

In the first full moon after New Year, which fell this
year on the twentieth of February, there was the annual
festival in Tashiding. The miracle of the self-filling chalice occurs at the time.

Since ancient days—more than eight generations ago—
this miracle has been ordained. From a designated spot
in the mountain river a small vessel of water is drawn
and poured into an ancient wooden chalice. In the presence of witnesses, representatives of the Maharajah of
Sikhim, the chalice is closed and hermetically sealed. A
year later at sunrise during the same full moon, the chalice is unsealed amidst due ceremony and the quantity of
water is measured. Sometimes the water has diminished
but sometimes it has increased considerably. In the year of
the great war the water tripled in quantity, which meant
war. Now the water has diminished by half, which means
famine and disorder.

This evil omen has been intensified by another sign.
On February twentieth there occurred a complete eclipse
of the moon. Never has there been so evil a sign.

．　．　．　．　．

The trumpets sound, the whistles shriek, the people in
costumes, as though from the "Snowmaiden," proceed to
the great stupa. The choir, singing, winds its way around
the crowds. Many prostrate themselves. The drums of the
lamas resoundingly thunder. At this moment darkness
falls athwart the clear moonlight! The golden fires of offerings gleam out as though against black velvet. A complete
eclipse occurs! The demon Rakhu has stolen the moon!
Never was it so until this day of miracle in Tashiding.

．　．　．　．　．

Said Asura Rakhu to the sun: "Because thou hast carried away Razayana by deceit, I shall swallow thee, god of

sun, at that time when, on the thirtieth day, you will unite the knots of the orbit!" And further Rakhu pronounced a prophetic threat: "In penalty that thou, moon, although recognizing me, commanded that I be cut asunder, I shall seize thee and devour thee on the date of the fifteenth, during the time of the full moon!" And attentively the people are watching the eclipse of the moon and sun and beat upon the drums and threaten Rakhu.

.   .   .   .   .

But there was also one good omen. At sunrise the head lama beheld garlands of fire starting to glow upon the peaks of the mountains.

.   .   .   .   .

When the moon was restored to the world, the dancing commenced around the main stupa, a typical Russian round. The songs are also like the Russian; their import is spiritual. "In a monastery dwells our Lord Buddha. We bring to him our offering"—so begins one song; or "Mighty is the sacred book but I shall find a spot for it close to my heart" or, "I recollect the sacred monastery."

.   .   .   .   .

In a white kaftan the artist who decorated the local temple approaches. We have arranged for him to go with us to paint the Blessed Maitreya. He will demonstrate the technique of the local painting.

.   .   .   .   .

Red, yellow, white, purple kaftans; women's sleeves of crimson, green and white. Peaked hats, fur-edged. The people talk, sing, and for two nights walk around the stupa.

.   .   .   .   .

They are touching their foreheads to the stone upon which the teacher, Padma Sambhava gave his benediction of the site. They walk around another stone bearing the imprint of the teacher's foot and the imprint of hoofs and paws of beasts. And again the chorus marches around the stupa, singing of the fulfillment of all desires.

. . . . .

Entering the temple, you walk along your left up to the wall of the altar. Within the temples of the Yellow Sect, in the center of the altar wall, is the statue of Buddha. Or now, perhaps Maitreya-Buddha is at the right. Sometimes the lower temple is dedicated to Padma Sambhava and the upper one to Buddha. These positions are closely related to the inner meanings of the teachings. Buddha represents heaven; Padma Sambhava the earth. Upon the side niches are images of Avalokiteshvara—a spiritual conclave of brotherhood, many-headed and many-armed, like our Russian Hundred-Armed One. There are also statues of the "Keepers of Lightning," of the founders of Monasteries and of sixteen Arhats, sitting in carved caves. Upon the altar are lamps and various offerings, seven chalices with water, a saucer of rice, censers with incense, a shrine with relics.

. . . . .

The walls are generally covered with frescoes, especially one wall, that of the altar. At the entrance stand the images of the guardians of the four hemispheres. In every temple will be found an image of the seven treasures vouchsafed to humanity; among them on a white horse is the image of the miraculous stone.

. . . . .

In a special compartment are kept the sacred books. The common dream of the monasteries is to increase the number of books; but books are expensive—a sacred volume costs up to a thousand rupees.

. . . . .

Especially touching is the service of the thousand lights, in the evening, here in the low frescoed temple, with its columns and ornamented beams. In the center

is a long table on which fires are set; along the walls also
stand rows of lights, and this sea of fires caressingly undu-
lates and sways, wrapped in a veil of smoke from the sandalwood, wild mint and other fragrances, which are consumed in the urns. During this service the singing, too, is
of exquisite harmony.

· · · · ·

Along all paths, the caravans of the pilgrims wind
their way. High saddles are covered with bright fabrics.
Wild white ponies are bearing the bulging-bellied luggage.
There are crowds of pilgrims seeking a resting place for
the night. Here and there are a few banners raised in
memory of the living and more often for the dead. A crowd
up to one thousand two hundred collects together—but a
peaceful, good crowd.

· · · · ·

At early dawn, long before sunrise, when the snows on
the mountain are still soft amber, the camp begins to stir.
The drone of life creeps along and broadens; the cadence
of early prayer mingles with the stamping of horses and
mules.

· · · · ·

In the morning, a procession makes its way toward our
tents. The head lama himself proclaims the bringing of
gifts. After him follow high uplifted trays with rice, with
the ribs of a ram, with sugar-cane, with ale and fruit. The
lama himself makes the offering to our traveling kitchen.

· · · · ·

Amidst the stupas are spread the tents of the pilgrims.
Here under a green canopy are sitting lamas from Tibet.
Women are turning the lengthy pages of the prayer book
for them. The lamas are intoning Tantrik songs, to the
sounds of hand drums and gongs. Where is Stravinsky,
Stokovsky, Prokofieff, where Zavadsky, to portray the
powerful modes of these stirring calls? And how fine is

the white-gold face of her who turns the pages before the singers.

Not far off, a group from Nepal are clapping hands in rhythmic beat and chanting. In the center, a woman, with features unmoved, ecstatically dances the Sherpa Dance, full of the fine gestures of conjuration. Sometimes she moves her hands in a fluttering motion like a bird and utters a weird birdlike call. It is indeed striking.

There the wanderers from Bhutan are praying under a red canopy. Before the distribution of the healing waters, a sacred procession walks around the stupas. In the front are trumpeters in high red hats; after them the lamas in tiaras, and behind are borne a long row of sacred books.

. . . . .

At sunset, within the tent, the head lama quietly speaks of the sanctuaries of Sikhim. He relates the "miracles" which he has heard, or has himself seen; of the buzzing of swarms of invisible bees; of the singing and celestial music; of the apparitions of sacred images. At our departure the lama pointed out two gracious omens. Upon our way, coming to meet us, were three brimming bamboo water-pails carried by water carriers and two woodsmen with full fagots of wood.

PEMAYANGTSE

Tashiding is one of Sikhim's prominent sites and belongs to the parish of a great monastery, Pemayangtse, and is a day's travel away. It is also on the peak, standing like a bulwark. It has been newly rebuilt. Its renovation has been done with such sensitiveness that even the most recent painting gives you joy by its fine and ingenious decoration. And the carvings on the casements are fairylike. And the tall heavy doorways lead you into the wooden temples of Russia. Dignified are the head lamas with their festive purple garments and with their impressive red tiaras adorning their heads. Nevertheless one recalls with most pleasure the eighty-year-old abbot of Tashiding, ever zealous and careful to improve his structure, with his economical eye penetrating everywhere.

. . . . .

Behind the gates of Pemayangtse three-hundred-year-old ancient trees are standing as guardians—like the fairy forest of Berendey. A tiny street of the lamas' homes is like the suburb of Berendey, painted and ornamented with its many-colored porches and stairways.

. . . . .

Here is "Heaven's Sacred Mountain" and upon its peaks shines a small mountain lake. There is also a small temple erected on the spot where the founder of the Red Sect in Sikhim lived. From Dubdi, the founder passed to the Sacred Lake and thence into the ancient Sanga Chöling.

The four most ancient monasteries of Sikhim are Dubdi, Sanga Chöling, Daling and Robling. And the meanings of their names are noble ones: "Palace of Meditation," "Island of Secret Teaching," "Island of Lightning" and "Island of Happy Striving."

. . . . .

An excellent monastery is Sanga Chöling; nor do we forget Daling with its blue-white, porcelain-like entrance amidst a bamboo grove. Here at the altar is preciously kept a sealed box containing relics of the founder of the monastery. There are banners—gold on a black background. In Sanga Chöling there are no relics, but there lies a stone made sacred by the blessing of the founder; when the life in the monastery is undefiled the stone is firm, but each besmirching of life makes the stone crack.

. . . . .

Here are those tiny doors, beloved to me in Novgorod and Yaroslavl. Here is beautiful fresco painting. Here are the polychrome ornaments entwining all casements of the windows and doors. Here are the same rounded backs of pilgrims devoted to the faith, and the fires of dedicated offerings. Our coolies are also lighting a fire—a true widow's mite. And above them adamantly rises "the Keeper of Lightning."

. . . . .

Although the teacher, Padma Sambhava, was never in Pemayangtse, yet in the monastery are kept the things which belonged to this founder of the religion. The things are kept sealed but on some occasions are shown; a garment, headdress, beads, tiny bells of a wondrous chime, two magic daggers and a small exquisite image of Buddha.

. . . . .

And the trumpets sound more thunderous in Pemayangtse and the dragon guardians seem more terrifying and the influence of the monastery is greater. The ruins of the palace of the Maharajah are near. According to the biblical custom the first Maharajah was chosen to reign by the head of the religion. But there is no figure of Maitreya in the big monastery.

. . . . .

A few solitary temples with a single fire before them, surrounded by peach and rose flowers and intertwining orchids and wild peonies, more closely indicate the path of simple attainment of the Teaching.

. . . . .

Out of the forest walks a peasant and his head is adorned with white flowers. Where is this possible? Only in Sikhim.

. . . . .

Are the inhabitants of Sikhim poor? Where there are no riches there is no poverty. The people are living simply. Upon the hills, amidst blossoming trees, stand the quiet little houses. Through the colored branches shine the bright stars and glimmer the snow-covered peaks. Here are people carrying their vegetables; here they pasture their cattle and smile kindly. Here with fairylike music they walk along the steep paths in wedding processions.

Knowing of reincarnation they quietly cremate the bodies. And they are singing. Mark, they are often singing.

Verily, one can sing under a canopy of various flowers and plants. Orchids, like colorful eyes, cling to the trunks of the giant trees. Pink, purple and yellow bouquets are strewn along the way like bright sparks. And these are not simply plants; many have their ancient powers of healing.

. . . . .

Nature awaits here full of gifts. Come hither and be cured. Charura, Parura, Orrura are the three important curative fruits against cough, cold and fever. Charura is like a yellow cherry; Parura like a green chestnut and Orrura like a yellowish-green crab-apple. All three are sharp to the taste and full of tannin. Here is the red bark of Aku Ombo, to cure wounds. Salve against fever is Sergi Phurba, like a dry giant bean. Chuta, the dry bitter root, will cure swelling and heal the throat. Bassack is a brown powder for colds. The red-stemmed Tze produces magenta; bitter Purma is for incenses. A broth from the roots of Berekuro is effective for women's ailments. The flowers of Dangero heal the stomach, much like the flower of the red rhododendron; while the leaf of Dysro is a disinfectant for wounds. Memshing Pati is a sacred plant in Nepal, where it is used for head ornaments at festivals. Endless are the useful plants awaiting the best application and study.

The leaves of the herb Ava Duti are said "to soften" stones, just as do the "snow-frogs"[3] in the Himalayas. Therefore if upon a stone you see the print of an elk's foot or the paw of an animal, it seems they have eaten or touched this wondrous herb. Turning again to legends: near Phalut on the road to Kinchenjunga grows a precious plant, the black aconite. Its flower lights up at night, and by its glow one locates this rare plant. Here again is the trace of the legend of the Russian fire flower, that enchanted

---

[3] "Snow-frogs"—a legend which attributes to snow-frogs the ability to soften stones.

blossom which fulfills all wishes—and which leads us not to superstition but to that same source wherein so much still lies concealed.

. . . . .

Before our gates a strange gift was found. The branches of a fir tree, rhododendron and some other plants were there, with their leaves pointing to our house, and covered with a flat stone. This is Sunnium (a conjuration) and the man who raises this offering receives upon himself all which is sworn upon it, whether of good or evil, sickness or sorrow or joy. For many days it lay there and even horses shied at it. The same conjuration we observed in the suburb of Jaipur; there in the middle of a street, in a flat basket, lay a lamb's liver, flowers and three silver rupees. None touched them. These conjurations are of very ancient origin.

. . . . .

Everywhere are legends of the accidental discoveries of sacred spots, the revelation of which was followed by dumbness and even death. Thus it is told that one Shikari (a hunter) in Assam, accidentally wandered into a sacred place and beheld its mysteries, and when he attempted to reveal them he was stricken dumb.

. . . . .

On the shore of the sea a stick is moving. It moves on alone and near the top of it is tied a lighted tinder. Thus do the conjurers of the coast of Malabar invoke their conjurations to burn the house of an enemy. Doctor Jones of Calcutta tried to overtake such a stick but it "walked away" beyond his own pace.

. . . . .

A legend from around Mongolia: "A venerated mother died and her son was desirous that a high lama possessed of exalted powers should perform the services over her. But such a lama could not be found. The son at the moment of death deposited the spirit of the departing one into a sandalwood casket, strongly sealed this sanctuary and himself invited the best lamas from Tibet. The lamas concentrated upon the casket; one of them began to change in countenance, first becoming red, then blue from exertion. Then suddenly the casket burst into splinters before the eyes of all. This lama was able to free the spirit and thus could perform the service."

. . . . .

The people here know everything; they have heard everything. One can remember and disclose all things in the twilight: of "Nam-Yg" (heavenly letters)—the letters and sacred books which are falling from heaven; of rings of silver or turquoise which change their color as a sign of foreboding and warning; of *Si*, the stone bead, sent from heaven to guard the health; of the finding of objects which disappear afterward. All this is known.

. . . . .

A woman was very pious and dreamt that she might receive the image of Buddha. Working in the morning amid her flowers she discovered an image and brought it into her shrine. But soon she forgot it and Buddha disappeared from the shrine. Next time the woman found in her garden a whirling sparkling stone and put it into a coffer and forgot it. Then the stone disappeared. Neglect always results in the disappearance of the bestowed happiness.

. . . . .

Do not record the things which can be read in books but those which are related to you in person; for those thoughts are the living ones. Not by the book but by the thought shall you judge life. Understand the sparks of the primordial bliss.

. . . . .

In the twilight under the flowing stars, in the purple sheen of the mist, sounds the soft voice of the lama, telling his calm tale of the "King of the World," of His power, of His action and wisdom, of His legions, in which each warrior shall be possessed of some extraordinary gift. And he tells of the dates of the new age of general well-being.

. . . . .

The tale is taken from an ancient Tibetan book, wherein, under symbolic names, are given the future movements of the Dalai Lama and Tashi Lama, which have already been fulfilled. There are described the special physical marks of rulers under whom the country shall fall during the reign of the monkeys. But afterwards shall the rule be regained and then will come Someone of greatness. His coming is calculated in twelve years—which will be in 1936.

. . . . .

When the time came for the Blessed Buddha to depart from this earth He was asked by four lords of Dharmapala to bequeath to mankind His image. The Blessed One consented and designated the most worthy artist, but the artist could not take the exact measurements because his hand trembled so when he approached the Blessed One. Then said Buddha, "I shall stand near the water. Thou shalt take the measurements from my reflection." And the artist was thus enabled to do so, and executed four images, modeled from a sacred alloy of seven metals. Two of these images are now in Lhasa and the remaining two are still hidden until the appointed time.

. . . . .

One Tibetan ruler married Chinese and Nepal princesses in order that through them he might attract to Tibet the two sacred images of Buddha.

. . . . .

Twelve hundred years after Buddha, the teacher Padma Sambhava brought the teachings of the Blessed One closer to men. At the birth of Padma Sambhava all the skies were aglow and the shepherds saw miraculous tokens. The eight-year-old Teacher was manifested to the world in the

Lotus flower. Padma Sambhava did not die but departed to teach new countries. Had he not done so the world would be threatened with disaster.

. . . . .

In the cave Kandro Sampo, not far from Tashiding, near a certain hot spring, dwelt Padma Sambhava himself. A certain giant, thinking to penetrate across to Tibet, attempted to build a passage into the Sacred Land. The Blessed Teacher rose up and growing great in height struck the bold venturer. Thus was the giant destroyed. And now in the cave is the image of Padma Sambhava and behind it is a stone door. It is known that behind this door the Teacher hid sacred mysteries for the future. But the dates for their revelation have not yet come.

. . . . .

Wherefore do the giant trumpets in the Buddhist temples have so resonant a tone? The ruler of Tibet decided to summon from India, from the place where dwelt the Blessed One, a learned lama, in order to purify the fundamentals of the teaching. How to meet the guest? The High Lama of Tibet, having had a vision, gave the design of a new trumpet so that the guest should be received with unprecedented sound; and the meeting was a wonderful one—not by the wealth of gold but by the grandeur of sound!

. . . . .

Why do the gongs in the temple ring out with such great volume? And as silver, resound the gongs and bells at dawn and evening, when the atmosphere is tense. Their sound reminds one of the legend of the great Lama and the Chinese emperor. In order to test the knowledge and clairvoyance of the Lama, the emperor made for him a seat from sacred books and covering them with fabrics, invited the guest to sit down. The Lama made certain prayers and then sat down. The emperor demanded of him, "If your knowledge is so universal, how could you sit down on the sacred books?" "There are no sacred volumes," answered the Lama. And the astonished emperor, instead of his sacred volumes, found only blank papers. The emperor thereupon gave to the Lama many gifts and bells of liquid chime. But the Lama ordered them to be thrown into the river, saying, "I will not be able to carry these. If they are necessary to me, the river will bring these gifts to my monastery." And indeed the waters carried to him the bells, with their crystal chimes, clear as the waters of the river.

. . . . .

"Talismans. A mother many times asked her son to bring to her a sacred relic of Buddha. But the youth forgot her request. She said to him, 'I shall die here before your eyes if you will not bring it to me now.' The son went to Lhasa and again forgot the mother's request. A half day's journey from his home, he recalled the promise. But where can one find sacred objects in the desert? There is nought. But the traveler espies the skull of a dog. He decides to take out a tooth and folding it in yellow silk he brings it to the house. The old woman asks of him, 'Have you forgotten again my last request, my son?' He then gives her the dog's tooth wrapped in silk, saying, 'This is the tooth of Buddha.' And the mother puts the tooth into her shrine, and performs before it the most sacred rites, directing all her worship to her holy of holies. And the miracle is accomplished. The tooth begins to glow with pure rays and many miracles and sacred manifestations result from it."

. . . . .

A man searched for twelve years for Maitreya-Buddha. Nowhere did he find him, and becoming angry, he rejected his faith. As he walked along his way he beheld one who with a horsehair was sawing an iron rod, repeating to himself, "If the whole of life is not enough yet will I saw this through." Confusion fell upon him—"What do my twelve years mean," he said, "in the face of such persistence? I will return to my search." Thereupon Maitreya-Buddha himself appeared before the man and said, "Long already have I been with you but you did not see me, and you repulsed me and spat upon me. I will make a test. Go to the bazaar. I will be upon your shoulder." The man went, aware that he carried Maitreya. But the men around him shrank from him, closing their noses and eyes. "Wherefore do you shrink from, me, people?" he asked. "What a fright you have on your shoulder—an ill-smelling dog full of boils!" they replied. Again the people did not see Maitreya-Buddha, for each beheld only what he was worthy of seeing.

. . . . .

The lama says, "There are three kinds of teaching— one for the stranger, one for our own, and the third for the initiated who can retain. Now through ignorance they slaughter animals, they drink wine, they have property and eat meat and live squalidly. Does religion permit all this? Where is beauty, there is teaching; where is teaching, there is beauty.

The people here are sensitive. Your emotions and desires are transmitted so easily. Therefore know clearly what you desire. Otherwise instead of Buddha you shall behold the dog.

. . . . .

That which is hidden in the past is not of importance— that which in age-old books, copied and unfinished, lies covered with dust. For the new construction, that which now resolves itself into life is important. Not through library shelves but through the living word is measured the possibility of future structures.

. . . . .

Under Kinchenjunga are secreted the caves in which the treasures are resting. In stone coffins the cave dwellers are praying, torturing themselves in the name of the future. But the sun already has defined the future; not in secret caves but in full sunlight one perceives the worship and expectation of Maitreya-Buddha. It is now three years since the Tashi Lama solemnly and openly dedicated the great New Image in his Tashi-lhunpo. The intense, invisible work progresses.

· · · · ·

The Tashi Lama is now on his way to Mongolia by way of China. Unprecedented is this event through the ages. Mystery! Incidentally, it may be that only the abducting detachment passed through Sikhim and the Lama himself moved on to Mongolia.

· · · · ·

On a sacred morning upon the mountain started to glow rows of fire—another mystery!

· · · · ·

Just now the wave of attention is turned toward Tibet—behind the mountain rampart events are stirring, but Tibetan secrecy is great. Information is contradictory. Whither disappeared the Tashi Lama? What military manoeuvers proceed on the Chinese border? What transpires on the Mongolian line? A year of events!

· · · · ·

Sikhim is called the land of lightning. Of course, lightning also occurs here but is it not simpler to call it "the land of future steps"? For it would be difficult to imagine a better threshold to the mysteries of the future than this unexplored, rarely penetrated country of rocks and flowers.

· · · · ·

As behind a tiny silver apple on a saucer, do the hills and steps of the Himalayas reveal themselves. Hundreds, perhaps more, are the monasteries in Sikhim, each crowning the top of a summit. A small temple in Chakong; a big suburgan and monastery in Rinchenpong. Upon the next mountain appears gleaming white Pemayangtse, still higher, Sanga Chöling. Tashiding is almost unseen. On the other side of the valley is Daling and opposite Robling and still nearer Namtse. One may behold the monasteries for a distance of forty miles for we must not forget that here one can see extremely far.

. . . . .

And again before us is the wall to Tibet. And not the backbone of the lizard but the snow-white girdle is outlined upon the peaks of this wall—the girdle of the earth. Let us point the arrow northward—there must be the base of Mount Meru.

. . . . .

The Talmud relates that the dove brought the first olive branch to Noah from Mount Moriah. And Mount Moriah and the mountain Meru both lie in Asia. Here is the beginning of all things. Here is the source for all travelers and all searchers. Here is raised the first image of the Blessed Maitreya—Messiah—Muntazar[4] Thrice powerful M! Here above all disputes, the teachings have raised up the olive branch of the new world. Here is ordained the universal commune.

. . . . .

Someone voluntarily approached and touched our tent! Who is this man, with his long black braid and a turquoise earring in his ear, and garbed in a white kaftan? It is the Lama, Pema Don-dub, the local ikon painter. We ask, "Can you paint for us the Blessed Maitreya, exactly like the one in Tashi-lhunpo?" He consents and now he sits on a tiny rug in the corner of the white gallery, and with various pigments, paints the Image full of symbols. He prepares the fabric for the painting and covers it with *levkas* (a mixture of chalk on glue), and irons it with a shell. He works exactly like Russian ikon painters. In the same way does he grind his colors, heat them on a coal pan; and thus does he keep an additional brush in his

---

[4] Muntazar—the Messiah now awaited by the Mohammedans.

thick black hair. His Tibetan wife helps him to prepare his colors.

And so, in the corner of the white gallery the ingenious, many-colored image is being conceived. And each symbol upon it more clearly defines the Blessed One. Here is the frightful birdlike Garuda and wise Magi and Ganeshi, elephant of happiness, and Chintamani, the Steed, bearing on its back the miraculous stone, Treasure of the World. A sacred cycle of chosen symbols. And upon the image and the hands is laid pure gold.

Like our ikon painters, the artist lama chants hymns as he labors. The chants become more fervent; this means he is beginning upon the Image itself.

And another wonder occurs, only possible in this land. In the deep twilight when the waxing moon possesses all things, one hears through the house the silvery tones of a handmade flute. In the darkness the artist lama is sitting upon his rug, playing with rapture before the image of Maitreya-Messiah-Muntazar.

The Strings of the Earth!

Talai-Pho-Brang.

PART III

PIR-PANZAL

(1925)

WHERE have passed the hordes of the great Mongols? Where has the lost tribe of Israel concealed itself? Where does the "Throne of Solomon" stand? Where lie the paths of Christ the Wanderer? Where do the bonfires of the Shamans, Bon-po, of the religion of demons, glow? Where is Shalimar, the gardens of Jehangir? Where are the roads of Pamir, Lhasa, Khotan? Where is the mysterious cave, Amarnath? Where is the path of Alexander the Great to forgotten Taxila? Where are the walls of Akbar? Where did Ashvagosha teach? Where did Avantisvamin create? Where are the citadels of Chandragupta-Maurya? Where are the stones of wisdom of King Asoka? . . . All have passed by way of Kashmir. Here lie the ancient ways of Asia. And each caravan flashes by as a connecting link in the great body of the East.

Here are the sandy deserts on the way to Peshawar; and the blue peaks of Sonamarg; and the white slopes of Zoji-La. And in the flight of the eagles is the same untiring spirit; in the fleet steed is the same unalterable motion. Nor does the world of roses and shawls of Kashmir resemble that forgotten and hidden world of Kashmiri blades.

. . . . .

"Sacre du Printemps"—when we composed it together with Stravinsky, we could not conceive that Kashmir would greet us with its very setting. In Ghari, camping out by night, when the vivid spring sky became afire with stars and the mountains were azured, we observed rows of fires upon the mountains. The fires started into motion, separated and strangely circled about. Then the mountain slopes became aglow with these fiery processions. And in the village below, dark silhouettes began to whirl about brandishing resin torches on long staffs. The flaming circles proclaimed the end of winter frosts. And the songs proclaimed the Sacred Spring. This is the festival of the Ninth of March.

· · · · ·

"Bulbul," the nightingale, sings on the apple tree. The cuckoo reckons out a long life. White linens are spread on the meadow and a samovar is boiling. Red and yellow apples and sweet cakes are passed around to those seated upon the spring grass. The eyes of the violets and the white and yellow narcissus are woven into a many-hued carpet. At evening, flocks of ducks and geese completely cover the tiny islands over the lakes. Small bears steal out on the spring glades. But none fears them—unless the mother-bear is with her cubs. . . .

· · · · ·

The river banks are sloping. A line of boatsmen steer their canopied boats. . . . Upon a broad road the oxen drag themselves and the wheels grind along. Three-hundred-year-old plantains and tall poplars guard the ways. And the teeth of the encountered travelers gleam often in the smile of greeting.

· · · · ·

In the sheds lie the sleighs—veritable Moscow sleighs. In the yard, a crane screeches above the well. The straw roof is overgrown with green moss. Along the road are gnarled willow trees. And the greetings of the children are noisy. But where is this? Is it in Schuya or Kolomna? It is in Srinagar, in the "City of the Sun."

· · · · ·

Tiny, big-bellied pillars—small ornamental designs—steep little steps of stone—the gilded roofs of the temple—creaking, ornamented window-shutters—rusty locks—low little doors with their "curtesy"—carved balustrades—slanting tiles on stony floors—the odor of old lacquer—small windows with diminutive panes. Where are we then? Is this the Kremlin of Rostov? Are these the monasteries of Suzdal? Are they the temples of Yaroslavl? And what of the endless flocks of daws? What of the naked branches behind the windows? This is the chief palace of the Maharajah of Kashmir. How curious is everything which remains from antiquity. But the modern additions are hideous.

. . . . .

Upon the road are many Fords. In the hotel dining room one sees the faces of Americans. In the jewelry shop, side-by-side, hang two paintings—one of the view of Delhi, the other the view of the Moscow Kremlin. Among the crystals into which one gazes for destiny; among the sapphires of Kashmir and the Tibetan turquoises, are shimmering green Chinese jadaites—and like a garden, many-colored are the borders of the embroidered kaftans. Like precious shawls the rooms of the museum are strewn with minute Iran-designs and "Gandhara," belabored by destiny, unifies the cleft branches of West and East.

. . . . .

In the styles of the temples and mosques; in the angular carved dragons; in the tent-like, sloping hexagonal tower, is seen an unexpected combination of the old wooden churches of Norway and the Chinese pagodas. Out of one well is drawn the Romanesque Chimera, the animal ornaments of Altai and the tiny animals of Chinese Turkestan and China. The Siberian paths of the nations have carried afar the same meaning of adornment.

. . . . .

The fort of Akbar stands firmly planted. But after you have climbed the steepnesses and flights, you may perceive that the old bricks and the clay-beaten cement barely hold together. The arches are ready to give way.

. . . . .

Nishad, the garden of Akbar, occupies the site from the lake to the hill—a high place. The structures are modest and upon the corners are the little towers so beloved by him. They are characterized by simplicity and brightness.

. . . . .

Shalimar—the garden of Jehangir—is also in character with its possessor, standing "for itself." There is less of outward show, but more of luxury—of that luxury which brought the descendants of the Moguls to poverty. The last Mogul, in Delhi, secretly sold furniture out of the palace and destroyed the valuable facings of the walls of Shah Jehan and Aurungzeb. Thus ended the great dynasty.

. . . . .

The weaver of Kashmir accompanied the making of each of his designs with a special chant. Such a searching for rhythm reminds us of the great harmony of labor.

. . . . .

No song relates why the mountain "Throne of Solomon" bears this name. This is a place of such antiquity. Janaka, son of Asoka, had already dedicated one of the first Buddhist temples here. Seven centuries later the temple was rebuilt and consecrated to Mahadeva. . . . But whence comes the name of Solomon? The mountain received the name of Solomon from a legend that Solomon, desiring a respite from the conventions of a sovereign's life and from the burdens of his court, transported himself upon a flying carpet to this mountain with his favorite wife. Here, again, we come upon the mention of that "flying apparatus" possessed by Solomon. A similar mountain is in Turkestan and in Persia.

. . . . .

It is not alone the mountain "Throne of Solomon" which transports the consciousness into biblical spheres. In the valley of Sindh the prophet Elijah is reverenced

in a special manner. Most stirring are the legends; how
the prophet sitting in his cave saves fishermen and travelers. Under various aspects, at times benevolent, at times
stormy, the prophet appears to defend the works of justice
and piety. Mohammedans and Hindus, divided by many
differences, equally reverence the prophet Elijah.

.   .   .   .   .

Purple iris will always recall Moslem cemeteries. They
are covered with these flowers. But there is also joy. The
lilacs have blossomed, lilies of the valley are nodding and
the wild cherry tree glistens.

.   .   .   .   .

After the "miniature design" of modern Kashmir, the
eye rests before the ruins of Martand and Avantipur. Here,
also, the ninth and tenth centuries have flowered. Here
the solemn fantasy of the Asiatic cradle of the Romanesque merges with the joyous cult of Vishnu. One feels
also that here, against the background of the sapphire
foothills of the Himalayas, have stood mighty structures.
They are but partly revealed. The sloping, massed hillocks conceal entire palaces and cities. The spectacle of the
might of Asia is not yet revealed. Gleams of it only may
be noted upon its fragmentary pages. Loving hands will
complete the beautiful realization.

.   .   .   .   .

"Hail to Thee, Hakaura, our Horus, God of Existence,
Defender of the Land, bridling the desert by the serpent
of His Uraeus, dispatching the arrow without the aid of
the bow, as does the Goddess Sekhmet. The king's word
would turn the Asians to flight." So speaks the hymn in
honor of Senusert the Third. Two phrases have a special
meaning: "Shooting the arrow without a bow"—action at a
distance. "Bridler of the desert by the serpent of His Ura-
nus"—reminds one of the most ancient cult of Asia—the
wife and serpent. The snakelike capitals of the pillars of
Asia and of the Mayans speak of the same cult of the wise

wife. The old plaque found in Kashmir tells the same tale. In the middle sits the king of serpents with the magic flower in his hand. The king is endowed with two pairs of hands, dark and light, because wisdom has a complete armor. Before the king is a woman with a veiled head, and to her the king entrusts wisdom. As the background to this entire group is a multitude of snakes which have risen and united their heads. And around this central image is a procession of individual figures of rulers each wearing around his neck the image of the serpent. This sign of wisdom forces the humanlike and animal-like djins to serve and help the owners of the ancient sign. Into a long trumpet far-off the djins transmit messages. Djins bring flowers for the adornment of life. Djins, in the guise of animals, transport themselves through the air. They bring caskets with gems. They are present in the guise of sentinels. So is preserved the ancient symbol of wisdom.

. . . . .

"Gulidjan-Marda"—"Illo-Aladin-Shabasha"—"Illaila-Suleiman"—thus the rowers call to each other. Oars with corded blades cut the yellow waters.

. . . . .

Modern Srinagar is not more than one hundred and fifty to two hundred years old. Of the ancient "City of the Sun" nothing remains. The old mosque remains only as a shell. In the ugly rivets of the "wharf" are seen traces of the reliefs of the excellent stones of the ninth and eleventh centuries. There are separate fragments; nothing binds them with the dirty small houses of the present day.

The old bridges must soon crumble. Who originated the canals of Kashmir? Who lined the roads with so many poplar hedges? Was this not done by some of the nomads from Central Asia, where winter necessitates the marking of the paths, and where canals are needed for irrigating the sands? Where did these *shikara*—the light, gondola-like boats—originate?

. . . . .

Along the even bank one travels at the end of the tow-rope. And the yellow banks remind one of the Volga or the Mississippi. The river Jhelum is the nerve of Kashmir.

. . . . .

Vular is the largest lake, the most beautiful and the most stormy. For two nights our boat was dangerously driven against the clay bank. We should still have remained there, still be working there, were it not that the "ark" might have cracked. On this lake everything is so attractive. Toward the west is Pir-Panzal, glimmering with its snows. To the north and east are the massive mountains. To the south stretch the distances of Srinagar. Before sunset an astonishing Valhalla rises up over Pir-Panzal, and in the morning the eastern mountains are crystal blue. Upon the sandbanks flocks are herding and each horse is visible upon the far-off bank, so unusually transparent is the air. Near the eastern bank is seen a small island on which stand the ruins of a temple, and often the fakirs and the sadhus in meditation are seated there. The world of religion is less apparent in Kashmir.

The details of the ruined temple on the island could be transported into any Romanesque cathedral, for the Goths wandered far, and everywhere sowed the seeds of their style. The adornment of the women's caps recalls the Gothic *fibula* save that instead of red enamel we see red glass inlaid in copper.

. . . . .

Around the boat soar lovely little swallows. On deck, the hoopoes strut about. Above the fields the song of the skylark resounds. In the center of the village is a cemetery—a hillock strewn with stones, like our northern *zjalnik*. Upon the hillock is a chapel with a green, tent-like roof. Venerable, scrawny plantains are standing guard over the quietude. Near the villages are the remains of temples and "town-sites" in ruins—sandy mounds with their sand-strewn antiquity. Toward evening the rowers commence their drawling songs—"like the *burlaks*." And packs of dogs pierce the air with their howls. From the far distant North to the South one finds the same structure of life. It is amazing!

· · · · ·

On the northeast of Lake Vular the mountains converge. In this pass there is a kind of compelling power. The village, Bandapur, has quite an individual character, and when you reach the post office you can understand the importance of the site. Here, to the mountains, turns the road to Gilgit. You pass up to the first ascent and watch the windings of the rising path. Upon the peak of the very summit is the first night camp. Then on, the path lies first along the very edge where the snow still gleams white as a narrow strip, afterwards sinking far down into a new gateway. Gilgit and Chitral are especially guarded. If the road toward Ladak is difficult, then Gilgit and Chitral are positively forbidding. Violet and purple rocks; and snow peaks, beautifully blue. Each turbaned rider attracts one's attention; is he not perhaps from the North? Each pack of loaded ponies draws one's eye after them. A significant corner!

· · · · ·

The Russian words—*sunduk, karaul, samovar, tchai, chaprak, sudi-sudi, kavardak, kolpak*[5] —and many other words, resound strangely but distinctly in the speech of Kashmir. The braided bark-shoes remind one of other northern paths.

· · · · ·

The boatman is preparing a Kashmiri dinner for us. Six cooks arrive. The table is strewn with blue iris. Since morning, we have received nothing except for tea. Sobra, his brother Ramsana, skillful Ibrahim and other unknown brothers and uncles are here—and even perhaps the hun-

---

[5] Trunk, help, tea-kettle, tea, horse-blanket, here-here, upside down, pointed cap.

dred-year-old grandfather himself sitting with his *hookah* in the kitchen-boat. All are busying themselves over some mystery. Finally, at seven in the evening the mysterious dinner makes its appearance. Twenty-seven courses are served in turn and each has to be tasted. The sum of the inventiveness of this sextet of cooks comprises: Almond soup, Namki polaw, Mehtee, Tabak Maz, Kabab, Roogan Yosch, Dupiaz, Batha Kurma, Abgosh, Alubukhar Kurma, Chana Kurma, Marzewangan Kurma, Subzee Kurma, Namki Kabab Akhtabi, Koofta, Koofta Tikea, Dampokhta Kokarpootoo, Kandee Roogan Yosch, Metla polaw, Thula Shoom, Rewash, Methazoont, Metha Thool, Deesee Alu, Plireenee, Thula Halwa—thus is termed this apotheosis of mutton and spices. And how is it possible to tell them that just the ingeniousness of the dinner is so foreign to us!

. . . . .

Kashmiri singing. Seven men in white turbans, one red-headed, with long *sitara*. Three have *saazes*. Further on sits the most skilled one, before two *tablas*. At the corner are two singers, and in the center a woman singer, in blue shawl and silver bracelets and strings of beads. They sing songs of Persia and Arabia; Urdu and Kashmiri songs. And, as in the reliefs of Assyria, the woman raises her forefinger or her left palm or crosses her hands upon her temples. Sometimes—like a "duckling"—she jumps up and softly runs around the circle. The Persian song "Suram" is the song of farewell and eternal remembrance. The "Shakhnaz," the Arabian song: "The richest one will not carry his wealth with him beyond the grave." Or: "When Christ ascended—all servitors extolled him." And the song of Urdu runs: "Two friends—it matters not how distant— will think the same thoughts. The world is naught—and all must depart from it." "Kochur," the Kashmiri song, says: "Thou walkest upon the road but art not visible to me. Thou gavest me the wine of life and walkest away from me. Everything depends on God." "If I see but one man or woman, I already behold the entire world." "Kamach," the

Kashmiri song, runs: "They say their praises of Christ in all manner of words. Better was He than sun and moon."

And thus, on a red carpet, eight Moslems, of their own accord, glorify Christ and creation until the hour of midnight. Following them, all the boatmen move in time with the white turbans and sway as they chant. And the *saazes* drone like the whispers of the forest. And our Confucian Chinese repeats over and over in Tibetan *yakpodu*, meaning "good." And then the Victrola resounds with Rimsky-Korsakoff's "Song of Lel," sung by Chaliapin, and the turbans of the Kashmiris nod understandingly. There is one consciousness! The program finishes with the "Song of Akbar." And the entire midnight has passed without the least friction. And what has been mutually understood is accepted with a kindly smile.

Can one change such a communion of understanding into the vulgarity of ugliness? Possibly one can. We were shown the shameful letters which were sent to the natives by foreigners—shameful questions of the flesh. Can one substitute for the smile the mawling grimace? Of course it is not difficult. One can invoke a whole horror of ugliness. One can destroy this feeling of universal good. One can depart with the impress of searing banality. One can always go into the darkness of ignorance and prejudice.

· · · · ·

As in Sikhim, so in Kashmir, one is amazed by the spiritual understanding. One has hardly enough time to crystallize one's thoughts, when one's companion has made his complementary gesture. And how many fine thoughts one can sow by way of the intuition!

· · · · ·

Once again rhythmically the rowers call to each other—"Amposch-pamposch"—"Dazgir-Kashmir"—"Shah-an-Shah-Padi-Shah." And the meaning of these calls is "The land of roses," "The temple," "King of Kings," "Lotos," "Man," and "All is well." . . .

. . . . .

We live on the foothills of Pir-Panzal. The storms, continuous, blinding, last three days in succession. The hailstones are the size of dove's eggs. The stars are like candles. And each week there are earthquakes.

In Siberia, upon the steep hillocks are similar townsites girdled by thundering torrents. Cedar and pine groves austerely guard these dwellings and high above glimmer the white caps of the mountains. Here are woodpeckers, turtle-doves, orioles, musk-deer and mountain-goats. In just this same way, we live in the yellow, unpainted sturdy house. If there is sun, all is fragrant with evergreen, but if there is storm . . . For three days it thundered and the glare of lightning blinded one cruelly during the night. Rings of lightning! The gushing rains poured down, and hail suddenly blanched the green hills. What a storm!

. . . . .

The series "Banners of the East" unfolded: 1. Buddha the Conqueror before the spring of life. 2. Moses the Leader upon the summit, surrounded by the glory of the heavens. 3. Sergius the Builder, laboring with his own forces. 4. Watch on the Himalayas. 5. Confucius the Just, the traveler in exile. 6. Yen-No-Guyo-Dja, Friend of the Travelers (Japan). 7. Milarepa, the One Who Hearkened— at sunrise comprehending the voices of the Devas. 8. Dorje the Daring, who stood facing Mahakala himself. 9. Sahara the Beneficent Arrow, never slackening in its missions of benevolence. 10. Mohammed upon Mount Hira (the message of the Archangel Gabriel). 11. Nagarjuna, Conqueror of the Serpent, beholding upon the lake the vision of the Ruler of the Nagi. 12. Oirot the Messenger of the White Burkhan, the legend of Altai. And those already in the Museum: 13. Mother of the World. 14. Signs of Christ. 15. Lao-Tze. 16. Tsong-kha-pa. 17. Padma Sambhava. 18. Chalice. 19. The Ancient Serpent.

. . . . .

In Mongolia there is a custom of great antiquity. In moments of national disaster or danger, the lamas would ascend the high mountain and with conjurations would scatter white paper horses—the horse as a symbol of Buddha, of strength and happiness. And these steeds of Valkyrie, the resplendent horses, would float out, whirling, and carrying help to the unknown stricken ones. Procopius was wont to sit on the Dvina blessing the unknown seafarers: and these lamas upon the mountain ridges of Asia have sent horses to the far-off stricken ones. In this sending to the Unknown is seen the same concern for the general happiness. Such customs of lamas are precious. This is not "sitting beneath a tree," nor requests flung into space; not the ornamental gestures of a ritual; but a "command" for help to the far-off stricken ones—a heavenly voice demanding that human ills be alleviated.

. . . . .

Two other touching images must not be forgotten: Mani, the founder of so-called Manicheism, in the third century was crucified upon the gates of the city in Persia for his belief in the synthesis of teaching and for his idea of the Commune. The other one, Guru Kambala, gave his head as a symbol of devotion and service—and Kambala and horses, in their essence, both enter into the "Banners of the East."

. . . . .

Manicheism lived long. In Italy itself, Manicheans, persecuted, existed until the fourteenth century. Perhaps it is from them that Benozzo Gozzoli adopted the themes of the Pisan frescoes, of the four encounters of the Prince Siddhartha-Buddha, which enlightened his consciousness. Instead of the Hindu Ruler, there is a cavalcade of Italian *signori*. And in certain Eastern conceptions, as if somewhere from the depths of understanding, one perceives the characteristic fantasy of Gozzoli with his sumptuous

ornate rocks and his pine trees; with his gilded horse-blan-
kets and staffs bearing vivid banners. Tamed "Pardus" of
the East sit behind the saddles, and the turban gracefully
surrounds the helmet, as upon the coat-of-arms (insignia)
of crusaders. What is it? The echoes of crusades, about
which even Herri met de Bles dreamt? Or has the more
ancient organization of synthesis, of Mani believers, penetrated and linked the consciousness of East and West. How
many unexplained manifestations! How many names slandered! How many truly enlightened researches are buried
into one heap with the cast-off refuse. Future studies and
researches must be undertaken in an unprejudiced spirit
with an eye only to truth and justice.

. . . . .

Another detail linking East and West. Do you remember
the Turfan Mother of the World, with the child? Perhaps
Nestorians or Manicheans left this image in the center of
Asia. Or more correctly, this image has remained, transmitted from times still more remote. Kali, or Kwan Yin—
who knows how many ages old they are? Behind them is
concealed the wife and the serpent. The antiquity of the
symbol is already incalculable. Not toward the page of the
Bible, not toward the symbols of the Kabala, does this
image point. Continents no longer existing have molded
the beauty of the Mother of the World—this light-bearing
essence. Only ignorance insists on the lack of knowledge
of antiquity.

. . . . .

You may wonder how we fare without theaters. But
we have drama here each day—only without a stage, in
actual life. Perhaps a Chinese theater—with legends about
unheard-of peoples; perhaps the threatening monologue of
the policeman; perhaps the ill-omened ballet of the Kashmiri merchants—*Schaitans;* perhaps the drama of a boat
beaten by the waves; perhaps the procession of horses or
the peaceful evening songs, or a *furioso* of hail and earthquake. Nor does one have to hang frayed curtains, nor

must one make up one's face, when the whole world participates in the mystery of evolution; when renewed understanding triumphantly enters into life, in new creations of universal beauty.

. . . . .

In Mongolia the march was proclaimed by the sending of an arrow to the Prince-noyon. And the arrow which came flying to Feodor-Tyron also came from the East.

. . . . .

George rides upon a horse from Yarkand; and the Chinese and I on horses from Khotan. My horse has a star; the Yarkand horse bears a Chinese brand, the cross within a square—a sign of the coat of arms of Tian.

PART IV

LADAK

(1925)

INDRA, Agni and Surya—air, fire and the sun! The Hindu Trimurti-Trinity remains behind. The ancient Sarasvati of the Vedas, the great Ind, leads us to its snowy sources. If the Ganges is as a greeting—the seat, contemplation—then the Ind suggests motion, unswervingness, impetuosity. And how alluring and unfailing have been the ways of the movement of nations through the Hindu Kush and Pamir!

. . . . .

Again a caravan. Again, days and dates are readily forgotten. The character of the day becomes more important than its number or name. Like the Egyptians who named the years according to their qualities—"the year of battle," or "the year of lean crops"—one marks only the quality of the days. Perhaps, the day of the horse—when the mounts fell through the snowy bridge; the night of a wolf—when the packs stealthily approached the camps; the dawn of the eagle—when the golden eagle with a whir of wings sped upon the tent; the sunset of the castle—when as though sprung from the fiery copper peak, the vision of a castle arose unexpectedly. In place of a turban, from out the stone there rose before us the shaggy cap—the way toward the land of Buddha.

. . . . .

The qualities of Buddha are as follows: Sakya Muni—the wise one of the clan of Sakya; Sakyasinha—Sakya the lion; Bhagavat—the Blessed; Saddha—the Teacher; Jina—the Conqueror.

Thus spoke Buddha to the zealots and hypocrites: "Your rules are degraded and ridiculous. One among you walks naked; another will not begin to eat from a pitcher or platter, or refuses to sit at the table between two companions or two dishes. Another will not accept alms from the house where a pregnant woman lives or where he encounters a dog. Some will not eat from two vessels and at the seventh gulp refrain from eating. One will not sit upon a bench or mat. One lies naked upon thorned plants or upon cow's dung.

What do you expect, voluntary workers, for your 'hard' labors? You await alms and respect from the laity—and when you achieve this reward, you become deeply wedded to the comforts of the temporary life and do not desire to renounce them. When you see visitors approaching from a distance you immediately assume the appearance of having been discovered in profound meditation. When you are offered coarser victuals you hand them on to others, keeping for yourself all the dainty morsels. You succumb to vices and passion; you assume the mask of modesty. Not such, is the true asceticism."

. . . . .

It took Buddha six years to convert Kashyapa. He even lit the fires of altars which were strange to him before the stubbornness of the set convictions of Kashyapa could be broken, and Buddha could add to new teaching the "old authority." For whenever beauty, scientific reason and vital enlightenment are invoked, the "old fortresses" are especially invulnerable. One must realize all the difficulties of Buddha in breaking down prejudices, if it took six years for one man to absorb the beautiful simplicity before he could extinguish the useless fire of unnecessary superstitious offerings.

. . . . .

His was the task to live for eighty years constantly teaching; to see how under one's very eyes the teaching was perverted; to realize how many rulers and priests accepted the teachings only out of self-interested motive; to foresee the shells of a new conventionality already prepared. . . .

He who contained within himself the understanding of the uselessness of power, exclaimed: "Go, oh beggars, carry salvation and benevolence to the people." In the one word, "beggars," is contained his complete gospel. The time has come when from out the gilding of the idol there stands forth the image of Buddha, the great teacher, who preaches against killing, against intoxication and excesses. This powerful image appears, summoning men to a revaluation of values, to labor and to achievement.

. . . . .

Many times the teaching of Buddha was purified, but it was again quickly covered with the soot of prejudices. Its vitality was disfigured into a heap of treatises and of metaphysical nomenclature. Why, then, be astonished if there still remain erect the walls of the monastery of Lamayuru, stronghold of the faith of Bon-po with its Shaman invocations, founded long before the birth of Buddha?

. . . . .

Nevertheless this brought about a healthy realization: they became accustomed to purify the teachings. Of course it was not the heralded synods in Rajagriha, Vaisali and Patna which brought back the teachings to their original simplicity of the community. But strong-spirited individual teachers sincerely tried to reveal again the beautiful image of the teaching: Atisha, defeating convention, wrestled with the somber survival of the sorcery of Bon-po. Ashvagosha, the creator of the entire Mahayana of the north, applied the form of dramatic productions for the sake of conviction and visualization. The bold Nagarjuna reaped wisdom on Lake Yum Tso from his discourses with Nagi, "King of Serpents." The Tibetan Orpheus, Milarepa, surrounded by animals, hearkened to the prophetic voices of the mountains. Padma Sambhava conquered the forces of nature—powerful figure, distorted by the conventions of the Red Caps. The clear and active Tsong-kha-pa was beloved of the entire north as founder of the Yellow Caps.

And many others—solitary figures—who understood the predicted evolution and purged the gospel of Buddha from the dust of conventional forms. Their works, again, were covered by the musty layer of mechanical ritual. The conventional mind of the "man of everyday," though he accepted the teaching of Buddha, tried to clothe it with his own prejudiced understanding.

. . . . .

Neither from Alara Kalama, or from Uddaka Rama-putta could Buddha find a saving decision. The reformer, who strove toward reality, could not be satisfied by the misinterpretations of the Rig-Veda. Buddha walked far off to the secret places of the mountains. The legends bring the bold searcher even to Altai—and the legend of the White Burkhan is being preserved upon Altai in all its reality. Near the mysterious Uruvela, Buddha approaches the simplest expression of all his attainments. And on the shores of Naranjana he is illumined by the decision to pronounce the words concerning general welfare: of the renunciation of the personal, of the significance of labor for the general well-being, and of the meaning of knowl-edge. To establish a scientific approach to religion was a true attainment. To expose the self-interested priests and Brahmins was the summit of fearlessness. To reveal the true levers of hidden human forces was difficult beyond expression. Of unusual beauty is the coming of the King in the image of a mighty mendicant!

. . . . .

In the conception of the evolution of humanity, the figure of Buddha, the Enlightened One, takes an unques-tionably beautiful place.

. . . . .

Buddha had to hear bodily the tremor of destruction of his native city, Kapilavastu. Confucius had to tread the path of exile from place to place. And his cart in which he wandered is placed in a Temple together with his works and musical instruments. It is not to be wondered at, because at the base of the teachings of Confucius lies the same idea of cooperation. Let us remember his teachings: "When the hearts of mortals shall be kindled by love, then the whole world will be as one family. All men will in themselves be one man, and all things, by virtue of the astonishing mutual order and union, will appear as one and the same element." . . . "Hypocrisy is the most hateful vice." . . . "He who only covers himself by the semblance of virtue resembles an evil-doer who in the daytime appears as an honest man and at night busies himself with stealing the goods of his neighbor." . . .

"Beware of those who make themselves the exponents of virtue rather than its followers. Be not deceived by their scientific arguments. For although they may be understood as the expression of the soul's convictions, they are nevertheless only the fruits of a corrupt mind and the intellectually corroded impulses of the heart. Those who discourse with apparent sensitiveness on humility, on general well-being, are not always examples of those virtues." . .

"Temperance, simplicity in attire, propriety, the pursuit of science and art, aversion to flatterers, love of the humble, lack of greed, prudence, steadfastness, righteousness, goodness, are the prescribed virtues." . . .

"Acquire science and the fine arts. Apply the precepts of wisdom." . . . "The avaricious one, himself being restless, becomes for others a terrifying and disgusting object. Let prudence dictate thy actions." . . .

"To discriminate between men, whether they be good or evil, there is no better way than to look into the pupil of the eye; because the pupil of the eye cannot conceal the vice which is hidden in the heart." . . .

"Do not let the humble ones feel your high position nor display to your equals the preeminence of your merits." . . .

"There is nothing which cannot be obtained by persistence. Each day I can bring a basket of earth, and if I persist in it, finally I shall raise up a mountain." . . .

"Man must become the coworker of heaven and earth." . . .

"All beings nurture each other. The laws of the movements of constellations are carried out simultaneously without impeding each other." . . .

"The action of heaven and earth is divided into endless currents, influencing each being individually; their general action effects great transformations—therein is the greatness of heaven and earth."

"Conscientiousness, humaneness and valor are three universal qualities; but in order to apply them, sincerity is needed."

"The man who has not determined his destination cannot be considered a great man."

"Is there not a panacea for all that exists? Is this not love to humanity? Do not do unto another what you do not wish for yourself."

"If a man can govern himself, what difficulty could he encounter in governing a state?"

"A sage is firm but not stubborn." . . . "Be slow in words and quick in action."

"A wise one expects all from himself; the mediocre one, all from others "

"I love the glow of virtue which does not proclaim itself in loud words and pompous movements. Noise and proclamations are secondary things in the reformation of peoples."

"The ignorant one who prides himself on his knowledge, the nonentity, the one desiring freedom excessively, men who return to the ancient customs, all are subject to unavoidable misfortunes."

"An archer provides an example for a sage. When he does not reach the center of the target he searches for the cause within himself."

Proclaiming the general well-being, Confucius was compelled to have his cart of flight ever at hand. . . .

Our old Chinese speaks in whispers about Confucius. These old thoughts seem like the footprints of ancient Chinese travelers, who have given us so much useful information about India and all Central Asia.

.   .   .   .   .

If behind the present idol of Buddha it is difficult to perceive the lofty image of Buddha the Teacher, then it is still more unexpected to hear in Tibetan mountains beautiful words about Jesus. Yet Buddhists preserve the teachings of Jesus, and lamas pay reverence to Jesus who passed and taught here.

There have been distinct glimpses about a second visit of Christ to Egypt. But why is it incredible that after that, he could have been in India? Whoever doubts too completely that such legends about the Christ life exist in Asia, probably does not realize what an immense influence the Nestorians have had in all parts of Asia and how many so-called Apocryphal legends they spread in the most ancient times. And then, how much truth is veiled in the so-called Apocryphal legends!

Many remember the lines from the book of Notovitch, but it is still more wonderful to discover, on this site, in several variants, the same version of the legend of Issa. The local people know nothing of any published book but they know the legend and with deep reverence they speak of Issa. One might wonder what relation Moslems, Hindus or Buddhists have with Issa. But it is still more significant to see how vital are great ideas and how they penetrate even the most remote places. Never may one discover the source of such legends. But even if they originated from ancient Nestorian Apocrypha, at present it is instructive to see the widespread and deep consideration paid to the subject. It is significant to hear a local inhabitant, a Hindu, relate how Issa preached beside a small pool near the bazaar under a great tree, which now no longer exists. In such purely physical indications you may see how seriously this subject is regarded.

. . . . .

Legends say that Jesus was not killed by the Jewish people but by representatives of the Roman government. The empire and the wealthy killed the Great Teacher who carried light to the working and poor ones. The path of attainment of light!

. . . . .

Let us hearken to the way in which they speak of Jesus in Asia. In the legends which have the estimated antiquity of many centuries, it is related that Issa (Jesus) secretly left his parents and together with the merchants of Jerusalem turned toward the Indus to become perfected in the highest Teaching.

It is related that, "He passed his time in several ancient cities of India such as Benares. All loved him because Issa dwelt in peace with Vaishas and Shudras whom he instructed and helped.

"But the Brahmins and Kshatriyas told him that Brahma forbade those to approach who were created out of his womb and feet. The Vaishas were allowed to listen to the Vedas only on holidays and the Shudras were forbidden not only to be present at the reading of the Vedas, but could not even look at them.

"Issa said that man had filled the temples with his abominations. In order to pay homage to metals and stones, man sacrificed his fellows in whom dwells a spark of the Supreme Spirit. Man demeans those who labor by the sweat of their brows, in order to gain the good will of the sluggard who sits at the lavishly set board. But they who deprive their brothers of the common blessing shall be themselves stripped of it.

"Vaishas and Shudras were struck with astonishment and asked what they could perform. Issa bade them 'Worship not the idols. Do not consider yourself first. Do not humiliate your neighbor. Help the poor. Sustain the feeble. Do evil to no one. Do not covet that which you do not possess and which is possessed by others.'

"Many, learning of such words, decided to kill Issa. But Issa, forewarned, departed from this place by night.

"Afterward, Issa went into Nepal and into the Himalaya mountains." . . .

" 'Well, perform for us a miracle,' demanded the servitors of the Temple. Then Issa replied to them: 'Miracles made their appearance from the very day when the world was created. He who cannot behold them is deprived of the greatest gift of life. But woe to you, enemies of men, woe unto you, if you await that He should attest his power by miracle.'"

"Issa taught that men should not strive to behold the Eternal Spirit with one's own eyes but to feel it with the heart, and to become a pure and worthy soul." . . . "Not only shall you not make human offerings, but you must not slaughter animals, because all is given for the use of man. Do not steal the goods of others, because that would be usurpation from your near one. Do not cheat, that you may in turn not be cheated." Issa said: "Beware, ye, who divert men from the true path and who fill the people with superstitions and prejudices, who blind the vision of the seeing ones, and who preach subservience to material things."

Upon his return to the land of Israel, Issa taught: "Do not be subject to despair; do not desert your homes; do not defile the nobility of your feelings; be imbued with hope and with patience. Raise up the fallen and sustain the hungry; succor the ailing in order that you be entirely pure and just upon that last day which I am preparing for you. If you would perform deeds of benevolence and love, perform them with a generous heart. And let there not be in these deeds the hope of gain or any calculations of profit."

The legends continue thus: "Then Pilate, ruler of Jerusalem, gave orders to lay hands upon the preacher Issa and to deliver him to the judges, without however, arousing the displeasure of the people."

"But Issa taught: 'Do not seek straight paths in darkness, possessed by fear. But gather force and support each other. He who supports his neighbor strengthens himself.

" 'I tried to revive the laws of Moses in the hearts of the people. And I say unto you that you do not understand their true meaning because they do not teach revenge but forgiveness. But the meaning of these laws is distorted.' "

"Then the ruler sent to Issa his disguised servants that they should watch his actions and report to him about his words to the people."

" 'Thou just man,' said the disguised servant of the ruler of Jerusalem approaching Issa, 'Teach us, should we fulfill the will of Caesar or await the approaching deliverance?'

"But Issa, recognizing the disguised servants, said, 'I did not foretell unto you that you would be delivered from Cæsar; but I said that the soul which was immersed in sin would be delivered from sin.' "

"At this time, an old woman approached the crowd, but was pushed back. Then Issa said, 'Reverence Woman, mother of the universe; in her lies the truth of creation. She is the foundation of all that is good and beautiful. She is the source of life and death. Upon her depends the existence of man, because she is the sustenance of his labors. She gives birth to you in travail, she watches over your growth. Bless her. Honor her. Defend her. Love your wives and honor them, because tomorrow they shall be mothers, and later—progenitors of a whole race. Their love ennobles man, soothes the embittered heart and tames the beast. Wife and mother—they are the adornments of the universe.'

" 'As light divides itself from darkness, so does woman possess the gift to divide in man good intent from the thought of evil. Your best thoughts must belong to woman. Gather from them your moral strength, which you must possess to sustain your near ones. Do not humiliate her, for therein you will humiliate yourselves. And all which you will do to mother, to wife, to widow or to another woman in sorrow—that shall you also do for the Spirit.'

"So taught Issa; but the ruler Pilate ordered one of his servants to make accusation against him.

"Said Issa: 'Not far hence is the time when by the Highest Will the people will become purified and united into one family.'

"And then turning to the ruler, he said 'Why demean thy dignity and teach thy subordinates to live in deceit when even without this thou couldst also have had the means of accusing an innocent one?' "

Thus the legends of Asia weave such an image of Jesus, so ennobled and near to all nations. And Asia preserves in its mountains such legends. And it is not astonishing that the teachings of Jesus and Buddha are leading all nations into one family. But beautiful it is, that the light-giving idea of unity is expressed so clearly. And who shall be opposed to this idea? Who will lessen the simplest and most beautiful decision of life? And the earthly Unity is so easily and scientifically merging into the great Unity of all worlds. The commandments of Jesus and of Buddha lie upon one shelf. And the signs of ancient Sanskrit and of Pali unite all aspirations.

. . . . .

Another version also speaks about the life of Jesus in Tibet: "Near Lhasa was a temple of teaching with a wealth of manuscripts. Jesus was to acquaint himself with them. Meng-ste, a great sage of all the East, was in this temple."

"Finally Jesus reached a mountain pass and in the chief city of Ladak, Leh, he was joyously accepted by monks and people of the lower class." "And Jesus taught in the monasteries and in the bazaars (the market place); wherever the simple people gathered—there he taught."

"Not far from this place lived a woman whose son had died and she brought him to Jesus. And in the presence of a multitude, Jesus laid his hand on the child, and the child rose healed. And many brought their children and Jesus laid his hands upon them, healing them."

"Among the Ladakis, Jesus passed many days, teaching them. And they loved him and when the time of his departure came they sorrowed as children."

. . . . .

Said Jesus of skilled singers: "Whence is their talent and their power? For in one short life they could not possibly accumulate a quality of voice and a knowledge of the laws of harmonies. Are these miracles? No, because all things take place as a result of natural laws. Many thousands of years ago these people already molded their harmonies and their qualities. And they come again to learn still more from varied manifestations."

. . . . .

Still many other legends and manuscripts relate of Issa in Asia.

. . . . .

After the vital conception of general well-being indicated by Jesus and preserved by Buddhists, one cannot but recall the words of Eusebius in his book, "Life of Constantine": "In order to attach to Christianity greater attraction in the eyes of the nobility the priests adopted the outer garments and adornments which were used in pagan cults." Every one who knows the cult of Mithra can appreciate the justice of this remark. A devout neo-Platonist and worshiper of the ancient philosophy, Clement of Alexandria, taught Christian bishops.

. . . . .

Ignorance! Russian princes perished in the tents of Khans for their refusal to reverence the image of Buddha—yet at the same time the monasteries of Tibet were already preserving the wonderful lines about Jesus. Cyril of Alexandria brought about the destruction of the woman ascetic Hypatia, but it was to her own pupil, Cinesius, that the bishopric of Ptolemy was offered even before he accepted baptism.

Superstition! Jerome advised the newly converted Christians to trample upon the body of their pagan mother.

Cynicism! Pope Leo X exclaimed, "How useful to us is this allegory of Christ!"

．　．　．　．　．

It should not be forgotten that Origen, who knew the meaning of the ancient mysteries and understood the true significance of the teaching of Jesus, even he could speak in the words of "The Acts": "And all the believers were together and held everything in *united possession*. And the estates which were sold and all properties were distributed to each according to his need. And each day, dwelling unitedly and breaking bread in their homes, they partook of their food with joy and simplicity of the heart."

Origen understood why this general well-being was important and saw profoundly into the truth. Because of this, the Church, sometimes extremely liberal in bestowing the title of saint, refused him this title; but even enemies did not refuse to call Origen a teacher. For he approached the teaching scientifically and did not fear to speak of what was evident to him.

．　．　．　．　．

Of what was Origen accused? "Lives of the Saints" thus speaks of him: "Origen, the wonder of his age by reason of the prodigiousness of his mind and the profundity of his erudition, was condemned for heresy in two Alexandrian Councils and, after his death, in the Council of Constantinople. Origen did not think correctly about many truths of the Christian Church. Expounding the non-gentile teachings of the pre-existence of the soul, he did not reflect properly upon Christ, believing that a certain number of spiritual beings of equal worth were created, of whom one strove with such flaming love that he became united with the Highest Word and became its bearer upon earth. Holding to the heretical belief in the incarnation of the God-Word and the creation of the world, Origen did not rightly comprehend the death of Christ by crucifixion, representing it as something which had its spiritual counterpart in a spiritual world. He attributed too much to the acts of natural forces with which our nature is gifted. . . ."—Admirable were the councils which could speak against the infinite cosmic meaning of matter!

· · · · ·

Sergius, Builder of Communities, forebade his coworkers to accept alms. Food and other articles might be accepted only in exchange for labor. Hungering, himself, he offered his labor. The building up of communities and enlightenment alone preoccupied this remarkable man. His refusal of the office of Metropolite and his refusal to wear precious metals appear in his life as natural acts, without any pose. His life was one of indefatigable labor; he chose young, completely unknown coworkers; he preached simplicity, as above, so below. The refusal of personal property was not because of any command, but because of his realization of the harm of this idea. In the ranks of builders of communities, Sergius retains a great place.

They are not so numerous—these builders of a life which responds in its inner meaning to the future evolution. And we should carefully record these names of future illumination, extending their lists until our day.

· · · · ·

One of the great Mahatmas of India says:
"You were told that our knowledge was limited to this solar system: *ergo*, as philosophers who desired to remain worthy of the name, we could not either deny or affirm the existence of what you termed a supreme, omnipotent, intelligent Being of some sort beyond the limits of that solar system. But if such an existence is not absolutely impossible, yet, unless the uniformity of Nature's laws breaks at those limits we maintain that it is highly improbable.

Nevertheless, we deny most emphatically the position of agnosticism in this direction and as regards the solar system. Our doctrine knows no compromises. Neither affirms or denies, for it teaches only that which it knows to be the truth, therefore, we deny God both as philosophers and Buddhists. We know there is in our system no such thing as God, either personal or impersonal."

. . . . .

Amid strife and in the manifestation of truth, upon the chariots of time ascend the law-givers of human welfare: Moses, the untiring leader; Amos, the austere; Buddha, lion-conqueror; Confucius, justice of life; Zoroaster, flaming poet of the sun; Plato, transfigured and reflected in his "Shadows"; Blessed Issa, great in the immortal sacrifice; solitary Origen, the wise commentator; Sergius, great teacher and ascetic. All walked untiringly; all fell victim to the persecution of their day; all knew that the teachings of general well-being would inevitably come to pass; all knew that each sacrifice for the sake of the general well-being was but the approach of the way.

. . . . .

On the mountain they tell of these teachings and listen to them simply. And in the deserts and upon the steppes people sing in their daily life about eternity and about the same general wellbeing. The Tibetans, the Mongols, the Buriats, all remember about this happiness.

. . . . .

And upon what do the peoples of Asia ponder? The Altaians remember the White Burkhan—they even suffered in their expectation of Him twenty years ago. Upon the summit of Herem they are turning to the White Burkhan:

>Thou who dwellest behind white clouds
>Behind the blue skies—
>Three Kurbustans!
>Thou wearing four tresses—

White Burkhan!
Thou Spirit of Altai—
White Burkhan!
Thou peopling within thyself, in gold and silver,
A nation, White Altai!
Thou who illuminest the day—
Sun—Burkhan!
Thou who illuminest the night—
Moon—Burkhan!
Let my call be inscribed
Within the book Sudur!

The White Burkhan commands that the idols be burnt and promises great yield to the people's lands and pastures. And so the general well-being will also reach to the encampments of Altai. Thus is being transfigured the ancient legend about the coming of Buddha to Altai.

How ponder the people of Asia? The Buriats are singing:

You will say: Sun stand still!
What means its setting?
You will say: Century await!
What means its aging?

You will say: Moon be still!
What means its wane?
You will say: Century await
What means its aging?

You will say: Snow remain!
What means its melting?
You will say: Elders remain!
What means their passing?

You will say: Cloud be still!
What means its hiding?

You will say: Elders remain!
What means their passing?

Mongols are singing:

He who has no possessions which he would
gather with thoughts of gain;
Who has naught with which he would not have
strength enough to part;
Who thinks firmly—he possesses the lasting and
beautiful delight.

Yes, the thought of Asia is strong. Under a turban, and
a fez, and a tubeteika— a resourceful mind and an ability
richly applied.

.   .   .   .   .

The ancient Chinese have preserved the beautiful hymn
of the Mother of the Sun, calling her Ruler of the East!

Part V

LAMAYURU–HEMIS

(1925)

AMONG the manuscripts in the ancient Chinese watch-towers were found dictionaries and the biographies of famous women. Such was the modernity of ancient peoples.

· · · · ·

When you already know the beauties of Asia, and are accustomed to all the richness of its colors, nevertheless they again astonish you, and again elate your feelings, so that you feel able to accomplish the impossible.

· · · · ·

Flies, mosquitoes, fleas, earwigs! All possible gifts has Kashmir. Our departure was not without bloodshed. In Tangmarg a band of ruffians attacked our caravan and began to beat our men with iron rods; seven of our men were hurt. It was necessary to preserve order with revolvers and rifles. In Ghund, our hostlers fed the horses with poisonous grass; the horses began to shiver and finally lay down. The entire night they had to be walked up and down. My horse, Mastan, suffered especially, and also Sabsa, that of George. The drivers made fires around the ammunition box. A wildcat crept into the tent under George's bed.

· · · · ·

Sattar Khan (our caravan leader) brought five ragamuffins: "This is a special guard from the village. For in the neighborhood many Afridi (from Afghan) are wandering. They may rob." The ragamuffins slept near the tents. Nobody came to rob.

. . . . .

Did the ancient Goths not compare Kashmir with the Tyrol? Or with the Rhine? Transparent, ephemeral, flitting is the beauty of Kashmir. It is difficult to imagine oneself in mighty Asia. Further, further—beyond, to the rocks and amber sands.

. . . . .

Wet, rainy Baltal. We had not yet succeeded in spreading the wet tents when there arose a new provocation. A policeman came with a report that our people had at that moment just destroyed a sanitary post and had seriously insulted the doctor. Fortunately, the guard at the railway station did not confirm this evil invention. We again bid our men not to answer any insults. The caravaneers insisted upon our spending an extra day in Baltal because of their fear of avalanches on Zoji. We discussed, walked, reconnoitered on the mountain and with hesitation decided to move on. There were no avalanches, although as always on the edges of the mountain, there may have been separate falling stones. Upon the pass, as usual, was an icy wind. The fur coats became lighter than gauze!

. . . . .

The Balti had a stomach ache. Thoughtlessly, we gave him cognac. At once, three more "became sick"; and when we gave them laxatives they began to demand the same medicine as we gave to the first one.

. . . . .

In the field near Dras remarkably beautiful women were working. They were of an Arabian type, dressed in black shirts with black bands on their heads. We thought these were Dards but were told they were Afridi, who came to the summer pastures from Afghan; these are the ones of whom the people are afraid.

. . . . .

There are stories of how caravans were looted: one Tibetan caravan was captured by the Amban of Sining. The other was destroyed completely by a Mongolian Ja-lama, who, beginning his career as a statesman, finished as a feudal bandit. His *khoshuns*, up to now, are marauding in Tsaidam.

. . . . .

There are stories about the high interest which is extorted by the Sinkiang officials and army officers. All loan money on interest, exacting up to twenty per cent per month. It is terrible.

. . . . .

We encounter the passing caravans. All sorts of people—Dards, Baltis, Ladakis, Astoris and Yarkandis. The tongues are completely different. It is like an exodus of nations.

. . . . .

After Zoji all changed. Kashmir remained behind with all its poisonous herbs, cholera and insects. Crossing the icy bridges over a thundering river, we seemed to cross into another country. People seem more honest; the streams seem more health-giving; the herbs are more curative and the stones are multi-colored. And the air itself seems exhilarating. Mornings are brisk—as of the first autumn frosts. In the afternoon there is a clear dry heat. The rocks are purple and green of hue. Grasses are golden like rich carpets. And the recesses of the mountains as well as the slime of the river-bed and the healing aromatic herbs—all are prepared to contribute their gifts. Here verily great decisions are possible.

. . . . .

Beyond Dras we encounter the first Buddhist message. Near the road are two stone *stelae* representing Maitreya. Nearby, a stone with the image of a rider. Is this rider not upon a white horse? Is this not a messenger of the new world? It is remarkable that this first Buddhist emblem happens to be just the image of Maitreya.

. . . . .

In Maulbeck, we visited a typical Tibetan home of the old order. We climbed up on a slanting ladder as on a raised bridge. Within was the house chapel, and an odor of incense. We found a portly hostess—a widow. From the balconies is a wondrous view, encompassing all the mountains and a fantasy of sand formations. The rooms are peaceful. Upon the floor near the door, a girl squeezes out vegetable oil for lamps. Behind her is the skin of a yak, and her head is crowned by a weighty headdress of turquoise.

. . . . .

In Dras is the first sign of Maitreya. But in ancient Maulbeck, a gigantic image of the Coming One powerfully stands beside the road. Every traveler must pass by this rock. Two hands reach toward the sky, like the summons of far-off worlds. Two hands reach downward like the benediction of earth. They know that Maitreya is coming. Is it not about this gigantic image that Fa-hsien wrote in his diaries? So it would seem.

. . . . .

The Monastery, Maulbeck, with two temples and endless ruins, crowns the rocks with an unusually heroic chord. As a precious bronze wedge! And the country of forgotten heroism is asleep. Forgotten is the legend of Herodotus about ants bringing gold from the shore of the Indus. But some remember about this gold. And Gessar-Khan promises to open the gold fields upon a certain date to the people who will be worthily able to meet the coming tide of Maitreya—the age of universal unity ordained by Buddha himself.

. . . . .

Ladaki drivers, who are Buddhists, wash their hands and heads, and rinse their mouths before each meal. And they sing resoundingly and joyously. And my black hostler begins a dance on the road. We go merrily. We observe the colors and silhouettes of the rocks.

Whoever built Lamayuru and Maulbeck knew what was true beauty and fearlessness. Before such expanse, before such decorations, Italian cities pale. And these solemn rows of stupas are like joyous torches upon tourmaline sands. Where will one find such decoration as the castle of "Tiger's Peak," or the endless ruins of the castles crowning all the slopes near the Tibetan Kharbu? Where lies a country equal to these forsaken spots? Let us be just and bow before such true beauty.

. . . . .

It is amazing. Here in Lamayuru, in this very stronghold not only of the Red sects but even Bon-po, among the row of images stands a great image of Maitreya. It was placed here about two hundred years ago. Even here did this knowledge penetrate. Maitreya alone binds firmly the Mahayana and Hinayana including Ceylon. In this reverence are united Yellow and Red sects. There is magnificence in this reverence of the future.

. . . . .

The caravans, meeting, greet each other. They always inquire, "Whence do you come?" They never inquire, "Who are you?" Movement has already effaced personality. Above the caravans sound the calls, *"Shabash"* (good way ahead) or *"Kabarda"* (danger, attention). And truly, on the steep banks of the yellow, thunderous Indus, there is always danger of a cruel, swift tide, a sweep of sharp stones which can brush the horse into the whirlpool of the torrent.

[119]

. . . . .

Saspul is an open, merry place. Around it are many monasteries. At the very road is a small monastery, and within it a gigantic image of the seated Maitreya. On the side also stand giants, Manjushri and Avalokiteshvara. In the front temple is an ancient stone *stela* with the same images, which dates from the tenth century or earlier. The lama of the temple talks with knowledge about Maitreya. This temple has been little noticed in descriptions.

. . . . .

Maitreya stands as the symbol of the future. But we also perceived the signs of the past. Upon the rocks are images of deer, of mountain goats with twisted horns, of horses.

Where did we recall similar images? Why, on the stones of North America; upon Siberian rocks; the same technique, the same stylization, and the same reverence for animals. Few are the human images. We saw only one—an archer and several rows of people, perhaps representing a ritual. Through these images, America and Asia stretch hands to each other. On the wall of a semi-grotto where we paused for rest, the hands of some unknown travelers had also left the figures of animals.

. . . . .

Basgo is an ancient monastery upon the sharp cliffs. Such a whimsical and variegated line, without any minuteness, is seldom seen.

. . . . .

The Ladaki villages are not ill-smelling. On the contrary, one often smells incense, wild mint, sage, apples and apricots.

. . . . .

We passed Kalatse. There upon the bridge was nailed the hand of the "robber," Sukamir, who attempted to conquer Ladak for Kashmir. A cat had devoured this venal hand—and in its place it was found necessary to borrow the hand of a dead lama, lest the symbol suffer. Already missionaries are in Kalatse.

. . . . .

Encampments from Srinagar to Leh: Ganderbal, Kangan, Ghund, Sonamarg, Baltal (Zoji), Matayan, Dras, Kharbu, Kargil, Maulbeck, Tibetan Kharbu, Lamayuru, Nurla, Saspul (Basgo), Nyimu. The last may be omitted if the night-lodging is prepared in Leh.

. . . . .

Wheat does not fear an altitude of twelve thousand feet, and barley is adaptable as high as fifteen thousand feet. Horses are fed with barley instead of oats. A certain veterinarian attempted to prove that barley was very harmful for horses but all Tibet in practice has proved the opposite.

. . . . .

In the time of war and revolution the trade of Turkestan and India was increased. In Leh the former political inspector of Gilgit is stationed as special trade agent.

. . . . .

Bearded vultures, white-tailed eagles and European falcons of brownish-gold are perching upon the sapphires and tourmalines of the mountains.

. . . . .

On New Year the Tibetans bring to Buddha freshly blossoming greens, because the Tibetan New Year is at the beginning of February. And in Lhasa at that time they prepare for work in the fields. What then is there better and fresher and more symbolic of striving to offer to Buddha than the fresh seedlings, this first message of the awakened life?

. . . . .

Either one must accept what exists in its full reality or find recourse in personal superstitions. Of course, reality is precious. But then, one must take the actual living facts. These facts will bring their offering of tender verdure to Buddha; they also will evoke dreams of the unity of the peoples. They will give rise to the structure of the new unions. But these facts one can verify only in the desert beyond the accessible boundaries, outside of the sphere of influence; where there are no slanderers, no liars; where one thinks all afresh; where decisions do not depend upon any outlined regulations.

. . . . .

We are looking upon the inexhaustibly rich rock formations. We note where and how were conceived the examples of symbolic images. Nature, having no outlet, inscribed epics with their wealth of ornamentation, on the rocks. One perceives how the forms of imagery blend with the mountain atmosphere. Just those forms, thought out in the West, here begin to live and become convincing. One may expect the appearance of Kuan Yin; or Lhamo prepares the element of destruction; or the image of Mahakala may issue from the mass of the cliff. And how many enchanted stone knights await their liberation! How many enchanted helmets and swords are hidden in the chasms! This is not the unlifelike Durandale from Rockamadura. This is the real tragedy and achievement of life. And Bruguma of Gessar Khan is kin to Brunhilde of Siegfried. Crafty Locke runs along the fiery rocks. And under a tremendous banyan tree, in an orange mantle, sits a Sanyasin, in all ways and manners the same as in the times of Gautama Buddha.

. . . . .

Over the mountains rings out the "Forging of the Sword" and the "Call of Valkyrie" and the "Magic Fire Music" and the "Roar of Fafner." I remember Stravinsky once was ready to annihilate Wagner. No, Igor, this heroic realism, these harmonies of achievement are not to be destroyed. And the music of Wagner is also true, and rings remarkably in the mountains. Ragtime and fox-trots will not supplant Wagner. Upon the Tyrolian rocks and in the Villa at Pisa, Wagner became filled with a true enthusiasm and his sweep is fit for the heights of Asia. Humanity still lives by beauty.

. . . . .

An unusual fire in the village Nyimu! I was awakened by the exclamation of E.I.: "Fire! Fire!" I awoke and saw the silhouette of E.I. against a background of undulating bluish flame; gradually the fire died out. It appears that E.I. approached the bed and touched the blanket. The bluish flame, warm, odorless, flashed up. E.I. tried to extinguish it with her hands but the flame spread more and more strongly. Then she called me. The fire ceased as it began, without leaving the slightest trace on anything. Unforgettable was this leaping flame, unconsuming and vivid. The tent was entirely illumined. As always during phenomena, only afterwards we could talk over all the unusual details of this fire.

. . . . .

Dr. Francke relates the words of his Tibetan fellow traveler at the source of the Indus, in view of certain heights: "Behind them lies Ba-yul, the country of tall beings. Only highly developed people can find out something about the life in this Ba-yul. But if a simple man approaches the snowy boundaries he sometimes hears only voices incomprehensible to him."

. . . . .

A Ladaki song:

> Through the gates of the east entered the Hindu
>   Faith.
> Say, did you pass by way of the sacred word?
> The Persian kingdom erects the gates of the south.
> Did you pass through them?

The celestial message of China opens to us the
　　western gates.
How did you pass the way of the Chinese sign?
And the gates of the north belong to Gessar Khan.
How did you pass the way of the sword stroke?
Did you pass the gates leading to Lhasa, where lies
　　the way of the seekers of truth?
The east—the gates of India. There, hallowing the
　　sacred word and custom, we rested.
The Persian kingdom possesses the gates of the
　　south.
There we revered the border of the noble ones.
The celestial message of China opened to us the
　　western gates.
Affirming the dates it gave us happiness.
The gates to the warrior, Gessar, are on the north.
By the clash of swords we passed these nations.
And through the gates of Lhasa, seeking for truth,
We passed, testing in silence our spirit.

The geographical oddities of the song evidently result
from the accumulations of different races.

·　·　·　·　·

Another beautiful Ladaki song:

One is visited by wisdom and one is only an
　　onlooker.
Some can achieve wholly naught, therefore one
　　must test himself here.
But to him who already comes with wisdom, there
　　is special bliss.
Does the High One need the wisdom of nine signs?
And does the mediocre one need the same?
Are you coming as friend of high estate or do you
　　only desire a purse?
Did you come without threats?
Do you wish the covenant of friendship?

There are three kinds of enemies.
There are three kinds of friends.
Would you enumerate them?
There are three enemies:
An enemy who induces sickness,
An enemy who hates the spirit,
An enemy who avenges in bloodshed.
We did not come as enemies,
We are friend to you.
We name three friends:
Our Liberator Buddha,
The union of a harmonious family,
The union of love and blood.
Here are the three friends.
Verily, it is so.

· · · · ·

We recall the beautiful little book of Claude Bragdon, "Episodes of an Unwritten History." We could furnish him with several more episodes. It is always pleasant to meet Bragdon. All that he does is so sincere and fine.

· · · · ·

Pay attention to the blending of Kuan Yin, Aryabalo—Avalokiteshvara. Gessar insists upon the structure of the temple, Aryabalo.

The name of Gessar has reached as far as the Volga (Astrakhan).

· · · · ·

Gessar is being identified with Assur.

The temple of Gessar Khan was built upon the site of the manifestation of Avalokiteshvara.

The people of Ordoss place before the house five colored banners, the colors of the rainbow, awaiting the coming of the great being—"Tengiras Ochirtai."

· · · · ·

The abbot of the monastery Wu-t'ai shan in the book, "The Red Path to Shambhala," describes many details of

[125]

the way into this forbidden place. At the end of it there is a characteristic detail, to the effect that the traveler saw on the very edge of the safeguarded place, a caravan of Mongols with salt, although they did not suspect the nearness of the dwelling.

A Buriat lama gives the information that when he went to Shambhala he was led by an underground passage. The passage sometimes became so narrow that one could hardly push through the thoroughbred ram, which was being led into the forbidden place.

Mongolian lamas indicate several "safeguarded" places in the boundaries of Khangai and Gobi. There came several hurried messengers from the Himalayas.

Near Kalatse many places are pointed out which are dedicated to the name of Gessar Khan: 1. Garuda—of Gessar Khan. 2. Saddle of Gessar. 3. Tambourine of Bruguma, wife of Gessar. 4. Spinning wheel of Bruguma. 5. Castle of Gessar Khan—a high rock—a white spot indicates the sign of a door.

. . . . .

On Sumur upon the rock is an image of a crowned lion. This lion is upon Tibetan and military banners.

. . . . .

Mongols speak about the coming of "Meru."

. . . . .

In the spring in Ladak is a festival of Gessar, celebrated with singing and archery. From the names of the songs one may weave a complete garland about Gessar.

Let us remember the names: Gessar the Conqueror; Gessar and the Treasury of the Giants; The Wisdom of Bruguma; Father and Mother, the All-powerful; The Return of Gessar and Bruguma; The Voices of Heaven; The Conjuration of the Arrow; The Four Victories of Gessar; The Prayer of Gessar; Upon the Peak Shrar; Gessar the Ruler of Lightning; The Victory Song of Gessar; Praise to Gessar.

[126]

These titles alone proclaim the path of folk-consciousness, of the national dignity and the dream about the hero of freedom.

Both Ladakis and Mongols await fighters and builders of life. They endow them not only with a leonine courage but with serpentine cunning and the tirelessness of a stag. How wondrous it is to observe the growth of the consciousness and its forging of heroic symbols!

.　.　.　.　.

The images upon the rocks can be ascribed to three periods: the Neolith, the ancient faith of Bon-po and the superstition of a later period. In the technique of the images themselves one can distinguish the firm, succulent stylization of antiquity and the restrained, sharp line of later drawings.

.　.　.　.　.

The name of Orion is often connected with the narrative about Gessar Khan, On Altai, the mountain Beluha is called Outch-Sure. Outch means Orion; Sure, the dwelling of Gods; thus correlating to the Mongolian Sumer and Hindu Sumeru. Upon the mountain Outch-Sure one ascends by a White Khatik. The heavenly bird upon the mountain Outch-Sure has conquered the dragon. Tsagan Ubugun, white old man, is always near to the Great Bear.

.　.　.　.　.

They say in the caravan that the Mongolian soldiers—tseriks—carry special banners and sing a hymn composed by them about the approach of the time of Shambhala.

From border to border, from mouth to mouth.

.　.　.　.　.

One does not care to give to the local images any ethnographical or geographical character. Let them go as banners: "Sanctuaries and Citadels." Let them, by their general tone of heroism and attainment, themselves speak for this country.

[127]

. . . . .

Spitug is a powerful monastery, the first, according to the teachings of Tsong-kha-pa. Here are not ruins, but a living and working community. The abbot of the monastery and his coworkers are learned and strikingly keen men. Before one has yet completely spoken, they are ready to continue your finished thought correctly. In Spitug lies the image of Maitreya and the knowledge of the prophecies. In one of the divisions of Spitug in Leh in a special compartment stands a great image of Dukar, Mother of the World, with numberless eyes of omniscience, and with the arrow of justice. At her right, stands Maitreya—the Coming One. At her left, the many-armed image of the Avalokiteshvara, this conclave of the Brotherhood of the Great Unity. One should remember the correlation of these three symbols. This correlation has never been remarked upon or explained.

In both branches of Spitug, the murals are excellent, with strong tones and feeling of balance. They have promised to procure for us the same artist who painted these stirring walls.

. . . . .

To our camp came riding a missionary from Yarkand. On yaks, he had just crossed Khardong Pass, losing all sense of days and dates. His watch had stopped. He repeated constantly: "It is a staggeringly hard journey." He told us that the worst spots were Khardong and Sasser Pass, while Karakorum, though higher was easier. He praised highly the people of Turkestan. He informed us that the Amban is already awaiting us and considers us his guests.

. . . . .

The monastery Sheh, seven miles from Leh, is wonderfully laid out. In it is a tremendous, two-storied image of Buddha, the finest mural of any seen by us thus far.

In Trikshe also are the great images of Buddha, Maitreya and Manjushri. The paintings are somewhat simpler.

[128]

We did not see friendly lamas there. There was only an old Mongolian lama who, judging by his erratic laughter, was not quite normal.

One must also see the reverse side of Buddhism—let us go to Hemis. On approaching one already feels the strange atmosphere of darkness and dejection. The stupas have strange fearful images—ugly faces. Dark banners. Black ravens fly above and black dogs are gnawing at bones. And the canyon tightly incloses itself. Of course, the temple and the houses are all huddled together. And the objects of service are heaped together in dark corners like pillaged loot. The lamas are half-literate. Our guide laughs. "Hemis, a big name, but a little monastery." Of course, small, not according to size, but to inner meaning. Here is apparent prejudice and greed. The only fine thing about it was that upon the neighboring sharp rocks, at morning, the stags appeared and, standing long upon the cliffs, turned their heads to greet the sun.

It is an old monastery founded by a great lama who left a book about Shambhala and these manuscripts are lying down below, out of sight, probably feeding the mice.

. . . . .

Regarding the legends of Jesus—first there was a complete denial. To our amazement denial first comes from the circle of missionaries. Then slowly, little by little, creep in fragmentary, reticent details, difficult to obtain. Finally it appears that the old people in Ladak have heard and know about the legends.

. . . . .

Such legends about Jesus and the Book of Shambhala lie in the "darkest" place. And the figure of the lama—the compiler of the book of Shambhala—stands like an idol in some sort of fantastic headgear. And how many other relics have perished in dusty corners? For the Tantrik-lamas have no interest in them. It was necessary to see this other side of Buddhism.

And how simple it is to brush aside this grime and dust of fanaticism! How simple to restore the stirring mural paintings! How easy to purify and to cleanse the finely wrought statues! Nor is it difficult to bring the monastic organizations back to the full meaning of the working order, according to the teachings of the greatest Lion (Sinha)—Buddha.

.   .   .   .   .

"I am the King of Ladak"—thus the slender, slight man in Tibetan garb, approached us. He is the former King of Ladak, who was conquered by Kashmiris. His is a fine, intellectual face. Now his means are very limited. And so we speak at tea, and we tell him we love his country and his people who are remarkable for their calmness and honesty. We speak of the teaching and the guest in a fine, subtle way, remarks that the Yellow and Red Sects are now almost alike in many observances. We speak of ancient things, of the finesse of the work. The king invites us to see his palace, which rises high upon the rocks overlooking Leh.

We climb the steep, uncertain staircases. We pass along the dark crossings. We pause, rapt in joy, upon the terraces and balconies, from which, before us, spreads the vista of all mountains and sand-mounds. We must bow in order to enter the low, tiny doors which lead into the house temple. The temple is dedicated to Dukar, the resplendent Mother of the World. In the center again stands her image. On her right hand—Buddha.

Although the king now lives in Stog, the summer palace, nevertheless, before these images are fresh flowers. On the walls hang many finely colored banners. The general feeling of the paintings here is finer than in Sikhim, and one feels the great influence of Tashi-lhunpo.

Near the palace, in a separate temple, is placed the gigantic image of Maitreya. The wall painting there is very majestic. Often, the murals of Italy or of Russian churches, were either too detailed or too general in parts. But here one is startled by the unusual combination of breadth of understanding of the general parts, with their richness of detail. The figure of Maitreya is two stories high—up to the waist in the lower floor, and on the higher floor, the Image itself. Perhaps this division of the statue was done as an afterthought, but its idea is quite remarkable. It is as though the common man should not perceive at once the entire grandeur of the symbol. One must ascend the upper way in order to reach the Image—as though of a higher world. The lower floor is bathed in twilight while above, through the narrow windows without glass, the rays of the bright, all-penetrating sun pour in. And near you are great number of stupas and the glistening sand and fantastic networks of the gates.

. . . . .

The Mongolian lama has arrived and with him a new wave of news; they await our arrival in Lhasa. In monasteries, he says, all are discussing the prophecies. He is an excellent lama and has already traveled from Urga to Ceylon. How far this organization of the lamas is penetrating everywhere!

We are talking with the lama about what happened to us near Darjeeling. It must be recorded. We were going in an automobile near the monastery Ghum. Approaching us there appeared a porte-chaise, carried by four servants in white garments, while the lama himself sat in a remarkably beautiful garment with a crown upon his head. He had a bright, welcoming face, with a small black beard. The automobile had to slow down, and the lama smiled and joyously nodded his head. We thought that this was the important abbot of a large monastery. But afterwards we discovered that lamas are not carried in porte-chaises, nor do they wear crowns when traveling. Nor do lamas in Sikhim appear in such beautiful garments. No one ever heard of such a lama—and a face like his we found nowhere. The chauffeur slowed up the automobile

while driving before the lama, which enabled us sharply
to observe his face.

. . . . .

The last flight of the Tashi Lama had a heroic character. Three hundred armed lamas accompanied the vision-
ary refugee. Each of them, and the Tashi Lama himself,
led an extra horse by the bridle, because the flight was
hurried—and pursuit threatened them from all sides. A
message was brought to them, just in time, that five hundred Lhasan horsemen were hastening to cut off escape on
the Nagchu Pass. The Tashi Lama succeeded in turning to
the side and escaping through a gorge. A snowstorm rose
and the pursuit was cut off.

So, full-armed, amidst an incessant galloping, an historic flight occurred—the fulfillment of the ancient prophecies, so important for the future, took place. According
to an eyewitness, the monk-artist Gelong Champa Tashi,
the Tashi Lama took with him from Tashi-lhunpo only
the pictures of Shambhala. Out of them, on the way, he
gave two to well-known Khutukhtas; and here in Ladak
was Rinpoche, from the Chumbi, who told us that now
the shortest way is only through Shambhala! In many
monasteries the images of Maitreya are being raised and
restored!

From hand to hand among the local inhabitants
the prophecies and new commands are traveling. With
excitement they are comparing the dates which have
already been fulfilled. And they prepare and await, await,
await. . . .

Someone comes in the evening and whispers about a
new manuscript of Shambhala. We ask him to bring it.

One must be in these places to understand what
occurs! One must look into the eyes of these coming ones,
in order to realize how vitally important for them is the
meaning of Shambhala. And the dates of events are not a
curious oddity for them but are connected with the structures of the future. Though these structures are sometimes

dust-ridden and perverted, their substance is vital and stirs the thought. Following the development of thought you realize the dreams and hopes. And out of these fragments has been pieced together the real departure of the Tashi Lama—an important one. The new web of the world!

Three years before his departure, the Tashi Lama ordered that frescoes be painted on the walls of his inner chambers. In these frescoes in clear symbols are represented all the wanderings of the Tashi Lama through various countries.

·　·　·　·　·

Throughout Ladak are scattered stones with images of a cross, apparently Druid or Nestorian. The most ancient and now forgotten country preserves the Druid signs and all possible later symbols.

Not far from the site of Buddha stand most ancient tombs called ancient Dard graves. Their age is of course considerably more than a thousand years.

·　·　·　·　·

Three items of information reached us in one day about the legends of Jesus. A Hindu said to us: "I have heard from one Ladaki official that according to the words of the former Abbot of Hemis, there was a tree and a small pool in Leh beside which Jesus taught." (This is some new version about a tree and a pool, unheard before.)

The missionary says: "A nonsensical invention composed by a Pole who sat in Hemis several months." (One may ask why invented, when it coincides with other versions and proofs.)

Another says: "Is it not a Nestorian legend? Among them were many legends and true ones. But missionaries know nothing about it."

So the subject is being discussed. Thus slowly the news begins to leak out. The chief thing is the unusual depth of the legend and the wonderful meaning it has to the lamas throughout the entire East.

A good and sensitive Hindu spoke meaningly about the manuscript of the life of Issa. "Why does one always place Issa in Egypt during the time of his absence from Palestine? His young years of course were passed in study. The traces of his learning have naturally impressed themselves upon his later sermons. To what sources do these sermons lead? What is there in them of Egyptian? And why does one not see traces of Buddhism—of India? It is difficult to understand why the wandering of Issa by caravan path into India and into the region now occupied by Tibet, should be so vehemently denied."

The teachings of India were famed far and wide; let us even recall the description of the life of Appolonius of Tyana and his visits to Hindu sages.

Another speaker reminds us that in Syria a slab was found with an inscribed governmental edict about the persecution of the followers of Jesus as enemies of the government. This archaeological find must be curious for those who deny the historicity of Jesus the Teacher. And how does one explain the tiny coins used by the early Christians in the catacombs? And the first catacombs themselves still exist.

There are always those who love scornfully to deny when something difficult enters their consciousness; but then, knowledge is transformed into seminaristic scholasticism and slander is cultivated as a fine art. In what possible way could a recent forgery penetrate into the consciousness of the whole East? And where is the scientist who could write a long treatise in Pali and Tibetan? We do not know such a one.

. . . . .

Each day the lama rejoices and astonishes us. He has seen so much and knows so much and is able so keenly to discriminate among the people. Just now he has brought us the information that a name very close to us is mentioned in the most ancient prophecies. There is not the slightest bigotry in the lama and for the defense of the foundations he is even ready to take arms.

He will whisper: "Do not speak to this man—he will babble everything." . . . "And now I had better leave you." And there is nothing personal felt behind his motives. And how ready he is to move farther!

. . . . .

Leh is a remarkable site. Here the legends connected the paths of Buddha and Christ. Buddha went through Leh northwards. Issa communed here with the people on his way from Tibet. Secretly and cautiously the legends are guarded. It is difficult to sound them because lamas, above all people, know how to keep silent. Only by means of a common language—and not merely that of tongue but also of inner understanding—can one approach their significant mysteries. One becomes convinced that every educated Gelong knows much. Even by his eyes one cannot guess when he agrees or inwardly laughs at you, knowing more than yourself. How many stories these silent ones can tell of the passing "savants" who have found themselves in the most ridiculous positions! But now has come the time of the illumination of Asia.

. . . . .

Wonderful voices have the Ladakis. Their robes strangely recall the Russian Byzantine ornaments. Often instead of the fur slung behind the shoulders, there is a short mantle of cloth with embroidered designs, which gives the impression of the ancient *corsno* (Byzantine mantle-cloak). Their high embroidered hats are like those of Boyars. In their girdles are metal depositories for a pen and a pair of reed pipes, and with these latter they fill the evening with ringing melodies. During the hours of their work in the fields the Ladakis wear on their heads wreaths of barley and flowers. And the songs—such ringing joyous sound—are like the nature of Ladak itself!

. . . . .

Once again came the King of Ladak. As a result we are to live in his palace. From this site of the sermons of Issa, from its high terraces, one must paint a series of all that can be seen from here. In these high places, purified by winds, occurred the signs of great communions. Of course the places have changed. Destructions and constructions succeeded one another. The conquerors have brought new accumulations, but the basic silhouette remains unchanged. The same heavenly frames as formerly are crowning the earth—the same glowing stars and the tides of sand like a sea congealed. And the deafening winds, sweeping up from the earth. . . .

. . . . .

And here is the site of Buddha. It is eroded by time. A legend speaks of a "great and very ancient structure." But now the abutments of cliffs and rugged stones speak only of destruction. The old hewn stones have gone to the structure of later stupas, which in their turn have already crumbled. One fact is evident—you stand upon a place of ancient habitation. Not far off is an old village and a sharp-peaked heap of ruins—remains of an ancient fortress merged together like a monolith.

. . . . .

The days are filled with our settling in the Ladaki palace. Crowds of people are coming: envoys from Lhasa, Tibetan merchants, Ak-sakal the Elder, Tasildar from Kashmir (the district chief) and, again, the King of Ladak.

. . . . .

The old King Lama came himself. In spite of his poverty he brought with him about ten accompanying lamas and relatives. From the conversation it became apparent that the family of the king knows of the manuscripts about Issa. They also informed us that many Mohammedans would like to possess this document. Then followed conversation about prophecies connected with Shambhala, about the dates and about that which fills reality with beauty. The old King Lama departs and the crowd in white kaftans bow before him in reverence, simply and beautifully.

As simply yesterday in the street did a woman, walking out of the field of stubble, approach and stretch out a hand of greeting. They are now harvesting the golden barley. Rows of people with flower wreaths on their heads, carry on their backs sheaves of golden wheat and sing stirringly and joyously, in golden full-voiced garlands of song.

. . . . .

And so we live in a Ladaki palace. The ruins of Italian castles pale in comparison with this picturesque pile, this mass which rises in the chalice of the many-colored mountains. Where have we seen such lofty roof-terraces? Where have we previously walked upon such ruined alleys? Of course in the painting of Mehesky—the Moon people[6]. Of course, these are the very same towers. Only here are dwelling not the Mehesky, but descendants of Gessar Khan. All Kings of Ladak trace their descent from the heroic Gessar Khan.

. . . . .

How wonderful that George knows all necessary Tibetan dialects. Only without a translator will people here speak about spiritual things. Now one must absorb, with full knowledge, with clear, true approach. Curiosity is not fitting. Only insistent love of knowledge!

. . . . .

The eighth of September. Letters from America. Many messages will miss us here. The letters traveled for six weeks—but successfully reached the steamer.

---

[6]   Painting of Roerich, 1915.

. . . . .

Upon the walls of the room chosen as the dining-room are painted vases with many-colored plants. On the bedroom walls are all the symbols of Chintamani—the stone of the treasure of the world. And the carved pillars, black from age, support the dusky ceiling with its big Berendey-like balusters. Little doors are above a high threshold and the narrow windows are without glass. And before nightfall the wind blows freely through the passageways. The floor is covered with bright felting from Yarkand. And upon the lower terrace a black dog barks—Tumbal, and the white dog, Amdong, are our new fellow travelers. During the night the wind whistles and the old walls shake.

I am painting in the upper chamber which has its exit upon all the roofs. Its doors have broad carved casements and the pillars have intricately frescoed capitals. Stairs, steps and dark ceilings are patterned by age. Where have I seen this chamber before? Where have these bright colors sparkled? Of course in the "Snowmaiden"[7] in the Chicago setting. My dear ones enter and say: "Well, here is verily the true Berendey in his own chamber."

Berendeyevka ended sooner than we thought—the fall does not tarry. One must pass Karakorum before the autumn northeast wind approaches. The way to Shayok is passable only a week longer. Moreover, the people already have taken the bridges apart for fuel, and the water has risen to the height of a man. There remains the path through the Khardong and Sasser passes. Many varied imperative considerations cause us to hasten the date of departure. With a large caravan one becomes a subject.

. . . . .

Hence with horses, with mules and yaks, with rams and with dogs, we go on the old trail—but with the signs of new possibilities, we will walk upon the mountains. And then down to the deserts. Is it possible to descend from the

---

[7] Snowmaiden in Roerich's setting for the Chicago Opera Co., 1921.

mountains? But the element of the sand is also beckoning and the desert nights and sunrises are also glowing. And in this glimmer of beauty lies the whole conception and hope.

· · · · ·

Karakorum—the black throne. Beyond lies China—again the old patrimony of Buddha.

· · · · ·

On a red steed, unbridled, with flaming banner, rushes the Great Rider, in armor and blowing upon the sacred conch-shell. From him are darting tongues of flame and before him fly messengers—birds. Behind him lie the mountains—Beluha. Snows and the White Tara send blessings. Above him exultingly is held the gathering of the Great Lamas. Beneath him are the guardians and herds of domestic animals as the symbols of the site. This ancient Tibetan picture was brought to us on the last day of our life in Ladak.

· · · · ·

In the courtyard they complete the loading of the yaks. We are now setting out! And the day is sparkling.

PART VI

LEH–KARAKORUM–KHOTAN

(1925)

September 18th

A T last one can finally leave all of Kashmir's false-
ness and dirt. One can forget half-ruined Srinagar.
One can forget the attack made on our caravan by armed
bandits. The Moravian mission in Leh has some strange
restrictions and informs us of its consent to rent us one
of its houses on condition that I sign an agreement to do
no "Religious, semi-religious, etc., propaganda." No one
could explain just what meaning the mysterious *semi* and
etc. had. And who could pledge himself not to exceed the
incomprehensible limit of *semi* and *etc.?* We were able to
get along without the headquarters of the mission—in the
Palace of the Ladaki King. Only in the mountains does
one feel safe. Only in the desert passes ignorance does not
reach one.

. . . . .

September 19th

We learned how widespread are the legends about Issa.
It is important only to know the substance of these legends. The sermons related in them, of unity, of the significance of woman and all the indications about Buddhism,
are so remarkably timely for us. Lamas know the significance of these legends. And why do people resent and
slander these legends? Every one knows how to slander
the so-called "Apocrypha." For slander does not need a
high intelligence. But who can fail to recognize that many
of the so-called "Apocrypha" are far more basically true
than many official documents? The Kraledvorsky manuscript which was accepted by everyone happened to be
a forgery—while many genuine documents do not enter

into any one's consciousness. It is enough to remember the so-called Evangel of the Ebionites. Such authorities as Origen, Jerome and Epiphany speak about the existence of this biography. Irenæus, in the second century, knows of it—and where is it now? It is better, instead of useless discussions, humanly to reflect on the facts and thoughts which are communicated in the legends of Issa, "the best of human sons." Appreciate how close to contemporary consciousness is the substance of these legends and be astonished how widely all the East knows of them and how persistent is the repetition of them.

.   .   .   .   .

For a long time we loaded the yaks, horses, mules, donkeys, sheep, dogs—a complete biblical procession. The caravaneers are like a case of an ethnographical museum. We passed the pool where, according to tradition, Issa first taught. To the left remain the prehistoric tombs. Behind them, the place where Buddha, the ancient founder of the Order, went northward through Khotan. Farther on, ruins of structures and the garden which speaks so much to us. We passed by stony reliefs of Maitreya, which on the way, convey to distant travelers their parting word of hope for the future. The palace remained behind the rock, with the temple Dukar—the illumined, many-armed Mother of the World. The last sign from Leh was the farewell of the women of Ladak. They went out upon the road carrying the blessed milk of yaks. They sprinkled the milk on the foreheads of the horses and travelers in order to give them the power of yaks, so needed on the steep inclines and upon the slippery ribs of the glaciers. The women bade us farewell.

Up to Khardong, the ascent is easy. The hot sun set, and toward evening there sprang up a sharp, cold wind. We had to spread our camp on a naked Arctic plain, under the cutting wind. The Kashmiris very slyly would not show the Ladakis many of the things. And at twilight, by reason of the gale, there was an indescribable confusion.

And above us stood snow-covered Khardong! It rose unapproachably.

. . . . .

September 20th

We ascended the pass on yaks at three o'clock in the morning. These heavy, woolly animals are truly irreplaceable because of their soft step and steadiness; but, of course, only when they are broken in. For a wild yak is entirely untamable. Once, the Tibetans provided unbroken yaks for a Chinese regiment and immediately three-quarters of the riders were thrown to the earth. Our ascent was not difficult. The view from Khardong is majestic but the entire northern part of Khardong is one steep, powerful glacier. The descent was tiresome and dangerous. We had to walk and creep!

We saw how one loaded yak tripped and was slipping precipitately down the smooth rib of the glacier; but at the very edge of the precipice, the yak, straining itself, clutched down with his short strong feet. Many animals and people begin to be attacked by hemorrhages and headaches along ascents higher than sixteen thousand feet; on our way even now frozen blood is seen. Already we pass the skeleton of a horse that had fallen. With us all is well. After the crossing they tell us of an entire caravan that was frozen on Khardong, a caravan of Baltis comprising about one hundred horses was found frozen. Some of the men were found frozen holding their hands to their mouths as though screaming. Even now, in the fall, the fingers and toes soon become numb. One has to rub them with snow. It is almost impossible to paint. One can imagine how it is here during the winter. But beautiful is this threatening glacier! Far below is a turquoise lake. They say it is very deep. The entire path is strewn with gigantic boulders. Looking back, it seems as though the pass would be impenetrable.

. . . . .

September 21st

After the difficulties of the pass and glacier the road seems easy. After the piercing cold—heat and a vivid sun. The sands are hot; the mountains with their snowy rims, recede. Here are the beds of the streams. Sometimes a stream disappears into the stony masses and only the rumbling tumult indicates the flow of the invisible water. Briar roses and tamarisks are everywhere. And the natives in this valley of the Nubra River are friendly people. The river itself, in flood tide, can become a ponderous torrent. Now in the fall, its current is divided into many channels of unusually beautiful and intricate design. We go beyond the usual encampment.

We slept overnight in Territ, in a real Tibetan house. In our camp there are three parties: Buddhist, Moslem and Chinese. They are not without mutual suspicions of one another. They eat separately. Our old Lun-po happens to be the son of the Elder in Leh and is a big landowner. He has his estates and houses everywhere, in Leh, in Hemis and in Territ and in different places in Changthang. He told us how many monasteries were destroyed during the periods of past invasions. In one of his own houses here are such ruins, full of chips and statues and the remains of destroyed books. We are sorry that Lun-po came to us only during the last few days. He came, and to the question as to who he was, he proudly lifted his eyes and clearly pronounced "Bhoti," meaning Buddhist. He also tells us his brother is the treasurer in Hemis and knows how many secreted objects there are not shown to visitors. Lun-po wants to remain with us and to go to different countries. He wants to learn Russian; he begs only one thing: "Do not cut off my braid!" And his braid is really a wonderful one—black and down to his knees. We calmed him. No one will make any attempts against this symbol of his national pride. Apparently he already knows that in China the order has been given to cut the queues and that in

Tibet it is forbidden to show the tongue as a sign of devotion and gratitude. And Lun-po, in moments of pleasure, likes to show a broad and healthy tongue. He is a good companion for the heights and glaciers but hardly fits in a house. We are approaching his property and he begs us not to remain in the tents but to stay overnight in his house. With pride he shows us the gates (Chorten)—the walls of which are painted over with a vivid design. There are many fields and fruit trees. We sleep in a frescoed Tibetan room. A vivid cornice. There is a broad window, and a low broad door with a great ring for a lock. The sandy floor is covered with colored felt. In the designs of ornaments the swastika is often repeated. In the middle of the room is a heavy pillar and on a wide pilaster is an image of Chintamani, the Treasure of the World.

Every Tibetan estate is strangely reminiscent of the plan of the feudal palaces. The entire building is surrounded by a wall higher than the height of a man. The entrance is through thick gates. Behind the wall is a square of outer yard and here horses are neighing and fires are burning. From the yard you go as into an armor hall. Beyond it is the inner courtyard with many doors into the household living quarters. From there a ladder leads to the second floor, which also has many rooms. A similar ladder leads to a flat roof from which you have a broad vista of the far mountains, of rivers and the entire route. The corner of the roof is occupied by an elaborately designed chamber like a tower. And to the roof of this chamber leads another ladder. Ready for the defense, independently, stand the Tibetan estates.

. . . . .

September 22nd

It is a clear morning. On the edges of the road are whole hedges of briar roses. It is an easy journey. Ahead of us are golden sands and behind them the blue mountains, all shades with white caps of early snow. It is even hot. A mile from the road is an old monastery—Sandoling. We decide to enter: Perhaps our lama might be there? Through village dwellings, through stony streams, through rocky masses, dangerous for the horses' feet, we ascend. We were not attracted by the lamas in the monastery; but behind them there is something invisible—someone who knows much is leading Sandoling on the path of the future.

At Sandoling is the final outpost of Buddhism before the desert and therefore we wanted to know. What signs are in this monastery? There is a new altar of Maitreya with a new image glowing with strong colors. There is an excellent image of Dukar. It is pleasant to see the rich collection of banners—these banners were painted in Ladak. Among them are some very colorful ones of various fantastic subjects. All are trimmed with vivid silk. There is a good library. The head lama of the monastery is absent. Again we do not find our lama. In the early morning he had left on the road to the frontier. We shall hasten to find him. It is a long village. Another house of our Lun-po is here—but we shall go farther. The banks of the streams and the slopes of the mountain are covered with snow-white soda. The strata of the mountain slopes are blue, crimson and brown, indicating the vast abundance of metals. It somehow seems to us that radium must be here, in these blessed, unexploited regions.

.   .   .   .   .

September 23rd

The frontier site—Panimikh. Of course, on maps, the frontier is indicated through Karakorum—but upon the heights no one has established the frontiers—and human kind ends in Panimikh Of course, human endeavor often extends further, also. Beyond Panimikh, as was to be expected for our further passage, the bridge fell to pieces. This mysterious repairing of the roads was encountered by us in other localities.

We were told that in the village two *Sahibs* from Yarkand were stopping. We had hardly had time to unfold our tents when they approached us; they were two Swedish missionaries, one of them the ailing Germanson. They return to Stockholm. Germanson tells of the difficult places on the road. He speaks about Chinese Turkestan without any special enthusiasm.

Opposite Panimikh, behind the river, on the background of a red rock, as though glued, is a monastery of the Red Sect. Against the red background of the mountains, one cannot even see the approach to the monastery. It is as though, to save itself from enemies, the monastery had flown up and perched on the unseen ledge. Far to the left flows the Nubra, and our road goes to the right almost touching the row of cliffs. So, toward evening, we are nearing the foot of the pass, Karaul davan. There is a fantasy of mountain masses. We pause at the very beginning of the steep ascent.

The evening ends with an unexpected encounter with a Moslem. At the frontier of the desert there proceeds a talk about Mohammed, about the domestic life of the Prophet and about his reverence for woman. The talk continues about the movement of the Achmadis, and about legends saying that the tomb of Jesus is in Srinagar and the tomb of Mary in Kashgar. Again about the legends of Issa! Moslems are especially interested in these legends.

The moon rises in conflict with the bonfires. Finally the lama comes! In order to avoid the bridge he was led somewhere through a torrent. In the mountains, it is so everywhere. Even being familiar with thirty ways, you may not know the thirty-first. The lama will go on the pass by night; they prepare a lantern and an ax for him.

. . . . .

September 24th

Karaul davan, although lower than Khardong, seemed more difficult to us. Especially severe are the masses of enormous boulders along the descent. What gigantic work was entailed here, to polish and accumulate these heavy bulks! Near Territ was a path of briars. Here the trail of skeletons started. Horses, donkeys, yaks, in all positions,

and in all stages of decomposition. It is good that the evil
smell is little perceived in this cold air. Many skeletons
are congealed as if in a jumping position. It is like the
last leap of the Valkyries. Among the boulders, we are
squeezed together between the rocks. Omar-Khan's horse
fell. At the fording a sheep was drowned. Is it possible
that the great caravan paths of the past eternally came up
against these huge masses?

From behind a stone rises a strange figure in a woolly
Yarkand cap, a fur kaftan and a lantern. This is the lama
dressed as a Yarkandi. The moon rose early and the lama
crossed the comb of the pass successfully. The same day—
an unexpected discovery. It appears that the lama speaks
Russian. He even knows many of our friends. All the while
no one would have suspected such knowledge. When one
spoke Russian in his presence, not a muscle revealed that
he understood. And in his answers he never once showed
his knowledge of what we said in Russian. Once more it is
clear how difficult it is to appraise the measure of knowledge of the lamas. Toward the evening—snow and wind;
the servants and caravaneers decide to interrupt the march
for four hours, although we could still have proceeded
boldly for two hours. We gave in unnecessarily—and we
came right into a strip of the first snow. We pass the night
near the powerful glacier, amidst endless boulders. Two
more horses fell.

. . . . .

September 25th

The approach to Sasser Pass is higher than seventeen
thousand feet. There is a complete Arctic stillness. Glaciers and snowpeaks—a most beautiful spot. The billows of
the clouds roll by and open up new, endlessly new, combinations of the cosmic structure. There are broad lines; all
the ornaments and arabesques are discarded.

The people become more concentrated. Everywhere are
the bodies of animals. There are also human tombs, and
our people try to hide it from us. As if this could have

any effect on us! Omar-Khan lost two more horses. The *purga* (blizzard) is commencing. Overnight we are thickly covered with snow. The water in the pitchers freezes. It is impossible to paint because the hands become numb so quickly. It is good that in Kashmir we lined our tents with heavy material. Our fur shoes come in handy.

You, my young friends, I remind you to provide yourselves with clothes for heat and especially for cold. The cold approaches quickly and sharply. Suddenly you cease to feel your extremities. Have always at hand a little medicine chest. The chief considerations are the teeth and the stomach; also prevention against colds. Have bandages for cuts and bruises. All this has already been of use in our caravan. Any kind of wine on the heights is very harmful. Against headaches—pyramidon. One should not eat much. Very useful is Tibetan tea; it is really a hot soup and warms one very well. It is light and nourishing. The soda which is used in the tea keeps the lips from painful chapping.

Do not overfeed the dogs and horses, otherwise bleeding will begin and you will have to do away with the animal. The whole path is covered with the traces of blood. One must make sure, in advance, that the horses have already been on the heights. Many untried horses perish at once. On such difficult passes all social differences are erased; all remain just people, equally working, equally near to danger. Young friends, you must know all conditions of the caravan life in the desert. Only upon such ways will you learn to fight with the elements, where each uncertain step is already an actual death. There you will forget the number of days and hours. There the stars will shine for you as heavenly runes. The foundation of all teachings is fearlessness. Not in bitter-sweet, summer suburban camps, but on the severe heights, learn keenness of thought and resourcefulness of action. Not only during lectures, in well-heated auditoriums, but upon the cold glaciers, realize the power of the work of matter and you will understand that each end is but the beginning of something still more significant and beautiful.

Again the piercing gale. The fire becomes dim. The wings of the tent are flapping noisily—they want to fly.

. . . . .

September 26th

Sasser davan met us in every way most severely. Before dawn a pricking *purga* had commenced. We ascend to Sasser—this gigantic moraine is completely covered with frozen snow. We hurry to go farther because it will be still worse. Our entire path is marked with many bodies of animals. The icy trail along the edge sometimes narrows completely, only allowing of a horse-hoof. The horses proceed by themselves. We walked six hours through the glaciers. Gegen had an attack of bleeding; he fell from his horse. Especially dangerous is the ascent on the arched surface of the cap of the glacier. Sabsa, George's horse, is slipping terribly on the greenish ice. Amidst the glaciers, for a moment, the sun flashes—all the white kingdom dazzles with an unendurable glow. Straight before us appears a wondrous little black lake between white shores; and again everything is covered by the opaque *purga.* Beyond the glaciers we proceed along an Arctic ridge. Finally, to our astonishment, we see grazing camels. They travel as far as the northern foot of Sasser, and there take over the loads which were transported by horses and yaks through the Sasser. Some of our Ladakis going through the passes for the first time, never have seen camels and timidly they go around these long-bodied curiosities. The horses are snorting. My hostler, Gurban, looks back, and shaking his fist, threateningly repeats: "Sasseri! Sasseri!"

We pass by Sasser Sarai—a ruined stony square. We stopped in the beautiful valley beside the current of the river Shayok. On the right side of the stream passes the winter road to Turkestan. By this road one avoids the passes, but one has to cross the river very often, and in some places even to go with the stream. In September the

river reaches the height of one's shoulders, and is dangerous for horses and men. In addition, the road takes almost
a week longer. We shall go the shorter way. Unexpectedly,
we come into a narrow crevice between two purple rocks.
It is astonishing to what extent all signs of a road often
disappear. One has to pass these places more than once in
order to remember all the contours and windings of the
road—the unseen one.

The colors are beautiful. Behind us are the white giants.
And it is strange to realize that we have just descended
from them. To the left—many sharply outlined snow-peaks
and yellow slopes. Straight ahead of us—the light gray
bed of Shayok, with some reddish and bronze-green little
islands. Beyond them are purple and velvety brown rocks.
To the right flows the river and clouds of snowy dust whirl
about. The sky is not at rest. Milky white clouds, like
heavy threads, are creeping behind Sasser. Had we hurried
ahead one day toward Sasser we would have avoided these
snowy persecutions. The September monsoon of Kashmir
creeps along and pursues us over the mountains, changing
from a pouring rain into a severe *purga*. The restlessness of
Nature is reflected in the animals. The horses are kicking;
the dogs are snarling.

. . . . .

September 27th

At dawn, everything is again frozen. Everything is covered with a deep snow. The horses are shivering. Now they
will have to ford Shayok. Like black silhouettes, the riders
are hurrying upon the light shore. They have succeeded in
finding a fording place, where the water reaches up only
to the stomach of the horse.

After the broad valley we dived down at once into a nar-
row canyon. It was formed in an unusually fantastic way.
In the blue stream, the ice of the night was cracking. The
red walls were full of white cracks—like pages of runes.
Again, unexpected ascents and turns in narrow passes.
We emerged upon a broad valley surrounded by vari-

colored mountains. The varied shining layers in the mountain slopes reflect some inner treasures. On the slopes two lonely figures are moving—every new being astonishes one in this silence. Are these not treasure seekers? No, they are people from some caravan sent for roots and twigs of withered bush, for their fire. After this, all possibility of obtaining fuel is gone and one must make provision for several days.

Among the mountains are small, muddy lakes. On the mossy shores quick little wood-snipes are scurrying. The altitude of sixteen thousand feet does not frighten them. Ravens are cawing. There are very few eagles. On account of the lack of fuel we also stopped unusually early—by two o'clock. The people went with sacks to gather the roots of bushes. As on the frescoes of Gozzoli, the groups of faceted purple mountains appear, cut by warm brown hillocks. Light yellow swamp grass covers the deep valley. The black horses stand out with unusual sharpness against the light yellow background. They seem immeasurably big. Here in the spaces of Asia originated the tales of the Giant *Bogatyrs.* Either it is the height or the purity of the air which makes all proportions bigger, and the rider, who appears from behind a hill, looks like a giant. The middle-sized Kirghiz dog takes on the proportions of a bear. The scale of measurements is great here.

Mighty must be the streams in the mountains to leave such broad river beds filled with these eroded pebbles. Reflected in the beauty of the Grand Canyon you feel some tragic catastrophe. Near Karakorum you feel the long incomprehensible labor as of giants—is it not here that structures of the future were prepared?

What a wind! The skin is chapped as though cut.

It is very difficult with the languages—in the caravan one hears six languages absolutely unrelated to each other.

The provision of hay has disappeared. It is clear that the hostlers have fed their horses with the hay. Nazar-bey screamed something for a long time. Finally, we understood that our cook ate up the hay. The cook was deeply offended.

The lama is informing us about various significant things. Much of this news is known to us—but it is instructive to see how, in various countries, the very same conditions are being reflected. Different countries are as under glasses of different colors. Again we are astonished at the knowledge of the organization of lamas. The whole of Asia is pierced as with roots by this wandering organization.

It is astonishing how quickly the news spreads without any mail communications. And then, these caravan fires, like glow-worms, attract unexpected listeners. Quicker than by couriers, flies the winged news to the bazaars. And they whisper beside the long pipe. . . . Understand!

. . . . .

September 28th

It is a cold night. Everything is firmly frozen. The entire day was woven out of beautiful yellow and red tones. First we proceeded upon the steep, crumbling slopes of the red gorge. We passed the old stony rampart—the remains of military fortresses or frontier posts. Below were the iridescent, yellow, green and ultramarine little streams. Afterwards, we crossed to the broad old river bed—the hillside Debsang. For six hours we went along all sorts of solemn sand formations. They are like pyramids of giants; like cities with cragged walls; like solitary watch-towers; like gates to some forbidden countries; like monuments of battles, long-silenced. It is a full variety, never repeated, colored with infinite feeling. I would like to stop here for a week. But the caravaneers are looking at the sky where the icy Kashmiri dragon already shows its stormy wings.

E.I.has been on horseback all the ten days. She does not like small decisions. She had never been horseback riding and here she suddenly went on horseback through Karakorum. And always she is valiant and the first one ready. Even her knee injured in Kashmir has somehow ceased to trouble her. It is simply astonishing!

In the evening we reached Debsang davan. It became still colder. It would be better if Debsang were called Ulan Korum, meaning the Red Throne. At the entrance protrudes a powerful rock like a red cap.

Be cautious with the mountain streams. They rejoice one with their crystal purity but in the water behind a turn there may be a dead horse or a camel with a bloody jaw.

. . . . .

September 29th

We passed Debsang. We went out upon the roof of the world. It is impossible to call it otherwise. All the peaks have disappeared. Before us there are seeming covers as of some powerful inner domes. Looking at these sandy domes it is impossible to imagine one's self at an altitude of eighteen thousand feet. Limitless spaces. To the left, far off, is Godwin's White Peak. To the right on the horizon are the masses of Kunlun. All is so variegated and glorious and sweeping. The blue sky merges on pure cobalt and the grassless cupolas are domes of a golden hue. And the far-off peaks are silhouetted like pure white cones. The file of the caravan does not disturb the silence of the highest road of the world.

The hostler asks: "Why it is that here, at such a height is such an even surface? What is there inside?"

We read a Latin inscription upon a stone, concerning the camping of the Fillippi Expedition here. The men think that a hundred cases of the expedition were buried in this place.

There is a sharp wind blowing. We are hurrying toward Karakorum. We reach it but the crossing has to be left until tomorrow morning. Karakorum means Black Throne. Its black cap had been seen for several miles, but when we reached it, it was already too dark to sketch or to take photographs. In the evening we decided to go to

Suget davan and Sanju davan instead of Karghalik. It is true that Sanju is also higher than eighteen thousand feet and is considered difficult, depending upon the amount of snow, but this way we save six days. Besides, on the way to Karghalik there is much water, and some of the men complain that several times a day they have to go waist-deep in water, and in October this is dangerous.

. . . . .

September 30th

Karakorum. Again everything is frozen. The morning begins with a stinging blizzard. Everything is covered with mist. One cannot sketch nor photograph. Vaguely the black cap of Karakorum at times gleams through.

All that we now see has nothing in common with what we saw yesterday. Thus we proceed under the sharp wind from seven o'clock to two in this rarefied air. The pass itself is broad but not difficult except for those on foot. One has the strange sensation of feeling breathless even at the slightest movement. Upon the crest of the pass is a small pyramid of stones—those who pass, in spite of their breathlessness, do not forget to set a landmark to commemorate the conquest.

The descent is not steep, but the wind becomes stronger. It is necessary to cover the face with something, and one remembers the usefulness of Tibetan silk masks for traveling. During the day the snow slows down and beautiful white panoramas appear—whole masses of snowy cupolas and cones. There are even no birds.

At six o'clock we pause on a broad river bed. Around us in the deep silence is a whole amphitheater of snowy summits. The delicacy of the pearly tones is a sight never seen before. There is a full moon—and the silence of cold, pure, undefiled nature. We cross the highest road of the world, eighteen thousand six hundred feet. We cross the frontier of China. Our Chinese meditatively utters: "Chinese soil!" and for some reason shakes his head.

. . . . .

October 1st

We reached the division of the road to Kokyar or Sanju. Opposite Baksun Bulak is a wondrous white mountain—so fine, so untouched and delicate in its profiles. The bright sun reminded me of the frozen Fjords of Norway or the blue fairy-tale of Ladoga in winter. But here it is all more broad and more powerful. Before us, in the distance, are mountains etched with white outlines, as upon the old Chinese landscapes. Near the road grazed two Tibetan antelopes—one raised its head and gazed long at the caravan. The Buddhists did not shoot them: "We have enough food with us." Someone else will betray the confidence of these slender creatures. Right at the road lies a donkey with a fragrant load of cinnamon. Where is his owner? The people explain that this tired little donkey has been left to rest until the next caravan. There are no wild beasts here. And no traveler will break this special ethic of the caravan. We also saw loads left by some people on Sasser. They remained untouched.

. . . . .

October 2nd

In the frosty sun of the morning, before our camp, the snowy Mount Patos was clearly outlined. Thus, the Mahatma Ak-Dorje, passing from Tibet, named this highest summit of the Ridge (Patos phonetically, but Aktag in the local dialect). The mount stands above the division of road to Karghalik-Yarkand and Karakash-Khotan. The path Karghalik-Yarkand is lower—there are only two passes, not very high, but therefore having many rivers. The Karakash-Khotan path is higher and more mountainous. The passes are higher but on the other hand shorter.

The mount towers like a cone between the two wings of the white ridge. The lama, upon hearing about it, whispers: "The great teacher was not against true Buddhism. He said 'The true Buddhism is a good teaching.' "

The day started peacefully. We continued from seven o'clock on, up the gradual incline of Suget davan. The ascent is almost imperceptible and it is not startling to see so many skeletons. The peace of Nature forces you to forget the altitude. Near the road lies a woolly little dog just as though alive. By three o'clock imperceptibly, we reached the Pass itself. It is well always to ask about the northern side of the Pass; this side is always severe. And so it was here. The straight and easy way was suddenly carved out into a powerful, jagged ascent. In the distance were spread the white purple mountains covered by a some-what mournful design. A blizzard commenced; and into the bare spots of the snowy dust, pitilessly resounded the almost bluish-black sky. The path was completely covered.

Four caravans had assembled, comprising up to four hundred horses. The loaded, experienced mules were first sent ahead; we followed them. The entire descent was covered with the black zigzags of the silhouettes of horses. The air vibrated with the shouts of "Hosh! Hosh!" And everything crept down, stumbling, gliding and shoving. It was dangerous. The people were astonished at the early snow. We reached the stopping-point only at nine o'clock in the evening, by moonlight. The Turks quarreled with the Buddhists. Nazar-bey wanted to lead us somewhere far off. The Chinese rushed at him with a whip. The human quarrels affected the animals. The horses began to snort. The affair ended with a fight of the dogs—wild Tumbal hurt Amdong very seriously.

E.I. goes on horseback for more than thirteen hours without dismounting. It shows that the usual so-called fatigue may be conquered by something else, more powerful.

. . . . .

October 3rd

Again, the piles of stones; red and yellow bushes appear, very beautiful against the warm white haze of the sands. A meager willow appears beside the stream. Partridges and hares are seen. But as a whole, surprisingly few animals. We passed by some old walls transformed into heaps of stone. The people are anxious to reach the Chinese post, Kurul or Karaul-Surget. Gradually we descend. Already some kind of flat walls are seen. Somebody runs out from behind the gates—then scurries to hide. Some one comes out to meet us.

Amidst the wide hot plain, surrounded by snow mountains, stands the clay square, Kurul. In the distance, enticingly glimmers Kunlun. In the fortress are twenty-five soldiers, Sarts and Kirghiz and one Chinese officer with a secretary and translator. We saw no arms. Only in the narrow room of the officer hung a big single-barreled gun with a cock, like a duck's head. With this instrument one cannot shoot very much.

If Shin-lo, this Chinese frontier officer here, would only know how touched we were by his hearty reception! Isolated in these far-off mountains, deprived of every means of communication, this officer by his help and kindness reminded us of those traits of the better China. It was so important to us—because we go to China with sincere friendship and an open heart! And we met and said farewell to Shin-lo most heartily. Out of friendship we even unfolded our tents on the dusty yard of the fort. The people wanted to remain here at least one more day, because the desert has already begun. They rejoice. But we regret something unrepeatable. Crystals of the summits, will the lace of the desert sands replace you? Other caravans arrive. They talk around the camp-fire. Conversation, smiles, pipes and rest. They whisper: "In Bhutan, they await the coming soon of Shambhala."—"First was India, then China, afterward Russia and now will be Shambhala." . . .

"In the Temple under the image of Buddha is an underground boiling lake. Once a year they descend and throw into the lake precious stones." . . .

Thus a whole saga of beauty is being discussed. Camp-fires! Fire-flies of the desert! You stand like banners of the people's decisions.

．　．　．　．　．

October 4th

We had not passed a mile from Kurul when we reached the current of the river, Karakash daria, which means Black Nefrite. Along the streams of Karakash were found certain kinds of jade which gave to Khotan its past glory. One of the western gates of the Great Wall of China was even called the Jade Gate because through it used to be brought these beloved stones. Now in these places they do not even remember about the quarrying of jade. The color of Karakash daria, so bluish-green, itself recalls the best kinds of jade. It is a quick river, a joyous river, a noisy river. And this is the native country, not only of jade but also of gold. For several days Karakash daria becomes our guide. We pass several *Mazars*—venerated Moslem graves. One would think that their semispherical roofs, with a tower in the middle, were nothing else than the forms of an ancient Buddhist *Chorten.* When we approached the tomb of a saint, the Kirghiz guide jumped down from his horse and with a beautiful gesture offered his worship. It was difficult to expect from this clumsy body so beautiful a movement.

Fort Shahidula is abandoned—it is the usual lonely clay square. Besides, in these places, cannons have never yet made their appearance and have not threatened the clay walls.

It becomes hot. The altitude is not more than twelve thousand feet and above eighteen thousand it affects the breathing. We receive word that the yaks are ready for the passage of Sanju davan. Toward evening the *shamal* sprang up—the northeastern gale. For the first time we were in the midst of a real sand *purga*. The red mountains were hidden; the sky became gray. As high, thick pillars, the sand rose and moved slowly in a spiral, penetrating everything it encountered. The tents try to fly into midair. The horses slink down and turn their backs to the winds. All colorings disappear and only Karakash hastens on—as emerald as before.

. . . . .

October 5th

We proceeded through the entire day, along the Karakash. It is difficult to remember how many times we forded the river. In some places it reached up to the horse's belly, in other places it was lower than the knees. On one rocky edge the entire trail was washed away. We had to hurry and cross along separate boulders in the tumult of the current. Again came a severe stony road. Two horses of Nazar-bey broke their legs. Everywhere, the *shamal* of yesterday left its traces. Mountains are covered with a gray haze. All day, a cloud of all-penetrating dust hangs in the air. One's eyes smart. The whole coloring is changed. The sky has become purple. Only the joyous river glimmers as before with its greenish sparks. The first little encampments of the mountain Kirghiz appeared—*yurtas* covered the felts, or stony squares leaning against the rock. Small fields begin. Here are small Kirghiz women in high white head-dresses and red kaftans, some with peaked little Kirghiz caps. If only the photographs are successful! A picturesque group is set against the purple background of the sandy soft tones of the mountains. On a tiny gray donkey, is a woman in a bright red kaftan and a high head-dress. In her arms is a child in a light gray cover. Beside her is a man in a green kaftan with a red-peaked hat. Above them the dim purple sky. Who would wish to paint the Flight to Egypt?

Very steep lie the trails above the turbulent river. The camping site is in a sandy valley, in the middle of which is a dusty caravanserai. We have not the energy to stop in this yard permeated with dust. On the neighboring slopes it is also difficult to camp. There is either solid rock only, or soft shifting sands and neither of the two holds the pegs of the tents. With difficulty we find a spot. Gradually we discover the damage in the luggage. Here is a lock torn away; there a *yakhtan* has been soaked when the horse fell into the river.

Again, the camp-fires. Again there gather some sort of unknown woolly people. We must say, however, that none among these clumsy strangers did us harm. The notorious thievery of the Kirghiz did not touch us.

Again, some of the whispers of the camp-fires: "Burkhan Bullat (meaning the Sword of Buddha) appears at certain dates and then nothing will withstand it."—"Ulan Tserik became terribly strong."—"Everything that the enemies do will turn against themselves."—"More than a hundred years ago two scientist Brahmins went to Shambhala and set out toward the north."—"The Blessed Buddha was in Khotan and from there decided to go northwards."—"In one of the best monasteries of China the doctor of metaphysics is a Buriat."—"In the big Monastery the head Abbot is a Kalmuck."—"On the picture of Buddha the Conqueror the fire of justice flashes from the sword of the Blessed One."—"The Prophet said that Damascus would be destroyed before the new era." Thus the pilgrims are whispering on the way of Gaya, Sarnath or to Mecca. We meet long files of gray-bearded *Akhuns* and veiled female figures on the road. They are hastening before the approaching winter. They are a speedy mail.

The day ended with a *shamal*. Gigantic clouds of dust like an invisible transmigration of the peoples. One must know also this threatening image of Asia. Where else are there such extremities of heat and frost? Where else are the winds so unbearable after midday? Where are the rivers so treacherous when they overflow during the floods and where are the sands so pitiless? And where else is the gold not removed from the banks? Where else are so many skulls gleaming white under the sun? The broad hand of Asia!

. . . . .

October 6th

Again we make our way along the Karakash. We come to a great old Kirghiz cemetery, *mazars* with the semispherical vaulted roofs. Low tombs surrounded with staffs and with horse-tails hanging on the ends. Unquestionably these *mazars* are very often old Buddhist Chortens. Beyond the *mazar*, we leave the stream of Karakash and begin noticeably to ascend the mountain against the current of a mountain stream. The gorge gradually narrows here. At the left in the yellow sandstone mountain we notice caves several stories high. They are like the caves of Tun-huang. The natives and caravaneers say that they are old Kirghiz houses, but of course, we recognize here the remains of a vanishing Buddhism. The approaches to many of these caves have been worn away by the elements. High above, like aeries, remain the isolated entrances. It is characteristic that these caves are hidden not far from Sanju Pass as if they protected themselves by these mountains, from the waves of Islam. The hostler, Gurban, a Moslem, knows of other similar caves in these regions but is somehow apparently scornful of them. The caves nevertheless are very imposing.

An immeasurable antiquity emanates from these mountains. The sandy haze elevates them seemingly into the skies. And the mountains, instead of signifying limits and obstacles, tempt us once again upward. We reach the very bottom of Sanju. We had heard that there was no snow on the Pass but we had hardly received this information when the Kashmiri dragon overtook us and everything began to be covered with snow. It is a piercing storm. We are huddled together, awaiting the belated tents. The caravan arrives in the dark. From the Pass, a black avalanche of yaks is rushing on, and while running, almost tramples down the camp. Noise and rumble. Snow and cold. But the camp, crouched in the gorge, looks unusually picturesque. Something, as of the paintings of old Bosch or

Pieter Brueghel. The fire-light shines on the bronze faces. Through the dark one sees the horns of the black, invisible yaks. The wings of the tents flutter like birds. On the rocks is the gigantic shadow of Omarkhan. Again there are whispers of the desert: "Near the holy mountain Sabur is seen an unknown ancient city. There are many houses and Chortens." Tomorrow we must arise with the stars. It is a long way—and at day-break snow and wind will start up again to assail us.

. . . . .

October 7th

Nevertheless, the dragon overtook us during the night. Every thing is covered with snow and frozen. We try out the yaks. We hurry on. The seventh pass is Sanju. It is the steepest one—eighteen thousand three hundred feet. But it is not long. How clingingly the yaks proceed! We are again astonished at them. The saddle strap around the chest of my yak gives away with a snap. We must bind it with cords because on the steep descents one strap will not hold. Only the very summit of Sanju is dangerous. There the yak must skillfully jump across the crevice between two upper crags of a bare rock. There you must resign yourself to the surefootedness of the yak. Gegen falls down from his yak, but happily only bruises his leg. It might be worse. Of course on the northern side is a great amount of snow. We must hasten; and slipping on the sharp zigzags, we descend steeply. It is best not to take mountain sticks with sharp points—those with flat metallic points are better. In the silvery fog, the snow mountains completely merge. It is a pity to bid farewell to the heights, where, although it is cold, it is crystally pure and reverberating! There the word, desert, itself sounds like a challenge to all cities already transformed into ruins, or not yet thus fallen.

Why does it seem so sad to depart further from Kunlun, from the most ancient ridge?

The encampments of Mountain Kirghiz start again. The women and children are clean—one does not see the dreadful disfiguring skin diseases.

Down below in the sandy inclines are some dark hollows—caves. From these caves woolly yaks creep out and transport you into prehistoric times; then, also, the same thing happened. In the middle of the hillside, yellow worn-away hillocks are amassed. From them protrude stone blocks of most fantastic forms. Rhinoceroses, tigers, dogs and some sort of enthroned skeletons—it is all the work of water which has long since flowed away. The hillside is fenced by the warm purple mountains. One does not see snow in the direction of the desert. We stopped near an *aul* comprising nine *yurtas*. Within, it is clean. They bring out melons, watermelons and peaches which they get from the Sanju Bazaar or the Guma Bazaar. The mountains are alive with ringing echoes, barking and neighing thunder out like trumpets in the mountain gorges. The Kirghiz women show their embroideries but they will not sell; each works for herself.

· · · · ·

October 8th

It is a short tranquil passage. We stopped ten miles from the Sanju oasis. Isolated *yurtas* of Kirghiz are scattered about. Often there is one boy driving a whole caravan of camels.

Each day patients come to us with stomach trouble or colds. Once more we feel what the great sands of the desert mean—all-penetrating, searing, impeding the breathing. What regret; the mountains become visibly lower. The altitude of the path is not more than seven thousand feet, while the southern part of the desert is not lower than four thousand feet. It becomes warmer and warmer. A series of paintings, "Maitreya," is conceived. Again there are camp-fires.

"Rinpoche says that now the way is only through Shambhala—everybody knows that"—"Many prophecies are buried everywhere"—"Three campaigns of the Mongols"—"In the desert behind Keriya a subterranean river flowed above the ground"—"And when they dynamited the rock it was all not of precious stones"—"And there, where one cannot pass, one can go by underground passages." ...

Much is related and the matters of every day are interwoven with something great and already predestined. Much is being spoken about underground passages. But it is natural. From many castles, which are glued to the rocks, long underground passages were constructed to the water, and through these, donkeys used to carry the water. Gradually before us, rises a new picture of significant lives.

. . . . .

October 9th

Sanju—an oasis. We said farewell to the mountains. Of course, we shall return to them. Of course, other mountains are probably not worse than these—but it is sad to descend from them. The desert cannot bestow on us what the heights have whispered. As a farewell—the mountain bestowed on us something unusual. On the border of the oasis, just on the very last rock which we could still touch, appeared the same designs that we saw in Dardistan on the way back to Ladak. In the books about Ladak, these are called Dard designs, although apparently they bring us back to the Neoliths. And here, in Chinese Turkestan, on the shiny brown masses of rock, are again, as light silhouettes, the same archers, the same mountain sheep with huge twisted horns and the same ritual dances, rounds and processions of people. These are verily messengers of the transmigrations of the people. And there is some special meaning in this, that these designs were left on the border of the mountain kingdom. Farewell, mountains!

Groves of poplars and apricot trees appear, and beyond them spreads the kingdom of the sand. It reminds us of Egypt along the Nile, or of Arabia.

It is time for breakfast and we want to stop; but some riders are galloping toward us and beckon us to come farther. A *dastarkhan* from the Kirghiz Elders is already prepared. On bright patterned felts, heaps of melons, watermelons, pears, eggs, roast chicken are picturesquely spread, and in the center, is half of a baked mutton. Here are round

yellow cookies, with holes, looking as if they might have
been torn out of a painting by Peter Aerdsen. It reminded
us of dear Kluchino, Novgorod, of our excavations of the
Stone Age and of hospitable Efim. And here are the same
kaftans, and beards, and colored girdles and small caps
bordered with wolf fur or beaver. As a matter of fact, many
of these bearded men know single Russian words and are
very pleased if they possess some small Russian objects.
They know almost nothing of America. It would be good to
distribute among these people books in Turki about America. Thought should be given to this.

For the first time we saw Chinese soldiers, in uniforms
of the imperial times with red inscriptions on the entire
back and chest. Very ragged soldiers they were. The Kirghiz recruits were minus uniforms altogether. Can such
an army act at all?

One will ask, where then are the dangers? Where then are
the alluring attacks? Because in the cemetery in Leh there
are several monuments over the graves of murdered travelers. True, but all these people were killed by the Kashmiris
and Afghans. No one was killed by a Ladaki-Buddhist.
And then there is a special delight in the consciousness
that in the most distant unpeopled place you are safer and
less molested than in the streets of Western cities. A London policeman at the entrance of the East End inquires
if you are armed and prepared for danger. A night walk
in the suburbs of Montparnasse or Montmartre in Paris,
or in Hoboken, near New York, is far more full of danger than the paths of Himalaya and Karakorum. And the
tornadoes of Texas and Arizona—are they not equal to a
gale on the heights? And, besides, these dangers of nature
are essentially so joyous, so greatly awaken the vigor and
purify the consciousness. There exist collectors of caus-
tic exclamations of danger, but the most unsafe bamboo
or rope bridge evokes in you a stubborn resourcefulness.
What a pity, to descend out of the unpeopled spaces to the
whirl of the human crowd.

One stop beyond Sanju are said to be Buddhist antiquities.

. . . . .

October 10th

We emerged into a completely different country. Here Ladaki heroism is no more. No more are there the garlands of clear singing of the Ladakis. It is strange that only among Ladakis, did we find strong and agreeable voices. No more are there the castles on the waterless, courageous peaks. No more the *suburgans* and *kurgans* of fearlessness. The mountains have disappeared into a gray mist. How now to live, and whither to direct the eye? Here are peaceful, agricultural, ignorant Sarts, a forgotten oasis. Here are peaceful, agricultural slow Turki, who have forgotten completely that they took part in the marches of Jenghis Khan and Tamerlane. It is hot. In Sanju bazaar, it is sandy. From behind the clay walls and fruit-trees are a multitude of faces peeping out, full of fear and hiding—a whole crowd. The colorings remind one of the Nijni-Novgorod Fair. They offer us fruit and roasted mutton. Finally they bring us a gift of a Kirghiz dog.

Bells ring out and into the Maidan a Chinese official comes riding—again a very kind and obliging one. He is astonished that he did not receive a letter about us from the Am-ban of Yarkand but he explains that the Republic in China has discarded special notifications if there is a Chinese passport. And we possess a long passport under the name of Loluchi—which means Roerich. Are the Chinese officials of higher ranks so obliging? We hope that China will fulfill our expectations. When we received the passport they assured us of the help of all governors, of the deputation from the University of Peking. The Chinese official speaks about the passage of the Roosevelts, who turned toward Yarkand. He tells us of the ruins of the imperial palace twelve days from Khotan, which until the present day still yields antiquities. We understand it must be Aksu. Soon we start out on an old Silk Road. Here is the first place where antiquities can be found, because these places, as well as Khotan, are mentioned in the literature of three or four centuries before our present era. On the islands of the deserts, in the oases, were the strongholds of the last multitudes before the transmigration into unknown lands. Clouds stand erect on the horizon, but these are not the usual clouds—these are the plaits of whirling sands. Probably somewhere there is as a strong *buran*.

. . . . .

October 11th

Accompanied by the chirping of birds, amid the bleating of the herds, beside the joyous gurgling of the *ariks*, we left Sanju. Soon we turned away from the oasis and ascended along the sandy incline of a river bed and found ourselves in the real desert. The hills reclined in weak, uncertain silhouettes. The air vibrated on the horizon as though interweaving some new formations. The full design of the sand spread out—this is the veritable *Unencompassable*, over which passed the great hordes. Jenghis and Tamerlane passed just here and, as upon the waves of the seas there does not remain the trace of a boat, so on the sands remains no vestige of those movements.

Here rises the whole tenderness, the whole mercilessness of the desert. And the Kirghiz point to the hazy pink northeast—there is the great Takla Makan! There are buried cities. There is Kucha—the capital of the former Tokhars. Their manuscripts are known to us—but does one know how to pronounce these signs? By analogies one can read the letters, but the phonetic indications of the sound has disappeared. Farther on, upon the inclines of the mountains, is Karashahr—an ancient place. There, long before it was covered, according to the evidence of Chinese historians, the chalice of Buddha was brought to Karashahr from Peshawar. And still farther, are the foothills of the heavenly mountains where dwell the semi-dependent Kalmucks who remember their history, their mountains and the pastures and sacred mounts. And still further lies the great Altai, which the Blessed Buddha reached.

The shield of the sand quivers. The eradicable signs are ebbed away. We inquire about antiquities. Much has already been carried away from the desert—but still more remains hidden beneath the sands. One can find them only gropingly. And now after a strong *buran,* from these depths emerge new stupas, new temples and walls of unknown habitations. By the few signs, would you say where the most important things are buried? The inhabitants themselves in speaking are indifferent to the discoveries.

In the distance you see from afar the herds of wild kulans. From a distance, silhouetted, a rider approaches. From far he looks at us, stops, dismounts and spreads out something white. We approach and see a white felt on which are laid two melons and two pomegranates. This is a *dastarkhan* from an unknown traveler, met upon the way. An unknown friendly hand to a guest. This is a veritable enchanted tablecloth, blanching amidst the immeasurable sands. A greeting from the unknown—to the unknown.

We reached Sanju, an inhabited dusty farming site. There is a labyrinth of clay walls; already upon the children, one sees tetter, a thing which we did not see in the mountains. We could not find any antiquities. People tell us that two Chinese officials came and took with them all the Buddhist antiques, which the inhabitants had accumulated. If this be true—it means that imperial China begins to understand the significance of the study of the old monuments. One must see if this story is altogether true—or whether these officials did not take away these things simply for their own benefit.

.   .   .   .   .

October 12th

From Sanju to Pialma we proceed along the same Silk Road—and "silky" it is not only because the silk caravans passed there, but the road itself is silk and iridescent with all the combinations of sand; a milky desert with the finest designs of sand waves. The wind whirls the pearly dust and beneath your eyes new lacy meshes are created upon the surface of the ground. Old mile-posts are standing erect—the greater number of them half-destroyed. Behind us little bells are ringing. On a big gray horse the son of the neighboring Amban overtakes us. He is going on a leave of absence to Tun-huang—before him he has a journey of two months. He is curious—but very uncouth. He gives us some information concerning Khotan, speaks about the antiquities of Tun-huang. In Pialma there are also antiquities from Takla Makan.

It is a long passage. We proceed quickly from seven to halfpast four—but the people say that tomorrow's road will be still longer. We make our stop in a fruit orchard—it is infinitely better than in Sanju where the camels, donkeys, horses, roosters and dogs ceaselessly thundered their choruses through the entire night.

· · · · ·

October 13th

From Pialma to Zawa is about thirty-eight miles. We left before dawn under the sign of Orion. For the first time during the journey, we saw the beloved constellation. Again the desert. Toward ten o'clock it is hot, reddened and searing. The stirrup burns the foot through the boot. What must it be like in summer? It is not without cause that during the summer they travel by night marches.

At the right, one sees the blue inclines of Kunlun— they remind us of Santa Fe. On the left, the pink sands of Takla Makan—I recall the desert of Arizona.

The son of the Amban is singing Chinese *namthars*—sayings about Chinese giants. Unexpectedly sharp, with nasal inhalations, with shouts and the beating of some sort of inexplicable rhythms and final cadenzas. It is difficult to associate this with the epos of giants.

Under the necks of the horses the small straps of bells are ringing. Red tassels wave beneath the reins. So, did the great hordes thunder here.

. . . . .

Three doves flew with us for a long time. Where could they come from in this desert? They were messengers; they brought us to a remarkable place, an old worshiped *mazar* and mosque. There in the midst of the desert live thousands of doves protected by legend. Every traveler throws them a bit of corn. This benevolent spot is much worshiped. The sight of these countless flocks of doves breathes forth a strange surprise to you. It is an unexpected San Marco. These doves are wayside messengers pointing out the way to the travelers of the desert. It is said "one Chinaman killed and ate such a dove and died immediately."

The day ends with the golden grassy steppe with *barkhans* which resemble *kurgans*. This is the beginning of the Khotan oasis and reminds us of Southern Ukraine. In the evening there is sadness—Amdong has perished. The Lhasan mountain dog could not withstand the desert heat. What a pity! Amdong reminded us so much of a Finnish dog; he was so woolly and quick. Now there remains only black Tumbal—a ferocious one frightening the population. In order not to lose this guardian also we shall carry him in a palanquin tomorrow.

. . . . .

October 14th

From Zawa we go to Khotan. The entire path is along an oasis. An unbroken line of villages, small bazaars and gardens. They are harvesting the corn and barley. Again donkeys and horses are performing all kinds of domestic work. Again the women have covered faces. They have small boyars' hats and white veils as on the Byzantine miniatures. Gradually, unnoticeably, we are entering the bazaars of Khotan itself. There remains little of the ancient city. Khotan was known for its jade, its rugs and its song. From all this naught is left. The carpets are modernized; imitations of jade are common; of the songs there are only the simple Moslem songs accompanied by a very long two-stringed "guitar." There now remain the industries connected with silk, cotton, maize and dried fruits.

There is still an unattractive narrow bazaar and dusty alleys between the clay structures.

Ancient Khotan was ten miles away from here, where the village of Yotkan is now. As often happens, the most interesting sites are those covered with mosques and *mazars.* The flow of antiquity from Yotkan has almost ceased.

We stop temporarily in the dusty garden square in the center of the city. We are trying to fight for a house in the suburbs. It is not easy to obtain, because apparently it conflicts with some one's interest not comprehensible to us. In the beginning the Chinese officials are decent. The honorary sentinels comprise a guard of soldiers and beks. But they inquire if we will live here for a long time. Visits to the Taotai, Amban and Military Governor. Everywhere we have tea in little saucers with not elaborate sweets. Without delay come the return visits. The Military Governor has a green coach lined with purple. The Taotai has a two-horsed carriage and each horse has a separate wooden arch above it. The bridles are all Russian.

Then comes a luncheon at the Taotai—it lasts from two to six. More than forty courses. The victrola jangles out Chinese legends and songs. Of course the rhythms are very complicated and the variety of instruments can hardly be reproduced by the noisy records. At the end of the luncheon the old official of the *yamen* becomes drunk and wailingly grumbles something, probably funny.

. . . . .

A native merchant suggests: "Instead of hiring help, buy a dozen girls. The price of a good girl is thirty rupees." But we do not intend to buy girls although we are listening to it seriously because we are accustomed not to be astonished at anything; however, it is permissible to be astonished at the sale of human beings.

. . . . .

It begins! Kerim Bek who was stationed with us happens to be a blackguard. The stupidly smiling Amban says: "In the house you can paint but *outside* not." We inquire

[171]

the reasons. He smiles again still more stupidly and says the same thing. We ask him to confirm this notification in writing. But he absolutely refuses. We point out that it is precisely with the purpose of artistic work that the expedition has been sent and that it is included in our passport. The Amban smiles thrice stupidly and repeats his unaccountable prohibition.

. . . . .

The most vivid spot of our entrance into Khotan was the arrival of Tumbal in the palanquin. The Ladakis brought in his woolly majesty to the bazaar with loud songs. The black creature scowled and sat very important. The crowd rushed to the palanquin but immediately flew away from it along the entire bazaar howling: "A bear!" All the officials coming to see us considered it their duty to inquire about the fearful beast and the Military Governor, wanting to look at our Tibetan animal, for safety's sake took George by the hand. Wonderful guards are these Tibetan wolfhounds!

. . . . .

October 24th

We return home in the evening from the Taotai. The raven horses of "the honorary escort" become startled and frighten our horses. By moonlight, the towers of the Confucian temple with their gongs silently stand. The gongs have been silent all the time.

The road lies northward. Straight ahead, low over the horizon, brightly lies the Great Bear. . . .

PART VII

KHOTAN

(1925-1926)

O UR faithful Ladakis had intended to go with us to
the most distant parts. In Khotan they soon became
somewhat depressed. They wandered through the bazaars;
they complained that the people pulled their braids; they
grieved because of the Chinese officials. They assured us
that the Chinese Taotai would order them beaten. They
said that the Taotai himself had killed a man. At last the
whole sack-garbed crowd of Ladakis came; they smiled,
they shifted about, they crowded close to one another, they
repeated what good *yum-kusho* (mistress) and *yab-kusho* (great
gentleman), we were; and finally with tears they begged
us to let them go home. They hinted that if we would go
further on our way at once they would remain with us,
but that in Khotan it was impossible to live. They left
us very touchingly, hurrying through the snowy passes.
Although it was only the beginning of November they
were held back in Sanju where the crossing had become
impassable. We then appreciated the advice we had had,
to start as early as possible, because just after our passage,
there started a continuous blizzard and the severest frosts.

We did not even consider their statement that it was
impossible to live in Khotan; but soon we were convinced
that our simple friends, who had valiantly gone through
all the skeletons of Karakorum, had become saddened in
Khotan, not without cause.

The strangest symptoms began. Not only did they not
want to give us a suitable house, but they assured us that
we would have to live at the bazaar where it would be more
convenient for the Taotai to *watch* us. When we ourselves
made an effort to find a suitable house in the outskirts,
there was a mass of obstacles which we had to overcome

fearlessly ourselves. Our well-wisher, Kudai Berdi Bai, and the Afghanistan Aksakal helped us greatly to procure the house, but the Amban permitted us to make an agreement only *for one month*. He signified through this that we were undesirable tenants, yet neither would he permit us to leave. The permission to sketch was *not* given. A repulsive Bek was stationed to watch us. Finally there came a new Amban and the affair became still more complicated.

The Taotai's child became ill. They asked E.I. to come and help. The cure was successful and all three officials came seemingly to thank us. But their conduct was outrageous. They laughed, gesticulated, spat and said that our passport was altogether *unauthentic*. They proposed to insult Mr. Cheng-lo (the Chinese Ambassador in Paris) for giving out such a passport. Everything, verily, assumed ugly proportions. But these were flowers—the berries appeared the next day.

The Amban came and said that a telegram had been received from Urumchi, from the governor of the province, with the demand to expel our Expedition, and precisely through Sanju. This meant a return through a path closed by snow in winter.

Of course we were already accustomed to the hypocrisy of the officials of Khotan, and we did not doubt that there was no telegram and that the whole story was a fraud. "However," added the tempestuous Amban, "if you will personally ask Mr. Taotai maybe he will show some clemency." One should note that the officials did not permit any of our telegrams to pass, and we had to search for an opportunity to send telegrams to New York, Peking and Paris, by roundabout ways through the consulate in Kashgar. Besides this, the Amban pointed out that the officials had the complete right to take away all my artist's equipment.

The next day the Taotai changed his anger into clemency. And *on account* of the cure of his son by E.I., he notified us that he would not expel us by way of Sanju. But his clemency, because of the cure of his son, quickly evaporated and the officials threatened to search our house. Finally on December 29th the search took place. Our arms, three guns and three revolvers, were sealed and taken away. They said that in Kashgar we might receive them back. The permits from the British officials to carry arms were not even taken into consideration. When the enormous case was brought into the room for the packing of the arms, even the Chinese stepped back, murmuring "a coffin." E.I. added "This is the coffin of such type of officials." It would seem that the inventions of oppression were already exhausted, but ignorance prompted one more "game." They notified us that our American papers did not interest officials and demanded pre-war passports. With this, the "wise" officials of Republican China demanded nothing less than the old imperial passports. Quite accidentally we had with us an old passport and the Certificate of the Swedish Order of the Northern Star. The "buffalos" copied this and the other one, and pretended to send it somewhere.

The demand for a pre-war passport after nine years of Chinese revolution showed us that the officials of Khotan are not only ill-qualified, but that they are limitlessly ignorant; and to remain here would be even dangerous. We plan to go immediately to Kashgar and Urumchi in order to find a more sensible administration. My dear friends, if you want to try out your cold-bloodedness and patience, go to the city of Khotan. Here Taotai Ma, and Amban Chang Fu, will teach you with all their medieval resourcefulness. Before our departure, we heard a rumor in the bazaar that serious trouble was brewing for the Taotai. It is rumored that he received the position of the Taotai and the star from the governor of the province, for the murder which he himself executed of the military governor of Kashgar last year; however, it is revealed that the murder was accomplished not by him alone but also by the soldiers. Now one may believe that all murderers must become Taotais.

The details of the murder are medieval. The captured man was crucified and after two days of crucifixion the present commander of Khotan shot at him at such close range that the blood spurted upon the victor. At the same time his soldiers were also shooting with him.

I am writing with sorrow for the Chinese. I can imagine how the best Chinese will blush for such contemporaries! Let us recall the tales of Sven Hedin, how Chinese officials searched his trunks for Russian soldiers; how Filchner gave his signed waiver to the Amban that he had no claims against them for robbery; how badly Prjevalsky fared in Khotan; how Kosloff was forced to enter the court of the Amban with twenty Cossacks to quell the lawlessness. It is sad to realize and to see that the new order of the state has not yet changed its gloomy medievalism. Let the Amban get along without the aid of a handkerchief for his nose—that is not important. But let the Amban at least know something.

During the search of our things, the Amban recalled several times that the Russians at the frontier of Manchuria *broke his teapot*; all his petty rancor revealed itself in this information. And another very heinous crime did the Russians do; think only, they vaccinated the wife of the Taotai from Aksu!—This felony is related with rancor. During the search of our things, E.I. indignantly said to the Amban, who ordered that the yakhtan containing her own things be opened: "Look, Amban, there is my corset." And so the wife of the Taotai from Aksu was avenged! Our Chinaman is indignant and shocked. While he, a Chinese officer and diplomat, with a literary reputation, stood by, they usurped and carried away our arms! They deprived the Expedition of its means of defense. He says: "This is the work of robbers." Local Moslems come, advise and warn and try to show sympathy. One can imagine what these quiet, cowed people, who have lost their identities, have to bear. One can imagine how much the Chinese intellectuals, students and youths have to stand, they who are so sensitive to the grime of license.

It is necessary to find ways to depart. We must go, in spite of the frost. The camels are ready. The old Chinese whispers: "Tell the escorting soldiers, if they have guns, to go in front and not in the rear—Chinese shoot from behind." The banner of the Expedition is ready. It will be carried in front. Tzung sewed it; red with yellow and the inscription in black: "Lo, an American Art Officer."

. . . . .

The Amban does not know anything about art. The Bek—of Mongolian descent—instructs him politely by means of the following ancient legend: "In olden times in Kucha lived a celebrated painter. Once, as a deposit against a loan, he brought his painting representing a head of cabbage and a butterfly and asked three thousand *sar* (equivalent to two thousand seven hundred dollars). A boy, who was taking the place of the owner, gave him the requested loan. The owner returned. He was indignant that for a cabbage and. a butterfly, one should give so much money. He chased away the boy and considered the money lost. Winter came and on the appointed day the artist brought the money and asked to have the painting back. They took out the painting and the owner, to his terror, saw that the butterfly had disappeared from the picture. The artist demanded his complete picture as described. The owner was upset. The painter said, 'So you have unjustly thrown out the boy. But now only he can help you.' The owner called the boy. The boy for three days kept the picture near the fire and the butterfly appeared again. Then the boy said: 'You have not appreciated the artist, but he is so perfect that his colors have all the qualities of nature. The butterflies appear in the warm summer-time. For the winter they disappear. The same happens also in the painting. Only the warmth of the fire recalled the butterfly to life in winter as well. So perfect is this painter.' And the owner was ashamed and adopted the boy and made him rich for his wisdom." So does the Bek teach the Amban, but even the Buddha said in the Sutras: "The greatest crime is ignorance."

. . . . .

Among the Moslems, news has spread about the destruction of Damascus. The Moslems are indignant. Precisely by harming the sanctuaries and by pillage will this breach be most easily defined forever. In Paris they cannot even imagine how quickly through the depths of Asia fly bird-messengers. However, the flow of Moslem thought deserves great attention. One Moslem asked us why Muntazar, Messiah, Maitreya, all start with the same letter M. Is this not the very same *manifestation?* They also asked about Buddhism. They listened very attentively to the statement of Buddha being also a man, but being great through his supreme knowledge; of Buddha reverencing womankind; of Buddha having himself shown the manifestation of Maitreya. One day Kalmucks came from Karashahr. They came to make obeisance before Buddhist objects which we possess. Kalmucks know that here Buddha passed going northward. It is interesting to notice that Sir Charles Bell in his last book about Tibet points out that Buddha might have been of Mongolian descent. Nepal is populated by Mongoloids and the tribe of Sakya might have been sprung from them. Then, especially interesting is the direction of Buddha northward. All signs, all that remains, must be examined anew. The gigantic image of Maitreya, on the rock near Maulbeck, is often mentioned and described. It does not occur to one that the whole huge rock ought to be investigated from all sides. But when we were already in Khotan quite accidentally we heard about a Chinese inscription on the reverse side of the rock. It was an immeasurable pity to have lost this possibility; because a Chinese was with us. And then, what could this unexpected language have meant? One can expect Sanskrit, Pali, Tibetan and even Mongolian! But why did a Chinese hand write upon the rock of Maitreya? Monuments should always be approached with an open mind.

The antiques in Khotan are really exhausted. During the two months, outside of two or three fragments, and a dozen imitations, nothing was brought to us. And the occupation of seeking for treasure has ceased. And the tales breathe of old communications already described by Sir Aurel Stein. Yotkan—meaning the site of old Khotan—is really populated by peaceful Sarts and covered by Moslem cemeteries. Just as Italian antiquarians often refer to the name of Bode, here also now they are continually speaking about Sir John Marshall or about Sir Aurel Stein. There have not remained any ancient objects in daily use. Life is congealed as happens before a wave of new constructions.

· · · · ·

Why, in point of fact, is Khotan considered a commercial center of Chinese Turkestan? We do not see the nerve of this commerce. We live on a big road branching to Aksu, Kucha and Tun-huang, to the Province Kansu and into the depths of China. But seldom do the bells of camels sound. Seldom does one hear the call of the donkeys. By such steps the rotations of industry are not being created. The rug industry has deteriorated considerably, it is now conventional and without life. Properly speaking the Khotan designs have completely degenerated. The jade has disappeared. And another characteristic pointed out by ancient authors has disappeared: singing has ceased, and has been replaced by fierce screams. In contrast with such singing, that of the Ladakis is full of rhythm and freshness. When a people has ceased to sing, it means that they are greatly depressed.

It is strange to think that this is the very same Khotan to which Fa-hsien in the fourth century of our era dedicated the exalted description: "This country thrives happily. The people are rich. They are all Buddhists and find joy in music. There are more than ten thousand members of communes and they almost all belong to Mahayana. They all live and derive their support from the commune. The villages are spread on big expanses and before the door of each house a small pagoda (Suburghan) is raised. They all are very hospitable and provide the guests with everything that is necessary. The ruler of the country placed us in Gomati, which belongs to Mahayana. At the beating of gongs all members of the commune gather for a meal. All sit in harmonious order and keep silence, and do not clatter with the dishes. . . . Some of us went on to Kashgar." . . To what extent can reality be changed! The present evidence does not relate contemporary Khotan with its past, just as the Appian Way or the Road to Ostia do not lead to the present Roman Rome.

It is a pity that Fa-hsien did not travel further than Kashgar in what is now Russian Turkestan, because everywhere there and even in Persia are traces of Buddhism, not at all discovered yet. And Bokhara is nothing else than *Vihara*, the distorted name of a Buddhist monastery. George successfully discovered this philological transformation in Paris and Pelliot absolutely agreed with him. Pamir, Afghanistan, Persia—everywhere are traces of those flowerings of culture, when as chronicles say: "The art was incomparable, and a work of art and a book were the best gifts."

. . . . .

Tsung had a dream. We three, E.I., George and I, with sabers, slashed Yang-tu-t'u. Tsung comes running to tell it and laughs: "A very good dream. Now all the victory will be yours, and Tu-t'u will fare badly." Tzi Han Chen interprets this dream and also smiles broadly with pleasure that, if only in a dream, Tu-t'u fared badly. Tsung emphasizes the importance of the dream: "If Tu-t'u treats the great guests badly things will fare badly with him and he will not live." So in far-away Khotan is rendered a verdict against Tu-t'u in Urumchi: "More than a year he will not live." We speak to the Sart about this decision. He laughs. "You have already replaced Kerim-Bek, evidently the truth will assert itself with Tu-t'u." Although Tu-t'u makes fun of the Peking government he himself is sitting in a furnace of hatred. Who will sit in his place? The Khotan robber, Ma, or Aksu or the one from Kuldja with his Manchurians? Any enterprising troops can easily take Sinkiang.

·　·　·　·　·

The pilgrims are passing on their way bringing new messages. In Urga a place for the Temple of Shambhala will be set. When the image of Rigden-japo will reach Urga, then will flash the first light of the New Era—truth. Then will the true renaissance of Mongolia begin. In Kucha, in the bazaars, recently two arriving lamas distributed images and a prayer of Shambhala. Here, also, the nuclei of revivified Buddhism have found shelter. The celebrated Suburghan near Khotan must be the place of one of the manifestations of the New Era. Khotan is the path of Buddha. Burkhan Bulat is near Khotan. The magnets of the ways are planted "as truly as under the stone of Ghum lies the prophecy about the New Era."

·　·　·　·　·

The Maitreya Series comprises seven parts: 1. "Shambhala Approaches." 2. "The Steed of Happiness." 3. "The Strongholds of the Walls," 4. "The Banner of the Future." 5. "The Power of the Caves." 6. "The Whispers of the Desert." 7. "Maitreya the Conqueror."

·　·　·　·　·

December 1st

One cannot imagine a more striking contrast than the tones of the Himalayas and Ladak in comparison with the desert. Sometimes it seems that one's eyesight is gone or the eyes are filled with dust. And where are the crystals of purple, blue and green? Where is the abundance of fiery yellow and vivid red colorings? It is like a gray and dusty storeroom! The all-penetrating corrosions of time cut the skin like glass and eat the tissues. The eye is so accustomed to tonelessness, that, not glimpsing any colors, it slides as into a void. Also, unnoticeably, a sand storm starts up and our black Tumbal becomes woolly gray. Sometimes the stars are beautiful. Occasionally we are reminded of the charm of the mountains by the faint blue range of Kunlun. The donkeys are bemoaning their lot. And the home-made mowing machines also groan. The gigantic goiters of the people are repulsive. Some say they are "from the water." Others, "this is already such a race." The size of the goiters seriously affects the nerves and psychology of the consciousness. The frost begins. The water in the creeks is covered with ice.

· · · · ·

The lama says that one very learned Buddhist in Ladak wanted to arrange a discussion with George on the subject of Buddhism. At that time the lama was timorous about arranging the discussion. He says: "I was uncertain whether your son could speak about the foundations of the teaching. Nowadays there are so many foreigners who call themselves Buddhists, but they do not know anything and judge according to untruthful books and commentaries. Nowadays there are many such pseudo-Buddhists. But now I am sorry that I did not arrange this debate in Ladak because your son knows everything. He knows more than many learned lamas. Here I have put various questions unnoticeably and gradually to you; and you have explained to me everything. It is a pity that in Ladak we did not have an opportunity to speak. Once I was traveling here with the great scientist, P. I asked him various questions but he did not answer them. He only became angry, because he did not know how to answer."

The lama would like very much to see the Khazars, a Mongolian tribe which remained after the invasion in Afghanistan.

· · · · ·

January 1st, 1926

The lamas often repeat the words of Buddha: "An oil lamp starts to smoke before extinguishing."

Instead of being able quietly to depart from the rule of the Taotai there arise new insults and senseless difficulties. Our things are already packed. The camels are ready. We feel joy at leaving dangerous Khotan. But January 1st, early in the morning, a messenger comes from the Taotai, and in embarrassment tells us: "Mr. Taotai specifies that you go through Tun-huang not through Kashgar." We say: "Our arms were taken away. To go through the desert without arms is impossible. Not only every expedition, but every merchant going through the desert has arms with him. Besides, money has been sent for us to Kashgar. Moreover, our co-workers, the Americans, go to Urumchi. And fourth, the Taotai himself has just approved our going to Kashgar."

The messenger smiles, "All this is true. But Mr. Taotai sent me to tell you to go through the sands to Tun-huang."

"But it is difficult to go there! But the Taotai himself said that there are robbers in the Province of Kansu!"

"Quite true. But Mr. Taotai changed his decision and indicates for you the path through the desert to Tun-huang."

"It means that we cannot see either Yarkand, nor Kashgar, neither Aksu or Kucha. All these orders of the Chinese officials bring insult to the United States!"

"Speak yourself with Mr. Taotai. Today is New Year and if you will beg Mr. Taotai *very well* maybe he will again change his orders."

"But we don't want to beg. We desire justice."

The messenger only smiles and suggests again that we go today to the Taotai.

Here also the people whisper to us a colorful detail. The case for our arms, without special reason, was made of a very huge size, like a coffin, and was carried on poles by four people. This procession went into the court of the Taotai during his festival lunch. The Chinese again whispered, "a coffin." And the Taotai himself became pale and ordered them quickly to carry the case out of his court into the *yamen* of the Amban. He knows that he is committing an offense for which he will have to answer.

We go to the Taotai. As is prescribed for the action of a tragic *Grand Guignol,* the drama must be combined with the sideshow. On our way we meet a procession carrying paper dragons, rocks, fish and all sorts of tinsel. They are coming in our direction to congratulate us on the New Year.

The conference with the Taotai exceeded all limits of patience. We told him about the necessity of changing American checks in Kashgar. We told him about the necessity of having our teeth attended to. We told him about the hurried necessity of communicating with New York. We said that by his conduct he offended the dignity of America. We told about all causes and reasons. But the Taotai answered that we could go either through the Sanju Pass back to India (which is obviously ridiculous because the Pass is covered with ice until June) or we could go through the desert to Kansu (without arms, though infested with robbers, against whom he himself had warned us); or we would be detained in Khotan. I pointed out that our forced detention was an arrest for which we gave no cause. The Taotai repeated the same words, insisting that our passport, which was given by order of the Peking government, was not valid. Is it possible that Mr. Chang Lo, the representative of China, at the League of Nations, does not know how to give a passport? But the Taotai had never heard of the League of Nations. I pointed out that in view of such offensive conduct, I desired to leave China completely. The Taotai repeated the same thing. The people behind the Taotai's back laughed and pointed to his head. We disputed unceasingly. It was impossible to follow up this complicated fissure of ignorance and madness. The Taotai was trying to annihilate our sympathy for China. We remembered one of our acquaintances, a progressive

Chinese, in America. Listening to my defense of China, he somehow withered and asked sadly: "And you yourself, have you already been in China?" I answered, "I am intending to go there." He added: "We shall speak after your return."

And so we returned to our house *arrested*. We sat upon our packed trunks and we ended the New Year's Day by composing a written address to the Consuls of Kashgar: "The Roerich Expedition on the eve of leaving for Kashgar has been arrested by the Chinese officials of Khotan without cause occasioned on the part of the Expedition.

"In view of the absence of a United States Consul, we are addressing ourselves herewith to the representatives of foreign governments in the city of Kashgar with the urgent demand that they show the most serious consideration in obtaining permission at once for the Expedition to proceed to Kashgar. In the event that permission of the Kashgar Taotai be insufficient we beg that they telegraph at our expense to the Governor-General of the Province of Urumchi.

"Three causes compel us precipitately to hurry on. These are: First, the necessity to communicate with our representatives from America; second, the necessity to see the doctor of the Swedish Mission; third, the necessity of receiving money in Kashgar."

And so we shall wait. Our letters at best can reach only in nine days, if they reach at all. We have received back five of our very important telegrams undispatched. Everything has become really dangerous, because the officials are in every way hindering our communications with America. Our arms are seized. Of what else do they wish to deprive us?

We have received a note about the seizure of our arms. It begins thus: "I am giving this paper for the reason that before me appeared a foreign man, Hulitzu, the other name, Loluchi, etc." It appears that Hulitzu means Roerich and Loluchi is also Roerich. Who can make anything out of this diabolic nonsense!

It is significant that America is again completely ignored in this manuscript. It seems that altogether the Taotai, even more than Columbus, doubts the existence of some kind of unknown-to-him America, which is called Mei-Kuo.

E.I. is very depressed. She set out with such an open heart. She says: "What shall one do with humanity; these are not men." George is very downcast: "But that China, which is shown to us in museums and lectures, has nothing in common with what is occurring!" Our Chinese has drooped altogether, and begs us not to speak of anything because they will kill us, "because these are thieves, murderers and dogs!" The lama whispers, "The Chinese never act differently." All this becomes dangerous.

Sir Aurel Stein gives in his book, as an authentic fact, that the Taotai in Kashgar for a few years of his administration transferred in his name to Hankow two million *taels*. We thought this communication impossible, although Sir Aurel Stein is an authoritative scientist. But is it possible? Is it possible? . . .And you, builders of new China, how hard it must be for you! And are you many? But of course the history of the world has always been created by the minority.

.   .   .   .   .

I hope that the Roosevelts had it easier. They happily avoided the sack of Khotan. And withal, hunting in the mountains saves one from daily communications with the Taotai and Amban. In the mountains no one harmed us, nor placed obstacles in our way. And there was no one to change his decisions daily. And after all, this is not a difference of psychologies. And our Chinese and the Moslems equally understand the whole dangerous absurdity of the situation. Just now someone offered to find a faithful man who would place our letter to the Consuls into the postbag, because today near the post office some suspicious watchers were noticed.

. . . . .

January 2nd

A merchant came inquiring about the possibilities of commercial connections with America. But what connections can there be if Khotan meets those coming from America in such hostility? One may not enter and may not leave. Such commercial connections!

. . . . .

The more hostile the officials are to us, the more sympathetically is the population inclined toward us. They offer to send over our addresses to the Consuls in a more certain way. Our people are sincerely indignant, especially at the seizure of the arms. They say: "They will never return the arms." Three Chinese advise us to go on Russian roads. They express the belief that the officials, as usual, want to extort a large bribe. Our case is being discussed from all sides at the bazaar. Today the Bek accompanied George even during his ride. It means that the surveillance over us is intensified.

I am writing all these details because it will be useful for others. Verily, it is instructive! We have a passport from the Peking government; a special letter of recommendation from the Chinese Ambassador in Paris; a wonderful letter from the United States Consul in Calcutta; a letter from the Victoria and Albert Museum in London; a letter from the Archaeological Society in Washington; letters from six institutions in the United States. With us is a Chinese, a former officer and diplomat. With us are books published about my paintings. With us are English, French and other passports. And even with this complete symposium, one risks falling prey to the tyranny of dangerous despots. All this is very instructive.

Just now they have brought a new "authentic" communication from the bazaar. Don't you see, during the search of our house many *machine guns* were found. Tomorrow they will discover that my pictures are wings of aeroplanes. They speak about a Great Foreigner who travels from Tibet on one hundred horses! On verifying this, it comes out that this is also about us.

. . . . .

January 3rd

They speak in the bazaar about the fight of the ten Chinese generals. They speak about the death of Chang-Tso-Lin. They speak about foreigners who brought four hundred cases of arms. On verification, it appears that this rumor is also about us. Today our letter to the Consuls left. The men are afraid to go through the desert without arms. It is impossible to foresee into how the present events will resolve themselves.

. . . . .

January 4th

A Sunday bazaar communication. At the bazaar the Kalmucks were betting about our success. And the forecasting was successful, as never before. And they ran to communicate it to us. The Taotai himself with his foolish raids is helping in the spreading of absurd rumors. We shall in some way or other leave, but he will strangle himself in his garden of madness. I have decided to communicate with America and to give up the plan of going through China. I have too many reasons against it. I undertook to paint but I did not agree to pursue foolish controversies with madmen. One can cross the highest mountains, one can find a common tongue with the most primitive tribes, but savages in dress clothes with decorations and many wives, are absolutely not acceptable and do not enter into any evolution.

. . . . .

They come to ask us to help a woman going through a difficult childbirth. Of course we are helpless. But the Chinese knows a sure remedy: "This is the devil sitting under the bed and it hinders the woman from giving birth. One has to shoot with a gun under the bed and the devil will run away and the woman will give birth immediately!" The Chinaman has another conjecture; he says with a very important air: "The Tibetans are fools. They think that in heaven there is only one dragon. This is foolish. In the heaven there are a dragon and a bird. One dragon cannot make rain." The Chinese also knows that there exists a district where only women live and they give birth only to girls. He dislikes *"revived corpses"* very much.

. . . . .

We are formulating our accusation against the Taotai for the Governor-General as follows: We accuse Ma-ta-jen Taotai of Khotan of the following: 1. Of a deeply insulting attitude toward the dignity of the United States of America and toward the cultural goal of our expedition. 2. Of his insulting refusal to take into consideration the letter from the Consul-General of the United States in India. 3. Of his insulting prohibition put upon the pursuit of artistic work in Khotan under threat of confiscating all art materials belonging to the expedition. 4. Of the insulting refusal to take into consideration all letters and authorizations from the American institutions which have organized the expedition. 5. Of the insulting behavior toward our personal dignity. 6. Of the insulting refusal to recognize as valid our Chinese passport given to us by order of the Peking government, through Mr. Cheng Lo, the Chinese Ambassador in Paris. 7. Of the refusal to take into consideration the letter given by Mr. Cheng Lo to all governors of Turkestan. 8. Of forcibly detaining the expedition in Khotan which ruined the scheduled plans of the expedition. 9. The insulting seizure of all our arms (two guns, one hunter's gun and three revolvers), which deprived the expedition of all means of defense, although every traveler crossing the desert carries arms. 10. Of the insulting and inhuman threat to send the expedition beyond the boundaries of China through the Pass of Sanju closed with snow. 11. Of the insulting refusal to take into consideration the presence in the expedition of a middle-aged lady.

12. Of insulting and inhuman intent to send the expedition to the desert in the direction of Tun-huang without arms, without money and with the members suffering from their teeth. 13. Of the insulting and humiliating change of his own orders each day. 14. Of the insulting and inhuman refusal to permit a personal consultation with the doctor of the Swedish Mission in Kashgar. 15. Of the insulting refusal to permit us to arrange our money affairs personally in Kashgar. 16. Of his insulting demand that we show the invalid pre-war passport, nine years after the revolution. 17. Of his insulting refusal to permit us to communicate with American institutions from Kashgar.

If Ma-ta-jen, the Taotai of Khotan, would like to follow the indications from the Governor-General at Urumchi he would strive to direct the expedition just there. His repeated refusals to permit us to proceed to Urumchi via Kashgar show his criminal intentions. The above-mentioned accusations force us to demand a full and immediate satisfaction.

. . . . .

Also one must notice that in all negotiations, we pointed out to the officials that such actions as theirs would reflect on the Chinese students and Chinese quarters so numerous and widespread in America. But it was clear that the fate of their compatriots did not interest the criminal officials in the slightest.

. . . . .

Our lama informs us that a lama known to him was going on a pilgrimage to Tibet and was arrested by Chinese officials. The lama gave a bribe to the local colonel of a thousand *lan,* a horse and two pieces of cloth. And in the night the latter let him through. The lama walked for nine days by crossing at night and during the day hid himself in the sands.

. . . . .

January 5th

Vedantists call Buddhists "Nastika." It means godless people. However, Vedanta also does not concede a personal god but knows only the principle. The formula of initiation of a Buddhist is: "I take refuge in Buddha; I take refuge in The Teaching; I take refuge in the Order." Does not this formula lead to endless knowledge—Buddha the man, the greater teacher of light, reverencing knowledge and summoning to go fearlessly along the path of general well-being. The entire contemporary evolution was foretold by Buddha—this lion of fearlessness and attainment.

. . . . .

An occidental newspaper from India reached us. Bose has discovered muscles in plants. Of course, if there are nerves, why not muscles. Bose is demonstrating just that page which is needed for the coming evolution.

. . . . .

January 6th

Another "wonderful" detail about Khotan. A month ago a woman servant came to be hired—a strange Moslem woman; she at once threw back her veil and started vulgarly to smile, offering her services. The cheeks were rouged. The eyebrows thick as a finger—in one straight line. One felt something specially sent, unclean. We refused. She left. Today an old Chinese complained about rumors which the Amban spread that he made dishonorable offers to the washwoman. The old man is again indignant. At once we remembered the rouged one. Travelers, be careful! The old man protests: "The Amban himself has a wine shop in Yarkand. If only we could get soldiers from the Consul!" If even a Chinese dreams of the Consul's soldiers one can imagine his mood.

. . . . .

The characteristics of the fifth Buddha: The North; the blessing of fearlessness; Akochir or Ak Dorje (the crossed

[191]

Dorje); the sound A; Tara; Visvapani (the many-armed, all bestowing) Maitreya.

.　.　.　.　.

In his article in the Shanghai *Times* of 1925, "In the wilderness of Tibet," Dr. Lao Tsin says, "in one of the sanctuaries I have seen one of its most remarkable characteristics—the mummified body of a scientist who, they say, died 350 years ago. Garbed in the costume of a Tibetan lama, as he was during his life, he sits in an armchair and appears like a man rather fallen asleep than dead hundreds of years since. Before him on the table lies an unfinished manuscript over which he was at work before his death. The body has turned yellow and dry with time, but as a whole it has kept incredibly well. Many legends were woven around these remains of the ancient Tibetan scientist. I was assured that three times during the period since his death, the body had changed its original position. And once it disappeared altogether and came back only after two or three days. Once the keepers of the temple, coming into the chamber where the remains were kept, discovered that the manuscript before him was completed with a message of the greatest importance for the whole world."

.　.　.　.　.

Okakura notes: "You can laugh at us having 'too much tea' but could we not also suspect you Westerners of the 'lack of tea' in your constitution? You have gained an expansion of your possessions at the price of all calmness. We have created the harmony without force against any attack. Would you believe it? The East in certain respects is greater than the West! The sky of contemporary humanity is broken in the cyclopic fight for wealth and despotism. The world moves gropingly in the darkness of egoism and vulgarity. One buys science with a bad conscience. One manifests good will, out of love for utility. East and West, like two dragons tossed by the turbulent sea, are fighting in vain to conquer the precious stone of life. We need 'Ny-uka' in order to heal the great disaster. We await the great Avatar."

. . . . .

Aurobindo Ghose says, "We say to humanity, 'The time has come when you must take the great step and rise out of a material existence into the higher, deeper and wider life toward which humanity moves. The problems which have troubled mankind can only be solved by conquering the kingdom within; not by harnessing the forces of Nature to the service of comfort and luxury, but by mastering the forces of the intellect and the spirit; by vindicating the freedom of man within as well as without and by conquering, from within, external Nature."

. . . . .

Alexandra David-Neel says in her article, "The Coming Hero": ("La Vie de Peuple," 1925, Paris.) "We can smile at these extravagant dreams but in those immense regions where they are accepted with unshaken belief and with the greatest reverence, their influence can become powerful and foreshadow completely unexpected events which the most skillful of politicians is unable to foresee."

Read the story of David-Neel about the old lama who brought flowers upon the glaciers. Read the tale of the lama about the coming of the time of Shambhala. From a local story-teller the lama is transformed into a participant in international events. David-Neel has brought from Tibet several new variants of the manuscript about Shambhala.

. . . . .

For a scientist the whole net of prophecies and very significant indications drawn across the entire immeasurable distances of Asia, represents a remarkable interest. A poet would say that the sand and stones were speaking because often the ways of this speeding information are absolutely undecipherable. And you need but relate a piece of information when, immediately, one gives you in reply a still more significant piece of news. And at this, the half-shut eyes are faintly glistening.

. . . . .

And so we live. Once we receive a piece of information from the heights, and once from the abyss. Today a soldier stopped our Chinese at the bazaar, caught hold of his horse by the bridle, and demanded money from him. Yesterday one of our "guards" stopped a woman on the road and tried to demand money from her. And in such a country they have left us without arms! It is strange that Prjevalsky also had unpleasant experiences just in Khotan. Marco Polo condemns the customs of Khotan. So we sit on our trunks amidst untold infamy. They brought us information from the bazaar that the Taotai is introducing the opium trade in Khotan.

. . . . .

January 8th

A number of members of the brotherhood of Buddha spent their time in quarrels and the Blessed One left them. The neighboring donors were repelled by the quarreling ones and the latter were humbled and came to Buddha asking him to forget everything not referring to the causes of quarrels among them. But Buddha said: "Such reconciliation will not be fundamental. On the contrary, fearlessly uncover all the roots of the quarrels and of your animosity. Only then will reconciliation be real."

. . . . .

Going to Asia do not take much food. Everything is there in sufficient quantity. Kashmiri agencies know nothing. They made us carry flour and rice with us. They warned us that there was no sugar. They made us take forage. However, everything is there and for the ten days of desert through Karakorum, not much provision is needed. It only makes the caravan senselessly long!

. . . . .

January 10th

How is our consciousness enriched by sitting in Khotan? It becomes clear that a life such as that in Khotan should not exist. Imagine the lives of one hundred thousand people plunged into complete darkness, divested of all light. Out of darkness are being born disease, vice, lies, treachery and ignorance. The people have retained only their small trade, achieved by cheating and treachery. The understanding of quality in the products has died out. The understanding about celerity in work has perished. The understanding of the victory of labor is demolished. Submersion in the slush of bazaars and a mutual strangulation goes on. Thus it cannot continue!

. . . . .

The lama who warned us that "Chinese cannot act differently" is predicting another occurrence. He says: "When they see that things cannot continue in such insolence and cruelty, they will assure you that nothing at all happened, that it only appeared so to us and they were always friends. Note that they transmit everything by word of mouth and that the frightened Beks will deny everything that they have seen and heard. The only proof is the receipt regarding the seizure of the arms."

You, builders of New China, remove the "buffalos" more quickly. The place for them is the zoo.

. . . . .

Our Khotan friend, Kudai-Berdi-Bai, relates with the humor of the East, about his visit to a miserly friend: "I come to him and he sits and washes heaps of silver coins which have become absolutely black. It appears that he keeps his riches in the ground and our earth is such that the silver gets absolutely black. And so I tell him, 'Dost thou see, even the silver gets black when it is hidden from people. And thy face will also get black in the other world, if thou wilt uselessly hide thy riches.' "

This is a tale from the practical East.

. . . . .

Great auriferous sands were recently found two days away from Khotan, along the Karakash, Thousands of gold seekers who worked on the stream of the river Keriya left their work and turned to Karakash. A few more gold-bearing rivers were mentioned. Of course, all this is exploited by very crude means. In natural resources Sinkiang is a rich province.

. . . . .

January 11th

The sensation of Khotan! Bazaar rumors came, about the dinner arranged by some official in Kashgar. It is being discussed at the bazaars in the most fantastic way. The Taotai officials, merchants and also many of the poorest inhabitants were invited to the dinner. The places were so arranged that the Taotai and the officials were among the most ragged beggars. The same thing happened with the richest man of the city. The host said: "Now we are not in office. Here we are all men, are all equals. Is it not so? Tomorrow you will be the head, Taotai, and today we are equal people." According to the echoes in Khotan the impression was very great. So it is being related in the bazaar. One cannot discern where the people's creation begins.

. . . . .

January 12th

Letters came from America. Through Kuldja from November 5th and through Tashkent from December 1st; almost the same amount of time as to Ladak from New York. Beloved friends, we read with joy about all works, exhibitions, lectures, the school, the propaganda of art among broad masses; because all this is so imperatively needed. You are bringing true joy into the life of youth and are kindling the heart-fires.

. . . . .

We heard about some gigantic statues in Central Asia. It is difficult to know which; maybe these are the celebrated statues in Bamian, the half-destroyed city between Kabul and Balkh. The height of one of these is 170 feet. Some consider them entirely of Buddhist origin. Others see in them the most ancient antiquity. The same unclearness as about the stone giants on the Easter Island.

. . . . .

Our Chinese is deeply offended by the officials. He does not want to go back to China. He hung on the gates some sort of tremendous vivid notice—black and red. In translation it means: "The American art officer, Lo, forbids any one to enter into the court who has no business there." It appears that "Lo" means Roerich!?! "Lo"—in Chinese, also means "alarm."

. . . . .

In Khotan there was a fire during the night. The Sarts interpreted it as due to the unworthy conduct of the officials against the good guests.

. . . . .

January 13th

A telegram came: "Washington undertakes necessary measures." But the arms were all taken away. And without arms I cannot attempt to sketch in unknown countries. I have a great deal of experience and reasons for this. Not only people but wild dogs have taught me this custom. Isn't it insolent to ignore all papers and to deprive us of all means of defense? There have been many cases of oppression of expeditions but such an act is not known in literature. I am placing the responsibility upon the government of the Chinese Republic.

.   .   .   .   .

January 15th

From America came a telegram so distorted that it was impossible to understand the meaning. The unseen friends from the bazaar brought the news about a big quarrel between the Taotai and Amban.

.   .   .   .   .

And even days of seeming inactivity are full of signs. Here is a remarkable little casket! There is news about the monastery near Kuldja! And there is Maitreya! There is information that often the ruler of a district of China simply doesn't recognize the money of his predecessor. And the people do not know where to keep their money. From everyday life, the discussion ascends to the problems of the common order of things. There are periods, called the "balls of events," when each circumstance rolls toward one and the same common end. It is now for seventeen years that we are watching the manifestations of the hastening of evolution. Between the tomb of that which passes away and between the cradle of the future, electrons of untold energy are gathering new formations. And the painter-hermit of the mountain abodes is tracing with surety the battle and victory of Maitreya. Confidently he is tracing the lines and the distinctions of those approaching ones, and the signs of those passing away! And quietly and indisputably he is signing the dedication: "Homage to the ruler of the law, to the exalted ruler of the northern country of Shambhala." In Burkan Bulat will be the Temple of Shambhala.

.   .   .   .   .

January 17th

The officials are intensifying their criminality. The Amban started to open packages addressed to us. Today he opened a package from the Shanghai bank. We shall say to him, "Do not forget, Amban, that it is just the Statue of Liberty which opens the way to the heart of America. Now all Khotan knows that we have received money. Yet you and the Taotai have deprived us all of means of self-defense."

The Amban notifies us that there is an order from Urumchi to open all letters and to seize our arms. But that instead of arms, they will give us military escort. I answer him that we cannot trust their soldiers, because they all run away at the sight of our one dog. However, three years ago an American expedition had to defend itself from an attack of a pack of dogs, by shooting. I point out to the Amban that the arms taken by him belong to the American institutions but again America is being completely ignored. I also tell him that his soldiers will end by shooting each other. The Amban did not have time to reach the city when, in confirmation of my remarks about the guard, the secretary came galloping to us, asking help in a serious surgical case. Two of the Taotai's closest bodyguards shot one another. Of course we are not surgeons. It appears that the officer of the Taotai was stealing some things and the other guard discovered it and, as a result, the two were seriously wounded. And from these thieves and assassins, the Taotai wishes to provide our guard. Our old man Ts'ai Han Chen says, "Formerly, for opening a stranger's letter in China, one was punished by having an eye taken out and a hand cut off. But here there are no officers but robbers." It will be enlightening to see how we will find the central power of the province Sinkiang, in Urumchi.

· · · · ·

January 18th

The first snow fell. E.I. is feeding the birds. Masses of speckled little birds surrounded her. Hindus often feed the birds during the winter months.

．　．　．　．　．

January 19th

We received a letter from the English Consul in Kashgar. Apparently they are making efforts to enable us to leave Khotan.

．　．　．　．　．

January 20th

There is a letter from the English Consul. He notifies us that following his efforts and those of the Kashgar Taotai, the Governor-General invites us immediately to proceed to Kashgar. We will see how and when the local "Governors" are going to notify us.

．　．　．　．　．

Toward evening the Amban notifies us briefly through Khudai-Berdí-Baí that a letter has been received from the Governor-General with permission for us to go to Kashgar. Even the commands of the Governor-General are being transmitted through the private note of a private man. What an organization! At our first meeting I said to the Taotai that Akbar the Great called travelers the best ambassadors of his kingdom and always took care to preserve good relationship with them. I can say now to the Taotai, "You, Ma-ta-jen, for three months have very actively created our mood and I did not hide from you that I would describe all that occurred. Confucius ordained that according to the committed evil, one must act, in *just measure.* China is a Confucian country and according to Confucius I have to write on your portrait: Ma-ta-jen, ignorant and cruel savage." And according to the teaching of Buddha, "ignorance is qualified as the greatest crime." And the same wise Confucius rejected all who rebelled against art and knowledge. However, we all had approached with a sincere desire to inscribe into our notes that the powers of China had become more cultured than during the times of the decline of the empire. And now let us again piercingly look into the eyes of the new officials. Does there not hide behind their shoulders an ignorant Ma-ta-jen?

. . . . .

People have started to move. Preparations! Out of all the trunks, the best are American—Belber. They do not bend on all passes nor let any dust through. The horse easily takes two trunks. Rather bad are the Kashmiri *yaktans.*

. . . . .

Our Chinese is rejoicing. He apparently feared direct assaults on the part of the Taotai. Now he recognizes that his following of "the customs" was superfluous. He made us bring firecrackers to the Taotai, the day of the completion of his new house. He arranged a procession with gifts when he came to Khotan. Against our wishes he brought cards to the new Amban. According to the results this was all in vain. He explains, that these are not officers but bandits, but he also agrees that one must abandon these customs.

. . . . .

As one might expect from these ignorant officials of Khotan, now they give us to understand that the command from the Governor-General came through their efforts. They do not know that in the letter of the British Consul the order of the receipt of the command is clearly outlined and they think that we believe them.

A *mafa* (a carriage) from Khotan to Kashgar costs twenty-five *sar;* a pack horse, six *sar.* (A *sar* is about one Mexican dollar.)

. . . . .

From the developed negatives many and necessary ones appeared to be spoiled. Some have lines and black spots. While still in India they warned us that these so-called tropical films give bad results. Generally all our regular films turn out. Well, but tropical films are all cloudy. And often a whole half of a film or more, is either white or black. Very good are *Agfa.*

. . . . .

The local bearded men are coming to talk over all sorts of things. Of course, the true intention is not revealed at once. Of course, they wish to hear about the new customs. They think that these customs could be good. They think that all men must labor. All is well and the tea is being consumed in full accord. But suddenly one drags from out his bosom a number of a London newspaper with a reprint of a drawing from a Moscow magazine, *Bezbojnik*. Allah also received his unlucky share there. The bearded one "naively" inquires, "But this seems to be Allah?" Of course it is evident and he concludes sourly: "We do not touch their Lenin. Then why do they offend our Allah? And then, do they know the whole Koran? Let them not offend us Moslems. We are many." The bearded ones sourly departed. . . .

. . . . .

In Cairo, near Napoleon's cannon-balls which stuck out in the walls of the Mosque, I asked the guide: "Why do you not remove these traces of war?" He answered: "We shall guard these marks of western sentiments."

. . . . .

A representative of Japanese newspapers was asked, "Is corporal punishment of children permitted in Japan?" As befits a great country, the answer was in the negative. Really, are many of the attacks on Japan just? The courage and honor of the Samurai, the warriors; the heroism and self-sacrifice of the women; the intensified labor of workmen and husbandmen give undeniable charm to Nippon. I never had any collisions with Japanese. On the contrary, there appeared sensitive Japanese friends. I recall my articles, long since, about Japan. I shall not refute them, but I even will reaffirm much of what was told. Eliseeff, in Paris, spoke about the methods of teaching in Japanese monasteries. It is very remarkable. Sudden questions and the demand that the answer should not contain the least intrusion of the personal. As in life, appear the episodes of the Japanese drama. The assassins are stealthily creeping to kill the crown prince. In the helplessness of the moment, the nurse exchanges him for her child. Shockingly subtle is the expression of her cold official mourning over the supposed prince when her mother's heart is torn with sorrow.

. . . . .

Tao-Te-Ching points out: "A sage places his personality in the last plan but nevertheless it appears on the first place. He considers his personality as if detached from him, and nevertheless his personality is preserved. Is it not because of this, that his ends are realized? Because he has no personal and private ends. He is free from self-exposition and therefore he gives light. He is free from self-affirmation and therefore is being distinguished. He is free from self-pride and therefore his merits are acknowledged. He is free from self-satisfaction and therefore he enjoys superiority. And because of that he is to such an extent free from any competition. No one in the world can compete with him. He who possesses the qualities of Tao is like a child—the venomous insects will not sting him; wild animals will not attack him, birds of prey will not strike him!"

Buddha ordains: "By introspection, by virtue and purity a wise man creates of himself an island which cannot be submerged by any floods" (Udanavarga).

. . . . .

January 23rd

Our Chinese and lama apparently know well a certain type of Chinese official. Everything happens according to their "prophecies." The officials repeatedly assure us of their friendship and put the blame for everything that happened on the Governor-General of the Sinkiang province. Now the officials have the problem, on what pretext to return our seized arms in order to restore everything to an elusive oral condition and to say: "All that occurred was the fantasy of travelers." For three months we passed through a wonderful schooling; something of the course experienced by us nevertheless remains unclear. For instance, why did the officials in every way prevent us from communicating with America and why did they return us the telegrams undispatched? Whereas, it is known to everybody that through Kashgar and the English Consulate one can always communicate. The local people at once warned us not to believe the officials. And to our questions as to why, since we did nothing wrong, the local bearded one repeated, "Because they are fools." But also in the actions of hopeless fools there is some sort of even distorted sense. It means, therefore, that here is concealed not only stupidity but even criminality.

. . . . .

A telegram came from New York: "American minister is acting."

. . . . .

Let us finish by a page of that China which we did not see: "Finally the yellow ruler, son of heaven, conquered the demon of earth and darkness. But the giant in his agony knocked with his head the solar arch and broke into fragments the cupola of blue jade. The stars lost their nests and the moon wandered without aim amidst the scattered fragments of night. In despair the ruler searched everywhere to find who could restore the heavens. He did not search in vain. From the eastern sea arose the ruleress, the heavenly Ny-uka, shining in her armor of flames. She forged the five colors of the rainbow in her magic forge and restored the heavens."

. . . . .

Let us not forget the colorful pollen of Japan which we did not yet see. "Komio, the regent of Nara, sang, 'If I shall pluck thee, my hand will defile thee, oh flower. Thus as I see thee on the bosom of the meadow, so I dedicate thee to the Buddhas of the past, present and future.' "

. . . . .

And again a page from the true East apostrophizes the Mother of the World: "Thou, Who hast covered Thy Face! Thou, Who hast woven the texture of the far-off worlds, Messenger of the Untold! Ruler of the Elusive! Bestower of the Unrepeatable!

"By Thy command the ocean becomes silent and the whirlwinds trace the outlines of invisible signs. . . And She who covered her face will stand on guard alone in the glory of the signs. And none will ascend to the summit, none will perceive the glory of the twelve-signed symbol of her power. From the spirals of light she herself has woven the sign in silence. She is the Leader of those who go toward attainment. Four corners, the sign of affirmation, are manifested by her as a benediction to those who have made their decision. . . .

"A silent command, all-penetrating, unchangeable, indivisible, irrefutable, blinding, generous, indescribable, unrepeatable, unharmed, unpronounced, timeless, unde-layable—the lightning manifested in the lightning!"

PART VIII

TAKLA MAKAN–KARASHAHR

(1926)

January 27th

TIMUR Bey is our new caravaneer. Wherever you look, there are some historical names; all are Shahs, Sultans, Beys. Even the most insignificant one appropriates to himself the title Akhun. He comes to weigh our things. The arrangement of the scale transports one into the Neolithic Age. On a beam hangs a stick with some "magic" circles and signs. A massive green piece of jade on a little string slides along as a counterbalance for the trunk and "the magi" in a round little cap proclaims the number seen by him alone. Truly we found such stones with holes from the Neolithic Age and we called them *grusily*, plumblines; but more correctly, these are weights.

We must go eastward and that is why tomorrow we go toward the west! The stops on the way to Kashgar are: 1. Zawa; 2. Pialma; 3. Zangu Chuda; 4. Guma bazaar; 5. Cholak; 6. Ak-kim; 7. Karghalik; 8. Posgam; 9. Yarkand; 10. Kokrabat; 11. Kizil; 12. Yangi Hissar; 13. Yaberchat; 14. Kashgar.

Our friends, the Kalmucks, passed us yesterday on the shortest way to Aksu and Karashahr. In the darkness of dawn, past our gates, rang the low-toned bells of their camels. They carried rugs from Khotan to Toin Lama. With them they also carried many valuable messages which can be appreciated by the Buddhist consciousness.

Again in our caravan there will be three currents: Buddhist, Moslem, Chinese. The last one is the weakest. The last invention of Ts'ai Han Chen—the banner of the expedition with the big inscription "Lo" (Roerich) which also means "Alarm," is put on a vivid red staff. Ts'ai Hang Chen took our cards to the officials and, as we expected, the rogues, Taotai and Amban, *assured* us that they had greatly *helped* us.

The *mafas* came for the lama and Ts'ai Han Chen. It is evident that these carriages have not changed since the fifteenth century. They would be good for any museum. Kudai-Berdi-Bai brought a *dastarkhan* in the shape of roasted mutton and pastry. Incidentally, the Chinese colonel also realized that something unfortunate had happened. Again loads; again woolly caps; again the ferocious roar of Tumbal. In the morning we started on the road. For the last time the little birds of Khotan came flying to us. And sheep came. Tumbal, like a black statue, became seemingly transfixed on the pile of baggage.

· · · · ·

January 28th

From seven o'clock in the morning we collected the caravan. We saw the type of work of Ladakis—swift, energetic. Worse is that of the Dardistans and Kashmiris. Good is the work of Nepalese, but worst of all, that of Khotanese. Such laziness and incapacity is hard to imagine. From seven to twelve they loaded forty horses with effort. We went through Khotan; again we were convinced that whatever bears the marks of old Khotan is not so bad and shows remnants of carving, of some ornamentation and proportion. But everything new has become a senseless heap of clay and pitiful stakes. At the bazaar you sometimes see faces, not wicked, but depressed and void of any expression.

It is clear that places like Khotan have exhausted their old sap and can be rejuvenated only by a radical reconstruction. The Chinese sit behind the clay walls of the Chinese city. They show no desire to cooperate with the population. They remain accidental newcomers, and do not think of making any improvements to help. Life has become dusty and brains have become dusty. A flash of vigorous lightning is needed.

From afar appears the silhouette of light gray Kunlun. It grieves one to depart from this remarkable range—it grieves one to realize that the Himalayas are again receding.

Again we have a guard of five soldiers. It is not known whether we are guarding them or whether they are guarding us. Karakash darya is frozen and the horses break through the thin ice. The morning is cold but by midday the sun is already burning. Buds are on the branches. Beside the road perch gray-crested larks. We passed nine wayside towers. Again Zawa, Ts'ai Han Chen says smiling, with a toothless mouth, "The Taotai of Khotan thinks that we will return again to Khotan. Such a stupid official!"

But now all thoughts of stupid officials are far from us because we are again in the desert. Again the purple of the evening sands; again bonfires. The caravan with our belongings is much delayed, and we wait quite at ease as though these things which so much complicate life do not exist. On the sands are many-colored feltings. The gay tongues of flame, fiery and courageous, whirl out toward the endless long evening clouds. In the evening, in Zawa, it was apparent that the bek and officer who were stationed with us smoked opium. George asked Ts'ai Han Chen to reprimand them. He said, "Of course, it is very bad, but to the chief protector of opium a statue is erected." And the light of the moon and the silence of the night were again permeated with human poison. . . .

. . . . .

January 29th

Before dawn we ourselves had again to arouse the whole caravan. Timur Bey went away somewhere and proved himself a sluggard. I began to call alongside the tents in Tibetan, "Long, long, long"—as the Tibetans cry early in the morning, rousing the people. On the hillock, a man with a big horn came out and began to blow a sustained note in all directions. It seems that it is the miller notifying the peasants that he is ready to grind grain. Again the desert. Again a *mazar* with doves. But now the traces of light snow are everywhere. The silvery tones have become more severe. The snowy mountains toward the left become more ethereal and more varied. But the sands are as wearisome as before. We have seldom become so tired. In the twilight—the message from the desert from the back of an unknown camel: "In Pialma the water has dried up." Well, we shall go somehow. At eight o'clock, in the darkness, under a dull moon, we enter Pialma. Here, awaiting us is the Swedish missionary, Nystrom (in Chinese, Liseti). According to his tales, he had many such cases as ours with the Chinese officials. The same hypocritical instability and insolent changing of decisions.

. . . . .

January 30th

The fog descends. Around us is the bluish-white fog and the circular plateau of the sands. Sometimes the sands assume a sculptural character or resemble the shell of a pearl. But still today we are going along a very flat plateau with rare low *burkhans,* thin abrupt little bushes. Half-covered, lies the skeleton of a donkey. Here, half-ruined towers—*potais*—stick out. Each one of them ten *li* apart. One can easily cross a *potai* in forty minutes. The waves of the sand merge into an even line on the horizon. What could disturb the monotony of this plateau?

In the desert of Khotan, a rumor reached us about the well-known traveler, Kosloff. They say that when Kosloff was in Karashahr, there was a "horrible dragon" living there, but the courageous Russian *bogatyr* conquered the dangerous dragon, conjured him, and sealed him in a glass jar. By this act the whole district was saved. They speak of the buried cities and they point with their hands toward Takla-Makan. A sort of reverence and superstitious fear resound as they pronounce the name of the great desert. In this direction are spread two narrow files of caravans. They go from Pialma for fuel. And here is nothing else. And no sounds. And no colors. And the pearly dust winds into a blue curtain. Like ancient catafalques the *mafas* proceed rhythmically and the purple wheels slowly turn. The red cloak of the Chinese officer shows flame-colored. As protection from the wind he has donned the most amazing yellow cape with the longest red cloak. Whence this invention? In it are buried some thousands of years.

To the left the file of a caravan departs. Where to? This is the direction straight to Tibet, to Chang-thang. Yes, so it is, they go to the Tibetan lakes for salt. And here is another memorable meeting! From afar, is silhouetted a small man. He walks boldly. His gait is not that of a Sart; and a Chinese does not go solitary through the desert. A cap with ear-laps. A gray cloak. Yes, it is a Ladaki. They will go anywhere, all alone in the desert. We meet. He shows all his teeth, and they start to gleam, and he stretches out his hand. "Djuli, Djuli," he greets. And he is attracted toward us. We find mutual acquaintances. We tell him whither each one went. One to Chang-thang; another through Kokyar; another was freezing in Sanju. And what is it that brings us so close to the Ladakis? Wherefore this common tongue? Wherefrom, this united valiant step? Wherefrom the courage of lonely marches? We wanted to keep this passing friend with us.

. . . . .

January 31st

After the wind and fog the vivid morning glows radiantly. We go as far as Chuda; the people ask us to defer the pass to Guma for two days. We shall do this. The Chinese department of the caravan disintegrated first. On the fourth day Ts'ai Han Chen already had the appearance of a corpse. Tang-ke-chang collapsed and even remained somewhere on the road. Sung lost his gloves and became irritated. The Chinese soldier lost his horse. Altogether it was again apparent to us, that, for a march, the Chinese are absolutely unfit. Ts'ai Han Chen excellently mounted butterflies. Chang was carefully preoccupied beside his bed because a proper Chinese bed has to look like a mountain.

Sung boldly attacked the Sarts. The soldiers and officers in caps resembled anything except warriors. And the guns with their muzzles hermetically stuffed-up and with the triggers bound up are transformed from an active apparatus into a symbol. It is true there are no robbers here, but in any case this entire troop would run at sight of the first organized column.

Again we find the bluish-white spots of snow. From the north side of each *barkhan* is hidden some such light, fragrant spot. Assuredly the snow gives to the ground an especial fragrance. One cannot believe that today is the last day of January—it is spring. The Turkis are working better today, and for this they receive a sheep. Poor ones— they appreciate every token. Apparently the proprietor of the caravan is pressing them. And what kind of a "ladder of octopi" is this? Gegen is again angry at the Chinese.

It is pleasant to come to the encampment before dark. Yes, yes, verily, it is spring. I have been painting.

· · · · ·

February 1st

Guma Bazaar. We marched through some fantastic sand formations. At times it seemed as though these were remains of stupas or towers. There is more snow. The white slopes give the impression of shores and between them it seems as though there were a sea. So convincing is the impression of the sea that one has to remind one's self that in the desert there are no such water surfaces.

Again a dusty garden is "prepared" for us; again beks and soldiers. We had hardly succeeded in spreading our tents before the Amban came. Our impression of him is better than that of the one in Khotan. The Amban knows about our Khotan troubles. He is indignant at the Kho-tan officials. He wonders how one can prohibit a painter from working and confirms the fact that the road to Tun-huang through the desert is very difficult. And for the

"T'ai-T'ai"[8] it would be impossible to go on such a road for two months. The conversation turns to childish themes. In Guma it is very hot in summer; it is hotter than in Kansu. In Urumchi it is now very cold; it is impossible to sit outdoors as we do here. In Guma the horses are not good but in Kashgar there are tall horses and the best pacing horses are in Karashahr. All this we also knew without him. With the Amban is his nine-year-old son. Afterward they put father and son into a vividly-colored two-wheeled conveyance—*mafa*—and all go away. And George has again to go on horseback to pay his return visit. There is a crowd at the gates. Above the clay walls a mass of heads in woolly caps peer out. The soldiers are noisily whipping the uninvited spectators, tomorrow we shall stop in Selyak instead of Cholak. In Cholak all the water has dried up.

The evening ends with Chinese dances. A procession with paper lanterns arrives. Before the gates of the garden, a close circle is formed and they begin to dance. First, an old man, a young woman and a camel. The young woman runs away from the old man; he catches her and the camel decoratively shakes his woolly neck.

Then the dance of the ship accompanied by a song. In a red paper boat swings "the beauty," and the boatman, in a role like Charon, is rowing at the bow of the boat. Afterwards dragons and horsemen on paper horses. They sing: "As in the heaven are being born the stars, so from the earth, are emerging the waters." It is not subtle but there is nothing common or insolent about it. Voices of grown-ups mingle with clear young voices. The darkness of the night is filled with the movements of a simple and not unruly crowd.

· · · · ·

February 2nd

A wintry white desert. The torrents are frozen. A flat plain abruptly commences after Guma Bazaar. On the

---

[8] T'ai-T'ai—lady

horizon are low snowy hills. On account of the water we had to stop in Selyak at one o'clock in the afternoon. We have not yet had such short crossings as these. Selyak is a simple clay serai for caravans, with a few gnarled trees amidst the silent desert. A gray sky. An eastern wind. Some camels, half a dozen dogs and the frightened children of the proprietor. Nothing else. And here strange information reaches us about Khotan. Karken Bey—alias Moldavak—who looked so remarkably like a European, proclaimed himself a Persian citizen, but proved to be a director of the Ottoman bank and a Catholic. This is, verily, a strange combination. In his workshop they are imitating carpets, following the ones found in the editions of the British Museum. With what firm in London or Paris is he connected? And in what antique shops does one encounter his imitations?

At the bazaar in Guma the women lifted back their veils from their faces in order to see us better. The veil, thrown back, is put together like a *kokoshnik* (Slavonic headgear). Probably the form of some *kokoshniks* developed from the raised veil. The bek in Guma is an absolute "Sadko" and he does not even have to use make-up. There are characters ready-made for all the operas of Rimsky-Korsakoff.

In the road the soldiers are telling our T'sai Han Chen the reason why their horses are so poor. "The officials bill the government twenty-five or thirty *scars,* but they themselves pay fifteen or ten." They all are speaking about the murder of the Kashgar Titai by the Taotai of Khotan. Somehow the murderer hastened to put an end to the arrested one, without the trial of the Governor-General. Everywhere are mercenary motives of some kind.

We had to leave Chang in Guma. He collapsed completely—an example of the destructive effect of opium. As soon as the smoker, from out his smoky den, comes into vigorous conditions of nature, he falls apart like a card house.

The water in Selyak is like weak coffee. The tea turns out to be ugly looking and unsavory. Again we are setting up the tents. Not far off is a lonely tomb with two animal tails on the bent stakes. I have been painting.

We are reading Vladimirtzeff's description of the life of Jenghis Khan. A fine, vital savant is Vladimirtzeff. Recently he has published several books and all of such virile content! And so needed for the time! It is a pity that Rudnief is silent. One ought to translate the description of the life of Jenghis Khan for America. This enterprising fundamental spirit will be valued there.

. . . . .

February 3rd

During the night the caravans pass by—the bells of the camels ring out as a complete orchestra. Finally one caravan walks against our tent and almost crushes it. From morning on there is a wind. The desert is completely white. The winter has started and through the entire long crossing we go as in the far north. We pass an old *langar* with the ruins of towers. The low trees stand out in silhouette and we can see Ak-kem—a small village with a few little huts. Our caravan is very much delayed and we sit and wait once more.

Again endless tales about the cowardice of the Chinese colonel T'ung-ling); about the treachery of Taotai; about the stupidity of the Amban. Never and nowhere before have we heard such unanimous condemnation of the officials. It is even boring to set it down; it cannot continue like this; new China will have completely to change the character of its officials. Sung fell twice from the horse. The Chinese department of the caravan is completely without luck. E.I. has been trotting on her horse from eight to four. This is astonishing. In some former time she must have been a rider.

From somewhere they are bringing very beautiful feltings, as coverings for the floor. In Khotan we saw none like these. A complicated mosaic design. Better than the carpets. Truly, koshmas and chintzes are the best of the local industries. The designs of the chintzes are the same as in Russia in the seventeenth century or earlier. I have been painting.

. . . . .

February 4th

From Ak-kem to Karghalik is a short but a cold crossing along the snowy desert. They say that in a day the snow will again disappear. Somehow the strip from Selyak to Karghalik is always exceptionally snowy. Maybe it is the influence of some range of mountains—other reasons are not apparent. The other peculiarity of the local places is that silver and even gold become absolutely black; probably the consistency of the soil contributes to this. Gradually along the extended outskirts we enter the Karghalik Bazaar. Alas! By its severe smell it recalls ill-smelling Srinagar. We ask why it is so dirty here, worse than in Guma. The customary reply: "Amban pu hao." That means a "mean Amban."

We receive quarters in the very bazaar itself amidst unbelievable dirt. We had to resign ourselves to our operetta escort, the beks, and look for a garden outside the city. We found a solitary house with a garden, Tomorrow, the gloomy possessions of the Khotan Taotai end. Will it be better? One thing this criminal could not spoil: he could not contaminate the air of the desert. A wonderful prelude to spring. The air is brisk.

The day ends again with dances. The dragon and the boat are seen again. But best of all is the dance on stilts. The natural artists reveal themselves. The same Russian dance concerning a young man's courtship of a maiden is accompanied by strings resembling the balalaika. Diaghileff and Bolm could find suggestions for their compositions. And the servants in red with paper lanterns are not bad. This little fragment of creation for a minute lit up the deadness of the desert.

Here are less goiters. Give to this people at least a small window of light and the vehement fire of the hearts will flare up.

. . . . .

Karghalik said farewell poorly. The beks, stationed with us, appeared to be idiots. We could not get any horses; finally one bek appeared on a wild colt which kicked Olla—the horse of E.I. The blow fell just on the leg of E.I. But happily it was softened by the Gilgit soft boots. And, truly, why should they force upon us these beks and soldiers? Besides discomfort and expense they do not contribute anything. Yesterday a Chinese came to be hired as a servant. As it happened, he remained in Karghalik after the murder of the Amban by the soldiers—many murders. We ask our Tsung why even the beks in Karghalik are bad. The stereotyped answer: "Amban is mean." (They pronounce it here not Amban but Ambal.)

The snow stopped at once beyond Karghalik. Apparently the snowy expanse ended; but then the white salt marshes started. We passed two bazaars. We passed wretched mosques and cemeteries and we entered the long Posgam bazaar. We do not stay in the tents but in the house of the elder, a big house with dark little rooms. Again many-colored feltings are on the floor; the table and armchairs are even upholstered with leather. Of course this house was pointed out to us by an incidental Punjabian from the bazaar because all the beks only hindered us from moving. When will these hopelessly monotonous habitations end, deprived of color and deteriorating in filth and wilderness? We have just passed a forge. Of course it would be wonderful for the details of a setting of the Nieblungen, but as an agricultural instrument it cannot be of any worth. In the little holes are half-naked men and children blowing into toy-like bellows. Take away the excitement of the caravan and everything will sink into a complete paralysis.

· · · · ·

February 6th

Almost the entire crossing to Yarkand is amidst the peaceful borders of oases. For a moment the rumbling surface of Yarkand darya glimmered. For a moment the colorful crossing on rafts amidst the icy shores flashed out, amidst the gathering of horses, camels, mules and *mafas;* and afterward the *mazars* and clay huts. And the heavy-topped trunks of the willows beside the road. Thus up to Yarkand itself, up to the clay walls. Again a house is prepared for us, in the bazaar itself; but there appears a deliverer in the shape of a Ladaki Aksakal. They lead us out of town and in a quiet garden we find a white house with quarters for our men, with red carpets and, most important, with the Lhasa language of the Aksakal himself. From Posgam our farewell was the salutation of the Punjabi—"Urus Kharosh." And here is the familiar Tibetan language. We visit the Swedish missionaries. We cure our old man, the Chinese; we listen again to different tales of the local customs; how Chinese officials are driving the population toward complete ruin, after which they easily govern the pauperized pariahs. A letter came from the English Consul. He invites us to stop with him. The local Asiatic bank also offers three rooms in Kashgar.

· · · · ·

February 7th

A day in Yarkand. Our people are eating mutton. Silence. A strange thing; absolutely all beg to continue with us. Even the Chinese soldiers of the escort say they would joyfully go further with us. A Chinese captain entered our service as a sweeper; also an officer, an Armenian, the major-domo of the former Amban; they all beg us; so that until we reach Urumchi we shall go in a strange international combination. We paid a visit to the local Amban. He makes a better impression than the Khotan "rulers."

When our Ts'ai Han Chen began to relate the circumstances of our Khotan captivity, the Amban became sincerely indignant. But the most remarkable thing is that, according to the words of the Amban, letters from Peking about our passage were received everywhere with requests to help us along. The Amban is indignant. How did the Khotan people dare to disregard the order from Peking?

Again we pass through bazaars as in Khotan. A slight variation. On the doorways of the *yamen,* instead of a cat-like dragon, there are pictures of a series of warriors with swords. At three o'clock the soldiers and the beks come to us and, preceded by a red umbrella, arrives the Amban himself. Then follows a peaceful tea-party. The Amban apologizes that he could not arrange a good lunch because of our hasty departure. After many agreeable compliments, we part. A Chinese doctor comes for Ts'ai Han Chen. The sentries stand in black turbans.

Chinese theater follows. They are trying out the horses. A peaceful medieval nonsense as in the paintings of Vinckboons.

From somewhere rumors creep into Yarkand about some events in China; about the movements of Feng, about the closing of banks in Peking; about the actions of the old dynasty! But no one knows anything and one cannot understand a thing.

. . . . .

February 8th

Buddha was opposed to prisons. He demanded labor and intensive work. In Darjeeling not long ago there was an interesting case. In a crowd an old lama was arrested. He did not try to vindicate himself and was put into prison. Then came the time to liberate him but the prisoner would not come out. He said that never and nowhere did he have such a quiet place, where there was no noise, where they fed one and did not disturb his meditation. With difficulty they persuaded the old man to leave the prison.

The lama says: "Do not beat people but let them justly work out their penalty." This remark is provoked on seeing that the beks are striking people and are planting furrows of hatred, protests and humiliation.

At the time of our departure we do not escape a fray. Yarkand itself makes a much better impression than Khotan; it is bigger in size and more varied in its trade; and even the clay towers and walls give a certain decorative impression. And there, beyond the tops of the trees, appear the mountains—the ridge of Kashgar, which does not leave our left the whole way. And everything becomes beautified; and tiny ice-covered lakes and blue rivers and brown hillocks appear against a blue background of rocky mountains. We love the mountains so much! Our own planet would be very mountainous!

Again trouble with the Chinese. It appeared that Ts'ai Han Chen has started to smoke opium and has begun to demoralize the rest of the caravan. We shall have to use severe measures. We are standing behind the boundary of a little village, Kokrabat. It will be announced that everyone who smokes opium will be discharged immediately.

. . . . .

February 9th

Again the *mazars*, the graves with banners. Little mosques for the *Namaz*. How much more touching is the *Namaz* in the desert on a little rug before the face of heaven, than the *Namaz* before a barren clay wall. Very humble, these by-way clay mosques, with crooked walls and toy-like turrets. Where did the creativeness of this country disappear to? For the whole time we have seen only one filigree earring, not bad, and a couple of silver buttons. In the sun, women on donkeys with bright green and scarlet *chekmens*, are gracefully riding by. It seems as though there are fewer goiters here than in Khotan. It is an interesting problem to investigate the cause of that monstrous growth of the thyroid gland. Aside from the quality of the water there must be other reasons.

A man rides past us with a falcon in his hands. The falcon hunt is still the favorite sport here. We are followed by flocks of meddling crows and ravens. We remember how in Mongolia you sometimes have to shoot them to rid yourself of the innumerable flocks of crows that attack the horses. We are going along the Kara-kum sands—meaning the black sands. A layer of chipped stones and pebbles gives a grayish pearly surface to the desert. At the left the masses of mountains continue. It is strange to think that beyond these mountains is already Russian Turkestan, and that these ranges end in the heights of Pamir. It is the first day, after three months, when the desert is really beautiful, colorful and varied. And the blue sky adorns itself with an especially subtle design of feathery white cloudlets. Upon the crests of the mountains the snow glitters. The pink foothills disappear into a blue mist out of which emerges the outline of the ridges. A bright day.

The men are anticipating the visit to Kashgar. Everything that is good in Kashgar is called foreign. The good houses are foreign. The good boots are foreign. The good horses are foreign. The good carts are foreign. We are passing two or three abandoned *langars*—inns. And in clouds of darkening dust we enter Kizil where we will camp. The crossing is considered a long one but we already have arrived at two-thirty. Kizil is a strange, half-abandoned place with silent clay squares of huts. A big old Moslem cemetery. From afar it looks like a whole big city of red clay. The holes of the old graves are black. The people complain about Ts'ai Han Chen. The old man smoked opium the whole night. We decided to let him go as soon as possible. We cannot retain in the caravan such an unpleasant example; Sung holds out better than the rest of the Chinese. He does not smoke and shows resourcefulness. We asked him why the little finger on his left hand was amputated. It appears he was a terrible gambler who lost everything, became poor, and in order to pay his debts, he himself cut off his little finger, and thus we have one gambler, one officer of the murdered Amban, one from the caravan of the murdered American, Langdon; one a confirmed smoker of opium—quite a variety.

Our Ladaki, Ramsana, adorned himself to such an extent that he even pinned to his chest two buckles from a garter. But the greatest desire of Ramsana is to carry a gun, and ride a good horse. He is eighteen years old and a useful man can be made out of him. His father is a Moslem and his mother a Buddhist. By some kind of marks the lamas recognized in him the reincarnated dead abbot of the monastery, but his father, a confirmed Moslem, interfered with his monastic career.

· · · · ·

February 10th

Mist; the north wind and dense clouds of mist. For long we journeyed through sandy corridors and deep creeks. For a long time we have not seen such an amount of all-pervading sand. Then gray salt marshes appeared and low hillocks of a bluish-brown tone. It became more beautiful, and when we approached Kingul darya with high shores, with a frozen high hanging bridge, with dams and with a cluster of houses and walls, it became quite lovely. Such landscapes one finds on old Chinese drawings. We entered into the long bazaar of Yangi Hissar. A house was prepared in the bazaar and as usual it was not good. We stopped in the Swedish Mission. The conversation was about Stockholm, about the curing of goiter with iodine and the movement of Feng toward Sinkiang.

They say that behind the grave of Mohammed there is an empty grave prepared for Jesus, in the time of his second coming. In Ispahan, in Persia, they keep a saddled white horse ready for the coming of the Messiah. Everyone in his own way.

Just now the Hindu merchants came to give us their "salaam" and to greet us upon our arrival. They show us photographs of the crucified Titai and of his murdered son. They recount the medieval details of this murder, without trial. In general the stories of Khotan coincide except for the details of the beheading. Here they say that the crucified ruler remained on the cross for two days, and that then his body was thrown out somewhere. And now the *mazar* (the grave) built by the ruler stands empty. In the papers little was described of this tragedy of crucifixion. Here continue crucifixions and treachery, the sale of people and generous remuneration for murderers. The hastening of evolution is necessary.

They say that near Kashgar are the ruins of a Buddhist temple. So it must be, because in these regions Buddhism existed; but it is interesting that we did not happen to hear previously about these ruins. That means that in Kashgar there are mosques and the *mazar* of Miriam and the ruins of Buddhism!

The evening is spent with the Swedish folk. A quiet supper. We hear tales about the richness of this country where not more than three per cent of the area is cultivated. In the near-by mountains, iron, copper, silver and coal are found. The murdered Titai intended to start certain developments, but now these possibilities have again been sunken into darkness.

. . . . .

February 11th

We bid farewell to the hospitable family of Anderson. The seven-month-old Sven stared with his blue eyes at E.I., caught her finger tightly and did not want to let her go. We spoke about the fertility of the district where, besides varied vegetables, many curative herbs: ricinus, licorice, digitalis and others, are growing wild. One can imagine how the plain would develop under the tractors of Ford. They speak about the absence of forests in these localities; but two days' march away (and the crossings are short) there is a wonderful store of coal. We take with us a piece of this product which does not fall below the best samples. And may it not be that here in the neighborhood there is oil? Or that there is radium in the mountains? At that, how easy it is to plant whole spaces with trees. While excavating, great stumps have often been found in these places as well as the trunks of former forests. It is only necessary to apply the least diligence and resourcefulness and the district will become unrecognizable. There is plenty of water during the summer; one has only to collect it in reservoirs. Now in February the days are just like spring. Only December and January are cold. The cold air of the night is of a refreshing nature. If the Chinese would only not fear everything new and if their officials were chosen according to merit and not according to their capacity for robbing! Otherwise, whence this incomprehensibly speedy enrichment of the Ambans and Taotais? By such means every manifestation of assiduity is only for the ends of the most speedy enrichment of the officials, immersed in opium and gambling. We stopped in Yaberchat, a small place four hours from Kashgar. We could easily have made the route to Kashgar in one day, but on account of the pack horses we had to stay in the outskirts, among heavy-topped willows and clay walls.

. . . . .

February 12th

Mist, low brush, naked willows and a bumpy road, with crossings over ice-covered streams. First we pass the new city of Kashgar. The walls are more imposing than the Yarkand walls. There is more verve and motion in the bazaar. Prisoners in chains are begging alms for their food. Between the new and the old city is a distance of about two *p'o-t'ai.* Toward us ride two "vividly red Chaprassi" from the English Consul. The Consul awaits us for breakfast while the house of the local bank is being made ready. The British Consul and his wife inquire sympathetically about the affairs at Khotan. In the bank they speak "about the character" of the Chinese administration. It seems that the Khotan Taotai is known in the whole province and nobody is astonished at his action. The caravan arrives. The things are brought in.

. . . . .

February 13th

The Chinese New Year! At four o'clock in the morning we are awakened by the noise of firecrackers and rockets. Behind the wall is a pillar of flame and shots are heard. We thought it was a fire.

Major Gillan, the British Consul, and his wife came. It appears that they are both Scotch. Among the Scotch we long ago found sympathetic people, and these belong to a fine type of Scotch clans. The Ladaki Aksakal comes. He is a Moslem who lived for a long time in Lhasa and Shigatse. The translator of the consulate comes. He complains of the increase of smoking of opium and hemp hashish. The rich permit themselves the luxury of using expensive opium, and the poor ones dope themselves with home-made hashish. The possibility of earning a livelihood is very poor here. Formerly about thirty thousand people went each year to other countries for their living.

And again endless tales about the enrichment of Chinese officials by pillage. When you are seated in a peaceful Chinese restaurant in America, remember about the robbers—the Taotais and Ambans—who are keeping the people in complete torpor. Let the sight-seeing motors to Chinatown remind you how millions of people are perishing in the darkness of ignorance.

The director of the branch of the local bank, A., comes. A new wave of information. Each part of the province has its own money, which is accepted with reluctance in the neighboring provinces. In Kashgar are *sars*; in Urumchi, *lans*, which have the value of one-third of a *sar*; in Kuldja, they have their own *lans*, which the population calls roubles. At that, half or a quarter of a *lan* is obtained by tearing the bill into corresponding parts. As a result of such operations the monetary symbols are turned into tatters, deprived of any designation. But when it is necessary to give the symbol its former value, one pastes under it some pieces of any kind of paper. One may receive *lans* of which one-half consists of an advertisement of a sale of soap or something as unexpected.

We see the Swedish missionary, Palmberg. In spite of the medical activity of the Swedish Missions, they are periodically subject to persecution on the part of the officials. Recently they even had to temporarily discontinue the work, and yet they are the only doctors in the whole large district. Not even at the garrison is there a doctor. The local inhabitants tell us that nowhere in the world do people know what is occurring in abandoned Chinese Turkestan, left as it is to the plunder of a handful of ignoramuses. They beseech us: "Write and tell to the world about the deterioration of an entire country into a savage state." Again prisoners in chains are passing, begging alms. This custom was common in the fifteenth century, but to see it in usage now astonishes one.

.   .   .   .

February 14th

We are sitting in semi-inactivity because the Chinese New Year is being celebrated for several days. I remember how the American Consul in Calcutta, dear Mr. Jenkins, figured out all the days of the year which were not affected by the holidays of the different local nationalities. There remained only fifty-two working days. And here they celebrated the European New Year and now the Chinese. The various explanations hinder greatly the calculations of the months. Moslem, Chinese, Tibetan—all these calculate different dates.

A Sart comes and says that near Kucha the inhabitants are destroying the remains of the Buddhist temples. . . . The reason is that many travelers and Chinese are interested in these ruins and frescoes, and it is difficult for the people to accommodate all these guests. They built a great fire within the ruins, and the frescoes were destroyed. One may suspect also another cause—the ancient iconoclasm of the Moslems. Whether by this or some other means, soon these small remnants of Tokhars and Uigurs will also disappear.

. . . . .

February 15th

In the morning we visit the Taotai. The impression is one of good-nature. The *yamen* has a more livable aspect. One does not see the tattered soldiers. There is no crowd of beks. Mr. Tao, the manager of the foreign department, is also present. Of course, our passports appear to be absolutely correct. The letters of recommendation are found excellent. And they express astonishment at the actions of Khotan. They will immediately send a telegram to the Governor-General about the return of our arms. During the day we saw the Swedish missionary, Torquist, and many inhabitants of the local colony. It is curious to notice that for a long time now, the Governor-General has attempted to leave Urumchi with his pillaged goods. But the neighboring province does not permit him to pass without the payment of a tribute of many millions. Thus, one of his caravans, comprising several wagons with silver, has already been confiscated. Now the "dignitary" is trying to transfer his capital to foreign banks. One also should note that after the murder of the Titai and his son, in Kashgar, their families suffered complete robbery. The earrings were ripped out of the ears of the son's wife. They brought a photo of the crucified Titai. Friends, look upon this brutality committed without trial and without thought of responsibility! Incidentally, they say that the Taotai from Aksu is already collecting soldiers to proceed to Khotan. The pillaged goods do not lie in the same place for long.

. . . . .

February 16th

The Taotai arrived. Boring conversations about the cult of ancestors, about astrology, about the weather. He looked at the photographs of my paintings. He said that he had already telegraphed to Urumchi about permission for us to proceed. These permissions for each step recall the most brutal times and we are bored by it, to the last degree. Even to complain about the rudeness of the officials, one needs permission. Passing through the city we again observed the local types. These are very cruel faces. Many more beggars and cripples than in Yarkand. We must exchange the remaining rupees. We are advised to take some gold. The Kirghiz are bringing it from the mountains. Hindus and Turki accept it gladly.

. . . . .

February 17th

The day for the exchange of money. The selection of a *tarantas.* A new driver—a Cossack refugee from Orenburg. An instructive scene in the bazaar. A *mullah* with a whip is chasing the people to the mosque. The lashes of the whip strike the backs, the shoulders, the faces. The enthusiasm for prayer is evoked with difficulty and many are hurrying to hide themselves in the side-streets. They say that *Medresse*—the schools at the mosques—are visited rarely. Even in the wilderness, the people expect more refined and more profound forms of knowledge.

. . . . .

February 18th

Not far from the village Artish, one can see, high in the rock, three windows. Of course, these are the Buddhist caves, explored by LeCoq and Stein. From below one can distinguish remnants of frescoes. No objects of especial note have been found there. The people adorn these caves with a legend. The old king had a daughter. Death from a scorpion's sting was predicted for her. In order to save her the king constructed a dwelling place for her in the rock, but her destiny was fulfilled. The princess wanted to taste some grapes. She drew up a basket on a rope and in it a venomous scorpion was hiding.

Fifteen miles eastward, in the middle of the cemetery, the tomb of Mary the mother of Issa is pointed out. The details of the legend are slipping away. Why, just Mary in Kashgar, nobody can tell. It is the same concerning Issa in Srinagar. Are there not some traces of Nestorianism and Manicheism here?

Along the bazaar, Kadi, the judge, passes pompously, with a whip in his hand. He is going to catch gamblers. Of course, the groups of gamblers quickly disperse and after the passing of the "guard" they at once collect again. Like opium, gambling is despoiling the population.

We enter a Chinese dwelling. Opposite the entrance is an altar with New Year's offerings and sweets. On the wall is a vividly colored picture of the "ruler" of the gods. Who is it? It is the same Gessar; it is the same one who is awaited. Each in his own way. The New Year is welcomed precisely with his image. Even in Kashgar which is almost Moslem, is hidden the Far Eastern belief. There, also, we see Kuan Yin, the Mother of the World, and Man-long-life (the synthesis of all ages). And one more image the "Ruler of Gods." This image is less intricate. There are only two figures—The "Ruler" and his guardian. The "Ruler," sitting at the table, is watching the flame of a red candle. In the forehead of the "Ruler," is a precious stone like a red star. The picture is of new and simple work, but very decorative. We went into the yard of a small temple. The temple itself is closed. The service is not performed. Opposite the entrance is a stage for the Chinese theater.

The setting sun is flooding the banks of Tumen daria. Alongside a narrow ridge you go toward the sandy slopes. Like a dead city, immovable and breathless, stand the clay walls above these slopes. The trees are naked. One can see very far. This is the first sight of what one may call a Central Asiatic city. And not under ill-smelling sheds of the narrow bazaars; not by the faces of lepers; but in the golden rays of the sun and in the immovability of the walls you realize that Kashgar is verily an old place.

. . . . .

February 19th

Many subterranean waters are in Kashgar. The flooding of the rivers and the rice fields gives a special kind of fever somewhat like malaria. There are widely varying symptoms: aching of joints; sleepiness, pain in the extremities.

It is not easy to receive money on checks from China. *Taels* were awaiting us since November, but now it is already the end of February and the post office delays handing over the money. The money may, of course, have been given out on percentage. They tell us that one of the local ambans refused, for a long time, to transfer the collected taxes to the Governor-General, because they were loaned out on percentage for the enrichment of the Amban. They brought photographs of the victims "of justice": rows of people with chopped off fingers or soles of the feet with cut tendons. The majority of them were unable or could not pay on time "to whom was necessary." Here are also photographs of the murdered Titai in his full "glory" with two ribbons crossed, with stars and with widespread legs. Here are also photographs of the developments of oil-wells, started by the Titai; group of the wives of Titai and other local officials. Old letters came from America from October 30th through Peking. It took three months and a half to reach us this way.

Apparently to find horses here is still more difficult than in Yarkand. At Dr. Yalovenko's, we found all drugs necessary for us. His little hospital is better equipped than the one of the Swedish Mission.

We drink tea at the Gillans'; we go with them to inspect a stupa. Near the river the road starts to become muddy. We cross a narrow bridge and ascend amidst the fantastic sand formations created by water and earthquake.

Of course, here was the most ancient part of Kashgar; here may be found Buddhist traces. The stupa itself has become a formless mass and only the remnants of the bricks lying at the bottom, reveal the construction. Its size is great; not smaller than the great stupa in Sarnath. In reality there remains only the base, and the whole top cupola has disappeared. It is difficult among sand slopes to distinguish ruins. How many of such masked ruins are buried underneath the currents of rivers and under the sloping Kurgans, under the typical Asiatic cover. . . .

It becomes cold toward evening. And, purple-silhouetted, stands Kashgar with a Chinese temple on the wall of the city. The silhouette is not devoid of calmness and grandeur but this is, as it were, a false grandeur, because the mass of the silhouette is transformed into the fragility of clay and sand buildings. Late in the evening, George Chu, the Chinese secretary of the British Consul, arrives with the good news that a telegram from the Tu-t'u of Urumchi has come, and that we are permitted to leave. But in spite of the request of the Kashgar Taotai and the British Consul, our two guns and three revolvers are left sealed and the permission to paint is not even mentioned, although the Consul and Taotai distinctly asked about it in the telegrams. Mr. George Chu smilingly says: "I learned English from an American teacher in Peking and I have been glad to help and to bring a good message to an American Expedition."

. . . . .

February 20th

We prepare the caravan in a hurry, in order to leave more quickly before the beginning of the spring thaw and before the flooding of the river. The journey to Urumchi is a good one thousand eight hundred miles. It is difficult to get horses. All the best horses are sent to Fergan where there is a big demand for horses from Russia.

We have to discharge Ts'ai Han Chen; he became completely mad yesterday and beat the Ladaki Musu; he is a victim to opium smoking. We go to express our gratitude to Mr. Gillan for his help in sending telegrams. I tell him how agreeable it is to find such cultural regard for the

tasks of our Expedition. I regret that in spite of his representation neither the arms nor the permission to sketch
have been given. I ask him to give us the text of the telegrams that he sent, for inclusion in our diary. Then some
talk about the exchange of rupees which rose in value to
the *sars:* There are rumors about the exchange of the current *sars* for a new currency. Nobody knows anything. Just
as the missionary Torquist says: "The Chinese are born
Confucians. They live as Taoists and die Buddhists." We
should like to see real Chinese. So much is being spoken
about the intensive work in Canton. Is it possible that
there they do not know about the dark life of Chinese
Turkestan? Is it possible that they do not know how one
robber usurps the place of another robber and crucifies
him—not for the people's welfare, not for justice, but for
personal motives and personal enrichment? And the help-
ers of the "power"—the rich beks—are treading with whips
on the bent backs of the poor.

· · · · ·

February 21st

It is impossible to find horses. All the good horses
have been dispatched to Andijan to transport goods from
abroad. Now they are demanding one *sar* a day for horses.
The price is unprecedented. We will have to take *arbas,* and
this means that to Urumchi we will have to go fifty-five
days instead of forty. It is one thousand eight hundred
miles. We must hurry because the thaw will soon begin.
Outside the city, near the horse-market, is an interesting
mazar, Gissarlik—a *mazar* which is said to belong to some
Mongolian count. There is a belief that if one throws a
piece of clay at the cupola of a *mazar,* one's moles fall off.

· · · · ·

February 23rd

It is not easy to receive money through the Chinese
post office. Since November, the post office has not been
able to collect one thousand six hundred Mexican dollars.

It is really ridiculous when one knows that the local general, by commission of the Governor-General is transferring ten thousand pounds of "personal savings" through here.

We went to the Taotai to talk about our arms and the permission to sketch. The Taotai came to a resolution, "Try to paint and if the police prohibit it, then stop." Our arms became rusted from dampness. When we pointed it out, we were told by the interpreter of the Consulate, "Do not make too much fuss about it." Again we felt ourselves in a country not of justice, but in a country of personal license. We were also told that if Tu T'u (the Governor-General) will *find us worthy* then he will permit us our arms and the possibility of work. Colossal indifference is needed to accept seriously all these sentences. It is interesting to know by what means and with what apparatus the Governor-General will investigate our "worthiness," for the work and for the arms. . . . But the "worthiness" of similar officials is evident to us without any special apparatus. Whence come these depths of ignorance? To cap the climax it was stipulated that we should not remove from the case containing the arms, any more than were permitted. That means, we should not take out the revolvers. As usual, the visit ended with assurances that they had helped us very much. Such hypocrisy!

· · · · ·

February 24th

The tales about the movements of the Chinese army of Sinkiang are interesting. A cannon is drawn by two horses. On each one of them sits a soldier. On the muzzle of the cannon also sits a warrior. When the horses stop, they add one more nag from a village. "An army" which went forth twenty thousand strong, at an expense of six million *sars,* reached the battleground about two thousand in number. They count the size of the army by the number of caps. Therefore, if there are not enough "warriors" in the carts, they put out caps on sticks. The calculation of cavalry is by men and horses, or doubly. Nowhere is this forgotten province written about as it actually is. Unknowingly some of the travelers don a dress suit, when they visit the Taotai, but it is time to tell what really exists. It is time to speak simply, in the name of human dignity. One may consider "seriously" the surviving customs of the inhabitants of the Solomon Islands, but a kingdom with four hundred million people cannot be looked upon in our times from the point of view of ethnographical curiosities. One ought in every way to help the true workers of China to bring the country out of its tragi-comical situation. We do not know what and how will be our further path, but the observations of the unembellished life of Sinkiang appall us. Sinkiang was conquered in its time by Mongols, Arabs, Chinese, Tibetans. The backs of the Sarts endured everything and they brought their *salaams.*

． ． ． ．

February 25th

If you have a Chinese postal money-order, it does not mean that as yet you have the money. China cannot even redeem a check for one thousand six hundred Mexican dollars. Whereas the local bank through Tashkent pays you immediately. Friends do not use the Chinese mail. The letters are opened, many things do not reach you, and money is not delivered to you. Again, one has to transport one's consciousness to the Solomon Islands and then one can understand better the actions of the Sinkiang company.

And here again the British Consul and his secretary, Chu, must take steps for us. Thanks to their personal influence, as a special favor, we finally receive that which is one's common right. We express to Mr. Chu our hope that we will meet him in the Washington or Paris Embassies. We exchange greetings with Major and Mrs. Gillan. Truly, they have helped us to leave Khotan. We ask each other where we shall meet again.

. . . . .

February 26th

We left. In the morning the Consul with his wife came to say good-by; the Secretary of the Consulate, Chu, the Director of the Bank, Anokhin; Dr. Yalovenko; the family of Krijhoffs. We said good-by. We sat for a while. Where shall we meet again? We pass through the Kashgar bazaars. We go through the sandy gray road. At the left, the Kashgar River glows blue; pools, rice fields, fever-beds. At the right are villages, and muddy lakes. A milky spring mist is overhanging. The crossing is not long. Toward three o'clock we stopped in a small village, Yamdom.

We have parted with Ts'ai Han Chen. He smoked opium and led women away from the bazaars and beat the servants. I remember his two stories. The horse under him was frightened and he fell down. For that he broke the horse's leg with a stone. Another story. An eagle came down and scratched his hand. Here the vengeance was subtle; a piece of meat stuffed with gunpowder was put out on a long wick. The eagle seized the meat and exploded.

The man who goes ahead as the scout is called *Dorogha* here.

Toward evening it gets cold. There is no snow. The mountains are not seen.

. . . . .

February 27th

Salt marshes, bushes, willows, small villages. A short crossing to Faizabad. By half-past one, we are already at the site. Nevertheless, in the book of routes, the way from Kashgar to Faizabad is divided into three days. Even at a slow walking pace one can reach it sooner. How thoroughly all the books with information about the "facts" must be inspected. Too many untrue "facts" are lying on the shelves of libraries and there is too much reverence attached to the printed word, without any revaluation.

Anew, anew, anew—through new consciousness and new containment.

And some people respect money as such! Just now wooden chips were brought to us with inscribed signs, and the people assure us that this is real money: And the best money, because it is issued by the gamblers. This authority apparently stands in high esteem. Everywhere in the bazaars are groups of men actively occupied in gambling. I remember hearing in some bank a furious exclamation: "I do not pay you with wooden chips." According to the local customs this remark was not exaggerated. The chip is brown, three-and-a-half inches long, and on it, inscribed by hand, are Chinese signs. People love this money because it does not tear. The redemption of these signs is very simple here. After the sign is worn out the government refuses to redeem it at the treasury, and the last owner of such a symbol liquidated the State debt. We investigated the sites of our further encampments and we found that these are not correctly given in the book of routes. We sometimes have to combine two stretches, otherwise we will not reach Urumchi even in fifty days. They sent us two soldiers as escorts—true bandits. We had to send them back.

. . . . .

February 28th

The whole night, till four o'clock, under the full green moon, they were singing all around in the different *kishlaks* probably in honor of the month of Barat. They sang wildly, but mellowed by distance, the notes sometimes resounded beautifully. The singing was not by Sarts, but by Torguts. How strange! How did Torguts come to Moslem Faizabad? Of course these are prisoners of former wars. Until now, they have retained their customs of singing their resonant songs under the full moon. Analyzing the nationalities, you can sometimes distinguish them by the remnants of their garments, sometimes by the language and sometimes by the ancient sacred chants. During the nights the melodies of their native land ring out. And somehow the heart readily responds to this call. It is instructive to follow the combinations of peoples covered by the sands of the deserts.

We rose early, at five o'clock, because the road is long—fifteen *p'o-t'ai*. It means a hundred and fifty Chinese *lee*, which means about sixty miles. First, salt marshes, greenish-gray; then dead sand, *barkhans*. The dust is opaque; the thin brush has been uprooted for fuel and because of this the entire desert is being completely devastated, while two stops away from Kashgar are wonderful coal and oil deposits. People themselves through their ignorance deplete their soil. Near the small rivers ice is still lying; and under the sun, it is already burning hot and it is difficult to move in furs. The site of the encampment is called Kara julgun, a small gray village. The caravan is late. We drink tea out of the local *kungan*. There is not enough black paint to depict this teapot. The sketches are multiplying.

. . . . .

March 1st

It seems to be the most desolate crossing. Almost the entire time we went along the sites of old destroyed forests. All the *barkhans* are filled with gigantic old stumps and roots. Apparently there was a big forest here but now people have carried away the wood. The sands have scattered it and one proceeds as though along a gnarled cemetery. The scanty brush cannot withstand the sand *burans*. Everything is gray. Gray also are the pools and the spring floods which have begun. On account of these floods we are making twelve *p'o-t'ai*, instead of eight. Ditches, stumps, sand slopes; the biggest Chinese road is comparable to a small trail. During the day we meet a few sparse caravans, but they, of course, cannot comprise the nerve of true commerce. Everything is dead.

The gray village Urdaklik. On the flat roofs silent figures linger, though they cannot see anything from their roof but the dusty horizon. And these people have no outlook or hope. Occasional travelers pass by them. During the night the fire of a caravan will suddenly flare up. And again the same oppressive silence. Geese and ducks are fly-ing toward the spring floods but here only the crows and rooks are keeping house. Instead of a plow, some wooden implement of the stone age. Is it possible that the beks and Chinese ambans succeed in enriching themselves at the expense of these people also?

Our Chinese escort has no luck. In three days, three "warriors" managed to fall down from their horses. What if there were a whole regiment of such *tseriks*, as they are called here? It is related that in certain Chinese armies the cannons are carried on the backs of people, and the enemies in the daytime shoot in the air and at night sit together at their gambling.

· · · · ·

March 2nd

Chinese Turkestan has been described from the archae-ological standpoint; the ancient conquest and the change of rulership have been recounted. But nothing has been related of the present consciousness of the country. Yet, in the progress of the world's evolution we cannot cover with silence this vast country forgotten by destiny. It is very instructive to follow the remnants of the Tokhar, Uigur and Mongol constructions, but it is also very instructive and astonishing to see into what the consciousness of the country has turned: Again the same sandy gray hopeless-ness.

The *buran* lasts the entire day. We go beside "the for-est"—to speak more correctly, the forest-cemetery. The surviving *kargach*—trees—are sticking out, crooked, brushy and horny. Instead of the sun there is a silvery circle. How clearly one sees the reason which impelled the great migrators and conquerors toward the west and south. Imagining a great migration, do not picture feet, shoes or hoofs—everything up to the waistline is drowned in a thick dusty cloud.

We overtake an old man. He is complaining about something. We understand that somebody has broken his shoulder and that they have driven away sixteen of his horses. Of course on the Karakorum heights, they are more ethical. During the day we meet three caravans of donkeys and half a dozen carts. We stop in Chuga. We covered fourteen-and-a-half *p'o-t'ai*. Is it possible that this is the greatest Chinese road? And can a government be called a power which keeps its chief artery in such condition? One has to cry out about this, as about every ignorant deed impeding culture.

E.I. caught cold.

. . . . .

March 3rd

It is especially absurd to realize that a whole day of exhausting travel is equal to two hours' ride by automobile or to an hour by aeroplane. The roads here could be utilized easily for automobiles and one would not even have to build aerodromes. Perhaps nothing would so awaken the people's consciousness as a steel bird with a message of good cheer and with necessary supplies. Through these aisles, with their files of dusty and overloaded donkeys, would be opened a crevice of reason. Sir Aurel Stein expresses in his books the fear lest the primitiveness of this country be disturbed by the building of railroads and other evidences of civilization. I always have been against uncultural evidences of civilization, but there are moments of such paralysis of a country that one needs every super-measure of enlightenment.

But the Buddhist knows the reason of the apathy of the country: In the Books of Kanjur it is said that if the country should reject the teaching of Buddha, the trees would wither and the grass would droop and welfare would disappear.

We make our way first along the so-called "forest," then salt marshes. We get into the flood of Yarkand darya; finally, we reach the clay walls and towers of Maral-bashi. Do not shoot at these walls with a cannon—-too much dust will remain! The long bazaar of Maral-bashi is dirtier and darker than the other bazaars, or equal to all others. We halt in a garden far behind the city. The Amban has sent to inquire our names. It appears that in the order of the Kashgar Taotai regarding our passage our name is omitted. No, with Chinese conduct of affairs you will not go far!

Among the *sars* which were given to us with such difficulty in Kashgar, many are valueless. There should be ten letters on them, but often the tenth, the middle letter, is torn out and then the money is no longer accepted. Carefully examine all money which you receive whether from the bazaar or from the governor's *yamen.*

George remembers that Prjevalsky was the first to speak about Tun-huang, but afterwards the honor of this discovery was claimed by other scientists. As early as the Seventies, Prjevalsky spoke about these remarkable cave temples.

Near Maral-bashi are a few lakes. Fish abound. But sometimes one finds poisonous fish.

A new insolence from the Amban. He informs us that he will send us soldiers if we will ask him. But we do not need soldiers and, according to the command of the Governor-General they are guarding our confiscated and sealed arms. How can we question the Amban about the fulfillment of the command of the Governor-General? It is insolent and absurd. Again the people say: "The Amban does not know any customs." Sung had to go in spite of fatigue and the late hour to bring the Amban to reason, to tell him that we do not need the soldiers but they are needed by the order of the Governor-General.

.   .   .   .   .

March 4th

They send new soldiers. They do not even look like people, simply like insects. We remembered the stories of M.; how he himself turned to flight thirty *tseriks* and how a whole regiment of *tseriks* surrendered to two gunners. Yes, apparently all this is not exaggerated.

We first went by a dismal plain. Soon, at the right, against the yellow sky, appeared the opal silhouette of the mountains. Welcome, beloved mountains!

Suleiman relates, "A giant was living here. He saw that the lake was too big and with his sword he chopped the slopes from the neighboring mountains and threw them here. Behind this mountain is a beautiful garden and holy people live there but nobody can enter without their permission. Sarts have tried to go there but nobody has ever come back." And Suleiman pointed to the southeast.

Soon an unpleasant experience is in store for us. Some people gallop to meet us and warn us that water has begun to overflow the road. We had to make a detour of twenty miles. One also has to place this against the account of our arrest and detention in Khotan. We lost the best time for travel. Now we will be delayed everywhere by floods.

Another tale: "Under Urumchi is a steep mountain and there also live holy people. Once a Kalmuck wounded a mountain ram and the ram led the Kalmuck to a holy man. The man asked the Kalmuck to remain with them but the Kalmuck asked to return home, and the holy man gave the Kalmuck a lapful of wooden chips. The Kalmuck took them and thought, 'Where shall I carry these rarities?' He took them and threw them out into the woods. Only two chips remained caught, and when he came home, lo! gold hung to his garments. And so the Kalmuck lost."

We are going further, near gray sandy mountains with vigorous strata. We pass an old tomb. Then we pass a *mazar* of a giant holy man. They say that even the trails of the hoofs of his horses have remained on the mountain The mountains become more beautiful and merge into the romantic silhouette of Bible lore. Not far from here is an ancient site, Haivar. Near the road are the remains of the Chinese fortress, Angelik. Then, again, sands and floods.

Another tale: "Not far from Angelik is an old house. Whoever enters it is lost in wonder at the rich adornments and the heaps of gold. If one takes a heap of gold the door closes by itself, and he cannot leave. And until he returns the gold, to the very last grain, so long the door will remain unopened. A similar place is near Uch-Turfan. There stands a structure like a city, one can even see the smoke but one can enter only on Fridays. But one cannot carry out gold from this site either. And in Kucha they found an underground opening like a whole subterranean passage. They brought thousands of wagons with stones to fill it in—but they could not. The stones are to be seen even now. The tomb of a saint was also found there. Thirty-nine doors were open into it but they could not open the fortieth. And so they covered it again." The people remember also about the predicted beautiful gardens and about foreign gold.

It becomes dark. We come to the village Tumshuk. Bonfires and stars, and dreams of the people. And for a long, long time, someone was praying, by the light of a bonfire. For what? Is it not for enlightenment? High stands the chalice of Orion. Around the bonfire barefooted youths are lying—this is our guard.

. . . . .

March 5th

If you want to give a gift to these barefooted night guards your desire is in vain. All that you give will be taken away by the Elder. . . .

One of the tedious crossings is to Yaka Khuduk. Again unbearable dust; hidden ditches. A burnt forest. Boarweed and shallow river banks. There are many boar. Often we travel under a single telegraph wire. This is the same line which transmits telegrams in an absolutely unintelligible shape. In the last telegram from New York, there was a series of unintelligible letters and only the one last word "Advise" was legible. To whom and about what? One may think that it is a very sly code or a mischievous joke, where only the last provocative word is comprehensible.

Another tale: "In Kashgar recently lived a holy man. He heard when people in the holy place were praying, although it took six months to reach that place. There is such a holy place behind the mountains. In the district of Orenburg also there lived such a man. He heard about the present and the future, and about the war and about famine. In two hundred years the Sarts expect a great saint, and perhaps earlier."

We stop on the dusty bank of Yarkand darya. Sometimes a wind rises and whirls tall cruel pillars of sand. Here are small clay huts, naked bushes and sandy river banks.

. . . . .

March 6th

It is very simple to give an idea of our passage of today! On a round dish place a good bit of gray dust; throw in a few gray pieces of wool and stick in fragments of matches. Let ants crawl over this bumpy plain, and for realism, blow it in order to create pillars of dust.

And so we creep along. We expected to stay in Chulan, but there the water is bitter so we had to make a detour in order to spend the night in a *kishlak* in New Chulan. At the approach to its gray clay huts a light silhouette of mountains is seen unexpectedly—the thresholds of T'ian Shan. E.I. 's cold is still torturing her.

Suleiman relates how now in this country two firms are dealing in sausage casings; one German (Faust) and one American (Brenner). The prices of casings have risen so unprecedentedly that the works have become unprofitable. It is very strange to know that the casings of the sausages in American markets come from Khotan and Aksu. The same obstacles occur in the cotton trade. In order to raise the prices they mix different unmatched varieties and in this way are ruining the value of the entire product. With silk, similar difficulties occur. It is impossible to obtain the delivery of an entire order of a quality equal to a chosen sample. It is impossible to obtain material of a chosen shade. All this reduces the industry to medieval conditions. The melons and the raisins are of good quality.

The amber sun melts into the dusk of the horizon. In the distances the eyes of the bonfires light up. Somewhere someone is sitting and weaving the design of rumors. In the dusk the songs thunder out. The noisy *Tamasha* is held.

. . . . .

March 7th

It appears that the water in old Chulan is very good, even better than in New Chulan. But the inhabitants of New Chulan decided to lure the passers-by and threw dead mules and dogs into the lake of old Chulan. The caravan is the nerve of the country and this case of luring the passers-by is quite typical. We went thirteen *p'o-t'ai,* as far as the small habitation of Chutu Khuduk, a battered-down little village. It seems incredible that this little station is on the greatest road of China. All along are sands, but on the left stretches a mass of mountains and the pearly foothills adorn the horizon.

Another tale: "Near the city Osch there is still a Mountain of Solomon. There even remain the little impressions where Solomon prayed on his knees."

We recall how the British Consul in Kashgar notified us that George's friend Allen Priest was in Urumchi as late as November. After Boston we met Priest on the threshold of the Vatican in Rome. And now we find him on the Asiatic roads—an active sensitive man. The British Consul says that he received the permission to go from Siberia to Peking. Will we still find him in Urumchi? There are people with whom it is agreeable to meet anywhere—where shall we meet our dear Americans?

It is long since we have seen so noble a sunset with such broad gradations of opal purple hues. The golden sun, somewhat dulled, lingered long on the crags of the far-off mountains. And it went leaving a soft fiery pillar. These mountains mark the limits of this country. Today there are no songs. The village is silent. In the outskirts on the plain are our tents. From above, Orion peers down.

E.I. has almost recovered.

. . . . .

March 8th

We approach Ujkul, first by sands; afterward two *p'o-t'ai*
of habitations; fields; altogether ten *p'o-t'ai*. They start to
sow. They are plowing. The plow is of the stone age. Two
oxen drag one horny wooden device. Can one plow deeply
with such utensil? The day is spring-like. A fresh wind
and the warmth of the sun. Ujkul is a long dusty village.
For a day there are a few occurrences in the caravan! A
horse fell; his head swelled all the morning, and at three,
he died. In the *mafa* of the Gegen, the middle horse fell on
a bad ridge. We feared we could not raise him. Thereupon
it was discovered that yesterday a cart fell down and the
entire load fell out. And the guarding *tserik* had hidden
this occurrence. When we reprimanded him he idiotically
smiled.

The cool evening approaches; we speak about the
decline of the Chinese language. There are forty thousand signs collected, but not one of them expresses the
letter R. In olden times there was a sign which approximately expressed this letter, but afterward it disappeared
out of the eight thousand signs used in daily life. One
asks oneself why dictionaries preserve thirty-two thousand
unnecessary signs? In these unnecessary tatters is seen the
complete decline of Chinese evolution. And as a result the
local people whisper: "Do not go into this yard; there are
Chinese!" or "Can one expect justice from Chinese?"

And how many young people are innocently dragging
after them the results of the ignorance and cruelty of their
fathers and grandfathers. How they must hasten to get
rid of such an inheritance! If all these many thousands of
signs have led them toward ignorance, one should quickly
liberate oneself from these skeletons of conventions. Valiantly and severely one has to cut out the decay of survivals. Otherwise, why have entire nations vanished so often
from the history of the earth? "Great Matter is weaving
its design and mercilessly casts out each useless thread

from its cosmic web." Why did Confucius have to keep his traveling cart always at hand? When the criminal power departs one will have to provide railroads and the possibility of growth and exchange for the people immediately. And how easy it would be to lay railroad lines along the plains here!

Today the water is especially bad. During the whole week the water was yellowish brown, and today it is soapy gray and ill-smelling—one cannot drink it. You may expect someone to draw the head of a Dungan from out the well in a pail. This has already happened!

· · · · ·

March 9th

From Ujkul we go to Aksu, the capital of the unsuccessful Yakub-bek, who half a century ago tried to liberate Turkestan from Chinese rule, but could not find allies. The road is dank with many ditches. The river Aksu—it means white water—has already started to overflow. The bridges, as everywhere, are dancing as though alive. And this is the chief road of China! Gray sky and a yellow plowed field. We remember America; we remember the beauties of Santa Fe, the Grand Canyon, Colorado and Arizona. Again we mentally urge our friends—the Americans—to know better the beauties of their superb country. We recall how all types of ungifted Jean Cocteaux in Europe offer Americans a special dish of nonsense. . . . But America is full of its own possibilities.

Imperceptibly we approach the borders of Aksu. The same little clay houses and stalls. As always, two cities. The old one on the muddy place. The new, a little drier, where the Chinese officials, Taotai, Amban and the Colonel live. Five days from here is the Muzart Pass toward the Iliisk district of the Kalmucks. We stop in the new city, in the garden of the Andijan Aksakal. It is dusty.

Today the first bloodshed occurred. Two tramps beat our *mafakesh* until he bled and almost took out his eye. Screaming. Noise. The tramps were caught. They bound them and took them to the Amban. And our revolvers are sealed, because the Governor-General (that is the Tu-t'u) does not trust our American papers of recommendation. The Governor of course does not know his province: he is busy transferring his riches to different banks through various fantastic ways, to get it more quickly out of this territory! The Lama begs us not to remain in Aksu a long time. The local bazaar is notorious for its thievery and perversion. It is getting dark. The Amban comes to visit us. An agreeable exception; he speaks English, a little bit of other languages: he was employed in the Russian Asiatic Bank and knows Allan Priest (now Priest is in Peking) personally. We converse a long time. The Amban begs us to remain for a day, otherwise he cannot arrange for two horses until Kucha. We tell him about the Khotan ignoramuses. He shrugs his shoulders and says: "Probably you are in China for the first time." A sympathetic type of young official, who is watching events and who knows the significance of many things. He will come for luncheon tomorrow. He is the first cultured Chinese we encountered here. He does not seem to have the aggressiveness of Chu in Kashgar. The Amban of Aksu is somewhat on the type of earnest Chinese students, whom one may meet in American and Parisian universities. We rejoice to meet this type because we had molded our understanding of contemporary China according to his type and not according to the *buffalos.* Let us see what will happen further.

．　．　．　．　．

March 10th

Early in the morning we heard familiar singing. Thus at dawn on the passes did the Ladaki sing their prayers; and so it is here. Our two Ladaki caravaneers are sitting under a tree and are singing harmonious hymns to Tara and the Lord Maitreya.

Pan Tsi-lu, the Amban, comes. We speak about Chinese problems, about religion, about the teachings of life. He complains very much about the life in Aksu. He dreams of leaving because he cannot do anything there. Being alone and a subordinate, he cannot start anything constructive. We wished him success in his intentions. The Amban brought two issues of Chinese papers of the ninth and sixteenth of January. We read how Chang Tso Lin has declared himself independent of the central government. We read also of the resignation of Feng.

· · · · ·

March 11th

The last Chinese in the caravan has exploded! It came out that Sung has spent each night in the bazaar playing cards. The amputated finger did not teach him a lesson. Of our Chinese, two turned out to be opium smokers, and two gamblers. And here the best of the Chinese whom we met—the Amban in Aksu—is anxious to leave this country and feels that he cannot do anything. And who will be the one to undertake, courageously and self-sacrificingly, to turn this dusty cemetery into a flourishing garden? Silver and copper and coal and oil—all are there; but there is no solicitous hand.

We go by a long path to Karakhuduk (eighteen *p'o-t'ai*). First the clay walls of the new city. Then the pearly desert. Then *burkhans* and reeds. We march until midnight. We stop at a Chinese inn. Another worry: the backs of the pack horses are rotting because the caravaneers never remove the saddles; and the luggage is permeated with a repulsive odor. In the future it will be necessary to regulate this caravan evil; horses, mules and camels are so burdened here that one cannot permit them to be devoured alive by worms. Tibetans pity the horses. But Kashmiri and Sarts consign them to the worms. It is difficult to believe.

· · · · ·

March 12th

The Sinkiang anecdote continues. Today our famous escort wanted to attach an arrested criminal to our caravan. With great noise we had to eject the uninvited recruit.

And the entire day has been such a beautiful one. We have been going through fantastic, ancient sand formations. The sun is already burning but in the shade there is still ice. There are no trees nor habitations—far around us is the desert, ending in blue cragged hills. The lines are simple and powerful. In such places one may expect old monuments. At sunset we approach a lonely *langar,* Toghrak-dang. Very high up on the sandy rocks, something is silhouetted. We have no doubt that these are openings of old Buddhist caves. And so it is. Some of them are outlined very high and the entrances to them are crumbled. But three caves are on a low slope. The ceilings and the walls are pretty well gone. Of course it is the Moslems who have destroyed the images they hate. Near the ground a little below are still seen the remnants of ornaments, covered over with Turki inscriptions. But the most enticing thing is the hollow sound beneath the floor. It means that below, in the buried part of the rock, are also caves, not even filled in. We do not remember any mention of this place in Stein. It recalls to us the Tokhar antiquities of the fifth to the eighth centuries. The caves face the East. Before the eyes of the hermits spread the broad mountain view—a good and beautiful place. Under the cave a mountain spring murmurs—not a waterfall but just a light little stream. The thin spring runs through a wooden trough into the wooden pail of the Sart woman. So, also, did the hermits draw their water here. Among the crumbled fragments many pieces of basalt glow darkly. Of course, beside the caves there were stupas and separate structures, which were covered by the avalanche of rocks.

Little bells are ringing; the postman is hurrying to pass us with two sealed bags of mail. From Kashgar to Urumchi the mail takes thirteen days.

· · · · ·

March 13th

The children from the *langar* hasten to gather the papers left by the caravan. One little girl finds a colorful label from a match box.

The exultation of the possessor is unbounded. We regret not having colored postal cards to distribute. If you want to find a place in a child's heart in the quickest way, do it through vividly colored little pictures. The children will take them with joy and will remember.

We bid farewell to the caves. We pass rich sand formations, like high waves with congealed crests, or like threatening outstretched fingers, or like towers with bridges, or like tents. After the mountains we descend again to the sands. Probably a *buran* from Takla Makan has swept past here. Everything is drowned in clouds of thick dust. We shall stop in Kushtami in a dusty *langar*. Again some people are quarreling noisily. On our way we meet several droves of horses. They go to the Russian border toward Andijan. The breed of horses is not fine. We are nearing the horse country and the breed becomes inferior: the values and reputations have to be carefully examined. This was apparent already in the jade, silk, horses; in the quality of singing, in ceramics, and many other things. And one should not be afraid to examine traditions because it is time to transport one's self from the past to the future. One can know the past but one has to direct one's consciousness toward the future.

In the yard of the *langar* is a band of professional gamblers. Near the place are two tents of Karakirghiz—notorious thieves. Exactly in this place an escort given by the Amban once robbed a traveler. One has to take special precautions. The village did not send any guards. If we had our rifles everything would be well, but the ceremony of the sealing of the arms was made openly in order that the servants and all the knaves along the road would know. One cannot rely upon the Chinese escort. The only guard is our Tibetan Tumbal.

· · · · ·

March 14th

As one might have expected, during the night an outrageous thing occurred. It appeared that in spite of our refusal, the prisoner went along with our caravan. During the night there was frenzied gambling. The prisoner lost much money. They bound him. . . . In a word, the Chinese have arranged for us an "honorary" escort. Quicker, quicker out of this region!

After the *buran,* everything merges into mist. The mountains disappear. Yellow fields and occasional black oxen at the plow. They are sowing. On the poplars the buds swell. But here and there, near the rivers, lies late snow. We should stop in the city of Bai. But we are terrified at the dirt of the bazaar and decide to go five *p'o-t'ai* farther to the small *langar.* We are standing in a field among old tombs—*mazars.* In the darkness we set up the tents. It is interesting to note that the Amban in Bai is a nephew of the Tu-t'u. Apparently he has a collection of nephews and to all are given positions of Ambans and Consuls. The Sinkiang Company! Today important decisions are made. There is a communication.

. . . . .

March 15th

A dull day. Purple-gray sky. Yellow fields. The mountains at the right are of a pale opal silhouette. In these mountains are caves. Three *p'o-t'ai* from Kizil, where we shall stop, the caves have been explored by Stein. The remnants of the paintings have been burned by the local iconoclasts. On the way we find huge herds of sheep and goats. Where are they being driven? The answer is the same: to Andijan; the sheep, and the goats and the horses and the bulls and the wool, everything is going for sale. The common dream is trade and communications with foreigners. At the same time, hordes of Sarts are going away to find work, because one cannot find any work here. To Andijan, to Kuldje, to Chuguchak—these are three arteries which attract the travel of the entire country. We go through a bazaar and again they are calling to us, "You go well, Urus." Where from is this? Tomorrow to Kucha we have a long way—eighteen *p'o-t'ai.* We have to leave at five o'clock.

. . . . .

March 16th

One of the most beautiful days. Up to seven o'clock it is freezing and then there is a hot sun. First a valiant desert, in pearly tones. Afterwards a crossing brings the most unusual sand formations, like congealed ocean waves, like hundred-towered castles, like cathedrals, like *yurtas*—and all in an endless variety. In the Toghrak-dang *langar* we feed the horses. Not far from there are two caves with traces of colored decoration. Two *p'o-t'ai* from Kucha on a slope rises a tower, Kizil karga—meaning the red raven. On looking back we notice that not far away are the dark entrances of caves. We dismount and hurry there over the sandy mounds. These are the same celebrated caves, it seems to me, some of which LeCoq reproduced. But, as always, reproductions do not give even a fraction of the real impression. One must come to this amphitheater of former temples toward evening, when the impression is intensified by the quietude of nature. One has to imagine all these cavern-shrines, not with darkened walls and vaults, but vividly and brilliantly frescoed. In the niches one has to imagine the figures of the Blessed One and of Bodhisattvas, which are now carried away. In one cave remain the traces of images of thousands of Buddhas. In another cave remains the place of repose of Buddha and a part of the ceiling. The bottoms of the walls are covered with Moslem inscriptions. Under the floor one feels hollow spaces. Apparently there is a row of unopened subterranean structures. One cannot consider these excavations completed if the hollowness of the hidden parts resounds so apparently. Not Lamaism, but traces of true Buddhism are apparent in the silence of these caves. Of course it is wonderful that examples of the frescoes have been scattered into the museums of Europe. But the walls of the caves remain denuded and the true image of the shrines has disappeared—only the skeletons have remained.

We are going to Kucha, passing a row of gardens. The city seems cleaner than the others. Why is this? The Elder, the old Mullah, forces them to clean the streets. Of course it is again impossible to halt in the bazaar. They mention a garden behind the city but how can one reach it in the complete darkness which has fallen? A savior appears; out of this same darkness emerges a white turban, and an unexpected friend, a Sart, leads us out of town. There is a garden and a house and stables. The hostlers beg that they may sleep in the kitchen. Why? In the house for the servants lives "a man deprived of a soul." They mean an insane man. And the whole group of healthy peasants is afraid of him. The cook calls the chicken-coop the little chickens' carriage. Here we are in the capital of Tokhars. Here it is that the Tokhar King, Pochan, was persecuted by the Chinese and flew out of the city on a dragon, taking with him all his treasure! Much is rumored about the gold in the Buddhist caves.

. . . . .

March 17th

The whole morning is spent in negotiations with *arbakeshs, mafakeshs* and *korakeshs;* at first everything seems impossible. Then after an avalanche of unnecessary discussion everything becomes possible. At first, as far as Karashahr, the road is estimated as twelve long days. Whereas, as everybody knows, eight days is the customary period. We peer into all these faces. And where are the traces of the Tokhars? They are not visible. Perhaps something of a more Mongoloid type appears in the features, but in general, these are the same Turk Sarts. And thus, the Tokhars disappeared leaving no traces and no one knows even the true pronunciation of the symbols of their writings.

So, before the eyes of history has come a nation, from whence is unknown; nor is it known how it scattered and disappeared without a trace. And not a savage people but one with a written language, with culture. Just so is it with their Tzar Pochan: whither he flew on the dragon is known. And it is strange to sit in this same country—in this pear-garden—and not know anything about the inhabitants who were here not long ago.

One cannot obtain objects of antiquity here either—"Somewhere, someone knows about them in Takla Makan."

. . . . .

March 18th

At one o'clock at night, drums, trumpets and singing began. Loud and shrill and persistent were the screams of "Allah." These are the Moslems preparing for the fast of Ramazan. During the day they have to fast, but at night they can partake of food aplenty. In order not to outsleep the period of eating, the good Moslems play and dance on the eve of the day's fast. The dogs barked a great deal and were running wild during the night. Ramsana got up in order to inspect the camp and he noticed that the government guards, the *tseriks,* slept heavily. Ramsana took away the rifle from one of them, went around the camp and fell asleep with the rifle. The *tserik* was startled when he awoke in the morning without his gun. Oh, these unhappy *tseriks!*

In the morning a Swedish woman missionary came. She has been in this country for fifteen years and not one convert! However, the missionary busies herself with doctoring and midwifery and here it is absolutely necessary because all these "cities" are without a single doctor.

Then the American day begins. We go to see the American firm, Brenner Brothers of New York. They are in the gut and wool business. An entire community of vigorous working people. A unique community with children and with a joyous realization of the growing work. The business is developing. With all the primitiveness of the apparatus one has to admire the fine results. Here they are assorting and washing the wool. Here, on a hand-made press they are pressing it. Here a line of camels are waiting to lift the white heaps of wool and to carry them abroad, to Tientsin and to the ports for Europe and America. In the whole artel there are no books; for the entire community there is one New Testament and an accidental volume of Korolenko. It is a joy to be able to give them old newspapers and two books. There are tales about the affairs of the Sarts. They praise the murdered Titai. They ask what happens in the world. D. is skillfully interpreting the local customs by way of religious discussions. In this way the intolerance and superstition which are spread by the Mullahs find resistance. And there is much intolerance. And many of the local Beys have planned to strangle the new foreign enterprise. D. and P. show themselves as pioneers for America in this country. They listen to our tales about America. D. tells about the mineral riches of the Torgut and Iliisk district.

The Kalmucks are excellent marksmen. The Kalmuck administration does not hesitate to make innovations. The people praise the Sarts for their work. They have initiative, ability and adaptability.

In the country are many narrators of legends and fairy tales which touch the questions of the Koran and religion. Often the listeners enter into a dialogue with the narrator. Often keen questions upset the routine of superstition. In Turfan there exists a curious custom of sending young men with an experienced guide in the guise of a story-teller through the whole country, even to Mecca. Thus a unique experimental university is evolving. Through this, one may explain the adaptability of Turfanians.

The gatherings and festivities usually end with a song about Issa (Jesus):

"As Issa went on his wanderings, he saw a great head. On the road lay a dead human head. Issa thought that the great head belonged to a great man. And Issa decided to do good and to resurrect this great head. And the head covered itself with skin. And the eyes filled themselves. And there grew a great body and the blood flowed. And the heart was filled. And the mighty giant rose and thanked Issa that he resurrected him for usefulness to humankind."

There are many legends about the flights of Solomon, and among the Kalmucks is very widely spread a legend about Jesus which is nothing else than one of the manuscripts already known to us, "Issa, the Best of Human Sons." Of course it has penetrated here not from Hemis but from another original source. Everywhere are spread the signs of beauty. It is time to gather them fearlessly without superstition.

Again information is given to us about ancient places. About many caves and stupas along Kizil darya. Part of them have been excavated and part of them are still hidden. Not long ago on the bazaar they sold "a trunk with antiquities" brought from Lob (near Lob-nor). There are tales about old cities along the stream of Tarim or Yarkand darya. There are people who know these cities. The fossilized bodies in the burial grounds indicate a very great stature, taller of course than Mongolians. The expeditions which were there, completed the easier and most apparent part of the work. Now there yet remains the more concealed work demanding greater construction and preparation.

In Kucha it is already warm. The young grass is getting green and is two inches high. We learn that from Karashahr to Urumchi one can go by the mountain road. It will be five days shorter. In this way, one can avoid the hot site at Tukson, where there is a descent into the Turfan Oasis (960 feet below sea level). In the summer in Turfan people bury themselves in the earth and cannot walk more than one *p'o-t'ai.* Besides the approaching heat, there is mud by now, on the great road. It is better to go through the Kalmuck territory, along the mountain passes.

· · · · ·

March 19th

Ramsana again took the gun away from the sleeping *tserik* and strolled around the camp. And again the *tserik* bowed to his feet and asked him to return the gun as otherwise the Amban would beat him.

They ask on what the comparatively high exchange of the Chinese currency is based. But all know that it is not guaranteed by anything and circulates like dry leaves by command of the Governor. Of course, this is one of the successive misunderstandings and justice will soon clarify it.

Until now in Tibet there exists a custom of specially prosecuting gambling houses and brothels. A certain lama called Gekö Lama, upon learning of the existence of such houses, takes a dozen lamas with whips and at the very peak of the orgy presents himself at the house. And then, there on the spot, all present are whipped.

Interesting is the Kalmuck song, "Of him who came earlier": "One man pondered long and forgot to come to the elections of a Noyon (prince). Another man did not sleep that night and came first. And he was selected Noyon, because he entered first. And so the former who pondered, sits and broods that for him no place was found in the *yurta* of the Noyon."

As in other countries, so here are many marks of treasures. Often on the rocks one can see tiny projecting piles of stones. These are the signs of treasures. In the monastery records one can find directions as to how at certain times of the day, according to the indications of the shadows, one may go from one pile to another to the site of the treasure. D. is called Ishan here, meaning the holy one, for his knowledge of religious subjects. B. has seen an ancient tomb recently. The tibial bone found there reached six quarters in length. The spot is in the direction of Lob-nor. B. has marked it. So there are interesting indications for the future.

· · · · ·

March 20th

We bid farewell to the workers' group at Brenner's. We again noticed that wherever there is labor there is joy. P. went on a *troyka;* D. and M. went on horseback to accompany us out of town. Again questions. Where shall we meet? They will discuss the newspapers and books we left for a long time. For our farewell they demonstrated to us the wonderful pace of their Karashahr horses. "Now you shall encircle a part of the Gobi," calls D. We are sinking into the milky desert. A *shamal* begins. It fills our eyes. We turn into a yellow mass.

Every day new significant information comes. "The Mongolian army has reached the river Urungu and threatens Sin-kiang." Nobody in Europe and America knows about the affairs of the local countries.

We are stopping in the village Yaka-arik.

Underground creeks are often used here. This corresponds fully to the tradition of underground passages, so prevalent in Asia. Precisely in Central Asia, are interwoven fairy tales and reality. European measures are not applicable here.

From Peking it was proposed to the Tu-t'u of Sinkiang that an aeroplane communication between Peking and Urumchi be established. The Tu-t'u answered that in this province this would not be practicable, because his people were wild and would flee to the mountains. Of course the people would not flee; but rumors of the various ignorant activities of the Governor-General would spread more quickly. The people would very quickly welcome these air messengers. The dream of the Orient about the flying carpets, which the people attribute to Solomon, would be reborn in their expectation of the iron birds. For in Tibet also the most ancient prophecies have envisaged iron birds and iron serpents. There are also, as in traces of the fundamental teaching of Buddha, references to the cosmogonic problems of planetary evolution and of the development of life. As soon as we began to speak about Buddhism, as of a realistic teaching, the woman missionary in Kucha hastened to leave us, saying, "The scriptures of Buddhism are taken from Christianity." But the Pillars of Asoka were standing before Christianity and in the first century before Christ the recording of the covenants of Gautama was already begun. One has to regard things more simply and without prejudice.

. . . . .

March 21st

Not long ago the travels of Sven Hedin appeared as an unprecedented heroism; and now E.I. is crossing the same deserts and heights with no thought that it is anything extraordinary. Now the representatives of Brenner are traversing the same expanses where Sven Hedin, according to his books, almost perished from lack of water. And soon iron birds will swiftly fly above these same places. And the fairy tale of the past will be replaced by the new fairy tale of the cosmos.

Since evening the cicadas have been singing. High stands the shining moon. There is the fragrance of grass. But at two o'clock at night the *buran* struck. Verily struck. It came flying like a dragon and roared threateningly until morning. The tent was all aflutter. We had to prepare ourselves in case the tent should fly away. And in the morning again the pearly Gobi desert. Mother of pearl and opal, and above, dull sapphire. On the road, in order, is spread out a big caravan. This is Brenner's, or, as they call it here, Belyan-khan which goes to Tientsin.

Approaching us, tinkling, is a kazan *troyka*. Two women and three Tartar girls from Chuguchak are going to Karaul. We passed fourteen *p'o-t'ai*. And we shall stop in the garden of Yangiabad. The last *p'o-t'ai* suffocated us again with their deep sands. Tommy is limping. He has malanders. He will be out of service for five days. In the evening everything becomes quiet. The silvery sun sets.

Here we are called Rerengi-Bey. It is our fifth name thus far.

. . . . .

March 22rd

We are trying to find out whether we can avoid Karashahr and go from Kurat through a Kalmuck encampment, by way of the monastery Sharasüme on the mountain road to Urumchi. The Kalmucks, as a nation, have slipped out of attention. It is instructive to go through their *ulus* for a week.

The Dungans, or Chinese Moslems, occupy a strange position in the country. They are frankly disliked by Moslem, Chinese and Kalmucks. The word "Dungan" itself is pronounced with a certain contempt. The faces of the Dungans are scarcely attractive. There is much cruelty in them.

We proceed as far as Bogar, a dusty bazaar site. It is divided into nine *p'o-t'ai*, but apparently it is more, judging by the time. Here the *p'o-t'ai* are counted peculiarly. There are short *p'o-t'ai* and long *p'o-t'ai*. Down a mountain is a long *p'o-t'ai*, uphill is a short *p'o-t'ai*. A strange measure of distance.

First we go by the opal desert. To the left are hills. Three *p'o-t'ai* before Bogar one comes upon a swampy oasis. On the road is mud. Big flocks of ducks and geese are on the wing. The hoopoes are strutting about in a most pompous way. They say of them: "These are former men." The end of the road is enveloped in clouds of dust.

A dusty garden. On the fence is sitting the son of the Amban. Politely Sung persuades him "It is not good to sit on a fence." But nothing helps, and Sung applies the customary means here and throws a stone. The boy disappears.

From all sides you hear the same remarks about the inaccuracy of existing maps. In some important sites and details are omitted. It is necessary to examine the transcription of the name. In some, non-existing names are introduced. Some are taken from the Turki, others from the Chinese, and still others, from some kind of local jargon which is not recognized anywhere. Even in the staff maps there are a great many errors which promise one much trouble on the route.

．　．　．　．　．

March 23rd

Was not Tamerlane a great disinfector? He destroyed many cities. We know what it means to destroy little clay cities full of all sorts of contagion. Here we have passed twelve cities. What can be done with them? For the people's welfare, one ought to burn them and plan new villages beside them. While the old is in its final decay—it is difficult to force the natives to turn toward new places. Here the Tung-ling of Kucha constructed a new city alongside the old city. Broad streets, underground canals. But the people are afraid of the new place.

We follow a broad plain. We pass Yangizar. We go further through a dusty forest. We shall stop behind Chader. It is dark. We have passed sixteen *p'o-t'ai*. The caravan is delayed. Sabsa's back is swollen. Mastan and Olla are keeping up remarkably. Nobody knows distances. The caravan arrives at one at night.

．　．　．　．　．

March 24th

A tiring day. It is hot. We are passing by a dusty forest and low shrubs. Up to Chirchi it is twelve *p'o-t'ai*. We pass a big caravan of Belyankhan. Another caravan of the same firm stands in Chirchi. The pioneers of America are working.

Today is the day of our institutions in America! The day of the founders. We are sending our thoughts to America, to the house of the Museum and the school, where the day is being observed. Our dear friends, it is as if we were present at your annual meeting. The distance does not exist. Traversing these spaces we recall the plains of the Mississippi and Missouri and the immeasurable steppes of Russia. We are even rejoicing at the caravan of Belyankhan. This is already cooperation with Asia. As though both continents, divided by a cosmic catastrophe, remembered their former unity. How much of Mongolian there is in the types of the later Mayans and the red-skinned

Indians! How much equal breadth there is in America and in Asia. And now in its moment of regeneration, Asia remembers its distant ties. Greetings to America!

. . . . .

March 25th

They show us another species of monetary symbols—some sort of greasy little rag and a dirty little bone. This is the situation of the local currency: *Lans* (or *sar* or *teza*) are equal to four hundred *dekhans.* But a Kashgar *lan* is equal to three Urumchi *lans* and an Urumchi *lan* is equal to three Kuldja *lans.* A Khotan *lan* is considered eight hundred *dekhans.* You will say it is nonsense. I agree with you. But because of this nonsense, millions of people are suffering. Can such differences in standards of money existing in one province be further complicated by wooden and rag signs? This is the reason that people ask why the value of Chinese currency has stood so high until now.

Nowhere are objects of antiquity to be found. Apparently the accessible upper layer of discoveries has already been exported to Europe and as for the hidden layers, let them remain for Asia itself. The dignity of the countries demand that they should wisely dispose of their true resources. But so far the Ambans are disposing of the people's treasures for their own benefit. The Amban of Yangi Hissar (designated as Consul to Andijan) lost many thousands of *lans* at cards. Now he has especially increased the taxes without limit and will not leave for his new position until he regains his loss.

Twelve more *p'o-t'ai* through the desert with small brush. We reach Tim. In the morning it is still cool, but by midday the sun is already burning. The caravans begin to travel by night as during the summer. Again tales about the heat of Turfan where, in summer, they bake little cakes on the stones under the sun. It is said, "There are many underground springs here, and also many underground passages." In the past they once tortured a holy man and he hid himself in a subterranean passage and came out after six months of wandering.

And another thing happened long ago: "Some people went in search of God in Barkul. They came to a king who considered himself a god. He sat and read a book and his cat held a candle before him. The pilgrims decided to test whether the king really was a god. They argued, 'If we let loose a mouse, will the king's shrewd cat run after it? If the king is a god then his power should stop the cat.' Thereupon they let a mouse loose, and the king's cat ran away and threw down the candle. The people now saw that the king was not a god.

"They went further. They met a shepherd who gave them bread and asked if he could be their comrade. They took him, but the shepherd did not wish to take his dog. He said that because of the animal, people would find them more easily. But the dog ran after him. The shepherd did not even have pity on him and killed the dog. Only to seek God!

"They approached a chasm-like crevice in the mountain. And as they entered, the stone door closed after them. What passed where the holy people dwell, no one knows. Some time afterward the shepherd who had been sent for something came out; he came to the city to buy bread at the bazaar. He offered them money, but the people were astonished at the coming of the giant and they refused to take his money, saying that for two thousand years such money had not been current. The shepherd quickly returned to the mountain and the king of the place hurried after him in order to investigate this wonder. But apparently the holy people have no need for kings, for the mountain closed. Nor could it be opened either by tempest or by prayer. The king brought his entire army but much as they labored at this mountain, and though they all perished in the attempt, the mountain did not open. And near this mountain is the tomb of the king. Such deeds there were and such underground passages there are."

A young Baksha overtakes us on horseback. He sings fairy tales and tells legends, and he "conjures devils"—"Baksha, sing the tale of Shabistan!" He takes out from behind his back a long-stringed *gejack*. He sings as he rides. He plays. The strings sound well. And somehow one forgets the dry sands and the hot sun. Two melodies resound. Now the higher one dominates, as if in supplication or command; again the lower thunders out its victorious affirmation.

Then the Baksha takes the tambourine and fills the desert with widely varied rhythms. We rejoice that on the last day in the country of the Sarts, we are accompanied by the song and melodies of the Baksha Sart. Tomorrow we shall reach the *ulus* of the Kalmucks.

At the left, to the north, out of the fog looms the ridge of T'ian Shan. Behind it are the Kalmucks and beyond it Semirechye. At the entrance to Tim is a great ancient stupa and ruins of old structures, banners of Buddhism. It is said that the mountain where Buddha was initiated was all aflame. But after the prayer of the Blessed One, snow fell and extinguished the fire. Ice and snow now encircle this mountain and it is difficult to find it until the predestined date.

A quiet warm evening, a milky spring sky. If one only could reach an encampment of the Kalmuck Khan without entering Karashahr and go there, by monasteries and mountains, to Urumchi! We are awaiting the Kalmucks. This is significant.

. . . . .

March 26th

A fair, beautiful day. First from the north, rose the range of T'ian Shan. All sapphire and amethyst. Then we crossed a row of fine sand formations. From below the hill flashed a blue mountain river. A powerful and overflowing one. We followed the river. In front of us, closed gates—the custom house. The boundary of Kalmuck soil. The first Kalmucks appear. George tries his Mongolian on them.

They understand each other. We stop in a *langar,* not far from Mingoi Saur (thousand ruins). The ruins are enveloped in a legend that a lama saw a light at a certain place. The people dug. They reached water and there appeared a water-serpent.

There is a belief that on these sites stood a large monastery containing the chalice of Buddha, which disappeared from Peshawar, and which is mentioned by Fa-hsien in Karashahr.

Now we are stopping by the river, near strata of coal. This is the first day without dust—again mountain air. The first tree is in blossom. The Kalmuck soil smiles. It is as though we were now walking around its borders. At night a full moon shines. Behind the river glow the shepherds' bonfires.

We recall the hopes of the Kalmucks. We recall how Chuntse, the first one, told us about Toin Lama. Later there came full information as to what this Torgut leader can achieve if he is able to accept what is sent to him. And should he fail to accept it—then a long farewell to Dzungaria! Of what avail to speak if one's palm is full of holes. . . .

. . . . .

March 27th

The crossing to Karashahr (or Karachahr, or Karachar). Soon the mountains recede and the river disappears toward the south. Again a dusty and famished desert. Again a village road, instead of a broad Chinese highway. On the surface is a great deal of inflammable clay slate. There is coal in the mountains. In a whirl of dust we reach the river opposite Karashahr. The crossing is on primitive rafts. There were such crossings on the small tributaries of the Volga. A multi-colored crowd; piles of balls; carts, mules, camels and horses. And again, in the city itself, there is nothing Buddhist. Still Sarts and Chinese. One seldom sees the faces of Kalmucks, marked as they are by greater keenness and alertness.

S., a representative of Belyankhan, meets us. He praises the Kalmucks.

We have to change servants. Our terrorizing Gorban, of whom everybody is afraid, happens to be very timorous himself. He is afraid of Chinese and of Kalmucks and trembles for his miserable rupees. Sarts are apparently afraid of Kalmucks and Mongols. They fear their keenness. We shall have to fill in the loss of Sarts in the caravan by Kalmucks. How illuminating it is to observe this nation which may now enter the pages of history. How refreshing it is to penetrate again into the mountains and to leave the sands and the dust. Even the horses shake themselves when they approach fresh water and mountains. At the sight of mountains our Tibetans, Tsering and Ramsana, fairly leap with joy.

Smile, Kalmuck soil. The Series "Asurgina" and "Orovani" is conceived.

PART IX

KARASHAHR–DZUNGARIA

(1926)

March 28th

KARASHAHR, in translation, means Black City. The Chinese call Urumchi the Red Temple (Hung-Miao-Tzi).

On this expanse are the countries of the Torguts and Khoshuts. Strange is the destiny of the Kalmucks. The nation is dispersed in an inexplicable manner. In Chinese Sinkiang, the Olets occupy the Iliisk district; the Torguts, Karashahr; the Khoshuts, Dzungaria; the Oirots, Mongolia; the Damsok are in Tibet. Besides these there are Kalmuck *ulus*, scattered in Caucasia, Altai, Semirechye, Astrakhan, along the Don, and near Orenburg. Near the holy mountain Sabur stand the remains of the city of the Kalmuck King, Aisha. In the scattered *yurtas* the signs of self-consciousness begin to appear. The prophecies of the forefathers tell of the coming dates.

A dispute between a Sart Bey and the Kalmuck. The Sart says provokingly: "You have no god." The Kalmuck answers, calmly: "If a Sart comes among us we feed him and give him drink, and we feed his horse and give him provisions on his journey. But if a Kalmuck comes to the Sart, he is not given food and his horse remains hungry. Judge for yourself, who possesses the essential. The Sarts defile the Buddhist teaching and mock the Buddhist images but the Kalmucks say, 'We revere your inscriptions.' But you have no images because when the first images were bestowed, you were far distant and could not perceive them."

It is difficult to dispute with Buddhists. Those who know the teaching can tell so much of the evolution of life; they speak about the messengers from Shambhala who go forth on earth, in various guises, for the help of mankind. Unprejudiced, they speak of the new social movements, recalling the commands of Gautama himself. But if we eliminate from these tales the stylization of language and images we encounter a teaching based on the true knowledge of evolution far ahead of its epoch.

S. praises the Kalmucks for the steadfastness of their word: "One does not need written agreements. It is not as with the Sarts, especially the beks and beys."

We encounter a few beautiful Karashahr horses. This is the identical breed which one sees on ancient miniatures and on the statuettes of old China. Some scientists considered this breed extinct. But here it is before us, vigorous, dark-bay, firm in gait. It would be good for other countries to examine this breed.

Tomorrow we will go to the encampment of the Kalmuck Khan.

. . . . .

Hardly has evening fallen before a new Sinkiang villainy occurs. S. arrives in great excitement and says that the Amban will not permit us to go by the short road and orders us to continue our route through the sands and heat of Toksun, the long and wearisome highway. An added insult, an added imposition, an added derision of the artist and the man. Is it possible that we cannot see the monasteries? Is it possible that an artist must go only by way of the dry sands We hurry to the Taotai. The old man pretends to be indisposed and cannot receive us. His secretary shouts from the balcony that we can go, that the Amban will arrange all that is necessary. We go to the Amban. He is not at home. His secretary says that the Amban "fears for us on account of the great snows on the mountain pass." We explain that there is now no longer any snow, that we do not have to go by way of high Teke-davan, that we will go through Sumun-davan, which is lower.

At seven o'clock they promise to bring us the answer. Of course the snow of the Amban is by no means of a white color. These Chinese are capable of ruining each day. These Chinese are capable of transforming each day into a prison and a torture. We await the evening and nevertheless prepare to depart. There come Torguts, returning from Kobdo.

. . . . .

A Khoshut lama comes. He asks us to heal his eyes. He brings us valuable tales. Not fairy tales but facts. Facts are needed. The lama from Uliasutai has written a book about the approach of the time of Shambhala.

. . . . .

In the evening the answer comes. The nephew of the Taotai and the postmaster bring it. Of course the answer is negative. In spite of the heat, of the humidity and dust, we must go by the long way, through hot Toksun. E.I. says she will die from the heat, but the Chinese smile and notify us that their Governor has a very small heart. We compose this telegram to the Governor-General:

Please wire instructions to the Magistrate at Karashahr to allow Roerich Expedition to proceed to proceed to Urumchi by mountain way. Health of Mrs. Roerich does not allow her to continue journey through the hot sandy desert of the long road. The mountain road permits to reach Urumchi much sooner.

Until the arrival of an answer we shall go to the encampment of the Torgut Khan and the monastery Sharasüme.

The sense of surveillance and compulsion is abominable. What work can be accomplished when behind one's back stands the order of the Amban and when the Governor-General has a "very small heart"? One's whole mood is spoiled and we are waiting again as though in some medieval Chinese dungeon.

• • • • •

March 29th

We arise with the dawn. All our men hasten to leave earlier in order that the Chinese may not have time to invent new difficulties. S. accompanies us for a long distance. In a broad-brimmed hat and in a. yellow, old military coat, he sits well-poised on his ambling horse as if he came from a New Mexican ranch. We go by the yellow steppe; high grass. The sun is burning hot. To the north is again a vague silhouette of mountains; separate great *yurtas;* herds of camels. The riders wear round caps of Tibetan cut. After nine *p'o-t'ai* we arrive at the encampment. The bazaar is cleaner than the cities of the Sarts. The white buildings of the post shine in the sun. The walls, the yards, the walks, are broadly constructed. They lead us through a broad yard into a big room. White walls, black Chinese furniture, bearskins. We drink tea. They bring a card from the Gegen-regent (the Khan being a minor). This is the same reincarnated Sengchen Lama whom we mentioned in the Sikhim notes. Tomorrow we shall see him. We shall stop in the field behind the encampment opposite the mountains.

A wonderful sensation. Kalmucks come and are speaking to our lama. The Kalmucks ask whether we have pieces of magnet. They ask about Tibet, about Mongolia, all this very carefully, until they know with certainty who we are. The women are in very beautiful, well-fitting attire. Behind the wall a military trumpet resounds—these are the Cossacks of Toin-Lama, the Gegan ruler. He has two hundred Kalmuck riders, who are taught the Cossack formation.

• • • • •

March 30th

A clear morning. Purple mountains. It will be hot. The distinctness of the mountains and buildings reminds me somewhat of Ladak. One might have rejoiced had there not occurred a Chinese villainy in the guise of a guard, who came with the insolent announcement that we must not remain here too long, and that it would be better to await the command of the Tu-t'u in Karashahr—in the middle of manured fields, dust and suffocating heat. Verily, one may choke from all the proposals of the Chinese. Now even the escorting soldiers have begun to reprimand us. They ought rather to guard our seized arms, which were thrown on the field without any watch. At ten o'clock we go to Toin-Lama, a friendly man, small in stature. Although according to custom the face of Toin-Lama is impenetrable, nevertheless, upon hearing the tales about temples in Sikhim and Little Tibet he becomes animated and wishes us all success. He stands as he listens to the message, but fear of the Chinese congeals the tongue of Toin-Lama. He mumbles: "When the time comes." But the time has come! Every one measures for himself. . . .

The house of the prince is white and clean and spacious. In the yards stand *yurtas* with golden cupolas. Dented walls. Banners. Some faces smiling, and some gloomy. One can understand how strong is Sinkiang oppression. The Sinkiang dragon coils around the semi-independence of the Kalmucks. But the mountains and the white walls are so joyous! Not even three hours pass without Chinese treachery. A whole crowd of "ministers" and elders arrives from the Gegen-regent with two Chinese soldiers. Do we not see that the Amban of Karashahr commands us to return to Karashahr immediately? All this is told to us at length and firmly, but there is no letter with it. We say that we intend to leave Sinkiang as quickly as possible, but that we await the answer from the Tu-t'u. And here we sit again in inactivity and await a telegram from Urumchi, without any assurance that our telegram was sent at all. It is impossible to work because even without moving we call forth persecution. Meanwhile the soldier goes to the bazaar and entrusts his gun to Suleiman. And so the soldier's gun is being entrusted to our groom and our arms are left sealed in the fields. In fine, where is logic, where is reason?

After three hours a *buran* starts. The mountains disappear.

. . . . .

Friends, you will think that I am exaggerating somewhat. If anything, I should be glad to understate, but the occurrences are monstrous. Again a crowd of Kalmucks come with Chinese soldiers and transmit to us the demand that we immediately depart from the post by command of the Karashahr Taotai. They are noisy and threaten. It means that one cannot work; nor can one visit Sharasüme. The whole purpose of the Expedition vanishes. One can only determine to leave Chinese soil as quickly as possible. Within two hours we go to demand back our passport and a letter stating the reasons of our expulsion. They give us the passports with an official letter that the *expulsion* is by command of the Karashahr Taotai, who accuses us of having *made maps.* They give us carts in order to send us away more quickly. I tell them that I am fifty-two years old; that I was honorably received by twenty-two countries, and that for the first time in my life I am subjected to expulsion and this from the territory of the semi-independent Torguts. What kind of independence? This is nothing but slavery: humiliating slavery, against all the customs of the East—to cast out a guest! And where shall we go? To the heat of Toksun? And can E.I. endure it? Her heart is absolutely unable to bear the heat. And where is the nearest border in order to hide from the Chinese torturers?

A tempest threatens in the mountains.

. . . . .

March 31st

We slept badly. We arose before dawn. I walk out in the morning twilight. I meet our lama. He is very upset: "I must depart at once. They want to arrest us."—"Who said it?"—"During the night a lama came whom I know from Tibet; he says that yesterday the Kalmuck Elders wanted to bind us all; but they were afraid of the revolvers."—"Take Olla and the Kirghiz with you. Gallop through the steppe to Karashahr. There we shall find you."

In five minutes the lama and the Kirghiz are already galloping through the steppe. The carts have come in the meantime. We start in a hurry to load. Threatened by the Chinese, the Gegen-regent does not even come to say good-by. More than once was he held back in Urumchi and now he is even more afraid. Even for the religious festivals, the Chinese only permitted him to leave Urumchi for four days. Although he is not courageous, still one cannot simply expel guests in order to please the Chinese. Some riders are encircling us and spying. Again we go by the same steppe but Karashahr has become for us truly a black city. In Karashahr we were prohibited from visiting the Buddhist temple. They doom us to creep along the hot sands for twelve days and stupidly prohibit us from touching the beloved mountains. From Karashahr, by reason of the order of the Tu-t'u, we were again made convicts under surveillance. But on the other hand we know that the poor Gegen is surrounded by Chinese spies and that often under a Kalmuck's kaftan is hidden Chinese identity. We come into the manured garden where we were before. From the gates they scream at us "Kapr" (meaning impure, a Moslem greeting). Sung rushes at the offender with a whip. The usual fight. The Sart runs away. We go at once to the Amban and on our way take along the postmaster, who speaks English. The Amban says that according to the telegram of Tu-t'u, we must go by the long way through the sands, in spite of the danger to the health of E.I. Of course we already heard that the Tu-t'u has a "very small heart." But, nevertheless, this cruelty astonishes me. The Amban does not deny that he ordered us to return from the encampment and that *we were prohibited from visiting the Buddhist temple.* We say that in that case we have nothing to do in China and we ask for a written statement of these prohibitions for communication to America. The Amban is confused and refers to the necessity of conferring with the Taotai. Once more it is confirmed that we are prohibited from visiting the temples and painting the mountains and that in order to expedite our journey we are sent on a long road. Where art thou, Confucius? Where is thy justice and sagacity?

Tiresome bargaining over the *arbas* begins. They demand, as far as Urumchi, 180 *lans,* while the usual price is not more than ninety or a hundred *lans.* So we finish the day among different "friendly greetings."

Kalmuck soil had smiled to us from afar, but on approach this was turned into the Sinkiang grimace. We recall the deeply penetrating Sikhim moods; we recall the grandeur of the Himalayas. It was not without cause that our hearts ached when we began to descend from the Karakorum heights toward Takla Makan. The Kirghiz related how the Torgut Elders held council after the receipt of the letter from the Amban: "Should we bind them? We are many and they are only three." The Kirghiz, Salim, is indignant at the Gegan: "This is not a prince; if he changes his word in an hour, he shall never be a Burkhan." And again we see the sympathy of the people and the rancor of the Elders and beks. The Lama is indignant because of the conduct of the Kalmucks. All this is illuminating! The former Kalmuck Khan was poisoned. A wiser counselor was killed. The Torgut Elders are far from awakening.

· · · · ·

April 1st

Different tales about the Kalmucks. The late Kalmuck Khan, under pressure or under influence, gave an important mission to a Chinese. The Chinese hurriedly went to Urumchi in order to legalize and to ratify the mission. The Kalmucks overtook him in the mountains and put an end to him together with his escort, so that not even any traces were found. Because their Khan was susceptible to such influence, the Kalmucks poisoned him. As the heir was a minor, the brother of the Khan, Toin-Lama, became regent. In June of this year, the Toin-Lama will give over the state seal (tamgha) to the young Khan, and he himself is going away as an ecclesiastic to the monastery in Sharasŭme. Shall the twelve-year-old Khan reign for long? Toin-Lama fell into disgrace with the Tu-t'u after he refused to give his soldiers for the expedition that was sent to kill the Kashgar Titai. A complete medieval darkness!

The prosperity of the Kalmucks is being crippled because the taxes are high. Besides the Chinese taxes, they pay the local Noyon taxes. It is hard for the people. The herds of the simple people are getting meager; and the Elders, taking their bearing from Sinkiang, have reached a point where they try to *bind* an American Expedition. In Khotan they threatened to expel us, and in Karashahr they brought the threats into action. We shall hope that the weather will be less bloodthirsty than the Tu-t'u of Urumchi, and that it will not suffocate E.I. This official sends a compilation of his orders to the British Consul, also to the British Museum; but it is not the dead pages of his orders but his actions, which give the image of the man. Only at first hand is it possible to see the true image of the government of Sinkiang. It is not for nothing that the best Chinese are calling the Sinkiang government, "Sinkiang Company." And until you see it on this site, you will not be able to believe in such human deterioration. Of course the Tu-t'u is old and will die soon and he cannot take with him to his grave the pilfered goods. But who will be the one to clean these Augean stables?

Verily I should much rather paint than depict these harmful, malevolent evils. But apparently it has to be so. Probably for some this will be useful. America awaits my paintings of the Buddhist heights, but let the Chinese government explain why we were not permitted to go to the monasteries. In Sikhim they met us with trumpets and banners; but on Chinese soil, with ropes. Of course, the Amban of Karashahr did not give me any letter. Well, it is not necessary. We have a letter with the seal of the Kalmuck Khan which clearly indicates the order of the Chinese officials. Quicker, away from the Chinese threat! Before us are the islands of Japan: before us the dreams, long-existing, to see the Easter Islands with their mysterious stone giants.

Soldiers were not sent today at all and so our confiscated arms have to guard themselves. The evening is ended with the tedious procedure of granting leave to three hostlers who are going away to Ladak. The young Tibetan, Tsering, wants to go with us. He does not love his stepmother, and he says that his father has become a stranger to him and he wants to go far away with us. The young soul is knocking at the window of new possibilities. How can one not take him?

. . . . .

April 2nd

The morning begins with the drama of Tsering. His Ladaki father, misinformed by the malicious grooms, forbids Tsering to go with us. If he does, he says, he will break his legs and arms. You should have seen the tears of Tsering. All trembling and swallowing his tears, he bids us farewell. What right do people have to deprive one of his happiness? In his desire was so much striving toward light. And now Tsering again will have senselessly to march with donkeys along the dry sands, serving ignorance. Poor boy! Sometimes we wonder if he is not going to run away. Of course this is difficult because the malicious old man and the no less malicious hostler will watch him.

Since seven o'clock we have been busy with the *arbas* and caravan. We are writing contracts. We are protesting on account of the unfitness of the horses and the soldiers who were sent. The delay makes us indignant. An American would be driven distracted by such a tempo. When will these people awaken?

ALTAI-HIMALAYA

At the same time comes interesting information. The Chinese are taking vaccine against smallpox, not from calves but from people, and so they are contaminating people with syphilis and other diseases.

The Mongols have occupied the frontier from Sharasŭme and are within a hundred miles from Ku-ch'eng or, about three hundred miles from Urumchi—from the residence of the Governor-General. If one draws a line from Kuldja to Ku-ch'eng, the Tu-t'u will find himself in a sack. Incidentally, the illustrious Tu-t'u has erected for himself a monument in Urumchi. Will not the Mongols remove it?

We are marching only four *p'o-t'ai.* Instead of mountains, instead of monasteries, instead of Maitreya—again yellow steppes around us. What right do the Chinese have to deprive us of seeing beauty? The departure of the three hostlers somehow refreshed the caravan. For some reason the people are joyous. Ramsana expects Tsering and assures us that he will come running to us today or tomorrow.

. . . . .

April 3rd

It is very cold during the night and hot at midday. Yellow steppe. A dusty stony road. Northward is a range of foggy mountains. We reach the dirty little village of Ushaktal. Again we have to stop near cattle yards. Indiscriminating are all Taotais, Titais, Ambans, T'ung-lings, who for centuries have been stopping overnight at the same miserable inns. From this little village goes the Koshut road to Urumchi. Along the Khoshut road it is only four days to Urumchi but by order of the Governor-General, we have to go by the long dusty, hot and ugly road for eight whole days. This is Chinese cruelty, to force travelers to go in the dust and suffocating heat and to know that alongside this there goes a short road full of mountain beauty. It is significant that not one of the Taotais and Ambans whom we saw could mention to us any celebrated contemporary Chinese artist or scientist.

You may imagine our feeling when we saw the canyon through which the short road passes, and we ourselves had to crawl in clouds of hot dust!

Again a variation of the legend about Turfan: "From a cave came out a tall man and went to the bazaar to buy something. He offered to pay for his purchases with gold coins which were a thousand years old. Then the man went back into the same cave and disappeared. And at the entrance was standing a stone dog. The dog wanted to jump into the cave after the man but he became petrified."

Ushaktal is the center for Khoshut horses. They are larger than those of the Torguts. At a distance of one *p'o-t'ai* from Ushaktal are traces of an old fortress of the times of the conquest of Andijan and Fergana. Many mosquitoes. Wild geese.

. . . . .

April 4th

"The old Khan decided to hand over to his sons the tamgas (seals) that they should rule the Khoshuns. There were tamgas of gold, silver, copper and one of wood. The Khan's wife told her favorite son: 'My boy, take the wooden tamga. Don't take the gold ones!' The Khans began to choose the tamgas and the old Khan said, 'The sky has created water. Let us test the tamgas with water. The one tamga which shall be higher shall remain higher.' And the wooden tamga remained on the surface of the water, but the gold and silver sank underneath the water."

On the Black Irtysh are many gold prospectors, tens of thousands of them. The gold is only slightly under the soil. The Tu-t'u sent soldiers to detain the seekers, but on reaching the gold the entire troop disappeared.

Today is a beautiful day. From all sides appear mountains—blue, sapphire, purple, yellow and reddish brown. Gray sky and pearly vistas. Alongside the bed of a broad current we reach Kara-Kizil. It means black-red. The name is correctly given because the mountains are of coarse granite, black and red. The silence of the desert. How much more agreeable are these isolated *langars* than the cities and dirty bazaars!

And only to think that we could have gone for four days through solitary mountains, amidst far-off snows! Today the first small pine appeared. The whole day, for seventy-four miles, there was only one small *langar,* with a bad well, a hundred feet in depth. For the whole day only two small caravans of emaciated mules. It is as if one did not go by a big Chinese road but through a new undiscovered country. From the mountains protrude layers of black slate and coal formations. And the whole desert holds its breath awaiting the steps of the future.

·   ·   ·   ·   ·

April 5th

It is simply a torture with the *tserik.* He goes to sleep in an *arba* and he fails to guard not only our arms but even his own gun. During the night the servants of some passing Amban wanted to put our horses out of the *langar.*

And the mountains are so beautiful! They stand, dark bronze, with greenish and carmine spots. Behind the mountains again lies the desert, with dark shingled slopes strewn with light-yellow bushes. A whole carpet of Asia.

During the day it is hot. An eastern wind brings some relief. We passed nine *p'o-t'ai* to the poor village Kumash. A pilfered and disrupted village. Two tumble-down and uninhabited *langars.* At one time there was something here. E.I. asks, "But Ambans and Taotais are traveling here. Is it possible that they are stopping in such dirt?" Suleiman laughs, "What does it matter to these Ambans? If they only have an opium pipe and a woman! They roll in any dirt!" Apparently, respect to the officials is not very great. Through travelers from Khotan a vague report penetrates about the replacing of Taotai Ma.

The *Barkhans* are silent. The mountains are hidden in blue mist. We are reminded of a characteristic case. The travelers from China to Tibet relate how a nurse with a child was left on the border as customs inspector. It happened that the border official smoked much opium and his wife was so busy in the household, that the nurse had to fulfill the duties of a customs official. This was printed in the Shanghai papers. .

Last year Kalmuck pilgrims were prohibited from going to Tibet to worship in the sanctuaries. Such prohibition is very significant.

Already today the Chinese torture begins. The heat which we would have avoided on the Koshut mountain path has begun. It is now very early spring. They say the snow in Urumchi has already melted. In the evening we reprimanded Suleiman for his habit of letting his whips pass over human backs. He is astonished: "How shall I deal otherwise with a Dungan or Chinese? Does he understand reason? Either he takes you or you take him. Why do you think that the Dungan *mafakesh* went so quickly yesterday? Because from early morning we gave him a good kick. But today he probably will come late." And in such manner are they living here—a whole chain of evil.

· · · · ·

April 6th

A hot day. First the desert with many mounds and rocks surrounding it. After passing eight *p'o-t'ai* we entered a beautiful gorge. We went through it for several *p'o-t'ai*. Bluish-black bronze rocks, all-creviced. Complete lack of water. Destroyed *langars* on the way. Probably the water disappeared and the people were forced to migrate. During the entire day we saw only one caravan of mules and two riders. The greatest road is truly nothing but a stony desert. From seven in the morning until half past four, no life is seen on the road. If we had gone by the mountain path, we would be in Urumchi tomorrow. We stay overnight in Argai Bulak. An isolated *langar* amid bronze mountains. They say that here was also war with Andijan. A cave is seen high in the sandy rock. The trails to it are entirely crumbled.

. . . . .

April 7th

On account of the inhuman Governor-General we are compelled to proceed through the hot gorge. Varied sand formations; all is much more beautiful in Ladak. Amidst the sands a vivid green strip of grass is suddenly seen. It means that from the rock, unsuspected, a spring of ringing water is flowing which spreads over the sand. To be sure, one could easily gather the precious fluid into a constructed canal; one could easily repair the stony road; but of course the improvement of the country does not enter into the schedule of occupations of the Chinese administration. After a small crossing we enter the burning plain. E.I. , stifling from the heat, says, "This is not a governor but an old monster!" Really to compel foreigners to take four extra days of burning road—it is stupid and inhuman. It is just the same as to say to an American: "You can go from New York to Chicago but only via New Orleans." Amidst sands, amidst the milky mists, glows azure Toksun. Only one day's distance is Turfan and out of its nine-hundred-foot pit rises the heat. One can imagine how easily in summer even the natives die from heat in Turfan.

In Toksun the trees are already vividly green. A thick verdure springs up from the furrows. We are standing on the shore of a river dividing into many tributaries. . . . If only there would not be dissension again! Today the dawn started with an ugly fight. Suleiman battered up Sung and the latter came running to us all covered with blood. It is necessary for us to get rid of Suleiman quickly. This brute does not understand reason. And his persecution is chiefly directed against Sung only because he does not steal. But at the base of all this, the Tu-t'u himself is responsible for all the fighting—he who has confiscated our arms and who has ordered them carried sealed as a demonstration to the whole province. If we had the revolvers the men would conduct themselves differently. It is hot; even at five o'clock the heat does not diminish and the night brings no coolness into the tents.

Toward evening they bring the horses to the river. They walk them up and down before us. Will we not buy? The price is from three hundred to one thousand *lans*. A beautiful light-bay horse. On the back is a black stripe. The posture of the head reminds us of a zebra of kulan. Is there not in the species of Karashahr horses, a cross with, the kulan?

At twilight the Dungan Chinese doctor comes. He speaks Russian. How is that? It appears that his wife is a Russian Cossack woman from Semirechye. And here she herself is coming, in pink trousers and a blouse; and with her is a dark little girl. And under the stars of Toksun rings out the soft complaint of her life. From her thirteenth year her family sold her to Dungans. She ran away. There came the revolution. Her relatives disappeared. Came famine. And now the Cossack woman appears in a Chinese attire. "I am weary; I have nothing to speak about with them. They are dirty. And now we are anxious again to go to my country. My husband wants to be there. I bought for myself a little girl, a Sart. I paid twelve *lans* for her. I made for myself a kind of tent out of linen and put it in the room in order to cover their dirt. In Urumchi many of our Cossack women, because of need, have married Chinese. The educated ones and good dressmakers married Dungans.

Here are many scorpions. Beware at night. Turfan and Toksun are notorious for their scorpions. A little one bit me—I screamed with pain for three hours. Then they tightly tied a string around my finger and applied opium. Be careful."

The Cossack-Dungan woman goes into the dusk with the husband foreign-to-her and with the purchased little girl, whom she calls Eudoxia. And so the Tu-t'u sent us not only into a furnace but also into the city of scorpions.

It is hot at night. The grasshoppers chirp ceaselessly. George is astonished that until now human beings are sold. And this goes on openly and businesslike. Maybe in the list of the commands of the Tu-t'u, presented by him to the British Museum, there is a flowery command about the sale of human beings.

. . . . .

April 8th

Because of the cruelty of the Governor-General we spent a horrible day. We dragged ourselves through the burning stony desert. On the horizon the hot air is all a-quiver. The far-off inexistent lakes become dense and the mirages melt and are transformed into a gray pitiless plain. The far-off mountains merge into the heat. Only to think that we might, by now, have been in Urumchi. We would have already read news from America. But because of the despotism of a monster we have to tramp needlessly over the foothills for three more days. We shall stop in the *langar* of Pasha Tsaigan.

On our way, we have been thinking. The Europeans are not justified in destroying the monumental conceptions of the Near and Far East. Here we have seen caves pilfered and stripped. But when the time of the regeneration of Asia shall come, will she not ask, "Where are our best treasures, which were constructed by the creative spirit of our ancestors?" Would it not have been better, in the name of knowledge, to study all these monuments, carefully retain them and create conditions fostering preservation? Instead of this, fragments of frescoes were taken away, only to perish because of change of climate. In Berlin, whole cases of frescoes were destroyed by rats. In some countries parts of the monumental constructions are piled up in the museums with no indication as to their original purpose and meaning. Our friend Pelliot is right not to destroy these monumental constructions, but to study them and publish his researches about them. Let individual works of art move freely on our planet, but the deeply conceived composition of construction must not be destroyed. The result is that the head of a Bodhisattva is in Europe and its painted boots are in Asia. Where then is the disinterested knowledge which first of all purifies and preserves and restores? What would the world of learning say if fragments of the frescoes of Gozzoli or Mantegna were to be scattered in different countries? Soon over the whole world speedy steel birds will fly. All distances will be within reach, and not ragged skeletons but evidences of a high creation must meet these winged guests.

During the whole of today we saw only one small caravan of mules and only one rider. The dead silence of the great road is comparable only to the lethargy of contemporary China. Youth will come and the deserts will flourish.

In the *yakhtans* the candles have melted; the yellow sun hides behind the amber mountains. Tomorrow should be cooler—we shall go beyond the mountains into the first zone of the Altai climate.

. . . . .

April 9th

We are passing the last ridges of the Heavenly Mountains of T'ian Shan. We pass beside the route to Turfan. On the crossroad is an old Chinese *stela* with half-erased inscriptions and ornaments. There, long since, in the depths of the centuries, someone sought to preserve with care the signs and milestones. Farther on, our road branches—one road goes through the mountain passes and the other along a river with fifteen fordings. Our people debate a long time, as if the direction of our road were a state affair. The council has decided to go through the passes. All this is being discussed so seriously in order that we should realize the seriousness of the crossing. But the anticipations are in vain. Both crossings are very easy and bear no comparison with Ladak and Karakorum. We descend from the mountains to a small river. The ruins of an old fort are visible. Against the dark blue background of the mountains, a light golden sand peak shines out unexpectedly. We are told: "There lives a holy man. Formerly he used to show himself to people. Now no one sees him, but we know he lives there. A kind of little chapel stands there. But the doors are not seen." Thus a legend is being created.

Again we go by a narrow, bumpy village road and no one can believe that this is the biggest or rather the only artery of a whole district, which contains the metropolis. It is strange and even monstrous to see such deterioration of an entire country. One thing is beautiful—the soft bells of a long row of camels. These are the true ships of the desert.

We stop in Tapan ch'eng (the city of the Pass). We have marched eleven hours. E.I. even kissed her horse. To Urumchi it is now only twenty-two p'o't'ai. It is very hot during the day. The stars twinkle with unusual brightness. For the first time we heard the gongs of the little Chinese temple.

. . . . .

April 10th

In the evening a *buran* sprang up. We fastened the tents down with all our spikes. We heaped the *yakhtans* around for weights and we spent the wretched night in the trembling little house. At two o'clock during the night the gongs sounded in the temple. But we could not find out what kind of night service it could be. By morning the *shamal* became even stronger. Everything was obscured in a gray-yellow dust. The mountains disappeared. During the entire crossing we proceeded against the whistling waves of the whirlwind. On the approach to the capital of the Tu-t'u, the villages became still more bedraggled. The road is still worse and the types of Dungans still more murderous and savage. The difference of prices for products is incomprehensible. Here ten eggs cost one *sar*, and in the next village they are half the price. The same with fuel and forage.

A gray desert with white layers of salt. The waves of dust are moving about and the tails of the horses are curling. It is easy to imagine that the whirlwinds of Asia can overturn a loaded *arba* with fifty *puds* (two thousand pounds) or can stop a *troyka*. There were special difficulties in pitching the tents in the dirty little village of Ts'ai-o-pu. The tents fluttered in the wind, everything was atremor and a layer of dust instantly covered everything. And so we sit, amidst the muffled knocks of the storm, amidst the layers of sand and dirt. Why did we have to go through this furious *shamal* when by now we could have been in Urumchi for three days? Apparently the Tu-t'u wanted to show us his country in its complete dejection. Our eyes fill with dust and the sand grits against the teeth. The noise and the blows of the wind remind us of the tremendous seas vividly chronicled in the newspapers during our last crossing of the Atlantic.

Sometimes the formations of the mountains particularly suggest the fusion of multi-colored fluids, and often the desert thunders with the chords of the ocean. The *shamal* does not stop by evening as our caravaneers hoped.

. . . . .

April 11th

This story is told in explanation of the gales: "The Chinese army was pursuing a Kalmuck giant. The giant was strong. He evoked the gale to his aid from the mountains and he himself galloped away. And the gale scattered the Chinese forces. But as there was no one to conjure the gale, so it has remained."

Today part of the horizon has cleared. The faint outlines of mountains glimmer with their snowy crests. Steely lakes gleam below, surrounded by white borders of salt. The gale continues. It has become freezing during the night. Instead of the *shamal* it is now a freezing Siberian *siverko*, which pinches the cheeks and makes the eyes water. We take out our fur coats. Apparently we have to experience all the peculiarities of the local climate. The desert has changed into naked, grayish-yellow, silent mounds. The mountains in the distance are azure. The road is not a short one. Judging by the time it will take, there are fourteen *p'o-t'ai*. Far away, between two hills they point out Urumchi to us.

Before we reach the Chinese city we pass through a former Russian concession. There is a broad street with low houses of Russian type. We read the names: "Conditerskaya" (Pastry Shop); "Yuveleer" (Jeweler); Bardigine Company. . . . The messenger from the firm of Belyankhan arrives and takes us to the living quarters which are prepared—a low white house with two rooms and a foyer. But a difficulty arises: In order to let us in they would have to dispossess two foreigners—and this is so distasteful to all. We go to G., the representative of Belyankhan, to take counsel with him. It appears that everything is completely filled in Urumchi. There are no houses. We shall have to stay in *yurtas* outside the city. It is better. George gallops away with G. to find a site for our camp. Some curious people walk around us and they all insistently want to know who we are, where we come from, for what purpose and for how long, how many people are with us, and what is in the cases.

We have dinner with the G's. The conversation is about our America, about the life there, about the intensity of work; about the signs "Keep smiling." Yes, yes, this sign is also needed.

For dinner at the G's, there is an entire table filled with foreigners. It appears that today is an important day. The Tu-t'u called the Dungans to him and announced to them that he had no complaint against them. At the beginning of March mobilization took place and it was announced that every one was called out, but that the Dungans were not needed. The Dungans were troubled, especially since the Dungan officials had been discharged from some posts. In the city itself a dangerous band of Dungans had been operating. Following the mobilization, about ten thousand soldiers were sent toward Hami.

· · · · ·

April 12th

Since morning our people have refused to move beyond the town to the *yurtas*. They are afraid of being attacked by robbers. With George we went to C., to Chu-ta-hen, to Fan (who is in charge of the foreign section) and to the Tu-t'u himself. For a long time we passed through the Chinese city. Triple walls; long rows of shops. The products are more varied than in Kashgar. C. is a sympathetic Italian who is in charge of the post office. He was astonished at all our experiences, and advised us to go via Chuguchak, through Siberia, to Japan—the same way that our friend, Allen Priest, went. Chu-ta-hen is a young Chinese who speaks several languages. He smiles, and becomes indignant about the events in Khotan and Karashahr, and assures us he is ready to help. He takes us to Fan and the Tu-t'u. We go through all sorts of gates and alleys; we have tea with both dignitaries, and both offer us much sugar and assure us that in Khotan and Karashahr mistakes were committed by the officials; that we are great people and that is why we must pardon small people. They assure us that a thing of this sort will never recur, and that we can be absolutely calm, in Urumchi. But as to any investigation—not a word. We go back through all these long bazaars. Entire alleys filled with ginghams, hosiery, cheap crockery and popular pictures. At home E.I. meets us with a surprise. At the very moment when the Tu-t'u was assuring us of his friendship and help and good will, our house was being searched in great detail by the Chief of Police, accompanied by a Tartar translator. Again E.I. was questioned about our art works; again the same absurdity was committed from beginning to the end. How can one believe the assurances of the Tu-t'u?

After dinner I go to arrange a passage through Altai through Siberia, just as for Priest. The answer may not arrive before two weeks. To find better quarters is impossible—all the houses are crowded. They say that in five days someone is leaving the city and so we may succeed in moving at least for a short time into more comfortable lodgings. Keep smiling! Keep smiling!

Today I spoke to three Chinese higher officials, thus: "I am fifty-two years old; I have been honorably received in twenty-three countries. No one in my life ever prohibited me from working freely on my peaceful art-work. No one in my life has ever arrested me; no one in my life has ever taken away my revolver as a means of defense. No one in my life has ever sent me forcibly in a direction which I did not desire. No one in my life has convoyed prisoners together with me. No one has ever treated me as a robber. No one has ever refused to take into consideration the request of a middle-aged lady based on a matter of health. But the Chinese officials have done all this. Now our only desire is to leave as speedily as possible the borders of China where they insult so flagrantly the peaceful cultural expedition of America."

All this was said. The Governor-General and the Vice-Governor do not comment. They give assurances that in Urumchi no one will touch me. But behind our backs at the same moment they are making a search and E.I. has, without reason, to open all cases and trunks. Keep smiling!

. . . . .

April 13th

We search for some sort of suitable house. In Urumchi it is most difficult. This night they have stolen a horse from G. During the night a high wall was broken and the horse was taken out of the stable. The dogs barked. The hostlers slept. The thieves worked and the horse disappeared. Of course the police will not find it. But maybe one can buy it back from the local Kirghiz.

The drums thunder. With red banners, the newly formed regiment marches. Real ragamuffins. But F. (the director of the Russo-Asiatic Bank), calms us: "This is nothing. Look at the soldiers near Hami. Wonderful bands they are!" Keep smiling!

Smilingly the Chinese tell us: "How interesting it will be for you to relate in America all your adventures." A very strange attitude toward themselves. Also they did not permit Priest to take photos in Tun-huang. However, in the six volumes of Pelliot these caves have long ago been reproduced.

F. arrives. He does not know how to return to Shang-hai. It is interesting to hear the tales of those who were trapped in this way. On the so-called imperial road, it is impossible. While on his way here, he was arrested, detained, and afterward he was under the fire of the Hunghutze who are sometimes better organized than the state troops. He tells of past events in Siberia. He relates many horrors. G. arrives. New tales about the atrocities of the regiment of Anenkoff: How the officer, V., hacked to pieces the families of sixteen officers in his regiment, having first attacked all the women. Where is the image of humanity?

. . . . .

April 14th

A vivid day, full of sunshine. The snow on the mountains of Bogdo-ula is glistening. These are the same mountains beyond which "live holy people." One may wonder; has not a site been reserved for them in Altai? Today the holiday of Ramazan begins. Drums, calls from the mosques and crowds of people.

It would be interesting to examine more closely the psychology of the local officials. Here are the so-called generals and ministers of finance, of commerce and education. One hopes that there is no minister of transportation; if so, how could one account for the exasperating condition of the roads? How does the Minister of Education enlighten the people? And where is this mysterious system of industry? When the Minister of Industry asked one sick man about the condition of his health, the latter said: "The same as your industry." And the Tu-t'u "modestly" said that the grateful population had erected a monument to him for the prosperity of the district!

The system of taxation is remarkable. For example, at the gold mines, taxes are being assessed according to the number of workmen, quite irrespective of the results of the works. Now on the Black Irtysh there are thirty thousand people excavating. Of course, all this leads to the depletion of the gold-bearing soil. We move into the little house near the Russo-Asiatic Bank. Probably we shall have to stay there two weeks.

· · · · ·

April 15th

Tales about the Tu-t'u. The Peking government has tried many times to replace him but the shrewd Tu-t'u has gathered signatures from the local beys and sent to Peking the "petition of the population" made up by him saying that only the presence of Yan the Tu-t'u had guaranteed the peace of the country. But the peace of the province of the Tu-t'u is the peace of Death. This administrator affirms that the construction of factories and the development of manufacture creates a workers' class and that is why one must not develop industry and build factories.

In 1913 this administrator suspected his eight relatives of treachery. He therefore arranged a banquet, invited all officials and during that dinner, with his own hands, shot the chief suspect; and the guards at the same table made an end to the seven others. In 1918 the Tu-t'u had a grievance against one of the Ambans. He sent the disfavored one to Hami and on the way the Amban was "pasted with paper" and by this unique method he was strangled. In the "Garden of Tortures" of Mirbeau this invention of evil was omitted.

Of course the collection of funds for the erection of the monument for the Tu-t'u was conducted throughout the whole district by forced subscriptions. And as a gift "from the grateful population" appeared an ugly copper figure with gilded epaulettes and stars. For the improvement of the morale of his officials, the Tu-t'u prohibits them from subscribing to the foreign as well as the best Chinese newspapers. It is monstrous to see all these medieval measures in the days of the evolution of the world. For a few sensitive young officials, it is very difficult. I remember the sad smile of the Amban Pan in Aksu. I understand why his only newspapers were from the postmaster Cavalieri. There is one hope: the Tu-t'u is very old, and his "benevolent" strangulation of the huge country cannot continue for long. One should not forget that the population remembers well those few Chinese officials who did not pillage and did not manifest their hatred for humanity. They speak highly of a certain Taotai of Chugutchak. They remember Pan-Tajen, the father of our acquaintance from Aksu well and warmly. When the old Pan-Tajen was buried, the whole city accompanied the funeral procession. Unlike the usual custom, the old official did not leave any money because he did not take any bribes.

Today is the holiday of Ramazan. The city is attired in vividly colored dress. The people pay visits to each other. In the morning about two thousand people listen to the sermon of a Mullah in the open field. Two Chinese visits—Chu-ta-hen and Fan, with translators. The young Chu-ta-hen openly sympathizes with us and his keen eyes can look straight at us. Fan more often averts his eyes. Now he has the new excuse that all our difficulties have come from the Peking government which did not notify Sinkiang about our coming. But from October 12th until today Fan had enough time to get in touch with Peking and there is no need to blame the fault of Sinkiang on Peking.

· · · · ·

April 16th

Strange information reached us about the pillage of the frescoes of Tun-huang. If this report is true, then such vandalism has to be investigated as an entirely unlicensed destruction of a uniquely preserved monument. They say, "Some American" merchants came, cut out pieces of the frescoes and succeeded in carrying away "many cases." It seems that Chinese pursued the robbers but, as usual, were unsuccessful; and as a result the monument is defaced. The world of learning should not fail to investigate the destruction of this unique shrine. Of course, Allen Priest, who probably was in Tun-huang during the fall may give authentic and detailed information. We can only set down this fact for information. How indignant Pelliot would be should he learn about the destruction of the monument which he studied and wrote about. Here the whole foreign colony knows about what happened.

Just now a regiment is passing in the street. Is it possible that this collection of ragamuffins can show resistance to any one? The shrewd Tu-t'u is playing on these torn strings. Sometimes he calls into life the Dungans; now the Moslems; again the Kalmucks and then the Kirghiz. Or he may bring out varicolored roosters and announce that he whose roosters will conquer, shall be first. And the rooster of a certain color is already prepared to conquer his rivals, thus accomplishing the desire of the administrator. Or, also, the administrator may invent a non-existing plot or a revolt. The slavemaster has much ingenuity. . . .

We are indignant about the plundering of Tun-huang. The looting of the mosques of the Trans-Caspian district is also mentioned. And in Merv, the Oasis of Anou, valuable mural tiles are cut out and looted. Damascus is also destroyed. What does this mean? Is it possible that certain cosmic laws are being fulfilled. "Those, going toward the abyss, continue the path of their destiny, in tremor." So it is said in the teachings of the wise concerning the fulfillment of dates.

. . . . .

April 17th

During the long travels events are slipping by; only lately we dreamed of a trip to the Easter Islands, and now they tell us of the submersion of these islands three years ago. Is it possible that the giants of Atlantis have forever been merged in the abysses, and the flow of the cosmos—this Santana of Buddhism—is fulfilling its unalterable course? During the period of our marches through mountains and deserts, some of the smaller stars became of first magnitude. And a new island with a population of ten thousand sank into the sea. Lakes have dried up and new unexpected currents gushed forth. The cosmic energy confirms the steps of the evolution of humanity. Yesterday's "inadmissible" fairy tale is already being investigated by science. The refuse is being burned and the ashes are fertilizing the seedlings of new conquests.

In the silence of the suburb of Urumchi, one speaks in a comprehensive way about the tasks of the evolution of humanity, about the movement of nations, about knowledge, about the significance of color and sound. . . . It is gratifying to listen to this broad reasoning. . . . Some islands have merged into the depths and out of the depths have arisen new ones, powerful ones.

· · · · ·

April 18th

A journey out of town arranged by Yan Chang Lu and Chu-ta-hen. We visited the temple "of the god-devil," with a portrayal of hell. A poor temple. The images are ugly. Chu assures us that this is Buddhism but afterwards he himself confesses that such "popular primitive religion" has nothing in common with Buddhism. Hell is represented very undecoratively. In an oblong space on the floor a group of shoddy figures, recently completed, is arranged. A unique garden of tortures. They are grinding the sinners with millstones. They are crushing them with a press covered with nails. They are ripping their abdomens; they are boiling them in tar; they are tearing them apart with hooks and are injuring the extremities of the sinners by all the possible measures within the compass of Chinese fantasy. Especially revolting is the conduct of the righ-

[293]

teous ones, who, self-satisfied and arrogant, watch the tortures from little bridges and balconies of Paradise. It is not indicated to what section of hell the Tu-t'u himself will be assigned. All this curio-museum makes a pitiful and meaningless impression.

Afterward we visit the statue of the Tu-t'u with all its lifeless copper "grandeur"; then the pavilions and the pond which the Tu-t'u has constructed. Later we ascend a mountain behind the river, to the Tao temple in which is the god-of-all-gods. On one side of him is a six-armed god of horses and animals; on the other side is the god of insects. The impression of the temple is somewhat better and finer. Probably this is due to its more solitary location on the mountain. From the nearby rock the whole city is seen and all the surrounding mountains and hills. This is the most satisfying spot that we have seen in Chinese Turkestan. After this the temple of the god of thunder remains to be seen; it is unattractive and of little interest; and then tea and a dinner with the tiresome sitting on the floor. The old Yan Chang Lu very soon becomes intoxicated and his son sends him home. A satisfying conversation with B.; the broadness of his views may well astonish one. From Bogdo-ula, clouds are rising. It becomes cold toward evening. We shall have to find time to go to old Urumchi which is ten *versts* away. The red temple, after which the new city is named, is there. Toward evening again a game of pegs. In the yard is a crowd of people. Swings, exercises, May-poles; all nationalities; many children. There is also a project to organize a club. It is simple, human. It is joyous to behold.

· · · · ·

April 19th

It has become cold. This does not save the god of water from much discomfort. On account of the drought the Governor-General gave orders that the god of water be taken from the temple, and that his hands and feet be chopped off. We have read about savages who whip the gods because of their lack of zeal, but it appears that these savages live in Urumchi and that their leader is the Governor-General who considers himself a master of Chinese science. But who knows whether the god was simply a lazy one? Did he not have the hostile intention of stirring up the people against the Governor-General? With such a number of gods one may expect all sorts of alliances of those hostile to the "government." The local inhabitants are so accustomed to such an administrator that the strangest things begin to seem to them quite natural. One cannot build factories—this is natural. One cannot prospect for oil—this is natural. One cannot receive newspapers—this is natural. One cannot have a doctor—this is natural. Everything becomes natural.

From the mountain crevices curl clouds of smoke—the underground fire of coal is creeping out and the most precious resources of the country are vanishing.

Toward Ku-ch'eng, in the Valley of Death, lie heaps of bones—traces of a butchery of many thousands. Most of these dead ruins stand as witnesses of butchery and treason. But the province is "calm." And only the cemetery vies with this great calmness. How will this calmness of death explode? Who will come? Whence will he come? Who will begin the internal revolt? In the silence of the cemetery it is difficult to understand which tomb will be the first.

During the night in the direction of Hami pass bands of ragamuffins, called soldiers. They say that the Tu-t'u believes that forcibly gathering the ragamuffins from the bazaars into the barracks frees the city from a dangerous element. But what will be the fate of these armed gangs and upon whom will they turn their rusty arms? A Shanghai newspaper arrives with a description of an assault by Chinese armies on an American mission and the killing of the missionary. Formerly, this information would have upset one, but now no one is even astonished. And how else? They ask us whether we are sure that the Chinese will give us permission to go to Chuguchak? We answer, "And where else will the Chinese put us?" They tell us that everything is possible. They relate cases of absurd prohibitions and violence. When we are astonished at the "local affairs" the natives ask us "Is it possible that in America and Europe they do not know about Sinkiang?" If we had known one-half of the reality we would never have continued our way through China.

On Bogdo-ula snow fell; one has to light the stoves.

. . . . .

April 20th

During the night everything became white. It has been a long time since we have seen snow mountains with all their fine crystalline lines. Mountains, mountains! What magnetic forces are concealed within you! What a symbol of quietude is revealed in every sparkling peak! The legends of the greatest valor are conceived near mountains. The most human words find outlet on snowy heights. Toward evening, snow fell also in the valleys, and the whole district took on a wintry character. Tsenkevich comes. We speak about all the subjects near to us—his wanderings and adventures; they comprise a complete epic. An inexpressible charm lies in the fact that people leave their native places and on invisible wings make the earth small and accessible. And this accessibility is the beginning of the attainment of far-off worlds.

. . . . .

April 21st

There is snow since morning. Bogdo-ula appeared all snowy and blue. It is strange. F. does not believe in the horror of some quarters in Bombay. He cannot believe that these shameful cages with women exist. But every chauffeur knows it, and without any desire on your part takes you to see this hell—is it for the existence of this, that the earth has endured so many thousands of years?

M. says, "The Chinese desire to be left in peace." I agree and I always stand for the inviolability of freedom—but then it has to be fundamental and not hypocritical. The most unpardonable things on earth are hypocrisy, ignorance and treason.

. . . . .

April 22nd

By six in the morning all is covered with snow. Along Bogdo-ula creep billows of milky clouds. . . .

"The old lama went forth to look for Manjushri, the ruler of wisdom. He walked a long distance and finally he saw a man who was wringing out skins. Before him stood a little pail with the water from the skins! Complete dirt. The lama inquired from the man as to whether he had heard of the path to Manjushri. But the man only offered him a drink from the dirty pail. The lama was dismayed and hastened quickly away. But he met a clairvoyant lama who reproved him saying, "Stupid lama; you met Manjushri himself and the very dirt would have become a beverage of wisdom if you had had the courage to taste it." So do they speak of the courage of contact with Matter. Very significant are the conversations of these days.

The Olets know of the legend about Issa as do the Torguts. The slander against this legend becomes still more incomprehensible. Every enlightened lama speaks confidently about Issa as about any other historical fact.

Highly interesting are the words of At-Tabari about the prophetic mission of Mohammed ("History of Prophets and Kings"): "The revelation of the divine messenger began with impartations of truth, which came to him as the morning glow. Then he was filled with the desire for solitude and remained in the cave on Mount Hira. And so to him came the eternal True One and said, 'Mohammed, thou art god's messenger.'

" 'I knelt,' God's messenger says, 'and I waited. Then I slowly left. My heart was trembling. I came to Hadija and said *to enwrap me, enwrap me,* and my fear left. And He came again and said to me: «Mohammed, I am Gabriel, and thou art the Messenger of God»' . . ."

The exclamation "Enwrap me" gives authentic occult character to the narrative.

"Varaka the son of Naufal said to Mohammed, 'This is the divine revelation which was sent to Moses, the son of Umran. Would that I might live until the time when thy people shall expel thee!'—'Shall I be expelled by them?' Mohammed asked. 'Yes,' he answered, 'Verily never has a man appeared with that which thou hast appeared, without having aroused hostility against himself. In truth they shall consider thee a blasphemer. They shall harass thee, shall exile thee and fight against thee.' The words of Varaka increased Mohammed's firmness and dispelled his unrest."

. . . . .

April 23rd

Again the sun is here. Information comes that the road to China is absolutely impassable. Every one without exception speaks of war, speaks of pillage, and of course of the approaching heat. This path is closed. It is also strange that outside of F. no one has heard about the exporting of the frescoes from Tun-huang. Of course Priest must know all about that affair.

What an old hypocrite is the Tu-t'u! It appears that this hypocrite even has a school of law in Urumchi. You can imagine what "law" is being taught there. And by what statutes of this law, are judged all the robberies and briberies ordered by the officials. Some say, "One has to study China from the front entrance—from the ocean." But it is more enlightening to know the hidden recesses where nothing is "aired," for otherwise one could not see the thousand-year-old atrophy. Of course, the Tu-t'u thinks that no one will reach him through the desert.

A letter has come unexpectedly from Sikhim, from Colonel Bailey. They write about the books that were sent to us. But the majority of them have never reached us. No news from America. Probably the letters also disappeared or are being held back.

What pure air we have today!

. . . . .

April 24th

We received an invitation from the Commissioner of Foreign affairs, Fan, to come for dinner tomorrow. Is this not hypocrisy? With one hand to prohibit everything and with the other to invite us for dinner! If this is "skillful" diplomacy then it is not at all skillful, because a clever action is judged by results. And of course a hypocritical dinner cannot improve our relations. It would be better to give us permission to visit the Buddhist monasteries. Incidentally, our arms have been taken away and have not been returned.

The list of guests is a most absurd one: the Catholic missionary is Dutch; Kalin, a German; Cavalieri, an Italian; Channishef, a Moslem; and some Chinese. We shall see.

G. tells us about the villages of "Kerjaks" in Mongolian Altai. These "Kerjaks"—Old Believers—have preserved their own customs. Their chapels, their readers of the scriptures, their food, and their complete isolation from "worldly men." They use neither vodka nor tobacco. They deal in apiaries and furs, fish and cattle. In the midst of the Dungans and the Kirghiz stand their three villages of fifty or sixty houses; and nothing new penetrates behind their fences. Probably they keep up relations with their fellow-believers in the Russian Altai.

And it is strange and wondrous—in the whole district everywhere they are praising Altai. There, the mountains are beautiful, the cedars are powerful, the rivers are swift and there are hitherto-unseen flowers. And on the river Katun, it is said, will occur the last war in the world and afterward peaceful labor.

A year ago an embassy went to Tibet from Mongolia comprising thirty Mongols and three Russians. On the Tibetan border twenty Mongols and two Russians died. According to the report they died of some kind of gases.

Of course, something may have happened in the districts of geysers and old volcanos or because of winter gales. But the fact is meaningful, especially because it is difficult to invent such a thing.

. . . . .

April 25th

The fins of sharks, fungi, red and white seaweeds, bamboo shoots, lotus seeds, pigeon eggs, trepangs, and many other slimy and slippery dishes. They flavor them with sweet rice and roses. We finish. In the pavilion of the Governor-General's garden are three tables; one entirely of Chinese, the second, entirely Moslem, where no pork is served. The third is an international one; there are represented China, Russia, America, Germany, Holland and Italy. Fan, the host, does not eat anything himself. He explains it on the ground of his strict vegetarianism. His seaweedy face is smiling, probably because he hates all foreigners deeply and is full of the subtlest hypocrisy. Is it possible that Fan thinks that this absurd dinner washes away every affront of the Khotan and Karashahr officials? Not one word is mentioned by Fan about an investigation of what has happened. And where are politics and diplomacy? On his face is only hypocrisy—so clear, so apparent. After dinner, we stroll around the pond, on the bank of which stand two junkas. Then the low bows of Fan.

We pass the statue of the Governor and we pay a visit to the hospitable C. The day ends well. C. takes us by motor through the encircling road. A fresh wind, and very clear—truly heavenly—mountains. The evaporation from the newly fallen snow makes the far-off chains of mountains and peaks ethereal and transparently sapphire. Nearer are purple hills, and dented clay walls flooded by the sun. It is so vivid, so fresh and beautiful! And even "the vegetarian" hypocrite Fan begins to be transformed into a jellied seaweed.

. . . . .

April 26th

The Kirghiz are galloping on small white horses. On their heads are many-colored, quilted helmets. Just like the ancient *kuyak* of Russian warriors. On the crown is a tuft of feathers of the horned owl. On the hand sometimes is a falcon with a tiny hood above the eyes. They appear like a group which might have come out of the twelfth or fifteenth centuries. And here in the street stands the motor of C., a powerful Packard which, without damage, went all the way through from Peking to Urumchi. The motor belonged to the Russo-Asiatic Bank, but the Governor-General forbade them to use the machine and they had to sell it at practically nothing. Merely by its appearance the Packard reminds us that the way from Urumchi to Peking can unquestionably be traversed by motor. And only human ignorance and hypocrisy repeat the same paralyzing "No!"

Again a cold wind. Again the heavenly Bogdo-ula is a translucent blue.

Here again is a truly favorable sign. A Tibetan lama to whom we gave a hundred *lans* in Karashahr (at an encampment) arrived today. He brought back the money, excusing himself because he could not accompany us. He did not succeed in selling his horses and sheep. And now the horses are thin and there is no food. There is no one to whom to sell the animals, and the herd of horses cannot be left, so he cannot go with us. He will remain here until our departure and then will return. This is typical of a fine type of Tibetan. He walked ten days in order to return the money and to explain the affair. Up to now we have seen nothing objectionable in the Tibetan-Buddhists. It is a pity that he could not go with us. He is very well read and speaks with an excellent accent. He drank tea and dried the cup. He ate pot-cheese and washed his plate and put the chair in its place.

We went out of town toward the lakes.

. . . . .

April 27th

Note the character of the negotiations with Fan. He is told that a certain river flows eastward, but he insists it flows westward. They call his attention to the maps, but he repeats what he has said. They point out personal evidence but he persists in his declaration. And so it is against evidence, against maps, against facts. How can one conduct transactions under such conditions!

The border between Mongolia and China is not clearly defined at many points. Sharasüme up to the present remains in an undefined zone. Of course the Chinese delay the final division in every way.

. . . . .

April 28th

Pilgrims are not permitted to enter Tibet. Some Khoshuts gathered together secretly and set out for Tibet in February. Will they succeed in crossing the border? Here they know about the black stone—they await the stone. The Buddhists also know about the legend of "Issa, the Best of Human Sons."

A series of details is communicated to us regarding the hypocrisy of the Tu-t'u and how he freed himself from undesirable officials. This is no longer old lacquered Chinese work, but the grimace of a ruined mask. And the dark idol of the Tu-t'u stands here, and on the dark body glow the gold epaulettes and the ribbons and stars. Broadly spread are the copper legs of the idol; and Fan, with the grin of a skull, bows low. One hypocrite commands, another hypocrite secretly grins, and the third hypocrite in Khotan cleans his rifle for treason. From where comes this custom in Sinkiang of making an end of "disagreeable" people after dinner, behind their backs? From what depths of hatred for humanity, from what centuries of darkness, came this technique of treason? And this darkness is being overlaid with "scientific" degrees. Tu-t'u is a master of arts. Fan is a doctor of sciences, a lawyer and a writer. And where are their writings against the fetishism to which they are prey? Where are their condemnations of the sale of human beings and of treason and lies which they slavishly serve?

Throughout the entire day there is the noise of a dry and burning *buran*.

. . . . .

April 29th

After a hot *buran*—a dry windy day. There is no rain. The Moslems, Tartars and Sarts are ridiculing the command of the Tu-t'u not to kill animals for ten days; to sell no meat, and to whip the god of water for the drought. The Buddhists, Kalmucks and Tibetans are simply deriding such fetishism. The Dungans and Kirghiz, as well as Moslems, also mock and scorn it. I inquire for whose benefit this absurd act of savage fetishism is conceived? It seems that this entire comedy is invented expressly for the Sinkiang Chinese. It means that the Chinese alone are still a prey to the primitive form of fetishism. We did not know this, believing that the Chinese were committed to "the justice" of Confucius. And is it not the Tu-t'u himself, in the depths of his soul, who is going to whip the god of water? Because "the god of water" belongs only to the Chinese; hence the whipping of the god is needed for the benefit of the Chinese only. And the Chinese "doctors" and "magisters" are seriously encouraging this vicious absurdity. And they occupy themselves with absurdity very strenuously.

As before, each night troops of ragamuffins are being dispatched in the direction of Hami. Against whom is this unique "mobilization" directed? Perhaps against some detachment of the people's army of Feng? Of course, all these ragamuffins dispatched by night are not soldiers but simply fetishes unfit for anything. Out of twenty-four cannon, which were given by Anenkoff, only two usually work. But probably the cannon are also looked upon only as fetishes. Today a big parade of "armies" has been ordered.

We ask ourselves, "Why did Fan arrange a dinner for us?" Is not this the beginning of some difficulties? In Khotan all the Taotai's persecutions also started with the forty-course dinner and an honorary escort and with the assurance, "We are your friends." All in all, here among the Sinkiang Chinese the word *friend* has a peculiar meaning and we cannot approach the local psychology with our own measures.

The compilation of the ordinances of the Tu-t'u is preserved in a museum; people delude themselves into accepting these moribund evil remnants as the fragments of former civilizations. People are led into error by the "scientific degree" of Tu-t'u and the vegetarianism of Fan. People are led into error, thinking that the remains of fetishism are hidden in far-off marshes and in solitary islands of remote oceans. No, here in the capital of Sinkiang, under the wise rule of the Tu-t'u, fetishism is set up as the state religion and is sustained by the commands of the "ruler."

Our letters and telegrams do not arrive. We do not doubt that they are held back. The policemen asked E.I. whether I keep a diary. E.I. said that the diary had been sent from Kashgar to America. If only our books would not disappear! Where shall one hide them in this kingdom of fetishism?

In Kam, to develop the fierceness and liveliness of the horses, they feed them with dry leopard meat and pounded tea. They tell of leopard spots which appear on the rumps of the horses.

Luncheon at Cavallieri's. With the Europeans is one Chinese. The conversation is about our ill-fated adventures in Sinkiang. Chu says, "Do not judge China by Sinkiang. Good Chinese do not come here." I tell him frankly that I am still hoping to see better Chinese. I would be happy to speak of China in terms of praise, but the entire Sinkiang province, with the exception of three men, did not permit any avenue for favorable conclusions.

We compare the joyous mood we experienced in Sikhim, in the Himalayas, in India, in Ladak, with the prisonlike feelings in Sinkiang. . . .

. . . . .

April 30th

Last summer nearly seventy Buddhist monasteries were destroyed in the Amdoss district. "The Dungan armies of the Amban of Sining used machine guns. Many Tanguts perished. The Gegen of Amdoss asked the Goloks for help. The Goloks responded to his call. During the course of the coming summer it is possible there will be clashes. The Dungans have destroyed the celebrated image of Maitreya."

A lama from Kobdo is collecting a fund for the construction of a new image. The Goloks have made a rule to draft for service three men from each house. In Labrang, barracks are erected for Dungan armies. And the anti-Buddhist movement is being supported. All of this has not been printed anywhere and it is very important for the future. In addition to the movements which are apparent to the world, an inner agitation goes on which one can appreciate only on the site itself. F. repeats, "Chu spoke correctly yesterday when he declared that respectable Chinese do not go to Sinkiang." F. doubts that anything will result from our protests. He says: "Here you get accustomed to this and to everything just as you do to the sand in the desert." He is not correct! Even in Khotan we were able to deal with the robber Kerim-bek. It is impossible to "listen with equal indifference to the good and to the evil." Now the chief task is to leave Sinkiang. E.I. has no illusions, she knows that we will have to face all kinds of difficulties. It is rightly said by the Hindus: "Bring one rupee and every one will believe; bring a million and they will doubt."

The Orenburg horse became sick. We bled him. We were told that we must lead him twice around the Kirghiz tombs, then he would recover. So the local "experienced" people tell us.

In Lhasa is a temple of Gessar-Khan. On either side of the entrance are the images of two horses—one red and one white. According to the legend, when Gessar-Khan approaches Lhasa these horses neigh. Will not the call of these horses be heard soon?

We are discussing news from Sining. "The long ear" of Asia works better than the radio. From Kashgar there is no reply to six wireless messages. The only thing that one may believe is that the messages are being detained and, instead of their intended destination, reach some entirely different place.

. . . . .

May 1st

At twelve-thirty, luncheon with the Chinese. The court is very effectively and colorfully decorated. Under a big canopy hung with many vivid rugs, tables are set for a hundred people. Three *yurtas* are standing alongside for the Moslems where all the food is prepared without pork under the special supervision of a Moslem. The entire foreign colony is present. There are Italians, Germans, English, Sarts, Kirghiz and Tartars. The Chinese officials are all present except the Tu-t'u himself. Opposite us sits Fan. He does not eat anything except bread. It is either his diet, or hatred, or the acme of suspicion. Here the brother of the Tu-t'u also sits—an old man who fell into disgrace with his ruling brother for his liberal views. During the dinner the first one to get drunk is the commander of the fortress. He begins to be offensive; he breaks a few wine glasses; he pushes a lady and finally kicks over the tray with ice-cream. This incident of the ice-cream forces the Chinese to take measures and the commander of the fortress is removed by the aid of the Chief of Police and his own soldiers. Of all the Chinese, the most indignant at the conduct of the commandant, is the nine-year-old son of the Tu-t'u. He even has tears in his eyes for true indignation.

A youthful chorus sings a few songs. Mrs. E. P. P. tells me, "We used to come to look at you through a crack in the door when you came to Kuindjy." It appears that she knew Kuindjy and his wife, V. L., and so in Urumchi we speak about Kuindjy! We recall how he fed the birds; we recall his fearless liberal speeches, his anonymous aid to students in all courses. The memory of Kuindjy does not rust.

After luncheon they play pegs and tennis. In a week they will open the club. On a small stage of the club, they are planning to give Moslem and Chinese plays.

In the evening new reports reach us concerning the events in the Amdoss district about the oppression of the monasteries by Chinese soldiers; about the entrance of Chinese armies into Labrang; about the destruction of the image of Maitreya. The dates are approaching.

Late in the evening Tumbal becomes furious; the people are bringing a big Easter cake and eggs from G. and M.

Tomorrow is Easter.

It is curious for us, passers-by, to hear what the Chinese and Sarts say about the movements in Central China. They whisper to each other and wink: "How will the Tu-t'u now get out of this? Because this time, by whipping the gods, one will not escape. And the cock fight will not help. . . . They dream about the unseen Cantonese who must clear away the pillaging ambans; who must control the merchants and give the district freedom of industrial and cultural development. About Feng, or as he is sometimes called, Fyn, one speaks with greater reserve. But Canton draws the people's attention. To the armies of Canton are attributed qualities, existing and non-existing.

. . . . .

They come and ask: "Have you forceps?"—"Why?"—"Well, to extract a tooth." On our travels, amid the bonfires, the scenes recalled pictures of Bosch or the Elder Breughel; and now it is like Ostade. Nevertheless, the tooth is extracted and the forceps are returned.

A Chinese comes: "Kumashka-yashka." "What is that?" we are laughing. Is not this a Sogdi dialect, or are the Yafe-tides here? It proves to be a "box of papers." You can imagine how combinations of idioms are created. One may recall the anecdote of two eminent archaeologists who found a stone slab on which the curious expression, Rázmo-crópo-godilós or Razmó-cropó-godílos, was discovered. A lengthy discussion occurred as to how to read the inscription, when suddenly the driver of their cart, listening to the argument, smiled and said, "All that it means in our language is 'The weather has been rainy.' "

Improved combinations of different languages have a strange effect.

As a result we have seen people who do not know even one language. A little bit of Kalmuck, a smattering of Tibetan, two or three Russian, Chinese and Sart words. And when such a linguist becomes excited, he begins to talk in all five languages, quickly, unintelligibly, but in his own opinion very convincingly. Also he is very uncertain about his nationality; with unusual ease he appears a Russian, a Chinese, a Torgut. That is to say "kumash-ka-yashka!"

. . . . .

May 2nd

A clear morning. Lamas are coming to congratulate us upon the holiday. They are saying: "Christ is risen." Well, western clergymen, would you rejoice with the Buddhists on their holidays? We open our trunk filled with Buddhist pictures—we hang them on the walls and, together with the lamas, admire the resonant colors combined with the deep scientific symbols of these figures. Only knowledge without prejudice opens up new possibilities. The "incidental" of yesterday aligns itself with the moving files of evolution, and today's "imperative" seems often to become simply an incidental experience.

Yesterday, at dinner, someone told us it was improbable that we should be able to leave Urumchi soon. Can this be possible? So much of the undelayable, so much of immediacy before us; and here is complete inertia. Sitting on the trunks! The suspense of each day! Nothing from America! Why are our friends not acting there? Even the date of the departure of M. and S. is not known. However, maybe something is lost either in the telegraph or in the mail. Or the telegrams will reach us in half a year from now. This also happens here. The telegram of April reached us in October.

. . . . .

May 3rd

Tsampa-lama came from Kobdo; he left his caravan of thirty camels in Ku-ch'eng. He himself was immediately summoned to the Tu-t'u, had a long conference and was given a *yamen* to stay in, an honor reserved for an official not lower than the Taotai. They are awaiting the arrival of two officials from Kobdo. Two Mongolian lamas remain under arrest as before. The rumors which reached us in Karashahr are being confirmed. A telegram is received about the transit vise. It means that we can move about May 15th.

Here we can no longer receive the information from Sining about the Goloks. Now we must attend to our carriages to Chuguchak and look over the baggage. A telegram, dated April 2nd, arrived only on May 2nd. To Bakhty (the border) the telegram takes only one day. It means that for about a month the telegram was lying in Chuguchak. One could have delivered a message from Chuguchak much more quickly by foot. If only there may not be Chinese persecutions!

. . . . .

May 4th

Nevertheless, they chopped off the feet and hands of the poor god of water for his lack of zeal. They had hardly finished chopping them off, when it began to rain. Is it possible that the Sinkiang god needs such severe measures? Rain and snow began to fall and the streets of Urumchi changed into black, slimy mud. One can imagine the condition here two weeks before our arrival. It is not without cause that they tell us that donkeys and horses often drown here. It would cost nothing to have the merchants pave the bazaar, laying a pavement before each tiny shop. But here the all-powerful Tu-t'u does not exercise his power. The "magister" of sciences is on good terms with the reservoirs of mud. It is another matter when he finds it necessary to shoot a suspected opponent in the back. It is related that about twenty years ago a nobleman was honored by the Chinese Emperor with an unusually high title. For the bestowal of the title, a dinner was arranged by a local Amban. After the ceremony and a dinner of the choicest, a soldier came from out the curtain, behind the back of the guest, and with a single swing of a saber cut off the head of the one honored by the Emperor's favor.

. . . . .

May 5th

In Turkestan one Mullah, because of the absence of an "unfaithful" one from the mosque, gave orders to pour forty pails of water over his crown. After the seventeenth pail the unruly "faithful" one died. What is there to do about such logic?

Everything has started to move more quickly. Already the drivers are found. Now we have to decide the route. Three alternative combinations are offered. First—Kuldja; from there by motor to Tashkent, and by a direct train to the East; the second—Chuguchak, Semipalatinsk, Novosibirsk; third—Topolev mys, Zaisan, Irtysh, Semipalatinsk, Novosibirsk. The third combination is enticing, where we go by boat along the Irtysh, through mountainous and hilly spaces. But are not the Chinese again going to hinder us? Opinions are divided. Some think that some sort of mischief will follow. Others think that this time the Chinese will feel a sense of shame. Personally I am not optimistic. Because in Kashgar also they assured us that there would be no further insolence, whereas, one of the greatest affronts was committed in Karashahr, beyond Kashgar.

We went with B. out of town in the direction of Bogdo-ula. Endless Dungan cemeteries. Rows of small *kurgans:* On the top always stands a pot, a vessel or chips of a pot; it is a sort of ancient *kurgan* rite for the dead. In spite of their Mohammedanism, the Dungans have kept some of their own inherent customs. The Chinese folk-religion and Shamanism have left their traces.

Filchner came. It seems that they permitted him all surveys.

. . . . .

May 6th

Packing. Arrangements with the drivers. Three *troykas* to Topolev mys cost 660 *lans.*

. . . . .

May 7th

The morning at Fan's. All are ostensibly amiable. It seems that he promises not to hinder us from going to Topolev mys along the Zaisan. Much news about Tsampa. As in Karashahr, we hear that the situation is serious. Ten million *lans* were given in payment to attract thirty Mongolian koshuns (Mongolian district) to the side of the Tu-t'u.

Toward evening we walked with B. on the hills surrounding the city. Again a cemetery. In the middle of the barren field are a dozen crosses and two monuments. The history surrounding one of them is tragic. A young man, K., returned to his father after the civil war. His relatives and his good friends attacked him, and in every way denounced him. Finally, they bound him and locked him in a closet where he hanged himself. And so, above the young man stands a high monument with a big black cross and with a tearful text. . . .

Today is as sultry as in July. The snow on Bogdo-ula has melted considerably. In eight days we shall go again on a far-off journey.

. . . . .

May 8th

Rumors are current: "The Amban of Sining fled with an army of twenty thousand under the pressure of the Tanguts." Is it possible that the Goloks are approaching? This is even now the beginning of something prolonged.

How strange it is to think that here there is fetishism, primitive spiritualism, superstition, the shrieks of Mullahs, the name of Confucius—and everything is bound together as with an unbreakable vise.

Soon our Geshe will go to his mountains. Today he tells us that the head of the medical school in Lhasa spoke to him about "Azaras," which is their name for the Mahatmas living in the mountains and using their profound knowledge for the aid of humanity. We have not previously come upon the word "Azaras." This is not Sanskrit. But how difficult it is to force the Geshe to tell us details! Soon he will leave. He will tell Toin-Lama all that the latter has lost. Fear is a poor counselor.

. . . . .

May 9th

Again heat, unseasonable for the beginning of May. Some say this will mean rain. Some "console" us by saying that the heat has really begun. The Chinese seemingly are trying to persecute E.I. with their procrastination. Everything is so complicated; there are so many questions and so many unusual conditions. One must hasten departure.

The head of the medical school told our Geshe that he himself met such an "Azara" in the mountains of Sikhim. It is difficult to ascertain more than the fact that there was a small house and that the "Azara" was unusually tall. Then the "Azara" departed from the place. The very same news is creeping through all Asia.

We went out of town. The cuckoo was calling. The hoopoes were on the wing and the crickets chirped. Toward evening, thunder. E.I. read notes about the foundations of Buddhism. How beautiful is the unfoldment when the shell of the last layer falls away; when labor and knowledge occupy their fitting place.

. . . . .

May 10th

The soldiers have stopped their drilling. It is a holiday. They say it is because the Amban of Sining is routed. The last Peking newspaper announces that Kansu and Sinkiang remain in the sphere of influence of the national army. For Sinkiang it is significant.

Suddenly everything has so developed that it is necessary to leave as quickly as possible.

Up to the present time there has existed a saga about Gessar-Khan: "To Gessar-Bogdo-Khan were sent seven heads, cut off from seven black blacksmiths. And he boiled the seven heads in seven copper kettles. He fashioned out of them chalices, and inlaid these chalices with silver. And so out of seven heads came seven chalices; and Gessar-Khan filled these with a strong wine. Thereupon he ascended to the wise Manzalgormo and bestowed upon her the chalices. But she took the seven chalices fashioned from the seven heads of the blacksmiths and scattered them into the heavens and the seven chalices formed the constellation Dolan-Obogod (The Great Bear). And she is preserving the dates."

How remarkably the symbols are fused into these unclear and apparently meaningless words which bind Gessar-Khan with the seven-starred constellation of the north. The Mongolian "Gabala" and the special chalices of the Bhutanese temples recall the very same strivings and hopes. Again the prophecy from the Tripitaka is repeated that Buddha "indicated that his chalice would become an object of search at the time of the new achievements of the world, but that only pure bearers of the Order would be able to find it."

"Ribhavas are rushing to Savitri-Sun after Soma," according to the wisdom of the Rig-Veda. In the center of the plate of Khyil-Khor, is enchased Mount Sumeru, and on its sides are the four countries of the world, like great islands around it—a point at equal distance from four oceans. . . .

The Lama proclaims, "Let life be firm as adamant, victorious as the banner of the teacher, strong as the eagle, and continue eternally."

. . . . .

May 11th

We are invited for luncheon. Filchner and the Catholic missionary are also present. Filchner, sunburned, in a leather jacket, seems full of vigor. His task is a curious one. He connects the magnetic researches between Tashkent and Central China. The measurements were made in Russia, but the Carnegie Institute carries out the work in China at great expense. And now Filchner is combining these two fields of investigation as he told us.

We recalled his experiences with the Goloks. He did not reveal his exact route.

The conversation with the missionary is interesting. He speaks of the new understanding of Buddhism, as well as the present need of understanding Nirvana. He speaks of the desire for an immediate coordination of Buddhism and Catholicism. He mentions his knowledge of occult miracles. He is conversant with the literature. It is significant.

. . . . .

May 12th

On the table lies a petition signed with a fingerprint. An impoverished Kirghiz makes the following complaint. Three years ago, near Manass, he and his nine-year-old daughter stopped overnight in the house of a Dungan. For their night's lodging, the Dungan demanded the daughter of the Kirghiz. The Kirghiz refused. The Dungan beat him and drove him out, but he kept the girl and has held her for three years.

It is the usual occurrence here, to abduct and sell children with the idea of work and more often, for the purposes of depravity. Why call hypocritical conferences about the slaves in Africa, when in Central Asia and everywhere in China the sale of human beings is a common practice? All business organizations of the country know of this institution of slavery, yet none demands its cessation. Where are, then, the protests and demands?

. . . . .

We received an invitation from the Governor General to come for lunch tomorrow. Again the same people—Fan, Filchner, the missionary and Cavalieri. . . .

. . . . .

In the bazaar, the rumor has spread about a march toward Kobdo. And the last visit of the Governor General to the Consul is connected with this rumor. The Taotai, the Altaian commander of the local armies, left hurriedly for Sharasüme. This circumstance confirms still further the rumors of possible military movements.

It is a clear and fresh day. If we could only leave! But this is not possible before Saturday.

. . . . .

The stone-like metallic mass which remains after cremation from the lower lobes of the brain is called Ring-se, meaning treasure. According to the size of this mass, the psychic development of the dead is judged. What a proof of materialism! On the border of Tibet, we saw such a "mass" after the cremation of one Mongolian lama. It looks like the precipitant of amber.

. . . . .

May 13th

In the morning the Mongolian lama arrives. What joy! What we have gathered in spiritual teaching from the south, he likewise knows from the north. He relates exactly what fills the consciousness of the peoples and what they await; and in thought of this his eyes become filled with genuine tears. Our friend T. L. was near Lan-chow for six months, and each day he spoke of the significance of the future of Maitreya. "We knew it a long time ago," says the lama, "but we did not know how it would come about. And now the time has come. But not to every Mongol and Kalmuck can we tell it but only to those who can comprehend." The lama speaks about different proofs and no one would have suspected such knowledge in this modest man. He speaks about the spiritual meaning of Altai.

After these sincere and serious conversations, a hypocritical luncheon with the Governor-General. Again we pass endless corridors of the *yamen.* Again questions as to our health, again toasts. Again the fins of shark, bamboo and fungi. This host assures us that the local Sarts are better than all peoples of the earth. Several years ago he declared the same about the Dungans and even willed that he be buried in a Dungan cemetery. But now the "current" is toward the Sarts and his will is already changed. And the Sarts are proclaimed to be the best nation. E.I. whispers, "What a horrible old man." In the manner of a funeral procession we go back through the corridors, little yards, and the Governor-General pays us "the highest honors" by accompanying us to the carriage. Not a word about the investigation of the affairs at Khotan and Karashahr, as if everything were over and all the prohibitions against the work swallowed during the luncheon.

One can insult, in every possible way, and afterward plaster it over with the fins of shark. Today they will seal our trunks in order that we may not be disturbed on the border. For three hours the absurd, dragging procedure of opening the trunks and the useless inspection of our things, continued. And when will this nonsense cease?

Toward evening, a provocation now familiar to us occurs. A repulsive Dungan attacked and beat Ramsana. When he was caught he claimed that he mistook Ramsana for a Chinese and that was why he beat him. A strange explanation! It is queer that this provocation occurs just on the day of the luncheon at the Governor's. During the evening they warn us of two dangerous places on the road to Topolev mys. There are robberies of Kirghiz. Of course, here the Governor gives us no escort! The escort is necessary only where it is safe!

They tell us how the Dervishes sometimes kill the "unbelievers." In the crowd, or while dancing, the Dervish scratches the *giaour*, with a poisoned nail and death sometimes follows the same day. Medievalism!

· · · · ·

May 14th

They gave us a passport to Peking as long as my own height. Such stupidity—to write in a passport the number and description of all objects! How many changes may take place on the road! Chinese of Sinkiang, why do you reveal yourselves to us in such a way?

It appears that our drivers are not Chinese subjects at all, but from Bokhara. Now there are many such chameleons. An utter absurdity with the passports!

The volcanic traces in the district of Chuguchak, Kuldja, Vernyi and Tashkent are interesting. The soil seems to be breaking like a gigantic dynamo; it continues for months at a time.

Today is the farewell dinner at G.'s. Oh, how many difficulties with the packing! Possessions—enemies of man! Will we really leave tomorrow?

· · · · ·

May 15th

And after all we did not leave today! The driver refused to load. All pressure and persuasions were applied, but the old man remained as if wooden. The chief reason is that Saturday is considered by Moslems an unfavorable day. How ridiculous! And the whole day is lost.

We heard tales about Karakirghiz—how in the sixties, the Kirghiz boiled three thousand Russian Cossacks in kettles. The same information that the Kirghiz recently boiled and burned people in ovens is reported. We are accompanied by a whole series of tales of robberies. The Kirghiz robbed thirty *arbas*. The Kirghiz rob travelers. The Kirghiz are holding a cliff, seven days' travel away. The Kirghiz have bombs. It is like a Karakirghiz-Thousand-and-One-Nights.

. . . . .

May 16th

We left just the same. After all sorts of arguments with the drivers, somehow we loaded. Of course the Chinese remained true to type. The last night Sung cried and told the lama that the police and the *yamen* prohibited him from going with us as far as the border. Who knows what is the meaning of this new intrusion in our life? Or Sung perhaps has given too good a report about us. Sung is completely upset.

All the good people of Urumchi are bidding us farewell. They are indeed cordial people.

At the left, the snow ridges of T'ian Shan glowed purple and blue. Behind them remained the Kalmuck *ultus*. In back, Bogdo-ula appeared in all its beauty. Amid the snows shone three peaks—and it was joyous and full of light. And the air was filled with the scent of wild mint and wormwood. It was so luminous that the Chinese dusk paled at once.

Just as usual we were stopped at the custom house. In spite of the six-foot passport, they senselessly inspected our arms. Farther. . . . Farther. . . .

We camped in Sanji, a village thirty-nine *versts* away. To stay beyond the village is impossible—it is dangerous at night, and besides this, our faithful guard, Tumbal, was left at the Consulate. We stop in a courtyard. An old Sart woman in white walks with dignity through the yard. Little girls with many little black braids scurry out of the hut. It is already six o'clock and the heat has not yet begun to abate. How will it be with E.I. when even today was so difficult for her. And what right did the Khotan scoundrel have to arrest us and detain us longer? We might have passed here more than a month ago when there was no heat. And instead of investigating the wretched insolence with which they treated us, they gave us hypocritical dinners and false toasts. Where is the justice of Sinkiang? Decadence!

In the evening, some strange types come again to inspect our things. Understand, Chinese of Turkestan! While travelers remain as nothing but suspected prisoners in your country, so long you, yourselves, will remain at the level of prison-wardens. It is time for you not to affirm that the westward flowing river flows to the east, as the "learned" commissar of Foreign Affairs insists on doing. They say, "China was formerly a great nation." There are enough of all sorts of "former" peoples, now is the time for living peoples. Some are so used to the local license, that they phlegmatically say, "Even if you sue them for a hundred years, they will make no investigation, and the decision of their court will depend on the number of thousands of dollars paid to the judges." So those who have lived a long time in the large cities of Sinkiang declare.

. . . . .

May 17th

By five o'clock in the morning it is already warm. The day is going to be hot. In the bazaar a man is tied to a pole. A criminal? Or one too clever? A dangerous one? A disfavored one? A slandered one? Bogdo-ula drowned in the mist, but to the left, during the whole day, stretched the chain of T'ian Shan. Truly celestial mountains. After the purple borders there are ringing blue crests and the snow is sparkling. Dear mountain snows! When shall we see you again?

It is sandy and dusty. By twelve o'clock, we have covered nine *p'o-t'ai*, or thirty-six miles. We shall stop in the Dungan village, Hutubi. The water yesterday was bad and today no better. On account of the heat we decided to leave by night in order to reach Manass at noon.

On the willow near the road, the nightingales are sing-ing. Sadig, the driver, volunteers to cover five more *p'o-t'ai* this evening and thus to shorten tomorrow's journey. The loaded *troykas* remain behind again. The old driver informs me that he will go, not according to conditions, but as God desires. I ask them to translate this to him: that he will return also as God wills. The passage between Olunbulak and Kuldinen is considered dangerous on account of rob-bers. Everybody advises us that the carriages should go together and that the arms be held loaded. The shooting usually starts from both sides of the canyon.

Toward evening the heat becomes still more intense. By seven o'clock there is no relief whatsoever. Because of our arrest and detention, we have lost two months and a half and by now we would have been long since beyond the boundaries of the Chinese Dance of Death. And is it possible that none of you, Chinese of Sinkiang, who con-sider yourselves civilized, will be indignant at the license of the Khotan official? Is it possible that I will have to leave the boundaries of Chinese Turkestan, with the firm conviction that this country is not fit for cultural inter-course? We would so sincerely wish to say a word of full sympathy for China! We would like so much to justify her! Instead of that we proceed with the feeling of prisoners who have escaped from the nest of a robber-band.

It is hot and stuffy.

. . . . .

May 18th

We arise at 2:30 at night. By all measures we urge on the ill-tempered driver and at half-past four we leave. The morning becomes cloudy. The clouds were changed into opalescent fissures. A cool rain is starting. The heat abates only after one o'clock. The mountains of T'ian Shan reflect many colors. The irises glow purple. The fresh grass is richly green and fragrant after the rain. Our mood was somewhat disturbed by another custom house and a third inspection of our passports. What for? Why go by the highways, if turning toward the mountains, one may cross without any inspections whatsoever! These inspections are for the *arbas* and for inexperienced travelers but an experienced horseman can always avoid these tinsel barriers.

The ruins of old Manass remind us of the massacre during the uprising of the Dungans. There are heaps of clay walls. Remnants of a temple. Empty casements of windows and doors. Manass is one *p'o-t'ai* farther. And altogether we shall make sixteen-and-a-half *p'o-t'ai* today. The same bazaars as at Manass. The same Dungans. Sometimes one sees a Kalmuck. Here are no Torguts or Khoshuts, but Olets, who occupy the Iliisk district and Kuldja. There is no difference in their appearance. Along the entire road are stretched caravans of camels, carrying a hundred thousand *puds* of wool, bought for export. The bells ring impressively. Sadik, the driver, says with special emphasis: "Wool toward Chuguchak!" The dream of the district to establish communication is being fulfilled.

We are stopping at the house of the Elder of the village. Here the courtyards are somewhat cleaner than in the Kashgar and Karashahr districts. They say that here also they will inspect the passport. If only they do not tear up this ancient curiosity! We should like to bring it back in safety and reproduce it.

During the day it seemed to us as though we were going, a quarter century back, along the plain of Central Russia. And now we sit in a dirty little white room. E.I. remembers that thus, twenty years ago, we sat in little huts in Meretchi or Veluni on the Neman, or under the walls of the monastery of Susdal. Or later, in the cells of Siena and San Gemignano. We have seen, we have seen, we have seen!

The day ended with the third inspection of the arms and the deciphering of our passports. An illiterate opium smoker came from the Amban. He read, syllable by syllable, our *three-arshin- long* passport. He asked us to take out the guns from their cases, and timidly touched a revolver. A long time he paced about the same place and mumbled something and then he left us under the responsibility of the inn-keeper. Can one include such officials in the evolution of humanity? Simply dregs. But these stupidly annoying dregs are capable of obscuring the shining mountains; are capable of transforming every peaceful mood into the feeling of a prison. Away with ignorance!

. . . . .

May 19th

What a good sign! So we are told. What is the matter? We hear some unintelligible music, a shrill clarinet like a bag-pipe, cymbals and a drum. This shrill noise continues the whole evening. What is the matter? It appears that nearby a man has died, and they are getting ready to bury him. Not without cause in Manass, in a whole row of little shops, there is a multitude of vari-colored, gaily painted coffins. They say it is a very good sign for travelers, if a man dies nearby. It is uncertain whether it was according to the sign or not, but at a point halfway on our road, a wheel broke down. We shall have to repair it at the nearest village.

Today the road is a short one—only forty miles. We arrived as early as half-past one. It is clear that we could do two-and-a-half *p'o-t'ai* more, but the whole matter rests with the impossible driver. We sit in Ulan Usun awaiting the carriage.

It is a vivid day. On the far-off mountains, it looks as though snow has been added. The receding ridges are enticing. The desert is covered with sappy verdure and purple iris. The grazing herds are clearly silhouetted. The Lama goes aside and turns eastward to pray. We catch the rhythm of his hymn of praise. He probably invokes the new era, the time of Maitreya, the approach of which all Buddhists know. Under the line of snow on the mountains are hidden several large Kalmuck monasteries. In each one are a few hundred lamas. The monasteries are mostly nomadic—in *yurtas*. But there are also temples, although we cannot see them. If you want, you can see an absurd temple of the devil in Urumchi, but it is forbidden to see the Buddhist monasteries. It is ridiculous and stupid.

The grass is so green and starlings and jays are calling in the foliage of Karagach. The cuckoo hastily counts the years. In the steppe stand pillars of smoke—they are burning reeds. These clouds of smoke from the "Polovetsky Camp" are characteristic of the horizons of the steppes. We recall the dreams—the paintings of the year 1912, "The Serpent Awoke" and "The Sword of Valor," when the fiery angel brought the sword of valor to the guards.

We are told that on Altai some special red lilies bloom in spring. Whence this general reverence for Altai?

It is hot. They warn us that here are many thefts. The Governor-General did not send the promised order about the passage. It is better so! At least we do not have to have the faintest feeling that the Chinese did anything for us except to offer affronts, violence and obstacles. From Ulan Usun is four days' ride to the Torgut summering place. It is equally distant from Kucha, Urumchi, and from Ulan Usun.

. . . . .

May 20th

Up at four. How beautiful! The mountains become pink. A purplish mist is rising. The grass becomes luxuriant. We left at half-past five, before the heat. We made nine *p'o-t'ai* (thirty-six miles) until Yan-zi-hai. A wonderful road. Fresh and sweet is the scent of the silver jilda. The birds are singing; we have not heard so many of them for a long time. We cross the plain strewn with the mounds of graves—traces of skirmishes and the Dungan uprising. Like a forbidding wall stand the silvery blue mountains. We come speedily at half-past nine to Yan-zi-hai, just on time. The sun is already scorching; everything is searing. Jubilant, we enter a small clay hut. We shall be here until twelve o'clock at night, and then by moonlight, in the coolness, proceed further to Shiho. The nearness of Russia is already felt, in something almost intangible. Either the streets of the villages are broader, or there are more plowed fields. The inns are cleaner! We sit again in a little clay hut. In the room swallows are busy under the beams; they have built their nest.

It feels as if the ground were shaken. In the district of Chuguchak are extinct craters. Not long ago the underground activity was so intense that they expected an eruption.

. . . . .

May 21st

We arose at one o'clock at night. In the darkness, in the beginning of a *buran*, we left at half-past three. The mountains hid themselves in clouds of dust. We thundered through a plain of coarse pebbles. At one o'clock in the afternoon we came to Shiho, making sixteen *p'o-t'ai*.

Halfway we stopped to feed the horses. A crowd of Dungans and Chinese gathered. They walked around, examined our carriage, tried to touch us. Veritable little animals. We recalled how, fifteen years ago, in Sharasüme, there was an Amban. From Urumchi, ten thousand Dungans were sent against him, but from Zaisan a battalion succeeded in approaching and the ten thousand Urumchi soldiers immediately dispersed. Now the son of this Amban, an Olet prince, lives a day's journey from Shiho. He completed his education abroad. In the direction of Shiho is also a big Kalmuck monastery. Shiho is the crossroad between Urumchi (six days), Chuguchak (six days), Kuldja (nine days) and Sharasüme (twelve days).

On our way we met three *arbas* with precious loads—marral horns. Probably they are coming from Russian or Mongolian Altai. They are going through Urumchi toward Ku-ch'eng—to China to be used for valuable medicines. In Shiho we were not admitted to the courtyard of a former Russian citizen. The quality of the road is much better here than in Kashgar-Aksu-Toksun. From the great expanse of pebbles, it would be easy to make an excellent road. But for the Chinese, the fewer the roads of communication, the more quiet. The less enlightenment there is, the more convenient it is for the "rulers."

The "ruling power" came for the passports. And it was a very poor power indeed, so ragged, so ill-smelling! And with what torture it tried to read, syllable by syllable, the innumerable hieroglyphics of the six-foot passports. We gave the passports to the official, not without fear; even without this, the corners of this "valuable" document are already worn from the endless inspections.

E.I. says, "If the Chinese would have received us well, much would have been changed thereby." Verily, much!

No news from America. Where and whence are we going to receive it? Up to May 16th we have received no answer to our telegram sent April 12th. The condition of the telegraph post, of the wires, of the insulators, spell, "Resign all hope." One has to tell H. they should not send telegrams by Bently. Here, even without the code, the words are distorted beyond recognition.

· · · · ·

May 22nd

The sands, up to Tcha-pe-dzi itself, cover sixteen *p'o-t'ai*. Light clouds have hidden the sun. Otherwise there would be an unbearable heat, and Sadik says that it would kill the horses. We have never seen so much wild game. Gold pheasants and partridges; geese, ducks, gulls and hares. The pheasants perch on the road before the very carriage. We left at five o'clock; we arrived at half-past two. They suggest it will be better to travel at night. Tcha-pe-dzi is an unattractive place. The houses are squalid. We stop just behind the village, near the river. Beyond, the crest of T'ian Shan disappeared and far ahead, toward the north, appeared the light line of the Tarbagatai mountains. In the steppe the Chinese tombs are crumbling like little *kurgans*. Again the ill-smelling ragamuffin comes and takes away our passports somewhere. Amusingly he compares our faces with the photographs. Endless police-quarters!

We learned who Tsagan-Khutukhta is. It appears that he is an Olet. He is now in Labrang. How instructive it is to compare the face of Maitreya from behind the Himalayas with that from the North. Only thus a true representation of personalities, events and faiths is constructed. Each country, not deviating from the truth, adds its own details and its own observations. The reports about Tsagan-Khutukhta coincide.

Jilda is blooming. The early honeysuckle is becoming pink. Toward evening all is fragrant with the new spring. There will again be a drama with the drivers. We will have to persuade them to move at night. We decided not to sleep, but to leave at eleven at night.

. . . . .

May 23rd

The pulse of the evening is one of unrest. Some wholly strange Chinese came with ten soldiers. They are fulfilling some mysterious mission of the Governor-General. They are going to Peking and Moscow. A net is being woven.

Advice has come: to leave at once; to muffle the bells on the harnesses and to extinguish the lights. All is unrest. We follow the advice and we leave under rain and wind with arms loaded. We march through deep sands, difficult for the horses. Eighteen *p'o-t'ai* to Ulan Bulak. It took twelve hours with two hours for feeding the horses. Ulan Bulak is a poor *langar*. There is no food. Seven *p'o-t'ai* from the *langar*, the sands change into the dark-pebbled hills of the Djair mountains. Everything becomes clear. Blinding, threatening clouds whirl. And in the direction of Chuguchak it begins to thunder. We stop on a little hill near a wretched Chinese temple. In front of us, for the last time, stretches the ridge of the Heavenly Mountains merging in mist. They are so heavenly in tone, so rich with their white crests.

So little is known of Kalmuck *ulus*. When and who will succeed in threading all the labyrinths of buried treasures? The whole distance quivers in the rainbow of evaporation.

The sapphire desert and ethereal mountains merge with the sky. The hills are adorned in gold. Verily thou art beautiful, Asia! Accept the chalice.

A couple of Dungans and Kalmucks are traveling with us. And the tone in which the Kalmuch speaks to us rings confidently and intimately. Naively he tells us how he wanted to hunt in the mountains but the local prince forbade him. Across the road ran six gray gazelles. One can imagine how much game there is in the mountains.

The carriages do not arrive again. For the third night we shall go without sleep.

.   .   .   .   .

May 24th

Only Ladakis and some of the Mongolian Khoshuns are fit for distant trips. All others weaken and lose their vitality and fall prey to melancholy.

We bid farewell to T'ian Shan. Ahead of us are snowless, small cupolas of Djair. Today is one of those unbearable days of which all the caravaneers tell. It is in the canyons of Djair that robberies and murders occur. The hills of Djair confront us very severely. An icy gale, rain, hail, and during the night, ice and snow. Our driver succeeds in making seventeen *p'o-t'ai* to Kuldinen in twenty-two hours. We arrive at half-past two at night. We are completely exhausted from dragging ourselves after the *arbas*, with loaded guns. Ottu is a miserable station in the middle of the road, sunken in mud. After us, come the Chinese. Their arrogance begins. They walk all over us. They spit. Here they have also built a bonfire out of manure which smarts the eyes. They pour oil on it and spill tea. We are glad to get away from Kuldinen in the evening. We have not seen any robbers. Now they say that the chief spot for robberies is not on today's road but tomorrow's, between Kuldinen and Yadmantu. In the snow we reach Kuldinen. We crowd ourselves into an ill-smelling little hut, and we sleep four hours without waking. And then, again, we load, and we again quarrel with the wretched driver.

．　．　．　．　．

May 25th

The entire day is a beautiful one. It is true that in the narrow canyons of the red mountains we may be attacked. We learn that somewhere near here, during the civil war, many hundreds of Russians were slaughtered by the Kirghiz. One senses a tension among our men. Seemingly, as though in spite, in the most narrow crevice, the axle of the second *arba* breaks, and the other four carriages remain interlocked. It is a most advantageous moment for robbers, but they do not appear. For two hours the men are busy with the carriage. On the road through the hills, three carriages overturn.

After passing red and copper mountains we descend to a green steppe which is surrounded by blue crests; again the purity of the colors is like a fairy rainbow. Map'an (thirteen *p'o-t'ai* from Kuldinen) is a joyous resting place on the steppe. On the outskirts of the village stand *yurtas.* Herds are huddled together. Kirghiz, in *malachais*, are galloping about like warriors of the fifteenth century. The Kalmucks have honest faces. We have not yet had time to find a camp-site in Map'an before a Kalmuck comes with information of extreme importance: "In the second month (which means March) the Urumchi Governor-General spread the rumor through the *ulus*, the camps of the nomads and monasteries that the Tashi Lama had been elected Chinese Emperor. He has not yet ascended the throne but he has already accepted the tamgha (the seal)." Only those who have been in Asia will appreciate the significance of this invention. Yet, of this invention the newspapers do not write and Reuter's does not telegraph; but just these invisible knots are creating the future reality.

A vast amount of news about the Tashi Lama will float across the Kalmuck and Mongolian spaces. For many years!

All the riches of this country, all its beauty, all its significance, await new ways, a new culture and self-consciousness. Appreciate the nature of this rumor about the new Chinese Emperor!

. . . . .

May 26th

Today our road is long; about ninety miles. We hasten through a verdant steppe. Everywhere are *yurtas* and herds. Above the distant Tarbagatai mountains are the signs of bad weather again approaching and the wind becomes cool. To the right are the four hills of Altai. We rush through the village Kurte where the road branches into the larger road toward Chuguchak, and the small, clay road toward Durbuljin. In Durbuljin are the same clay huts and a still greater mixture of nationalities. The predominance of Sarts or Dungans has disappeared.

We have many annoyances with the drivers; we must induce them to reach the Post across the boundary in one march. We are advised not to remain overnight in the Chinese Post, or in the zone between Posts (thirty miles). Thefts and robberies occur there. We shall strive to make all seventy-five miles to Kozeun in one stretch. If only the Chinese customs will not detain us! Even Sadik (the driver) is nervous and advises us not to remain at the Chinese Post.

Another anecdote: "In Urumchi lies the unburied body of the Chuguchak Taotai. Beside the corpse is a white rooster, which they have carried with the coffin from Chuguchak." Grievous are the affairs of the dead one; from Peking a command has been received to institute a posthumous trial against the former Taotai for his crimes, and until the trial is ended not to bury him and not to send the body back to his native land. These are veritable "dead souls"! And for the comic relief, the white rooster is also crowing. If one has not been in China, it is impossible to believe there are such Dances of Death. How little of China is known, especially in America. I remember Dr.

Laufer asked me in Chicago, "And why do they fuss over the Chinese, when they do not know them?" At that time we also knew only the "Museum" China, but not the reality of Sinkiang.

The albums of sketches are accumulating.

．　．　．　．　．

May 27th

The day with all its colors is a beautiful one. Blue mountains; a silky steppe. At our left, are the snows of Tarbagatai, and straight northward are the foothills of Altai itself—Altai, the center of Asia. There are herds in the steppe. Great droves of horses; and blackish gray and milky white *yurtas*. Sun and wind and an unprecedented translucence of tones. It is even more resonant than Ladak.

From morning on we have been tormented by the wretched driver. Nothing is in order and the carriages are falling apart. We have not encountered a worse fellow. After the performance of the driver, a sequence of Chinese interludes. The Amban had appointed a soldier to accompany us to the border of Kozeun. The soldier arrived, turned around at the gate, and said that he was going to drink tea, and we did not see him again.

After we had passed five *p'o-t'ai*, up to the border-line, the comedy began; but one could have cried from it. The seven-foot-long passport and the seals of the Governor-General helped very little. The half-literate customs official wanted to break the seals of the Governor-General. Then he wanted to count all our things. And finally he tried to take away entirely the Chinese passport which was given to us to go on to Peking and to which the visa was attached. With the greatest difficulty we induced him to abandon this scheme; nevertheless, the torture and inventions of the customs idiot took about four hours. Only by six o'clock could we make a move to pass, or rather crawl, the twenty-five miles to the next Post. We had not completed a mile before the wheel on the driver's carriage broke. Before us was the possibility of a night in the mountains, in the heart of the most dangerous locality. We had to return to the Chinese Post. And here we sit again in our tents. Perhaps it is for the last time, before a long intermission. The beloved mountains and tent bring back so many recollections. And the full golden moon looks unflinchingly into the flap of the tent. Today we passed a few nomadic monasteries where Maitreya is reverenced. Avoiding complications with the Chinese, we did not turn from our way toward the *yurtas* of the monastery. It was a pity, it is a pity!

. . . . .

May 28th

How solemn is this night. The end and the beginning! Farewell, Dzungaria! As a farewell she revealed herself not only with her blue snow mountains, not only with the chrysoprase of the hills, but also with abundant grass and flowers not seen for a long time: wild peonies, crimson red, yellow lilies, golden-heads of a fiery orange color, irises, briar-roses. And the air is pervaded with the breath of spring. We descended and ascended green hills. We righted the fallen carriages.

Near us rode the Kirghiz escort. The same Scythians, the same caps, leather trousers and half-kaftans, as on the vase of Kuleb. The Kirghiz pursued the wolves which crossed the road. One of the Kirghiz picked a big bunch of red peonies for E.I. There is one more crossing. And on the peak is a heap of small stones. This is the end of China.

Welcome, spring soil, in thy new attire! Continuous grass and little goldenheads, and the white walls of the border Post of Kuzeun. Soldiers approach and question us. They are generally anxious to do as is best for us. Where is the crudeness and ignorance which one might expect in this isolated little post unmarked on the map. A long and attentive inspection of the things follows. Everything is examined. They apologize for taking our time and for the bother to us. Here is the head of the Post, and here is the family of his assistant, an old officer. We remain overnight at the Post.

.   .   .   .   .

May 29th

This morning we rode as far as the village Pokrovsky (seventy miles) on a wonderfully smooth road. The mountains recede. They are getting lower. Kirghiz *yurtas*. Curious riders. The sleek, raven-black horse of the soldier trots vigorously. A green frontier cap. The first village is called Rurikowsky after the first ruler of Russia. A low clay hut. The white walls and meager gardens are already seen. The climate here is very severe. Vegetables do not thrive—the frost kills them. But now the summer heat has already begun. If only we could reach Topolev mys; probably our driver will not make it. And so it proves. On a straight slope the wheel of the wagon breaks to pieces. One must send to the commandant's post to Pokrovskoye to get another wagon. We stand for a long time near a private mill. The proprietor is unfriendly and does not give his wagon.

Here is Pokrovskoye. More white houses. The commandant is coming out. Here is the head of the guard, and here is the assistant of the commandant. Striving to surpass one another they establish us in their modest apartment. They ask more questions, ever more insistently. They expect enlightening answers. They want to compare their information with ours. Ramsana, not knowing the language, remarks: "They have good souls." We ask him how he came to this conclusion: "It is seen in their eyes."

It appears that our boat on the Irtysh leaves to-night, and the next one only after three days. The driver is responsible for this difficulty. But at the Post they rejoice and ask us to remain with them at least one day. They come to us in the evening and we converse until midnight.

. . . . .

May 31st

J. accompanied us on horseback to the steppe. We bade him a heartfelt farewell. We made forty-five miles to Topolev mys to Blue Zaisan. Mountains and hills. Flat *kurgans.* Gray grass and vivid red slopes. *Auls* of Kirghiz *yurtas.* Not without reason do they call Kirghiz "Kara-kirghiz" black ones. The escort, a soldier, relates many instances of Kirghiz robberies. The Kirghiz, Kurbanof, keeps a band of fifty armed riders. We rush through a gorge where twenty-two Kirghiz recently attacked and tried to strangle seven frontier officials with lassos. But the latter at once, at the point of the saber, captured and slaughtered sixteen people. Farther, near a hill, four Kirghiz attacked one soldier. He had a hard time getting away. Lately, Kirghiz have driven 150 horses away from the ranch of Feodoroff. In Chuguchak, the seriously wounded chief of the Post even now lies, struck down by the bullets of Kirghiz thieves. The peasants complain about the perpetual robberies. Four cows of our hostess were driven away. It is so difficult to subdue these robbers and the soldiers of the frontier are straining all their forces.

Our driver lost his senses completely. During forty-five miles we had nine stops and breakdowns. Finally, one carriage overturned, the wheels upside down. It is remarkable that the horses and driver were not killed. Blue Zaisan glows on the horizon. Behind it is the white crest of the Altai Chain. Is it not Beluha herself?

Here is Topolev mys, a squatting village with white mud huts. A reliable boat left yesterday and we will probably have to go by the *Altai.* We shall stop with old Feodorova.

We drink tea. We eat pot-cheese with sour cream. On the wall hangs an image of Saint Nicolas and the supplement of the magazine, "Neva": *"Lomonosoff Shows an Electric Machine to Catherine the Great."* The nephews of F. are coming—former soldiers. They speak intelligently about

China, Korea, and about Chang Tso Lin. They want to get some perch and carp for us from Zaisan. On the windows are red and purple primroses, and the omnipresent geranium. Our Gegen was taken for a Chinese general. How many legends will travel about our passage?

. . . . .

June 1st

Old Feodorova also complains about the Kirghiz. They steal everything. Every night one has to guard the herds. But, in general, life is well ordered. The driver, Sadik says: "They all lie in Urumchi about life. They live as they lived before." The soldiers say of the Kirghiz: "When you come to him—he shouts out, 'Friend, friend.' But he himself at the same time is scheming how to take away your gun and to shoot you with it." So the whole night one has to keep the gun in hand.

Instead of the *Altai* came the worst boat, the *Lobkov*. Well, it is not destined that we shall go on a good boat—the driver prevented it. The lake lies like a pearl net. Today the sanctuary is seen, the Kalmuck Mountain Sabur, or rather Saw-ur.

The *Lobkov* proved to be not as bad as reputed. We arranged for the lama and Ramsana on the top deck. We all found accommodations.

Again a miracle; while we are still on the gangplank, the stevedores gather around us and beg us to "tell" them. On the top deck we are surrounded by a circle of all ages. And all of them are burning equally with one desire. *To know.* Each one has his angle of approach; each one his information, but all have one fervent desire—to know more. And how they discriminate in what is told! What remarks they make! One wants to know the economic situation of the countries; another wants to know about politics; still another searches information about Hindu Yogis, saying, "That's where truth is." People who so desire *to know* will receive what they desire. A boy is coming. He wants to travel with us. Four are crowded in George's small cabin, and they speak in a friendly manner. The atmosphere of profanity is no longer hanging over the pier. The people's work is thriving.

. . . . .

June 2nd

"How I should love to study for thirty years without stopping, but the job interferes," says a workman on the boat. And his eyes burn with a genuine thirst for knowledge.

For the last time, I turn toward China. On my painting which is in Peking there is an inscription: "The Friend of China." Did my friendship lessen after seeing the whole Dance of Death of Sinkiang? Not in the least. It is my friendship to real China that has given me the right to record so many horrors. A hypocritical enemy would close his eyes at this horror of reality but a friend must point out whatever assails an unprejudiced eye. In the lancing of these ulcers lies the assurance of the success of future China. Out of the past, out of the ancient civilization of China, one can construct a bridge only to the future new consciousness, with understanding of the true evolution. But the present will sink into the darkness as a stained page of history. The governors and ambans of contemporary China will become horrible masks in the curio-museum, as little needed for humanity as the amputation of the hands and feet of the god of water. I sincerely hope that China may soon cast off all degradation and wash away the dirt which has accumulated under the silk of the outer garment. I wish success to all who understand the terror of hypocrisy and ignorance.

Quite impartially, I am looking into the eyes of those who try to ascend. What thirst for knowledge! This thirst moves mountains; it gives an unwavering courage to new constructions.

While it is yet night, we leave Lake Zaisan and go between the flat banks of the still narrow Irtysh. The water is shallow now, and the boat more than once touches the sand bank. On the prow they are measuring the depth. You hear the same exclamations as on the upper Volga. Villages of a Kirghiz type. Here and there are herds. Many geese and all sorts of other wild waterfowl.

Green hills appear. We shall reach the mountains by evening. Toward six o'clock we reach the village Bati. Little village houses already predominate. And there are the mountains, and tempests over the mountains. An astounding effect of the light steppe under the blue mountains and cloudy billows. This wealth of cloud we have not seen for a long time.

In the evening, in the dining room, a boy comes in: "And won't I be scolded for coming in?" He goes to his mother. He talks a great deal. He defends the Kirghiz. He insists the Kirghiz would not steal. He tells about the unknown Kirghiz mountain road discovered by him—"like a highway through the very crest." . . . He speaks about catching fish: "We caught pike. Two *puds'* weight—like a crocodile." He remembers meeting a bear: "I was afraid of him but perhaps he was still more afraid of me."

The late evening until midnight is occupied in conversation with a village school teacher, about Yoga, about secrets of India, about reincarnation. All these questions are as daily bread here and the people live by them. They correspond with one another. They ask involved and profound questions. Such village school teachers are many. They keep in touch with each other and are genuinely interested in scientific discovery and psychic research. Toward midnight we reach Novyi Krasnoyarsk. A crowd comes to the boat.

· · · · ·

June 3rd

Since morning we have been passing tall cliffs. Gray masses are blocked up to the very edge of the water. The Irtysh has become narrower and flows still more rapidly. There is the little wooden city, Ust Kamenogorsk, and beyond, the mountains end. The Irtysh spreads into a broad, smooth, flowing river and on the horizon the separate crests and pyramids of vanished mountains are still visible. Farewell, mountains!

We have decided to go from Semipalatinsk to Omsk by boat, along the Irtysh. It entails a change of route. But it is no better by train. Twenty hours to Novosibirsk; we would arrive there late at night. On the boat, there is more intercourse with people and more air. There are cool days now and cold nights. They say that for three years now changes of climate have been noticeable. There is no heat during the summer, but the winters are also less cold.

Late at night there is again a conversation and on the same themes. It is really remarkable, personally to be convinced of the direction of the people's consciousness.

. . . . .

June 4th

Semipalatinsk. Three o'clock in the morning. The cargo is transferred to another boat, the *February Eighth,* as far as to Omsk. We decided to go by boat because the Altaian line is slow and it takes twenty hours to Novosibirsk. Again we meet courtesy and the desire to help in all ways. They give us letters to S. in Omsk, where they will arrange reservations for us in the international sleeping car. We visit a bookshop.

A boat was dragged under the steamer. It was capsized by the current. In a friendly way they rush to help the poor fellows. On the steamer curious children roam about. There is respectfulness in them, no rudeness—there is the same eagerness for learning. The Irtysh has spread itself into a powerful, broad river, on which rafts float. They are manned by the Kerjaks, Old Believers: "If you tell them that you have eaten with Kirghiz, they will never permit you at the table. And they all command that one should cross oneself," explains the little boy. A proverb of the steppe: "If thy comrade is one-eyed, try to close one eye to be a pair with him."

The *auls* of the nomads disappear. The horseback riders are seen more rarely and the Siberians, seemingly hewn out of stone, begin to appear. Below Beluha, snow still lingers. Lately snow fell again. Meat is sold at eight kopecks a pound, and a good horse is worth eighty rubles. And to everything is added the firm, stubborn, Siberian: "However." The Siberians are not afraid of the Kirghis—it is, as they say, only some prank of the steppes, thievery, bravado. A Comanche or a Zuni in Arizona will also lead away a horse. And did the Scythians really hobble their own horses on the vase of Kuleb? So much is being created. And the soil—the soil of Buddha—is being transported. Again, many dates will be forgotten and one may not record them.

.   .   .   .   .

June 5th

The tales about the cruelty of the Chinese are penetrating even here, on the Irtysh. The traveling frontiersmen remember the Chinese tortures witnessed by them. The convicted person is put into a hollow pole filled with sharp thorns. The body is thrust with all its weight upon the thorns. Through the nose and the nasal tube and mouth is drawn a horsehair and they begin to saw. Or they draw a horsehair through the eyeball. All this, the frontiersmen see and carry the news to the cities. And the Kirghiz's pranks also are related everywhere. When a rich bey robber was recently caught and sentenced to be exiled to Kamchatka, two hundred of his tribe came and offered all their wealth as ransom for the elder robber. Only by firm measures, these robberies can be stopped, especially if the Chinese will cease to favor contraband, for which they receive big bribes.

The *yurtas* almost ended. Low pine trees and shrubs. Behind the window, two young workmen are conversing. They speak about the organization of their local theater, about difficulties with costumes and lighting. They speak as one seldom hears in a capital. The frontiersmen speak of Buddhism; they understand it is not a religion but a teaching. They appreciate that Buddha the man, is a real historical personality. They are interested in the manuscript about Issa; they discuss the vastness of matter. What accounts for this vital, clear thinking? Because it is the nature of the spirit to strive toward beauty.

A bearded peasant from Nijni-Novgorod passes. He grieves that people do not understand the value of practical unity: "And they tend only to separativeness in the village: but how much more useful it would be to work as a unit. If we only could have Ford himself among us."

. . . . .

June 6th

Some people are afraid of mountains and they insist that mountains stifle them. Are not these people also afraid of great works?

The Irtysh grows still broader. What a current! The water has become yellow and the white caps rise. Now we can well believe that Yermak might have drowned here.

On the piers, the crowd becomes more and more dense, as though the entire town had poured out on the steamer. One little fellow asks another, quite a small one: "Are you a Boy Scout?" It is interesting to see the ease of migration so characteristic of the peasant. Listen to their speech— this one from Kamchatka is now in Semipalatinsk; this one, from Kronstadt, is in Paveodar; this one was in Seul and in Bokhara; this one is from the borders of Poland; this one from Nijni-Novgorod, is now in Altai. Tomorrow is the last day of the Irtysh—Omsk. A train and again that beauty above which is the Sign of the Rose.

. . . . .

June 7th

The wind and the whitecaps changed into a cold downpour. The crowds on the piers hid themselves. E.I. is pleased—there is no heat, which she so feared. We ask ourselves: Have the Lichtmanns already started? The last letters from America were from the beginning of January and the telegrams from the beginning of March.

The charm of Asia! Not the contagion—but the enchantment, and it was always within us. Even before the "Polovetsky Camp" or the "Guests from beyond the Sea" was painted. And how shall we be without thee, Asia? But we have not left thee. And when shall we leave thee? And where is thy border, Asia? Who said thy border is along the Ural? What tasks can be accomplished without Asia? What structure can be made without the stones, without the covenants of Asia? The "Long Ear" of Asia hearkens to the music of the spheres. The "Great Hand" of Asia is raising the chalice. About the Long Ear of Asia are woven many tales. About the Great Hand of Asia, the epic is only being written. All great Teachers came from Asia. E.I. reads the letter of the Mahatma. This morning we passed the village Yermak and the place where the conqueror of Siberia was drowned. The workman explained: "He would have swum out but his heavy armor dragged him down." So the workman remembers the hero of these wintry lands.

. . . . .

June 8th

Omsk. A bridge across the Irtysh. Some "historical" buildings; a private house where Kolchak lived; the building of the Kolchak Senate; the house of the soldiers; the cathedral where the worn banner of Yermak is guarded; the half-destroyed prison where Dostoyevsky was confined; the top of an old prison of the seventeenth century. It appears that both trains which we needed have just left and we shall have to remain three days—until Thursday evening. We hear about my paintings and the high prices that they bring. There are more questions about Yoga, about India, about Buddhism and about the teachings of life; of the study of will and cosmic matter.

Newspapers write that we have "found" the legend about Christ. Whence comes this legend? How could we find what has been known so long ago? But we found something greater. We could establish that the story of the life of Issa, the Teacher, is accepted and lives throughout the entire East, on the borders of Bhutan and in Tibet, on the walls of Sikhim, on the peaks of Ladak and in the Mongolian *Khoshuns.* And in the Kalmuck *ulus* lives this legend—lives, not in the sensationalism of the Sunday papers, but as a firm, calm realization. That which for the West is a sensation, is for the East an age-old knowledge.

．　．　．　．　．

June 9th

The cold sun penetrates through the ornamented leaves of the Philodendron in the rooms of the Hotel Europe. Not to a hothouse, not to a botanical garden, but to Sikhim shall these leaves carry our remembrances—there, where from the river Tishta we ascended to Chakong, the very same leaves wound around the green mossy trunk, interwoven with the brilliant colors of orchids; and to a small temple in Chakong with the solitary temple guard, tall and stately, in a simple linen shirt; and to the evening legends of Lama Mingyur. And so this ornamented leaf shall lead now into the far-off country and near this leaf shall flourish the images close and dear to us.

We are going to the District Museum. It has an art and ethnographical department. From the big cities they have sent a series of paintings. There is not only Levitsky but also Musatoff and Levitan. To our surprise, we find also two of my paintings. Both are from the unfinished group which stood near the walls of the studio. One, "Boats" (1903) from the Suite, "They are Building the City." The other one, "Benevolent Tree" (a sketch). One should note that both are unfinished.

The local school teacher comes up and asks, in astonishment: "You are Roerich?"—"Yes"—"But you were killed in Siberia, in 1918?" Again the same fairy tale, which reached us in London and America. And how could we not be killed if there were "funeral services" and obituaries? But the one who was chanted away at the "funeral services" has since worked very joyously, has traversed oceans and easily ascended heights. Probably the "funeral services" helped; and the obituaries were very heartfelt ones.

. . . . .

June 10th

We are departing: the trains leave at midnight. Friends, I shall rejoice, upon the completion of the journey, to transfer to you the complete drawings along with these brief notes. But for this, it is necessary to settle down somewhere for a time, and to arrange the notes and albums. But where and when?

Kosloff writes about Khangai. Two statues are interesting—the black and the white—the good and the evil. But why are they in Scythian attire? Are these Taras? Or adapted stone figures? It is significant as is everything from the old district of Orkhon.

Today is Saban Tui, a Tartar holiday of the sowing. Races on horses and camels. The Tartars with loud bells gallop into the grove outside the town. They are celebrating the new sowing.

At midnight the train arrives. We are passing under the Sign of the Rose; under the sign of the holiday of the sowing. Greetings to Friends!

Part X

ALTAI

(1926)

A CROSS the entire heaven shone a rainbow. And not one, but two. And through the rainbow-gate rushed the broad Ob: The great Ob—birthplace of the wife and serpent.

. . . . .

The Shambatyon River rolls along rapids and stones. Who will brave it? On its other shore live the people of M. M., the most sacred letter of the alphabet, conceals the name of the coming one. The Kabala recalls the Shambatyon. Katun[9] rolls along stones—a true Katun. And as yet, the city has not been built on the new site.

. . . . .

Katun in Turki means woman.

"The Dodecahedron, significant of the feminine Origin, is being indicated in scientific terms which are connected with the dates of evolution. . . ."

. . . . .

"On Katun and on the Bia, brother will rise against brother. There will be great slaughter and then there will begin a new life. . . ."

. . . . .

And still others come and speak concerning the same year of Twenty-eight. The sun spots condense as at present only every seventy-seven years. And then finally comes the most inspired person and he also talks about the same year. What a wonder! One, through astronomy; the other, through astrology; the third, through writings; the fourth,

---

[9] Katun is formed from the root, "to roll."

through numerology; and all are concerned with the same thing. What a wonder! If one adds twenty-five to 1911 one gets the same result—the year 1936.

. . . . .

Stone—wondrous stone. The stone of Tigeretz. And simply—stone. The entire district is all stone!

. . . . .

Elen-Chadir, Tourak, Kuegan, Karagai, Ak-kem, Yasatar, Ekonur, Chegan, Arasan, Urul, Kuraghan, Alahoi, Jharhash, Ongudai, Eloman, Turgunda, Argut, Karaghem, Archat, Jhaldur, Chingistai, Ak-Ulgun, Hamsar.

All these are names; these names of rivulets, habitations and town sites sound like a chanting tune, like a harmonious peal. So many nations have brought their finest harmonies and dreams. The tread of tribes went and is returning.

. . . . .

Near Black Anui on Karagol there are caves. The depths and distances are not known. There are bones and inscriptions.

. . . . .

And when we crossed Edigol the broadness of Altai spread before us. It blossomed in all interblending green and blue shades. It became white with distant snow. The grass and the flowers stood the height of a man on horseback. One cannot even locate the horses in it. Nowhere have we seen such grassy vesture.

. . . . .

An Altaian overtook us. Timorously he peered at us. What kind of new foreigners had come to his country? He brandished his whip and disappeared in the resounding grasses—blue, gold and purple. The resemblance between the North American Indians and the Mongols is striking.

. . . . .

About the good Oirot all know. Also they know the favorite Altaian name—Nicholai.

Beyond Yalui begin the Altaian *Ails.* The peaked *yurtas* covered with the bark of the larch tree are darkened. The site for Kamlayne is seen. Here they do not say Shaman but Kam. Toward Anui and Ulala there are still Kams who "conjure forth snow and serpents." But toward the south, Shamanism has been replaced by the teaching about the White Burkhan and his friend, Oirot. Sacrifices have been abolished, being replaced by the burning of aromatic heather and by harmonious singing. They expect the beginning of the new era soon. It was a woman—a young Altaian—who sensed the new steps of the world and safeguarded the first austere law.

. . . . .

The road, washed away by rains, exhausted the horses. We stopped in Kurlyk. We shall have to sit through the night. But it is no hardship to spend the night in a place where the teaching of the White Burkhan and his benevolent friend Oirot were born. The name of Oirot has been accepted by a whole district. Here, verily, they expect the coming of the White Burkhan. In the cliffs towering over Kurlyk, the entrances of the caves loom dark. These caves penetrate deeply: their depth has not been ascertained. There are also secret passages—from Tibet, through Kunlun, through Altyntag, through Turfan; the Long Ear knows of secret passages. How many people have saved themselves in these passages and caves! Reality has become a fairy tale. Just as the black aconite of the Himalaya has become the Fire-Blossom.

. . . . .

When the white birch grew in our land, the White Tsar came and conquered our country. And the Tchud did not wish to remain under the White Tsar and went under the ground. And they covered themselves with stones"—"On the Ouimon they show you the Tchud graves covered with stones"—"On this spot the underground Tchud departed." The migration of the nations has been imprinted there.

. . . . .

Belovodye! The grandfather of Atamanoff and the father of Ognieff went in search of Belovodye: "Over the Kokushy Mountains. Through Bogogorshe. Over Ergor— by a special path. Whoever does not know the path will perish in the lakes or on the hungry steppe. It has happened also that the people from Belovodye have come out on horseback through special passages over Ergor. And also long ago it happened that a woman from Belovodye came out. High of stature, thin of figure, with face darker than ours. She was clad in a long skirt, a kind of sarafan. There are special dates for everything."

. . . . .

From the south and from the north, from the east and from the west, they are thinking of the same things. And the same evolutionary process is being impressed upon the best images. A center between the four oceans exists. Consciousness of the new world exists. Will the subterranean Tchud not return? Do not the Agharti, the subterranean people, saddle their horses? Does not the bell of Belovodye ring out? Does not the horseman ride over Ergor? On the ridges—on the Dalnyi and on the Studenyi, the peaks are aflame.

. . . . .

"In 1923 Sokoliha with the people of Bukhtarma went to search for Belovodye. Not one of them returned. But recently there came letters from Sokoliha. She writes that she did not reach Belovodye but she lives well. Where she lives, she does not write. All know of Belovodye."

"Since when originated the news about Belovodye?"

"The message came from the Kalmucks and the Mongols; originally they told our forefathers who lived according to the old belief and devotion."

[346]

Which means that at the base of information about Belovodye lies a communication from the Buddhist world. The same center of teaching of life is interpreted by the Old Believers. The way between the Argun , and Irtysh leads on to the same Tibet.

. . . . .

They write about the magnetic storms and the unusual temperature and about various natural phenomena due to condensation of the sun spots. Next year the effect of the spots will be still more significant. Unusual northern lights are possible. There may be shocks of the nervous system. How many legends are connected with sun spots, those menacing wrinkles of the luminary.

. . . . .

Ramsana left for Ladak. He could not stand the low places of the north. "Either I leave or die" Of course, Ladakis pass their whole lives on heights not lower than - twelve thousand feet. It is a pity for Ramsana. One can confidently depend on Ladakis to watch things. The Oirot drivers are not like the Ladakis.

. . . . .

Vakhramey counts the number of wagons and agricultural machines. The Old Believer's heart has assimilated the machines. Sanely he estimates the industry of Germany and America. Sooner or later they will certainly work with America. The people remember the Americans. They value the frank character of the Americans and are aware of the common traits. "Come to work with us!" they call to the Americans. This friendly call has penetrated throughout all Asia.

. . . . .

After discussing industry, Vakhramey begins to murmur, chantingly, some tale; I catch: "And receive me, thou most peaceful desert. . . . And how shall I receive thee? I, the desert, possess neither mansions nor palaces in me." . . .

It is familiar to me: the tale about Jasaf. "Dost thou know, Vakhramey, about whom thou singest? Thou singest about Buddha. Because the *Bodhisatv* has been transformed into Jasaf."

So Buddha merged into the Kerjak consciousness. The plowed fields led them to the machines and cooperation to Belovodye.

But Vakhramey is not only versed in the cooperative movement and in canticles. According to the covenant of the wise ones, he is not astonished at anything; he knows the ores and the deer; he knows the little bees and especially the secret traditions. He knows the herbs and the flowers. This is indisputable. And not only does he know how and where the flowers grow, and where the roots are hidden, but he loves them and delights in them. Gathering a great bunch of vari-colored grasses, that reach up to his gray beard, his face lights up. And he pets them. And caressingly he speaks of their usefulness. Here is verily Panteleon the Healer. It is not dark witchery but knowledge drawn from experience. Greetings, Vakhramey Semeonich! For thee, on Himalaya, does the Fire-Blossom grow!

.   .   .   .   .

And here is Vakhramey's sister, Aunt Elena. She is both a healer and a painter of verdure and a skillful writer. She also knows herbs and flowers. She can decorate any kind of casement with ochre and madder-lake and red-lead. On the doors and casements, she can paint all types of grass designs. Or she will adorn them with bright little birds and a ferocious yellow lion as a guard. No important letter in the village can be written without her . . . "And to whom art thou writing?—to thy son? Let me tell thee how to write"—And a long, compassionate, heartfelt epistle, full of poetic spirit, would flow forth. Such a capable woman!

. . . . .

"With the people of Bukhtarma we do not wish to associate! You see, they appeared as comrades but really came
to rob, and the most characteristic thing was their ancient
sarafan. . . . And so now they are called 'Sarafaniki.' Now,
of course, they have reformed. If you meet one—he turns
away his face, because he still is human and feels ashamed.
. . . Now we ought to have real American machines. It is
time to free the horses." . . .

Again one sees a striving toward vigilant cooperation.
And new herds are fattening on the high ridges. And from
the Studenyi summit one can see best Beluha itself—of
whom even the deserts whisper.

. . . . .

Everything bears the traces of the civil war. Here on
the highway, a Red regiment was destroyed by ambush.
Here in the Katun they drowned the Whites. On the
mountain ridge are lying the red Commissars. And under
Katanda, the Kerjak psalmist, an old believer, was hacked
with sabers. Many graves on the roads; and near them
grows thick new grass.

. . . . .

As birds on the branches, so from mouth to mouth
flit words forgotten and not recognized by any one. The
inhabitants in Trans-Baikal calls a spider *misguir*. And a
guest merchant is called *misguir*—according to the Siberian interpretation, simply a spider. What kind of Turki
idiom helped here? Wind, in the language of the people
in Trans-Baikal, is *hiyus*—this is completely beyond understanding. The root is neither Mongolian nor Yakut.

On the *taiga* toward Kousnetzk they eat fitches and
marmots. This is dangerous because marmots bring on
the bubonic plague. They say that the infection disappears
from the fur under the influence of sun rays. But who
can ascertain when the rays have effect and how much?
Whence came the famous Spanish influenza, so similar in

form to the bubonic plague? Is it not from furs? Mongolia is often the breeding place for epidemics. And the cattle plague is also very common. One gets used to everything. In Lahore, in Srinagar, in Baramula, cholera was raging when we were there. In Khotan there was small pox; in Kashgar, scarlet fever. One gets used to anything.

· · · · ·

Oirot horses are sturdy, as are also the horses from Kuldja and Olet. The Karashahr race horses and Badakhshans are not sturdy and are less adaptable for the mountains.

· · · · ·

The Mongols and Buriats are anxious to see various countries. They want to visit Germany and France. They love America and Germany. The need of broadening one's horizon is demonstrated by them in an ancient parable of a frog and a turtle: The frog lived in a well and the turtle in the ocean. But the turtle came to the frog and told him of the vastness of the ocean. . . . "In your opinion is the ocean twice as large as my well?" . . . "Much larger," answered the turtle. "Wouldst thou say three times as large as my well?" . . . "Much larger." . . . "And four times as large?" . . . "Much larger" . . . Then the frog chased away the turtle as a boaster and a liar. . . .

· · · · ·

The Popovtsi, the Bezpopovtsi, the Striguni, the Priguni, the Pomortsi, the Netovtsi (not recognizing anything, but considering themselves "of the old faith") afford many incomprehensible discussions. And toward Trans-Baikal among the Semeiski (Old Believers exiled to Siberia with their entire families), also are added the Temnovertsi, and the Kalashniki. Each one of the Temnovertsi has his own ikon closed with little doors, to which he alone prays. If someone else should pray to the same ikon, it would become unfit! Still more strange—the Kalashniki. They pray before the ikon through a little opening in a *kalach*

[350]

(a loaf of bread). We have heard much, but such obscure beliefs we have never seen nor heard of—and in the summer of 1926! Here are also Hlysti, Pashkovtzi, Stundisti and Molokans. Among the green and blue hills, among the *taiga* thickets, one cannot perceive all curves. Glancing at the beard and low fillet, one cannot judge what the heavy-garbed man whom we encounter is carrying with him.

. . . . .

Ust Kan is the last telegraph station. From there we sent the first telegram ever sent to America. The telegraph operator was upset. He offered to send it by mail to Biisk. He had never dealt with such a fearful animal as America! But we insisted. And he promised to send it after consulting Biisk.

It is planned to extend the railroad line to Katanda, in two stages from Beluha. Up to Katanda, even in pre-war times a railroad line from Barnaul was planned—connecting the heart of Altai with Semipalatinsk and Novosibirsk. They say that even *then* the engineers went through this line. "Yes? When, 'then'?" . . . "Yes, it is known before the war." . . . The mysterious "then" becomes synonymous with the "pre-war epoch." From Peking one can go on a "Dodge" up to Urumchi itself, which means also up to Kuldja, up to Chuguchak, up to Semipalatinsk. Life forges a vital web of communication.

. . . . .

Tales creep in from Kobdo. Every one is interested in conveying to us at least something of unknown Mongolia, of the land of magnetic storms, mirages of the sun, and cruciform moons. Every one wants to know about Mongolia. . . . Everything is strange. They tell of a sentinel who was eaten by dogs. He hacked seven of them, but could not save himself from the pack. A Mongolian commander in Uliasutai ate a human heart. There are some who say it was a Russian and some who think it was a Chinese. On the Iro and toward Urianhai there is much gold. Also on the Iro a strange boy who pronounced some prophecy was born to a Shaman woman. They whisper about the reincarnation of the Mongolian Bogdo Gegen. And others say that another unusual being was also born in China. But authorities do not recognize either the one or the other: Bogdo Gegen was never reborn either as Mongolian or Chinese, but always in Tibet. On the way from Uliasutai to Kobdo some wild people in furs jumped out and threw stones at the machine. They were so-called Guards! On the way to Manchuria from a cliff "mineral oil" flows into the desert. There also exist such magnetic places that even an automobile slows up.

Thus at the cross-road are woven complicated carpets of Asiatic design. And how can they exist without news? In this case, it would not be worthwhile to go to a far-off *ail* and to drink tea with a strong essence of tales. Mongolia attracts attention.

. . . . .

"Blacksmiths of Kurumchi"—strange incomprehensible people, who not only passed but also lived within the boundaries of Altai and Trans-Baikal. The generally accepted divisions of Huns, Alans and Goths are divided into manifold unaccountable subdivisions. To such an extent is everything obscured that coins with exact dates are sometimes attributed to completely non-correlating, temporarily established periods. Stagstones, Kereksuri, stone figures; walls of nameless cities—although all have been written about and counted, yet the paths of the peoples have not been clarified. How remarkable are the textures from the last Hun's graves which completed the famous Siberian antiquities!

. . . . .

There exists a legend about a Black Stone, which appears at the dates of great events. If you compare all the verbal dates of India, Tibet, Egypt and Mongolia, then their coincidence will remind you that apart from the record of historians, there is being set down another history of the world. It is especially significant to compare the testimony of completely unrelated nationalities.

.　.　.　.　.

The Kalmucks and Mongols recognize from traces left by horses and camels, the origin and the quantity of the cargo. They will say: "A horseman passed here, leading two horses. Two horses are worn out and the third one is fresh." Or "A herd of horses passed by and with the herd are two horsemen." . . .

Different occurrences from the recent wars were related to us. One horseman volunteered to force the surrender of a whole regiment. He took his comrade and a big drove of horses. "More," he said, "is not needed." He drove the horses in the direction of the wind and he himself went with his comrade to negotiate. He demanded, "Surrender your arms at once, otherwise I will lead my whole army upon you." They reflected, perceiving the pillars of dust from the drove; then they surrendered the army. And the audacious fellow commanded his comrade to go in advance and lead back the troop. Thus he forced a whole regiment to surrender. This is not a fairy tale of Jengis-Khan. It is a recent event.

Rumors even outride the motors—they will go on horseback for two hundred miles to drink tea.

.　.　.　.　.

Again they report: "It is rumored that you were lost." Is it possible that for a second time they will bury one? Whence is this unquenchable desire for slander and false inventions? They say that many imitations of my paintings are circulating. They tell amusing stories and even mention several men who in this way, using my name, earned money. They say that V. and R. worked that way. I had a chance to see a few imitations before the war. I remember one very large painting not uncleverly composed from fragments of various of my works. The poor collector who called me to approve his purchase, was immeasurably grieved. Friends, they may bring such imitations to you to the Museum. Look, beware! So often it happened that we saw paintings as well as whole albums falsely signed. I remember one painting by Rustschitz signed with my name.

They speak about the destruction of many of my paintings—"Call of the Serpent" is lost from the Academy. "The March," "Unkrada," "Building of the Walls," "Sviatogor" and others are lost. Of course they consider them lost—but who knows? The paths of objects are so unexpected. Collecting Old Masters, we came across such subtle play of life.

. . . . .

A woman traveler, a painter, visits us. A geological expedition comes. A conversation about artists: Juon, Mashkov, Kanchalovsky, Lentulof, Saryan, Kustodief hold their ground. . . . Benois is shaky. Dobujhinsky went to Lithuania. They do not mention Somof. They do not know that Bakst has died. The young ones are growing. Stchuseff and Stchuko go forward boldly. The woman painter walks about, sketches old corners, gates, window casements, various beams and the little horses on cornices, as though making an inventory before a distant journey. The various tiny horses will depart from the roofs. Let them depart, as well as the pattern of the chintzes. But with what will they be replaced? The "Viennese" chair and the fading calico do not bring in culture. Here is a task for the young: Give an image of the future life. From factory whistles and from the peal of bells someone has synchronized a symphony; though as yet it is unsuccessful, the whole conception is truly resonant. And thus for the building of a house an alert hand is necessary and dispassionate labor. Here Ikon painters from Mastersky, Palehovsky and Holuisky lent the work new importance.

. . . . .

In the East, they apply the externalization of sensitiveness not only to separate individuals but also to groups and seemingly to whole districts. The result is a tremendous experiment in the application of psychic energy. And all this is being done silently and anonymously.

Behold and be surprised: books, paintings, songs, dances and buildings—all these are sent out upon the waves of the world anonymously. Books are attributed, according to tradition, to a certain author, but he himself does not put his name upon the manuscript. Paintings are not signed; the name of the architect of Potala is not inscribed. On faience, on ceramics, on metal art crafts one can sometimes see the trade-mark but not the name. And in this fundamental anonymity the East has left the West far behind. One must learn from the East, but for that one must absorb the psychology of the East. The East does not love false visitors; the East easily discerns masquerading imitations. And the East will never forget its decision. The judgment of the East is rendered at the very first moment. All the patches of corrections only serve to intensify the clownishness of the imitative attire.

. . . . .

The discovery of Theremin: "We saw on the screen the motion of human hands which took place at the same time behind the wall in the next room." At last the "miraculous" becomes "scientific." Finally, one begins to turn to the real study of all of the properties of energy.

. . . . .

Just when we did not ask; just when we did not expect, he himself spoke and demonstrated his knowledge of special places. Our simpletons would have considered this a fairy tale or an unusual revelation; yet here he smilingly closed his yellow khalat and proved his knowledge of certain ones and where they live. "And with that place, now for fifteen years there have been no communications."

. . . . .

To the Tashi Lama in Peking came a group of Chinese asking for passports for the passage to Shambhala. This reminded us of the letter which was written from Boston to Shambhala. Whence and how has this Chinese group come together? Were they attracted by the wanderings of Lao-Tzin? Or because of older writings? Or by the book of the Abbot of Wu-t'ai-shan. Some time ago one would have ridiculed that fact but now a great deal has occurred. The literature has become so enriched that the recent invention and "magic" have passed into the laboratory of research. And the skeptics are indignant, but only because of their complete ignorance and unenlightenment. Even the most obtuse thinkers ask "What does it mean?" One may speak about the significance of that which happens but the fact itself by now does not remain unobserved.

. . . . .

They tell of the experiment of Manouilof, who has made researches into the sex of plants and minerals and also into the masculine and feminine origin of human blood. Experiment with the mineral "pyrite" gives a result long since indicated by the science of the East: "Pyrite produces crystals of two kinds—one a kind of cube and the other a form of dodecahedron. If the very same reaction is poured into the test tube with cubic crystals—one will get a discoloration of fluid—the masculine reaction. And if the same be performed with the dodecahedron crystals, a purple color results—the feminine reaction." For the West this discovery is new but the ancient formulae of the East speak of the dodecahedron as the Mother of the World—the feminine beginning. They also point out about the purple physical feminine emanation. You can imagine with what calm smile the scientist of the East listens to the "new" discoveries of the West. "Hemoglobin in the blood of animals and chlorophyle in the juice of plants are similar in their nature." And the scientist of the East nods, as a sign of an age-long assent.

Know! Know without fear and in the entire measure.

[356]

. . . . .

When at last will people walk out of the foggy twilight of "mysticism," to the study of sunlit reality? When will the darkness of the cave transform itself into the radiance of space?

. . . . .

The horns of the deer and the jet of Kabarga up to now are regarded as precious wares. One must make research into the healing qualities of the powdered horn of the deer. The spring blood which fills these woolly horns of course is permeated with a strong excretion. What is the difference between the musk of the Tibetan ram and the musk of Altaian Kabarga? The Kabarga feeds upon the nettle of the cedar and the larch. Altaians chew the gum of fir tree tar. All the properties of musk must be investigated.

. . . . .

We are stopping in the former chapel of the Old Believers. On the walls are still seen the four corners of the former ikons. In the next room a red chalice is painted on the wall. Wherefore? At the gates sits a white dog. He came with us. Whence?

. . . . .

The White Burkhan, of course, is also the Blessed Buddha. In the region of Ak-Kem are traces of radio-activity. The water in Ak-Kem is milky white. Pure Belovodye. Through Ak-Kem the fiftieth latitude passes. We recall the conclusion of Csoma de Koros.

. . . . .

About two o'clock in the night, on the second of August, east of the village Altaiskoye, a large, powerfully luminous meteorite fell. To the south of Verkhiniouimon, last year, on the summit of the ridges, stones and sand were erupted as if by an explosion. A pit was formed.

"Unspilled Chalice"—the most blue, the most reverberant mountains. Purity itself as in Phalut. And he carries from the mountains his chalice.

. . . . .

"The Blacksmith forges the fate of humanity, on the Siver Mountains." The grave of Sviatogor is on Siver Mountain. The Siver Mountains—Sumyr, Subur, Sumbyr, Siberian-Sumeru. The exact center from the four oceans. In Altai, on the right bank of Katun, there is a mountain. Its significance is being likened to the world-mountain, Sumeru. Sayn Galabyn sudur is "the narrative of the Good Era."

. . . . .

All the trees were charmed against harming Baldur. One mistletoe was forgotten—and the arrow from this very mistletoe struck Baldur. All the animals gave blessings for the building of the temple in Lhasa, but one, the gray bull, was forgotten and he was the one who, in the form of an impious king, rebelled later against the true teaching. Nothing that exists can be neglected in the structure. "Even a mouse will gnaw through the knots."

. . . . .

Katun is welcoming. The Blue Mountains are resonant. White is Beluha. The flowers are vivid and the green grasses and cedars are calming. Who has said that Altai is cruel and unapproachable? Whose heart has become fearful of the austere power and beauty?

On the seventeenth of August we beheld Beluha. It was so clear and reverberant. Verily, Zvenigorod![10]

Beyond Beluha there appears the crests of Kunlun so beloved to the heart, and beyond that "the mountain of the Divine Queen" and "Five Treasure Troves of the Snows."

---

[10]   Zvenigorod—The City of Bells.

[358]

And herself, "the Queen of the White Snows," and all the written and unwritten, the spoken and the unspoken.

"Between the Irtysh and Argun. Over Kokushi. Through Bogogorshi, over Ergor itself, rides a horseman.

Part XI

MONGOLIA

(1926-1927)

BANG! A shot. The bullet pierced the window. It is good that George had just gone away from the window at that very moment. Who shot? Was it intentional, or was it a prank?

．．．．．

We are forewarned: "But you will not depart." I answer: "We shall depart as always. We shall not delay even for one day." Our Americans arrive. Boris is with them. The doctor is annexed. After a long correspondence, N. K. is found. Ludmilla and Raya will go with us: the first thirteen-year-old girl traveler into Tibet.

The Tibetan Donyer (Consul) is coming. He brings a Tibetan passport and a letter to the Dalai Lama. The Donyer gives such passports to pilgrims. Our knowledge of Buddhism entitles us to receive the same attention.

Four Buriat lamas come and ask us to take them with us. They saw the banner of the Expedition—the image of Maitreya with Ak-Dorje on top. All the servants have put little signs of Ak-dorje upon their caps. And like recruits they walk through Ulan Bator Khoto. George put them through a military drill. We bought eight more rifles. Everybody is amused by a Lewis machine gun standing in the dining room. Let them know that we have enough arms!

Coincident with our maneuvers, a Mongolian detachment was practicing to storm the stronghold. And on the other side our convoy went through the same maneuvers. You can imagine how completely confounded were both parties when they confronted each other!

. . . . .

"The Ruler of Shambhala."[11] This painting coincides unexpectedly with the prophecy of the Lama. "The Great Rider appeared and the heads of all people were turned towards the west, but the hand of the Rider turned all peoples toward the East."

A representative from the Mongolian government comes and begs us to make a design for the temple-shrine where the painting "Ruler of Shambhala" will be placed with other venerated objects.

. . . . .

The publication of "Foundations of Buddhism," and "New Era" is being completed. It is difficult to give a fine form to the book in a little printer's shop. The former lama, now a lithographer, lovingly redraws for the book "The Conquering Buddha" with the fiery sword. Again the messenger from the Government comes. They beg for permission to translate "Foundations of Buddhism" into Mongolian.

. . . . .

Much expectation and excitement! Nevertheless, we did not delay our departure. E. P. tensely stands at the threshold and says: "I await the solution of Him, who solves all things." And here comes a telegram. G. hustles about; he knows much. One can sometimes converse with him about the most sacred legends. It was he also who told us of a Mongolian version of the visit of the Teacher to Mongolia. It is strange to have heard the beginning of the tale in India and its conclusion in Mongolia. Thus is the entire desert encircled by one intense thought. We do not know how Tibet will greet us. If Ladak, called "Little Tibet," is beautiful, then "Great Tibet" must be unusually majestic. But often humanity errs in its appraisals and the

---

[11] The painting of Nicholas Roerich presented to the Mongolian government.

small "proves to be great." Unprejudiced, without superstition, we shall observe the reality.

. . . . .

Again all sorts of difficulties and expectations. And again unexpected friends. Among them the Esperantist. They help us to depart and prove an attentive escort. Like towers, are the highly packed automobiles.

. . . . .

There is a fully accredited story that on the river Iro an extraordinary child was born. Shortly after his birth he pronounced a prophecy and then became normal. The prophecy proved to be the same one about the future Mongolia as was given to us by a lama in Sikhim. It is well remembered in Mongolia.

The action of will used at a great distance has been remarkably developed in Mongolia. Quite recently one young Mongolian lama wrote a book about the path to Shambhala. Books about this path written by the Tashi Lama, the Abbot of Wu-t'ai-shan, a Buriat lama, are also known. The aspirations of the Mongols all face in this direction. Many other neighboring nationalities also understand all the reality of the meaning of Shambhala. Some of the Mongolian lamas know a great deal. Whenever we asked them questions, their answers showed deep knowledge. But then, it is not so easy to win their confidence in spiritual matters. Of the monasteries close to Ulan Bator Khoto, the most far-famed is the so-called Manjushri Khit. From it the late Bogdo-Gegen was kidnapped. All places in Mongolia are enveloped in legend.

. . . . .

In the camp among the yurtas and the herds, upon the hills of the Gobi, the Mongols of our convoy are heard singing a song about Shambhala recently composed by a Mongolian hero, Suche Bator: "We march to the holy war of Shambhala. Let us be reborn in the sacred land." . . .

And thus, valiantly and resonantly, the Mongols send out their hopes. Even in new Mongolia they know the reality of Shambhala. In Ulan Bator Khoto, the site for the future Dukang of Shambhala is already fenced around. The Mongols know about the arrival of the Ruler of Shambhala to Erdeni Dzo and Narabanchi. They know about the great "Guardians." They know of the great times. They know of the Chalice of Buddha which, after it left Peshawar, was preserved in Karashahr and disappeared for a time. They know of the coming of the Blessed Ones to Altai. They know the true significance of Altai. They know of the White Mountain. They know the sacred signs above the ancient Suburgan near Khotan. They know the news from China. Through all the silent spaces of Asia is heard the voice of the spirit of the future. They know that the time of Maitreya is come.

. . . . .

In the automobiles, crossing the small rivers in the spring and because of the lack of roads, we have ten breakdowns a day. If one can traverse seventy miles it is indeed a lucky day. Ordinarily, one does not make even twelve miles. Many Kereksurs (old graves), Kurgans: traces of great migrations. A remarkable stone figure—they say that here lived a notorious bandit and that now he has become a guard of the Path. The travelers smear the lips of the statue with grease in order to request a favor. Konchak, our servant, stands for long before this image and repeatedly demands that we have a good road. On the way, skulls and bones, the corpse of a baby wrapped in a sheepskin coat. Turpans, wild geese, all sort of ducks fly toward the north. Herds of kulans.

. . . . .

It is evident that we shall not go far in our automobiles. The road is not marked. The local guides themselves confuse the direction. And, for the most part, the automobiles are altogether poor. If only we can reach the border, the monastery Yum-Beise. There we shall have to take camels.

. . . . .

We hear legends. That which was told us about the visitation by the "Ruler of Shambhala" to monasteries in Narabanchi and Erdeni Dzo is confirmed in various palaces. Yum-Beise is an unpleasant, windy place. The monastery itself is not an inviting one and the lamas are not gracious. Beyond and above the monastery, on the mountain, a tremendous phallus is erected. . . .

. . . . .

There are endless negotiations concerning the engaging of the caravan. They propose to go as far as Chibochen (beyond Anhsi) in three weeks. By the end of April it is not good for camels; by that time it is hot, the camels are shedding, and during this time their strength leaves them. An old lama guide, a smuggler, is found, who offers to lead us by a short road through uncultivated parts. Usually no one goes there, fearing lack of water, but the lama has passed there no less than twenty times and knows that there are wells, streams and springs. But at this season even on the general road the wells also dry up and for this reason it is best to take the short way. The only danger of this new direction is the presence of the bands of the notorious Ja-Lama. But he was himself killed and his fellows are dispersed. Notwithstanding this, the region is dangerous. The lama guide assures us that now one may pass these places safely. We suspect our guide—may he not himself have been in the confidence of Ja-Lama? He knows too much of him and is too sure that we shall pass safely with him. He knows how Ja-Lama made his prisoners erect his city citadel which we shall pass on our way. We decided to go by this new way, however.

. . . . .

Limitless seems the Central Gobi. White—pink—blue—and slaty black. The gales bury the flat slopes with a layer of stones. One must not be caught in this stony gale. The danger in the Gobi is that the wells may have dried. Sometimes the mouths of the wells are filled with fallen animals. One can avoid the lack of water by taking another direction to the east, although the Chinese bands infest these regions.

· · · · ·

Night. Fires. Sentries. Recently within this canyon a caravan was looted. Suddenly the night silence is broken by a loud rifle shot. The fires are stamped out. A line of our men, armed with revolvers, lies low. Who opened fire on our camp? From somewhere comes the barking of a dog. We call for a volunteer to reconnoiter. It is decided that if he begins to sing, all is well. A vigilant silence and, at last, out of the darkness comes a merry song: "A Chinaman, proprietor of a caravan, did the shooting. He got frightened at the sight of our fires and thought we were robbers."

· · · · ·

Nyerva, leader of the caravan, whistles to attract the wind in the heat of noon. Like a barterer of winds on the shores of ancient Greece, the Mongol whistles long in a minor key; and the tips of the desert grass stir as in a breeze. The breeze rises and the Mongol winks, calling our attention to this. Barterers of winds! What a subject for an opera or symphony.

· · · · ·

From the white pebbles on the bosom of the Gobi the hand of an unknown traveler has fashioned certain figures. There are sacred inscriptions; but there are also erotic drawings repulsive amidst the majesty of the desert.

· · · · ·

Again precautions are necessary. Again it is necessary to don Mongolian kaftans. We approach the city of the notorious robber Ja-Lama or Tushegun Lama. We will camp somewhere nearby for the night. In the dense twi-

light some objects loom dark behind the hills. A dog barks.
. . . Although Ja-Lama himself was recently killed by the
Mongols, his bands are not yet scattered. We did not light
our fires for the night. We double the sentries. In the
morning we hear the astonished exclamation—"Here is
the city above us!" On the hills high up are perched the
towers and walls—a veritable citadel. It is imposing and
picturesque. George and P. K., with rifles ready, go to
investigate, and the Mongols bid them farewell with warn-
ings of caution. We watch through our field glasses. But,
finally they appear on the wall—it means that the robbers
now have deserted the castle.

. . . . .

Ja-Lama was not an ordinary bandit. He was a gradu-
ate of Law from Petrograd University and became a high
lama of Tibet, possessing great occult knowledge. Would a
night-robber have erected this city upon a high elevation,
visible from afar? What thoughts and dreams fretted the
gray head of Ja-Lama, which was carried for long afterward on a spear through the bazaars of Mongolia? . . . All
through the Central Gobi, the legend of Ja-Lama will persist for a long time. What a scenario for a moving picture!

. . . . .

Some peculiar riders approach the caravan and ask the
Mongols about the amount of arms we carry. The Mongols
whisper and gesticulate, indicating something very great
and then inform us—"Ja-Lama's men; they will not attack
us."

. . . . .

We near Anhsi. Vague rumors reach us about some
Chinese troops. To encounter them would be worse than
Ja-Lama's men. We will encircle Anhsi by night. But Nivra
loses the way. Dawn finds us before the walls of Anhsi.
They turn the camels and hasten to cross the broad, swift
stream. By evening we shall already have left the boundaries of Gansu, and shall enter the region of Kuku-nor. On

the mountains are the ruins of fortresses—landmarks of the former rebellions of the Dungans.

Swift streams. Before us is the snowy ridge of Nan-shan.

. . . . .

The Central Gobi is ended. Interior Mongolia, waterless, with its eroded auriferous ridges, is ended. In the mighty bottoms of these departed streams are concealed all manner of remains of the giants of antiquity. It is the first of June. Already for ten days we have been camping on the silvery banks of Shih-pao-ch'ang. Nan-Shan glows in the sunrise. The mountain stream murmurs. Whitely gleam the herds of goats and rams. Riders speed by us—is there any news? Rumors are in the air. When shall we advance? They try to frighten us by telling us not before September. There are many reasons. The grass must thicken. The camels must fatten and their wool must grow; and also the treacherous swamps of Tsaidam must dry. The Blue River will also subside by fall. We await news from Su-chow and Chamnar, and in the meantime, sly Machen, pupil of the Chinese, overcharges us. The old cheat calls me "the American King" and frequently during the day gallops over from his camp to our own.

. . . . .

Because we successfully administered medicine to them, the Mongols request us to invoke the rain, because of the unprecedented drought. They offer us five dollars from each yurta.

. . . . .

In spite of all the machinations of Machen we moved on to Sharagol under the ridge named after Humboldt. We crossed the cloudy quicksands of the Sharagol river with its endless tributaries just in time. Konchok almost drowned his gray Chinese horse. We camp beside a mountain spring on the foothill before Ulan davan (sixteen thousand feet) on the road to Tibet.

. . . . .

The Tibetans relate that during the time of the flight of the Dalai Lama in 1904, at the Chang-thang crossing, the men and horses felt a severe tremor. The Dalai Lama explained to them that they were at the hallowed border of Shambhala. Does the Dalai Lama know much of Shambhala? The Tashi Lama knows far more.

. . . . .

On July fifth we celebrated the Festival of Maitreya. In the tent of Shambhala a long service was performed and neighboring Mongols came and sang with our lamas.

. . . . .

Mongolian "noblemen" drape around themselves the broad pleated medieval kaftans. They wear gray felt caps, as though from the paintings of Gozzoli, and sacred chains and amulets around their necks. Whirlwind and sandstorm. At two o'clock in the afternoon we had to box ourselves tightly within the tents and light the candles.

I draw a plan of a Suburgan on the site of Shambhala where the Great Guardian stopped for the night. On July eleventh Nyerva from Kumbum monastery brings the prophecies and the new prayer of the Tashi Lama to Shambhala.

For three days P. K. has been galloping to Mahoi for camels.

Three new books are being compiled. The peaks glow white with snow; the air is fresh and the stillness recalls our Himalayan heights, toward which our spirits yearn. The Mongols admire the views of New York. For them America is a Promised Land. They whisper: "It is the attainment of Shambhala!" Not a day passes without its conversations on miraculous America.

. . . . .

On July fourteenth the annual holiday of the Mongols is celebrated. They are building a new obo (a kind of Suburgan); there are races and festivity! The young people of our camp beg us to let them go to the festival.

Since morning we have discussed the need of a Pan-Asiatic language which, at least elementally, would reconcile the three hundred dialects of Asia. In the evening our lamas read the prayers to Maitreya and Shambhala. If the West could understand what meaning the word Shambhala or Gessar has for Asia!

. . . . .

The rain and wind begin. The middle of July is more like autumn. At night the rain beats on the mountains.

. . . . .

In the midst of the rain and storm, most unexpected news reaches us. Such conquest of space is amazing. There is even news of the passing here of the Mahatma forty years ago. Again a veritable buran and showers. It is cold.

. . . . .

On July twentieth directions of the utmost importance reached us. They are difficult to execute but they may lead to certain results. No one in the caravan as yet suspects our immediate program.

. . . . .

On the next day also important news came and once again our fellow-travelers did not know of it. Compare these dates with your events. Gold was brought from Ulan Davan. Once again the gale. Raya, who is already thirteeen years old, has never yet heard of Christ. Thus do the fundamental teachings vanish out of life.

. . . . .

July twenty-fourth. This is not only our day, but also the day of the completion of our Suburgan. Mongols help in the erection of it and bring the treasure—norbu-rinpoche—tiny stones and seeds to put into the chalice of the Suburgan.

Within is also laid the Ak-dorje and the Maitreya Sanga.
Lai—in Hindu means red.

. . . . .

The end of July: "I am going joyously into the battle."
Lapis exilis—the wandering stone. Yesterday the Buriats
foretold something impending. Precisely, "I am sending
the best currents for the happy decision of the works."
We decide to start through Tsaidam to Tibet on August
19th. We shall dare to cross dangerous Tsaidam in a new
direction.

. . . . .

Toward evening on the twenty-eighth N. V. came galloping along with his sword and the ring. We had hardly
time to hear him, when, down the canyon, in place of the
peaceful stream, swept a devastating torrent. This was the
result of the strange night-tumult in the mountains. The
torrent swept away the kitchen, the dining tent, George's
tent. Much was destroyed and many Mongol yurtas were
swept away. We walked up to our waist in water. Many
irreplaceable things were destroyed. N. V. told us that on
the eve of his departure, for some inexplicable reason, the
tankas sent by us to Y. were destroyed by fire. It is significant! Correlate!

. . . . .

We complete the Suburgan. The Elder Lama of Tsaidam
comes to consecrate it. Prince Kurlik Beise sends envoys;
he offers his caravan. It is significant because the Prince
usually molests travelers.

. . . . .

On August fifth—something remarkable! We were in
our camp in the Kukunor district not far from the Humboldt Chain. In the morning about half-past nine some
of our caravaneers noticed a remarkably big black eagle
flying above us. Seven of us began to watch this unusual
bird. At this same moment another of our caravaneers
remarked, "There is something far above the bird." And

he shouted in his astonishment. We all saw, in a direction from north to south, something big and shiny reflecting the sun, like a huge oval moving at great speed. Crossing our camp this thing changed in its direction from south to southwest. And we saw how it disappeared in the intense blue sky. We even had time to take our field glasses and saw quite distinctly an oval form with shiny surface, one side of which was brilliant from the sun.

. . . . .

On August seventh the Suburgan was consecrated. Gegen of Tsaidam arrived; about thirty Mongolian guests also came. We held the service to the Suburgan. They promised to guard the Suburgan of Shambhala. If only the Dungans would not destroy it!

There was revolt among our Buriats. They went to the Chinese with a false report about us. Instead of the rebellious Buriats we took three Torguts with us. They are good shots.

. . . . .

Following the false report of the Buriats, the Chinese soldiers, with an official of the Sining Amban, arrived. They examined our passports. Of course, again extortion. We paid the Chinese. The Mongols are indignant about this incident.

. . . . .

Unexpected guests come swiftly from out the desert. Toward evening a mysterious stranger, in a beautiful gold embroidered Mongol garb, came galloping along. Who was he? Hurriedly he entered the tent. Without naming himself he said that he was our friend, that he must warn us concerning an attack prepared against us on the border of Tibet. He warned us of the need of increasing our guards and our reconnoitering troops. Thus he spoke and galloped away. Who was he? Our lamas say: "He is either a thief or a robber or a collector for the monastery." No one liked the luxurious garments of the stranger. But he was a friend. He desired to help. Again an operatic episode.

. . . . .

On August nineteenth we started through Tsaidam to Tibet. A memorable night in Tsaidam—when we crossed the salt marshes. We could not stop but had to go a hundred and twenty miles without a halt. In the darkness of night the road is invisible and yet we crossed the most dangerous parts during the night without realizing it. On either side of the narrow path are bottomless pits. If the horse trips it is impossible to extricate him. One false step and all is finished. It was difficult but at last Tsaidam was crossed in a new and in the shortest direction. There are many errors on the maps.

. . . . .

When we passed Tsaidam, which is by no means as the maps indicate it, one unconsciously looked toward the west. There glowed the endless pink sands. We recalled that between Tsaidam and Kunlun the maps show a complete desert area. Of course, this entire space is unexplored. Whereas, in the folds of these hills there may be much which is remarkable. In this direction, from the regions of Khotan and Scherschen the ancient Buddhist monasteries might have spread. There may be interesting hermitages and monumental caves. But even the Mongols speak little of these regions. They speak of caravans lost in the sands, of buried cities—but all this is legendary.

. . . . .

The gesture of greeting of the Tsaidam Mongols is remarkable. They uplift their arms as though paying their reverence to the sun. It is so rhythmical and beautiful! It reminded me of the beautiful gesture of the Hindu Brahmins that I saw in Benares during the hour of morning prayer. In the same way I recall the beautiful gesture of the Mussulmans when they are paying homage to the old Mazars (tombs).

. . . . .

They talk about some foreigners who were in Taiginer and bought old things. Again they say that foreigners came and took away "Burkhans" from Tun huang. Evidently something took place at the celebrated cave temples. There is too persistent talk about it in different districts. Not a few things were stolen for the Museums of Europe—but they talk of these especial "burkhans" from Kashgar, from Urumchi to the very borders of the Tibet.

. . . . .

Half-devoured corpses of men and horses are beside the road. The traces of the recent battle of the Mongols and the Goloks are seen here. The Mongols are removing their yurtas and hurrying under the protection of Prince Kurlik Beise. Soon we approach the Naiji Pass, the point of which our unknown well-wisher warned us. All seems quiet but near the camp we find a fresh camp-fire and a lost long-pipe. The place has been recently inhabited.

. . . . .

In the morning we proceed as usual. In the front, George and P. K. Then all of us on horseback—we and the lamas. Behind at a distance the Torguts with the mules and further behind, the caravan with camels, guarded by Golubin, Konchok and Tsering. In front of us is a canyon between two hills. Elena Ivanovna, always sensitive, hears the distant barking of dogs. Suddenly across the canyon among the hills, armed riders begin to leap, hiding between the hills. Zangin Lama shouts out "arangan," meaning robbers. I give the order to turn back so that we can occupy the peak of the hill and be closer to the Torguts. On the peak, instead of being the attacked we become the aggressors and take command of the situation. The troop of Panagis stops, is evidently surprised at our unexpected maneuver. The Colonel with Oschir the Torgut and the

Buryat Buchaieff gallop toward them with threatening shouts. The rest of us, ready for battle, keep watch. The Panagis, unexpectedly caught, become confused and as a sign of submission lower their arms. One of them holds a long spear—the sign that war is declared. We wanted to buy the spear—but the Panagis said, "We cannot sell it. It is our friend." The chief thing is always to act boldly!

. . . . .

The next day another attack was prepared but a terrific snowstorm, mingled with thunder, dispersed the superstitious Panagis. And so we crossed Naiji. We admired the tremendous herds of wild yaks. One of them was killed by the Torguts. Before us was the snow ridge, Angar Dakchin, or Marco Polo. How strange to give European names to the mountains and lakes which have their own names from ancient times. Toward night, the Mongolian lama died of hemorrhage. It is sad.

. . . . .

Behind Angar Dakchin is Kokushili. The same Kokushi which is known to the Old Believers on Altai— the seekers for Belovodye. Not far from here also are the sacred borders. We pass the rivers successfully. They cannot be crossed on horseback in spring or in the summer. But now, in the fall the water is not higher than the reins of the horses. Only two horses sank. Even the Blue River with its swift current was not an obstacle.

. . . . .

We look for the Tibetan outposts. Why are they not here? Something glows white in the distance. . . . Snow— but there is no snow around here. Is it a tent? But this is something truly superb. It is a gigantic geyser of glauber salt. A snowy mass—glistening in the sun—verily, a sacred boundary.

PART XII

TIBET

(1927-1928)

October 6th

L IKE black spiders with long legs are hidden the black tents of the Tibetans, stretched upon the longest ropes. The border troops take our passport and suggest that we camp for two days, until they bring the answer of General Horchichab, that is the chief ruler of the Province, Hor, and the chief commander of the northern front. What flowery titles!

We camp in the middle of a marshy plain overgrown with thin, prickly weeds. On the horizon is the lake and dead mountains. I call them dead because this is a veritable cemetery. Long ago, these were great mountains, perhaps rivals of Everest; now they are eroded and crumbled into small stones. The deep valleys became filled, forming a hill of fifteen thousand feet, open to the brutal winds. Before reaching the most significant sites, before the heavenly Himalayas, one falls into horrible marshes. The horses are slipping and stumbling among the ugly clumps. There is not a bird, not an animal.

. . . . .

George slumps in his saddle and almost falls off his horse. We rush to him and take him off. He has almost no heart beat. Two strong doses of digitalis are administered. We rub his hands. He recovers.

Further ahead Elena Ivanovana begins to feel badly. From the rear guard we are notified that Lama Malonof fell off his horse and lies unconscious on the road. The doctor hurries to him. Thus inhospitably does Tibet greet us.

. . . . .

A multi-colored banner with a bent staff. Music—drums and bagpipes. The firing of a salute. Deep in the tent is the little figure of the General in a vivid yellow khalat. On his round Chinese cap is a crosslike Ak-dorje of rubies. He makes an ingratiating speech and again requests us to stay in his camp, if only for two days. Then the General accompanies us into our camp with banners and music and the motley crowd forming his suite.

. . . . .

The impression from our visit to Kap-shö-pa is one of insignificance. The banner has become bent; his sword hangs like a piece of futile theatrical property; under the precious stones, dirt is accumulated. This is old Chinese stuff which the Chinese themselves have rejected. It is no longer fit for life and has lost all its former decorativeness, because the quality of the handiwork is gone, as well as the finesse of the art. One perceives only mediocrity and ugliness. Probably the General thought that the impression from his yellow khalat would be very great. But even his closest bodyguard was ragged and adorned with buttons from three armies—none of these Tibetan; and in the place where a foreign button was lacking, a safety pin was stuck. The rifles were of doubtful fitness, but there were plenty of musicians.

Again drums and salutes from the guns. The General, with all this motley crowd, accompanies us to our tent. At the same time he is curious to examine our things, proclaiming that "the hands of small people must not touch the belongings of great people."

. . . . .

We are told that the General came to settle some uprising among the Horpa. At the same time he placed a ban on the hunting of the musk deer. It is quite incomprehensible why one is allowed to kill domestic sheep and yaks, when wolves and foxes and everything savage are protected. But the population holds to a different opinion and secretly hunts kulans.

. . . . .

Our Tibetan, Chimpa, is dying. He was useful to us during the encounter with the Panagis and when the Mongols decided to desert us after Naiji. But when Chimpa reached Tibet he asserted his real nature and at the crossing to the camp of the General he left us, took our five camels, our tent and severed relations. This was his gratitude for all our care during his sickness and for our priceless medicines!

Evidently even a Tibetan cannot withstand the local climate. This is the third death in our caravan. The Mongolian lama died from pneumonia. The lama from Kharchin died because of the altitude. Did not the bears sense the presence of a dead body when they crept closer to the camp the night of his death? And they did not have to wait long. By morning his corpse was left to them.

. . . . .

The General prepares to depart for Kham. Finally he accepts our gift and disappears. And the caressing two days are transformed into a cruel five months of encampment in summer tents, in a frost of sixty Celsius, under whirlwinds and gales, at a height of fifteen thousand feet. A major and some ragamuffin soldiers are stationed with us. We are forbidden to speak to the passing caravans. We are forbidden to buy food from the population. The caravan slowly perishes. Every day there are new corpses near the tents, and packs of wild dogs noisily divide their new repast. Of 104 caravan animals, ninety perish. Five men die—three Mongolian lamas and two Tibetans. Malonoff's body becomes swollen from an attack of his heart and finally he also dies. The wife of the major who was stationed with us gets sick of pneumonia and dies.

Gryphons and eagles fight with packs of dogs over the prey. My letter to the Dalai Lama is found torn on the road. The letters to Colonel Bailey, British Resident of Sikhim, and to the Consul General of the United States in Calcutta are seized. We are forbidden to return or to move on. In spite of George's knowledge of the Tibetan language we can only study Tibetan life in its starkness; but we cannot help our condition. They tell us that the telegraph between Lhasa and India is destroyed because now Tibet does not need communication with the "Pellings." They refuse to take into consideration the doctor's certificate about our illness. They say that our passport was lost on the road although witnesses deny this invention.

Instead of the General's promised permission to proceed we remain on a plain exposed to the winds. The Tibetans tell us that the General's messenger to Lhasa disappeared on the road. Instead of helping, the Major prevents us from buying food in the neighboring villages. He forbids communication with the passing caravans and is without any feeling of compunction in the exchange of Chinese dollars. The doctor is very pessimistic and prophesies fatal illness because of the increasing frost. N. V. offers to go in disguise to India, but without knowledge of the language and with his noticeable height, this would end disastrously.

．　．　．　．　．

The entire population of black Horpa, like small Niebelungen, seem full of unrest. They sleep in a seated posture. They eat raw meat. They are only covered with half-rags—black from the smoke of the fire—and skins. They whisper, "The entire district is now covered with snows such as never before. Our yaks and sheep will perish. We shall not have Tsampa (barley). Our children will die and we shall die. And all this misfortune is because our government treats great travelers in such an inhuman way."

The lamas predict that everything will turn out well, and that the messenger with a propitious answer is already coming, that tomorrow he will arrive. But the days pass. The frost and gale increase. On the white plain no one is seen. The last horses and camels are falling. During the night the shivering animals come close to the tents, pulling the ropes as if they are knocking. And at dawn, we find them dead. And our men, huddled in sheepskins, pull them a few steps away from the camp. Otherwise the dangerous wild dogs and gryphons, the grave diggers, would give us no rest. One pack of dogs—about fifteen—has already attacked me. Every day our fire-arms are at hand. The Major wants to buy our arms, but in this country one must guard one's arms.

· · · · ·

Again frost and gales. Finally there is an uprising followed by the secession of our Buryat lamas. They thought that by slander against us they would improve their position. They were completely unable to obtain work.

And so each day goes by amidst the frozen plain with the dull outlines of the dead mountains. Then we make a short move from Chunargen to Sharugen in the vicinity of the Bon-po monastery. Only about two hours of marching and again the same detention. We requested permission to visit General Kap-shö-pa in his encampment at Kham. We were told: "Me, me, me," which means, "No." We asked to be permitted to pass through Eastern Tibet again. Again, "Me, me, me." Everything is "Me, me, me." At the same time the General writes us letters about the "drops of clemency which are dripping from the resplendent fingers of the Dalai Lama." But weeks go by. And finally the governors of Nagchu themselves come.

It is quite unprecedented that both governors should at once leave their province and come personally. They come with black eye glasses, in woolly fur caps. They are noisy. They are astonished that we gave importance to the Tibetan passport and altogether conduct themselves unreasonably. One of them is a lama, rumored to have strangled the Amban of Sining. The other, a sly old Manchurian official. We endure all with great patience. Now they will transport us to Nagchu but it will be a continuation of the same detention. They will demand gifts. But somehow, somewhere, we shall move, though perhaps in the most roundabout way. Some of us hope that our detention will not exceed one hundred days, but it will be more correct to assume 150 days and several additional days for delays on the road. Thus we must count the entire detention as lasting half a year. Of course during this time the Tibetans have afforded us an unusual opportunity to become acquainted with their life, customs and ethics. Without communications with governors, generals, dzong pons, officers, elders and lamas, we would not have any assurance about the reality of Tibet.

. . . . .

The frost at dawn is cruel. As usual, below 70 degrees Celsius. In the morning the doctor's cognac is frozen. One can imagine what a frost it is, when the strong wine becomes frozen. The doctor is pessimistic as before and expects danger. The health of N. V. and P. K. is bad. Death is predicted for Ochir. Ludmilla and Raya—or as Tibetans call them, Milla and Raiya—keep well.

. . . . .

What tiresome hills are between Chunargan and Nagchu. The mountains have long since crumbled and now the heaps of pebbles and stones are eroding. There is not a bush nor a tree; only high mounds with thorny prickly grass distasteful to the horses. We were told that on reaching Central Tibet we would be astonished by the change of nature. But others smile and say that up to the very Himalayas we shall go through a cemetery of crumbled mountains. Poor Hor-pa. Their teeth are falling out from scurvy. The muscles are lax. They have less strength than thirteen-year-old Raya. Of course lean raw meat and a pinch of dirty *tsampa* do not make for health. And how immeasurable is their suspicion of each other! They do not trust; they are afraid; they constantly anticipate all sort of misfortune. Mongols, in spite of the sly Dunganese officials, are veritable freemen compared with Tibetans.

· · · · ·

Everywhere are the signs of the cross. The old Mongolian coins of Nestorian khans have a cross, and over an ancient Buddhist monastery near Peking is a cross. On the seat of the saddle is also a cross and the reins are also fitted out with a cross. Even upon the stones of Ladak and Sinkiang are crosses. Nestorians and Manicheans passed broadly through Asia. On the frescoes of the monasteries are crosses. In the design of the kaftan, on the beads, on the necklaces, on the amulets—always the very same cross: Not the swastika with the streams of fire, but of equal arms, the eternal symbol of life. On the Chinese hats of Tibetan generals glows a ruby, crosslike *dorje.* The steed of happiness carries its sign. All bronze fibulae, probably from the tombs, are formed of a cross in a circle.

· · · · ·

Everywhere are the same signs of Chintamani. The little pillars of the houses and the clay-beaten walls are marked by this thrice-powerful image. The mules, the wrought silver vessels, the military banners, the prayer banners, the wood-cut on the page of a book are strengthened by the symbol of power.

Compare the present tale with its original source: Now one says: "And great hunger descended upon earth and people perished and could not longer endure. Then the Blessed Bodhisattvas sent a shower of rice. There was such excess of food that not only were all the people fully sustained but they also brought mountains of rice and erected temples and chortens of it. The temples were of such dimensions that it took several years to walk around them, and one chief chorten could only be encircled in several days. This place exists upon an island where the true teaching of the Blessed One formerly flourished."

One must understand it thus: Great spiritual hunger descended upon earth. And people could no longer exist in such dreadful conditions. Then the Great Teacher sent a true shower of spiritual food. Humanity which was exalted by this benediction erected great monuments of spiritual achievements. The measurements of these achievements are unencompassable. The teaching of Shambhala exists in a fortified place. And its power will soon become manifest.

. . . . .

The monasteries of Bon-po of the Black faith, hostile to Buddha, have a curious interest. In the Black Faith, which as a Black Mass exactly inverts the ritual of the Buddhist faith, one sees only denial of Buddha, and denunciation of Buddha and of all Buddhists as enemies. If the Buddhists encircle the altars from left to right, the Bon-po takes the opposite direction. If the Swastika of the Buddhist turns in the direction of the sun, that of the Bon-po must be turned in the opposite direction. They have invented their own saints and special sacred books. They have invented a special protector who replaces Buddha; and if you study the biography of this legendary protector you will be astonished to find the same details and events as in the life of Buddha; he is also supposed to be of royal family. The Bon-po do not allow Buddhists to enter their temples, and acknowledge neither the Tashi Lama nor the Dalai Lama. For them the Dalai Lama is only a civil ruler collecting taxes.

They are very friendly with foreigners because they believe that foreigners have nothing to do with Buddhism. In the beginning they greeted us heartily and proposed that we study their books and visit their temples, where we saw many inverted Buddhist symbols. But when they understood that we were in sympathy with Buddhism, their attitude entirely changed. You can understand our astonishment in finding such things in a so-called Buddhist country. As I said, they are numerous and well-to-do

and are very self-assertive. It is not a secret sect and Tibetans told us that now Bon-po is again increasing. Not only
have these people an invented Buddha but they have mysterious deities of Swastika.

This recalls the prehistoric times, the primitive religion of fire-worship of the Druids which has here been
corrupted into the incomprehensibly strange deities of
Swastika. Instead of the sacred word, Aum, they use the
word "A." In the old occult teaching the same expression,
"A," is used for Materia Matrix. It would be interesting to
study the origins of Bon-po, as perhaps something of the
Druid and old fire-worship would be found.

· · · · ·

One cannot believe any statement. All around us is
death. For five months on the main road to China and
Mongolia only three caravans passed. The Tibetan nomads
whisper about the difficult times for Lhasa. Of course
under such conditions the country cannot exist. Finally
the governors of Nagchu become satisfied with the gifts,
and after receiving the information that our money is
exhausted, decide to send us out by a roundabout way
through Chang-thang to Namru Dzong, Shentsu Dzong,
through passes of twenty thousand six hundred feet not
marked on maps, to Saga-Dzong, across the Brahmaputra, to Tingri-Dzong, Shekar-Dzong, Kampa-Dzong and
through Sepo-la to Sikhim. Evidently they have decided to
show us all religions of Tibet so that no doubts should be
left in our mind about this country. It is not an easy way.
Nobody has yet crossed from Ulan Bator Khoto to Sikhim.

· · · · ·

It is inexplicable why the Dzong-pons, officials of
Tibetan Dzongs (fortresses), show themselves from the
most ugly side. The people tell dark tales.

The ruins of old Tibet are interesting: These ancient
towers and walls were molded by an aspiring type of people. Their builders knew about Gessar Khan and about

the Ruler of Shambhala. Here also were the Ashrams of the great Mahatmas. But now there is nothing left of this.

.   .   .   .   .

I recall the stones of the "Tchud"—tombs on Altai. There passed the Goths who penetrated all Europe with their influence. And here in the Trans-Himalayas we meet the very same ancient tombs. We find places of ancient shrines which carry one's thoughts to the sun-cults of the Druids. The swords of the northern inhabitants of the Trans-Himalayas might have been taken out of the Goth graves on the South Russian steppes. The fibulae of Gothic burials—do they not remind you of the buckles of Tibetan tribes. And why was the site of Lhasa some time ago called Gotha according to missionary chronicles? And whence the name of the tribe Gotl? Whence, where and how did the forefathers of the Goths migrate, driven out by glaciers and by the severe moraines? In the crystallized daily life of the northern Tibetans are there not found the ancient traits of their departed brothers? It is astonishing; one Hor-pa resembles Moliere. Another would fit the type of d'Artagnan. The third resembles an Italian corsair. The fourth, with long strands of hair, is a distortion of a portrait of Hals or Palamedes; and that black and somber one, with an aquiline nose, is he not the executioner of Philip the Second?

And finally in the district of Doring (meaning the Long Stone) we found a real field of menhirs such as in Karnak. During the two marches which followed we found three more small groups of menhirs. For me it was a great joy to see this indubitable sign of Druidic antiquity.

.   .   .   .   .

"Ki-hoho" rings out the call from the camp of Goloks. "Hoihe" answers our camp. And so the whole night the enemies are mutually warned about the incessant vigilance of our camp. But of course the Goloks are already informed about our arms and have taken well into consideration the extent of our military capacity. The verdict was in our favor, and today we shall see the friendly faces of the dangerous nomads.

. . . . .

The Black Faith of Bon-po is so in keeping with the black tents. Upon long ropes, like deadly spiders, the tents gleam black in a formless mass. Next to them are black spots: refuse or corpses. The dryness of the air lessens the ill smell of decomposition. The piercing wind scatters the dry bones. We recall the widely announced safe-passage of the Donyer of Urga. How remarkably different is Tibet at a distance. They talk and whisper about uprisings. . . .

. . . . .

At each encampment the same thing happens: If we camp in the usual village, there is no trouble in procuring animals. If the Elder lives in the village, then one may be sure of unpleasant discussions; and if one gets into a dzong or monastery he should be prepared for a delay. Nothing is prepared, in spite of several *da-yig* letters, which were sent long since. It appears that the *da-yigs* were not received; that by mistake they were sent in another direction. It appears that villages where there are animals are far off, and it will take several days to gather yaks and horses. Finally it appears that as usual the peasants simply do not listen to Dzong-pon and refuse to fulfill his order. Sometimes the Dzong-pon suggests that we conduct all negotiations directly with the peasants and write our own letter to the villages with our own seal. And the seal must be red. Otherwise we will have to stay near the Dzong for many days. It sometimes also happens that one Elder suggests to us to arrest another unruly one. He himself leads us to the latter's camp and advises us to bind him and deliver him to Lhasa. Our Torguts have sometimes bound the hands of the Elder tightly behind his back; then his relations come with tongues sticking out and agree to fulfill the order of the Dalai Lama. Or it may happen that the governor suggests to us to arrest the local Major and to take him bound to Lhasa. At such a possible turn of affairs the Major lowers his tone and becomes more civil.

. . . . .

Before Saga-dzong are two unexpected passes. One is shown on the maps; but the other, a larger one of more than twenty thousand feet, is not indicated. This road is shown on the maps only by a faint outline. Evidently no one ever traversed it. There is the other customary southern road. But the Tibetan government sends us through this unexplored northern path.

On the way the Elders refuse to give us animals and again, instead of the passport of the governors, they ask us to send a letter with our seal everywhere. For our wax seal makes a greater impression.

From the crest of the pass a powerful white chain of snowy giants has appeared. This is already Nepal and the long-awaited Himalayas, on the other side of the Brahmaputra.

Saga-dzong is also a small impoverished village. They eat the corpses of animals and they mix tiny pebbles with the barley. The mendangs are defiled by fallen dogs and all sorts of refuse.

. . . . .

The camp is full of excitement. We are approaching the Brahmaputra, the very one which has its source in the sacred Manasaravar, Lake of the Great Nagi. There is where the wise Rig-vedas originated; there one is near the sacred Kailas; there, pilgrims go, realizing on what a noble highway lie these sites. Already files of pilgrims are encountered; they are gloomy and ragged, and carry spears.

Amidst rocks and sand, lilac and purple, lies the Brahmaputra. In May the water is not yet completely risen. The water line on the banks shows to what extent the river rises in June with the snow thaw and rains. There is still greater reverence for the Brahmaputra than for the Blue

River. The Blue Yangtse-Kyang is the longest river in the world but the Brahmaputra, son of Brahma, is enveloped by a rich frame-work of legends. It links the sacred bed of the Ganges with the Himalayas; for Manasaravar is close to Sutlej and the source of the Great Indus. There also was born Aryavarta.

. . . . .

A Mongolian lama says: "There lived a remarkably versed and scientific Geshe. But he always walked in the most modest garment. Once the Geshe went to visit his teacher, the former abbot of a big Labrang. The vain courtiers of the abbot saw the humble visitor and sent him away. And again came the Geshe and again he was evicted. Then the Geshe went to a merchant in a bazaar and asked him to lend him a rich garment and the Geshe put into his girdle several stones which looked like nuggets of Chinese silver. And in this way he was at once permitted to see his teacher. The Geshe entered, took off his rich garment, took from out the girdle the stones, and put them all together in a corner. Then he bowed to the stones and the garment; and only after did he bow to his teacher.

The other asked, "Am I not your teacher? If so, why do you bow first to the stones and the garment?"

"It is true," answered the Geshe that you are my teacher, "but without these things I could not reach you, and therefore I bow to that which brought me to my reverenced master."

. . . . .

Near the Brahmaputra are five monasteries leaning against the rocks of Chatu-gompa. Two of them are of the Red Sect, and three of Bon-po of the Black Faith. The monasteries of the Black Faith look far newer and cleaner than those of the Red Sect. Out of the windows of a big Dukang or Red Monastery, straw sticks out; several lamas of hopelessly dilapidated appearance sadly stroll about.

The Black Believers, on learning that we sympathize with Buddhism, ask us not even to approach their monasteries.

. . . . .

With astonishment we look at the *sho*, the only copper coin of Tibet in circulation. We saw neither silver nor gold in the *dzongs* nor in popular use. Although the minting of the small copper coins is poor, yet how grandiose is the inscription: "The government is victorious in all directions." It is astonishing that the half-sho and the quarter-sho are bigger than the *sho* itself.

. . . . .

Now comes our crossing through the Brahmaputra near the monastery Schitu. There is a small boat, a ferry, with a carved horse on the prow. It is especially difficult to load the camels. The current is pretty swift.

. . . . .

Although Tingri-dzong is regarded as a strong fortress it has a pitiful toy-like aspect, which perhaps had importance previous to the invention of gunpowder. There is no monastery but only suburgans of the Red Sects with fearful images and stripes as signs of their allegiance to the Red Sect. We recall the same fearful images on Tantrik tankas. What can one not see upon them? Magic swords, flayed human skins, fearful images with projecting teeth, and inverted triangles. The entire synthesis of Black Magic.

. . . . .

Near Tingri-dzong Mount Everest looms up in all its glimmering beauty.

. . . . .

We meet people who knew Sven Hedin. They praise him and regret that he could not speak Tibetan. They have heard here about Filchner. Some legends are already invented to the effect that he left three boys on the Blue River, as well as a mouse, a weasel and prairie dog. How does this originate? Of course, had we not known the language our entire work would have been immensely difficult. It is fortunate that George's knowledge of the language is considered by the Tibetans second only to Sir Charles Bell. The latter was called "the officer of peace," because of the way he conducted his negotiations.

．　．　．　．　．

Here is the old monastery Chung-tu, which belongs to the royal monastery Saskya. Evidently much has transpired within its ancient walls. Here is an umbrella above a large suburgan—the sign of former royal distinction. And here are crumbled Chinese walls, memories of conquered Tibet. Here is a long file of ancient Suburgans—remembrances of the time of a peaceful age. Here are amassed old and new by-ways and structures.

．　．　．　．　．

Another ancient place: Shekar-dzong. When the Tibetans were bold eagles, they were not afraid of soaring up to the steep rocks to mount their stronghold-sanctuaries upon the sharp promontories. There is a wealth of decoration on towers, passages and temples. But now Tibetans have descended to the valley. The chieftains are afraid to live in the castles and huddle below. Only from afar are the old dzongs of Tibet attractive. The prices for products are high to the point of absurdity. A sack of twenty-nine pounds of poor grain, of which five pounds are stones, costs eleven *norsangs* which is about nine rupees in the dzongs. A little piece of barley sugar is about four or five rupees. A horse, for two days' travel, eight rupees; and a pack-yak, four rupees.

Our marches are not of even length. Either they are very short, not exceeding four hours on horseback. Or, suddenly, they last for nine hours almost at a trot. We hasten toward Kampa-dzong, the last dzong before the border of Sikhim. But where is the castle? For a long time we fail to recognize the bulky mass on the distant rock as a castle. Really this structure is placed so high that it merges into the rock. Dzong pen, the chief of the castle, is a trifle more friendly than the others.

Far higher than the dzong on the opposite rocks is a monastery, in which now only eight lamas remain. But in this very monastery is the courtyard mentioned in the "Letters of the Mahatmas." There was the school mentioned by the Mahatmas, but now this school does not exist. But the old people still remember that here was a "religious school." And they remember the "tall Azaras" from India.

· · · · ·

The last crossing—Sepo La. This pass is easier than the others. We pass the turquoise lake, where the river Lachen has its source. The torrents begin as modest streams which, after two days of travel, seethe and become impassable without a bridge. Here is the first aroma of the healing Balu, and the first low cedars. Before us are whole forests of rhododendrons in bloom.

· · · · ·

Zoji La, Khardong La, Karaul Devan, Sasser Pass, Dabsang Pass, Karakorum Pass, Suget Pass, Sanju Pass, Urtu Kashkariin Daban, Ulan Daban, Chahariin Daban, Khentu Pass, Naiji La, Kukushili Pass, Dungbudra Pass, Tang La, Kamrong La, Tasang La, Lamsi Pass, Naptra La, Tamaker Pass, Shentsa Pass, Laptse nagri Pass, Tsag La, Lam ling Pass, Pong chen La, Dong La, Sang mo La, Kyegong La, Tsug chung La, Gya La, Urang La, Sharu La, Galung La, Sepo La; these are the thirty-five passes, each from fourteen thousand to twenty-one thousand feet high, which are crossed.

· · · · ·

Of all our camels, two crossed the Himalayas. One is from Bulugun (northern Mongolia), the other from Tsaidam. They will be the first to reach Gangtok, the capital of Sikhim. We will present them to the Maharajah of Sikhim. Along the entire way from Nagchu to Gangtok the camels attract crowds of curious onlookers because these "animals" have never been seen here. From Lhasa to Calcutta, camels are not known. In Thangu, a house already awaited us: a dak-bungalow and even forgotten magazines of 1927. For more than a year we existed entirely without news of the outer world.

. . . . .

The fairy tale of the waterfalls! A whole symphony is in the patterned streams. For several days we descend. Nearby we pass all species of the vegetable world. Finally, palms appear and near the river pass two leopards, vividly yellow with thick warm black spots. They appear, greet us cordially and go away. All already is seen: the black-and-white bears of Chang-thang, antelopes and argali, the stone-like rams with curved horns; finally the well-decked leopards.

. . . . .

A modest Finnish mission is in La-chen. Kind Miss Kronquist, self-exiled in solitude among the rocks, relates tales about the avalanches which threaten all Sikhim. Is it possible that on the southern side of the Himalayas continues the same deadening process which has crumbled the peaks of Chang-thang? Inspired by the noise of the current of Lachen which sprang up and became stronger under our very eyes, we recall Imatra and Finland and the sympathetic Relander and Aksel Gallen-Kallela. Here are the same blue distances as in Finland.

. . . . .

We make our final calculations regarding the caravan. The American equipment withstood all trials. The Belber trunks crossed from America for four years through entire Asia, through all fordings and passes without any damage. The tents from Abercrombie and Fitch also withstood all gales.

. . . . .

The remaining part of the way to Gangtok was easy. The hospitable house of the British Resident, Colonel Bailey, greets us. We tell about our trip. The letters to America are sent off. We are given a trustworthy *sardar* to Darjeeling. We shall make the entire way from Gangtok in one day. But we will have to change automobiles three times, because on the Tista the bridge was recently washed away and it is necessary to change. It means three automobiles and ten miles on horseback in one day—a steep ascent from Tista through Peshok.

. . . . .

It is necessary to collect and compile all the expedition material. This may take a long time. George, the Doctor, N. V., and P. K. are also preparing their notes. Our fellow-travelers will quickly scatter—one to China, one to Italy, one to Australia. Everywhere they will recall the inexpressible beauty of the Himalayas. Our way led from the Himalayas, and back to them. Majestic is Karakorum and the icy kingdom of Sasser. Beautiful is Kunlun. Fantastic is T'ian Shan—celestial mountains. Broad in sweep is Altai. Decorative is Nan shang. Austere is Angar Dakchin. But all these are only the preface to the unutterable grandeur of the Himalayas.

. . . . .

In the Himalayas the great Vedanta was crystallized. In the Himalayas Buddha became exalted in spirit. The very air of the Himalayas is penetrated with spiritual tension— the true Maitreya Sanga.

. . . . .

Our friend in Sikhim, the lama, tells us that during the winter he had heard that large detachments of cavalry were standing before Nagchu; such information caused a great deal of anxiety. This proved to be only one of the rumors current about ourselves. During these years rumor made me a "French and American King," "Commander of a Russian Corps," and "King of all Buddhists." I succeeded in dying twice. I succeeded in being simultaneously in Siberia, America and Tibet. According to the words of Mongols of Tsaidam I carried on a war with the Amban of Sining. And according to the words of the Taotai of Khotan I brought a small cannon which would, in ten minutes, destroy entire Khotan and its one hundred thousand inhabitants. We became accustomed to all this and now are no longer astonished by "authentic" rumors. The Mongols firmly remember the "Ameri Khan": Thus the American has been visualized as a kind of warrior. Fairy tales about ourselves from Lhasa were related to us, in which we could only identify ourselves with difficulty.

. . . . .

It is wondrous and strange to pass through the same places where the Mahatmas passed. Here was the school founded by Them. Two days' travel from Saga-dzong there was one of the Ashrams—not far from the Brahmaputra. Here the Mahatma stopped, hastening on an undeferrable mission. And here stood the modest blue tent. Now when Europe argues about the existence of the Mahatmas, when the Hindus are significantly silent about Them, many people in the expanses of Asia not only know the Mahatmas, not only have seen Them, but know many actual evidences of Their deeds and appearances. Always awaited, the Mahatmas unexpectedly created in the spaces of Asia a great special existence. When it was necessary, They manifested themselves. And when necessary, They passed unnoticeably as ordinary travelers. They do not write Their Names upon the stones, but the hearts of those who know, guard These Names, stronger than the rocks. Why suspect a fairy tale, imagination, invention, when in living forms the knowledge of the Mahatmas is impressed?

In haste, moved by idle curiosity, you will not understand even a simple chemical experiment. Will those, who in futile conversation discuss the question of Mahatmas, achieve anything? Will their empty curiosity be satisfied?

How many people there are who would love to receive a letter from the Mahatmas! But would it change their lives? It would provide a moment of astonishment and confusion and then again everything would return to the old routine, leaving no trace.

Often we are astonished why people who know the Mahatmas are so widely different in their social positions. But why was Boehme a shoemaker? Are the dimensions of consciousness measured only by outward distinctions? The works of the Mahatmas and their instructions to the pupils, are related in a literature which is not nearly as limited as it seems to those who do not know it.

. . . . .

The average scientist talks about Mahatmas as pure illusion. These are the scientists who have never seen Mahatmas. But Sir William Crooks or Sir Oliver Lodge would not speak so. Vivekananda, who was always upholding the rationalism of observation, knew Mahatmas. Many Hindus know Them. But they safeguard Their Names to such an extent that they are even ready to deny Their existence in order not to betray, not to reveal.

Not to betray! What a charm is in this understanding of the Guru in the steps of ascent.

But many are knocking at the doors of the great science. Often they do not acknowledge it, even are angered if someone asks them about it. How many of the younger generation want sincerely to start correspondence with a Guru! They try to find a real teacher. Everybody knocks in his own way. And how many of them find disillusionment because they knock at the wrong door, or they lacked sufficient energy and necessary determination to receive a true answer.

"What laboratory could analyze those who approach the technical methods of knowledge?" Yes, verily, it must be a laboratory where labor and perseverance and fearlessness are the keys to the gates. In a sound rationalism, in a true and fearless materialism grow the wings of spirit, the wings of consciousness. We are not to be isolated from life—not destructive, but creative—such is the teaching of the Mahatmas. They speak about the scientific foundations of existence. They direct one toward the conquest of energy. They speak of those victories of labor which shall transform life into a constant festival. Everything suggested by them is not ephemeral and illusory, but real, and pertains to the most all-embracing study of possibilities, which are suggested to us by life, without superstition, without prejudice. The true followers of the Mahatmas are not sectarians or hypocrites. On the contrary they are most vital people; they conquer in life. Not for long do they go into the mountains to purify themselves by the emanations of prana. In the darkest places of Tibet they know something about the Mahatmas, they have some recollections and legends. But for the moment their attention is directed to the prophecies about the return of the Tashi Lama in his full glory.

· · · · ·

Despite all, the straight road—Mongolia, Tsaidam, Tibet and the Himalayas—is crossed: first on the trail of Ja lama; then in Tsaidam in a new direction, then through the dzongs of Tibet to the mountain passes of the "abodes of snows."

There is something of predestination in the dying of old Tibet. The wheel of the law is turned. The mystery is gone. Tibet has none to guard; and none guards Tibet. The exclusiveness of its position as guardian of Buddhism no longer belongs to Tibet. Because Buddhism, according to the Commands of the Blessed One, becomes a universal possession. There is no need of superstition for the deep teaching. Prejudices are inimical to the search for truth.

The first image of the Blessed One was received by Tibet from Nepal and China—received only in the seventh century, more than one thousand years after the Blessed One lived and taught; received after the time when in India the brilliant literature of the followers of Buddhism had been already collected. The first image was received only after the beautiful Viharas, before which the Dukang of Tibet stand as poor younger brothers, were rising in all parts of Asia. Now, when there begins to be concern about the revival of true Buddhism, this wave passes by Tibet.

. . . . .

Let us consider the Black Magic of Tibet. Let us recall the revived corpses, the celebrated Rolang-resurrection—which is nothing but a crude form of vampirism. Let us recall the wandering spirits who kill and do all manner of evil; and they are often the spirits of lamas. Let us recall all sorts of obsessions, how, under evil influences, people are completely changed and temporarily fall into actual insanity. Let us recall evil conjurations and invocations with which the lamas arm themselves to frighten the ignorant people. Let us recall the suicidal magic daggers, dark fortune-telling, spells, were-wolves, entities which have assumed the appearance of animals; and all kinds of inventions of an evil will. First of all, such dark practices of lamas do not give very good evidence of their uprightness. Second, the sorcerers of the Coast of Malabar perform the entire black necromancy much more powerfully. They are known, feared, but no one worships them and they are not regarded as sacred personages. Malabar "miracles" antedate Tibetan magic.

. . . . .

Many authors who have written about Tibet have called it the miracle of miracles. But this title could refer only to old Tibet or is due to the misconception of those writers, who have been hypnotized by tradition. Truly, one could rightly call a school founded by Mahatmas a miracle. But for many years such a school has not existed. Now individual Tibetan lamas possess the power to produce low forms of materialization, levitation, manifestations of will, clairvoyance and clairaudience. It is the greatest test of the lamas if when they doubt about you, you demand of them,

"Ask your oracle what I am thinking at present and what intention I have." Then at once they become confused.

In the mountains some astonishing manifestations actually occur, but they have nothing to do with the lamas. We recollect the incident of the remarkable fire in our tent, which was repeated in Chang-thang. We recall the wave of heat amidst the cruel frosts. We recall many manifestations of the higher energies. Truly it is remarkable just to pass through those places where until recently there were Ashrams.

. . . . .

It would be absurd to condemn the entire population of Tibet. The lamas again may become educated. Again an enlightened government may appear. And people again may become regenerate. Much of that which appears to us as fallen "has not as yet risen."

In the teaching of the Blessed One there are practical indications about the whole routine of life. It is very easy to know and apply them. But now those who have desecrated the high teaching, must understand that their criminal actions are condemned and cannot continue.

. . . . .

Tibet bids us farewell with sad news. Our three Torguts, Ochir, Dorje and Manji, forty miles from Gyantse, were attacked by Tibetans. Two Torguts were killed and the third wounded. They were robbed of their money and possessions. Hearing this, a well-born Tibetan says, "Formerly the bandits were in the north of Tibet, but they infest the entire country now." Thus speak the good Tibetans with hopeless gestures. And how many decent Tibetans and learned lamas must suffer because of the present conditions.

There was another story that our Mongols reached Lhasa, but there they were seized and thrown into the Tibetan jail. Anyhow, our poor Torguts experienced trouble.

Another rumor: Poor Tzering, our Mongol, has suffered greatly. On the way from Nagchu to Lhasa he was robbed and now is begging in the Lhasa bazaar. Our Buriat lamas already dream of leaving Tibet. Jangin, Lama, Lama Tashi and Konchok safely reached home in Sharagolchi, because they returned back from Nagchu at once.

. . . . .

The Tibetans who have come to Sikhim say: "Now comes the year of the dragon. The past year was the year of the tiger and after that will be the year of the sheep. Will it not be easier then?"—"According to the prophecy, the Tashi Lama will not return to Tibet before three years."— Much is being rumored. We are overtaken by our lama from Kharching. He thought of remaining in Lhasa ten years but stayed only three months. With him three other learned lamas from Tashi lhunpo are traveling.

. . . . .

News from Sikhim. The monastery in Ghum is growing. Some new structures are being added. The walls are covered with frescoes. The monasteries in Kalimpong and Kurseong are also improving. Geshe Rinpoche is helping everywhere. He erects images of Maitreya. In Ghum is the same abbot. Our artist, Geshe Lhariba, from Kham, is working as before. All is friendly and good.

. . . . .

I have been asked, "How shall you speak of Tibet after your experiences?" Truly I shall praise what is full of light and shall condemn what is obscured in darkness. I shall not forget that the Tashi Lama has aroused general reverence for himself—he who is the spiritual ruler of Tibet and of whom only good is heard. Everywhere the Tibetans themselves say of their country, "The customs of Panchen Rinpoche (Tashi Lama) were far different." And they await with eagerness the fulfillment of the prophecy about his return when he will be the sole head of the Tibet and the true Teaching will again flourish. Truly, one has the feeling that if the Tashi Lama were now in Tibet again, things would be different!

Thus we distinguish two Tibets: One is the Tibet of officialdom—of those officials of whom the Tibetans themselves assert that their hearts are blacker than coal and harder than stone. These are the ones who reflect so much prejudice and violence and falsehood, who desecrate art and petrify learning with degeneracy.

But we also discern another Tibet, even though it is smaller in numbers. This is the Tibet of the few educated lamas and of an even smaller number of enlightened laymen. This is the Tibet which guards the essence of the Teaching and aspires towards enlightenment. It is the Tibet of its spiritual leaders.

It is of course not enigmatic which Tibet is closer to our consciousness—the enlightened ones we value, and may the obscured and corrupt ones disappear in their own darkness!

In letters from America, friends have expressed their regret that the actions of Tibet have urged the necessity of such strong criticisms. But Truth is not blindness; on the contrary it must be far-sighted. Moreover, a small and valuable minority may yet produce greater results than the dying, decomposed majority.

．　．　．　．　．

The Himalayas and Sikhim enclose Tibet. Nowhere is there such glimmer, such spiritual satiety as amidst these precious snows. Nowhere are there such qualifying expressions as in the speech of Sikhim—to everything is added the word "heroism." Man-heroes; women-heroes; rock-heroes; trees-heroes; waterfall-heroes; eagle-heroes. Here to Sikhim came great hermits because where could one, in two days' travel, ascend from tropical vegetation up to eternal snow. All grades of consciousness are here revealed. Friendly is Sikhim. Friendly is the Maharajah of Sikhim. Friendly is the Resident. Friendly is Laden La. And again we traverse the sacred valley of Tashi ding, as a trove of mystery and treasures. This is considered a remarkable place by all Sikhim and Bhutan. And the fine old abbot of Tashi ding is still alive but has aged and does not descend from his sacred mountain. And again the proximity of great India.

Again the Hindu sings: "How may I speak of the creator himself, if I know the incomparable, inexpressible beauty of Himalayas?"

. . . . .

It is told in the prophecies how the new era shall manifest itself: "First will begin an unprecedented war of all nations. Afterward brother shall rise against brother. Oceans of blood shall flow. And the people shall cease to understand one another. They shall forget the meaning of the word, Teacher. But just then shall the Teachers appear and in all corners of the world shall be heard the true teaching. To this word of truth shall the people be drawn, but those who are filled with darkness and ignorance shall set obstacles. As a diamond glows the light on the tower of the Lord of Shambhala. One stone on his ring is worth more than all the world's treasure. Even those who by accident help the Teachings of Shambhala will receive in return a hundredfold. Already many warriors of the teaching of truth are reincarnated. Only a few years shall elapse before every one shall hear the mighty steps of the Lord of the New era. And one can already perceive unusual manifestations and encounter unusual people. Already they open the gates of knowledge and ripened fruits are falling from the trees."

. . . . .

Lama Rinpoche knows that on the north side of Kinchenjunga, there lies a cave. Very narrow is the entrance to it, but it broadens and brings one into a whole city. The high priest knows many things, and asks not to speak of them until the appointed time. The consciousness of Geshe is profound. He possesses some clairvoyance. As if emerging from a trance he talks of the most unexpected actions and persons who are at a great distance. When we were freezing at Chang-thang and E.I. was ill, he unexpectedly said to those near him: "How difficult it is for her! How she is suffering!" So we were later told. Using the old custom of the high lamas, Geshe does not lie down to sleep but rests in a seated posture. Geshe knows about Shambhala and its complete significance. He takes care to revive the teachings.

. . . . .

One more image of Shambhala, the Mandala of Shambhala will reveal to those who know some hints of reality. On the top is Yi-dam as the sign of elemental power, and a figure of that Tashi Lama who wrote the very secret book the Path of Shambhala. In the center of the image the snow mountains form a circle. You can recognize three white borders. In the center is a seeming valley with many edifices. One can distinguish two plans, as though they were the plans of towers. On the tower is He Himself, Whose Light glows in the predestined time. Below is the powerful legion leading victorious battle. The victory of the spirit on the great field of life.

. . . . .

The new era of enlightenment is awaited. Each reaches in his own way. One nearer, one further; one beautifully, one distortedly; but all are concerned with the same predestined. It is especially striking to see such consciousness at a time when not the printed page, but sound itself—the human word—directs the lofty expectation. It is so precious to hear and to repeat. The Motherland of Gessar Khan, Ladak, knows that the time of the regeneration has come. Khotan remembers the Signs of Maitreya over the ancient Stupa. The Kalmucks in Karashar are awaiting the coming manifestation of the Chalice of Buddha. On Altai the Oirots renounce Shamanism and are singing new chants to the Awaited White Burkhan. The Messenger of the White Burkhan, Oirot, already rides throughout the world. The Mongols await the appearance of the Ruler of the World and prepare the Dukang of Shambhala. On Chang-thang they extol Gessar Khan and whisper about the hallowed borders of Shambhala. On the Brahmaputra they know about the Ashrams of Mahatmas and remember the wonderful Azaras. The Jews await the Messiah at the Bridge. The Moslems await Muntazar. In Isfahan the White Horse is already saddled. The Christians of Saint Thomas await the great Advent and wear hidden signs. The Hindus know the Kalki Avatar. And the Chinese at New Year light the fires before the image of Gessar Khan, ruler of the World. Rigden Japo, the Ruler, is fleeting over the desert, achieving his predestined path. A blind one may ask, "Is it so? Is there no exaggeration in it? Perhaps some fragments of survivals are taken as beliefs of the future."

It means that he who questions has never been in the East. If you once were upon these sites; if you traversed many thousands of miles; if you yourself have spoken to many people, then you know the reality of what is related. You shall understand why, of these sacred matters, one speaks only in the stillness of the evening, in quiet penetrating tones. Why, if someone enters, do all become silent? But if you say to them that they may continue the conversation in the presence of the guest your words will be met with a reverent bow. And it is not you who receives the silent significant bow but the Great Maitreya Himself.

GLOSSARY

Advaita: A Vedanta non-dualist sect.

Afridi: Natives of the district around Peshawar.

Ails: Villages.

Akbar: The great Mogul Emperor of India, patron of religions, arts and sciences.

Ak-Dorje: Buddhist symbol of the thunderbolt.

Akhun: A reader of the Koran—a title indicating learning.

Ak-kem: Meaning literally white water.

Aksakal: Head man, or elder.

Aksu: An oasis on the northern route of Chinese Turkestan.

Alara Kalama: A renowned sage who was for a while Buddha's teacher.

Altai: The mountainous region of Siberia—a range of mountains continuing into Mongolia.

Alus: Villages.

Amban: Manchu title for a magistrate.

Amrita: The drink of the gods—Elixir of Life.

Apocrypha: Writings having pretension to the character of the sacred scripture or received by certain sects but excluded from the canon.

Arbakeshs, Mafakeshs: Owners respectively of arbas—carts, and mafas—carriages.

Arhat: A member of the Buddhist order who attained the fourth stage of the path toward Nirvana. He is no more subject to rebirth.

Arik: Irrigation channel.

Arshin: Russian measure.

Arya Samaj: A modern theistic sect of India.

Asoka: King of the Morya Dynasty. Most zealous in spreading Buddhism. Erected thousands of shrines and sent missionaries throughout the Eastern world.

Assur: A city in Assyria, ancient seat of a library from which earliest known tablets were excavated.

Astoris: Natives of the Astor district of Kashmir.

Asvagosha: The greatest Buddhist poet; probably flourished in the first century A.D.

Atisha: Founder of a school of Buddhism in the eleventh century. True predecessor of Tsong-kha-pa, founder of the Yellow Sect, Tibet.

Aul: Mongol village (Tartar village).

Aurungzeb: Mogul Emperor, son of Jehan, reigned at the end of the seventeenth century.

Avalokiteshvara: The greatest Bodhisattva of Northern Buddhism. The savior and deliverer. Generally depicted many-armed and many-faced.

Baber: Descendant of Timur who invaded India and established the Mogul Dynasty. (Died in 1530 a.d.)

Babu: A literate man, in Hindustani.

Baldur: The Giver of all Good. A figure in Scandinavian mythology.

Balkh: A city of Afghanistan.

Baltis: Natives of Baltistan—a district north of Kashmir.

Barkhans: Desert dunes.

Bek: Minor official of Chinese Turkestan.

Belovodye: Literally white waters. Attributed to the name of a place.

Beluha: The highest peak of Russian Altai.

Berendeyevka: Land of Berendey; reference is made here to the village of Berendey—out of the opera, "Snowmaiden."

Berendeys in "Snowmaiden": Characters in Rimsky-Korsakoff's opera.

Bey: A Turkish title of respect.

Bezbojnik: A Russian newspaper dedicated to Atheism.

Bhagavad Gita: The Lord's Song. The Epic of Krishna, one part of the Mahabharata which contains the two great Epics of India.

Bogatyr: Knight, in Russian.

Bogdo-Khan: Religious head of the Mongolian Buddhists, called "Living Buddha."

Bogdo-ul: The "Holy Mountain," south of Urumchi, capital of Sinkiang.

Bolm: A premier dancer in the Imperial Russian Ballet.

Bön-po: Pre-Buddhist faith of Tibet, based on magic rites.

Boyars: Old Russian nobleman—state counselors.

Bruguma: Wife of Gessar-Khan.

Buran: Hurricane.

Buriat: Mongol tribe living in Transbakalia.

Burlaks: Russian boatsman.

Bya: A river in the Altai mountains.

Caravanserai: A stopping place for the caravan.

Chandragupta Maurya: The first Buddhist King of India. Grandfather of Asoka. Began his reign about 322 B.C.

Chintamani: The Sacred Stone counted among the great Blessings of the world.

Chorten: A stupa, in Tibetan; a shrine over relics.

Clement of Alexandria: Church father and voluminous writer living between the second and third centuries.

Csoma de Koros: A Hungarian traveler and scholar, born 1790.

Cyril of Alexandria: Nephew of Theophilus of Alexandria during the fifth century. Responsible for the murder of the girl philosopher, Hypatia.

Dalai-Lama: The secular ruler of Tibet, living in the Potala at Lhasa.

Dards: The people inhabiting the valleys adjacent to Gilgit—Mohammedans.

Dastarkhan: A food-offering to a person of high position.

Da-yig-letter: Official letter sent to the authorities announcing the arrival of a person of high standing.

Dharmapala: Protector of religion.

Diaghileff: Director of the Imperial Russian Ballet.

Djins: Elementals. Nature spirits.

Doroga: An official in Turki.

Dr. Francke: Dr. Herman Francke, renowned traveler.

Dras: A site on the road from Kashmir to Ladak.

Druid: Pre-Christian faith of the Celtic tribes.

Dukang: A chief temple of a lamaist monastery.

Dukar: A female deity corresponding to the Tara—the Mother of the World.

Dzong: Seat of the government of the district.

Dzong-pöns: Head of an administrative district.

E. I.: Helena Ivanovna Roerich—wife of Professor Roerich.

Easter Islands: Islands of the Polynesian group in the Pacific.

Epiphany: Bishop of Constantine born about 310. Teacher and friend of Jerome and opposed Origen in his numerous writings.

Eusebius: Known as the Father of Ecclesiastical history. Born probably in Palestine about 265.

Evangel of the Ebionites: Sect of early church of second to fourth centuries, believing in Messianic character of Christ but not his divinity.

Fa-hsien: Chinese pilgrim of the fifth century a.d.

Fez: Turkish skull cap.

Fibula: Breast plate.

Gandhara: The Greek period in Hindu art. Also the ancient province near Peshawar.

Garuda: The bird, steed of Vishnu.

Gelong: A full-consecrated lama.

Gessar-Khan: A name of the great Coming One. Hero of a great Mongolo-Tibetan epic.

Ghum: Monastery near Darjeeling.

Gobi: The Mongolian desert.

Gopis: Shepherdesses, the devotees of Krishna.

Great Bear: A constellation.

Guma: A site between Khotan and Kashgar.

Hanuman, Rama and Ravana: Characters of the Ramayana. Hanuman, king of Monkeys, aids Rama, hero of the epic, in his war upon Ravana, king of the demons who has carried away Sita, Rama's wife and thus precipitated the great war. A great analogy between this epic and the Iliad may be seen.

Hatha-Yoga: The lower form of Yoga practices. A man who uses physical means for spiritual self-development.

Hinayana and Mahayana: the two Buddhist schools, respectively the "Smaller Vehicle" and "Greater Vehicle." The former is the School of the Southern Buddhists, the latter is the Northern School, but spread in Tibet, Mongolia, China and Japan.

Hookah: A pipe with a long flexible tube.

Hoopoe: Bird (Upupa epops).

Horpa: Natives of Hor, northeastern Tibet.

Horus: Egyptian God, last of the divine sovereigns of Egypt, said to be son of Isis and Osiris.

Hunghutze: The Chinese robber bands operating along Manchuria; chiefly escaped criminals.

Ikon: The religious paintings of Russia.

Indra, Agni, Surya: The ancient Vedic Trimurti or Trinity.

Iran-designs: Designs of Persian origin.

Irenceus: One of the early Christian fathers.

Jalnik: Old Russian graveyard.

Jehangir: Mogul Emperor, son of Akbar, the Great (1555-1605).

Jenghis-Khan: Great Mongol conqueror (1162-1227). Considered the greatest warrior of history.

Jerome: Church father, regarded as one of the most learned. Lived from 337 to 420 A.D.

K'uen lun: A mountain range crossing northern India and Tibet.

Kabala: The hidden wisdom of the Hebrew Rabbis of the Middle Ages. It was combined into a theology after the capture of the Jews by Babylon.

Kabarga: The musk ram of Altai.

Kaftans: An oriental coatlike garment.

Kalki Avatar: Kalki incarnation of Vishnu.

Kalmucks: A Mongolian tribe which migrated into Russia and Chinese Turkestan.

Kansu: Province of China, south of Lower Mongolia.

Karashahr (Karashar): An important site south of Urumchi.

Kashyapa: Chief priest of the Jatilas, sect of fire worshipers. After his conversion all his followers entered the Buddhist order.

Katun: A river in the Altai mountains.

Khalat: The coatlike garment worn by the Mongols.

Kham and Golok: Districts in Tibet.

Khatik: A ceremonial scarf, given as a reverential offering.

Khutukhtu: One of the highest ranks of Lamas in Mongolia.

Kinchenjunga: Sacred mountain in Sikhim.

King of the World: The Coming Ruler whose great avatar is now expected by Asia.

Kirghiz: A nomad race widely scattered through Central Asia, of Mohammedan faith.

Kishlaks: Winter settlement.

Kluchino: A village in the Tver government, Russia.

Kokochnik: The Russian women's native headdress.

Kokyar: A small oasis in foothills south of Kargalik.

Kolchak: A general of the "white forces."

Korakeshs: Owners of horses.

Koshma: Felt.

Kosloff: Eminent Russian scientist and explorer, now in Central Asia.

Kremlin: Central fortified section of ancient Russian cities, comprising the churches, palaces, monasteries and other buildings.

Kshatriya: The second of the four castes into which the Hindus were originally divided. This is the warrior tribe.

Kuacka: An ancient Russian headgear.

Kuan Yin: Chinese Goddess of Mercy.

Kucha: An oasis on the northern trade-route of Chinese Turkestan.

Kuindjy: One of Russia's great artists, under whom Professor Roerich studied.

Kulan: A wild ass (Asihus Kyang).

Kurgan: A Turki word designating a burial mound in Russia.

Ladakis: Natives of Ladak, Little Tibet.

Lama: Priest of the monasteries.

Lamayura: A monastery site near Leh.

Langar: An inn.

Lanka: The ancient name of Ceylon; described in the Hindu Epic of Ramayana as of great magnificence, the habitation of the demons. The Ramayana is the Epic poem of Rama and his war against the Rakshasas or demons and giants, when the monkeys, led by Hanuman, were his allies.

Lao Tzin: A contemporary Chinese philosopher and writer.

Lel and Koupava: Mythical characters from the opera "Snowmaiden" by Rimsky-Korsakoff. Characters from ancient Russian lore.

Lemuria: The continent which according to the esoteric doctrines preceded Atlantis.

Lhamo: Tibetan deity of destruction.

Li: A Chinese measure of distance, approximately 485 yards.

Mafa: A carriage in Chinese Turkestan.

Mahabharata: The Great Epic of India, in which the Bhagavad Gita is incorporated.

Mahadeva: Great God, title of Shiva.

Mahakala: Deity of Thunder.

Maitreya: The Buddha of the future, who incarnates in himself all the hopes of the Buddhist world, from the island of Ceylon to the lamaseries of Siberia.

Manjusri: One of the principal Bodhisatvas, Prince of Knowledge.

Marral: Deer found in the Altai region, the horns of which are powdered and made into medicine.

Martand: Temple three miles east of Islamabad—probably founded between 370-500 A.D.

Maulbeck: A monastery site near Leh.

Mazar: Tomb of holy men or saints.

Mem-sahib: Madam or mistress in Hindustani.

Mendang: An elevation of stone on the hilltops, usually facing east, affording a seat for meditating lamas.

Menhirs: Megalithic stone monuments.

Meru, or Sumeru: The name of a mountain said to be in the center of the Earth and according to the East, the abode of the gods.

Metropolite: Highest church official in the Greek Catholic Church.

Milarepa: Tibetan poet-mystic (1038-1112 A.D.). The Tibetan Orpheus.

Mithra: An ancient Persian deity, a sun-god. Deeply connected with the highest occultism, the tenets of which were expounded in the Mithraic mysteries.

Moraine: A line of rocks and gravel at the edge and base of glaciers.

Nagchu: A district north of Lhasa.

Nagis: Snakes, or snake-worshipers.

Nairanjana: A river in which Buddha bathed after renouncing the path of bodily suffering as a means to knowledge.

Nijni-Novgorod Fair: Far-famed peasant fair of Russia.

Norbu-rinpoche: Precious jewel.

Novgorod: Literally, new city.

Nubra: River in the Nubra district of Kashmir.

Obo: A cairn of stones which crowns the summit of a pass.

Om: A holy invocation regarded as the most sacred syllable.

Ordoss: A district in the southernmost part of Mongolia.

Origen: The most learned of all the Church fathers and all early Christian writers. Lived 185 to 254 A.D.

Orion: A constellation especially characterized by the three central stars.

Oirots: Known as the messenger of the White Burkhan or coming Buddha. The belief in Oirot has spread in the last generation. Within this time a woman of the Shaman tribe, perceived in the mountains a vision of Oirot, a giant white figure on horseback, who bade her tell her people that they must renounce their magic rites and await in purity the coming of the White Burkhan. Reference is here made to this legend.

P'o-t'ai: Flat tower of clay marking distances on the Sinkiang roads. The average distances between them are about 2 $\frac{1}{2}$ miles, although these constantly vary.

Padma Sambhava: Founder of the Red Sect, one of the two great Tibetan Sects.

Pali: The ancient language of Magadha in which the Buddhist scriptures are written.

Panaga: Tribe of northeastern Tibet.

Panteleon: Saint and healer who gathered herbs and healed through these homely remedies.

Pelliot: Professor Paul Pelliot, eminent French sinologist.

Pemayangtse, Dubdi, Tashi-ding, Sanga Chöling, Baling: Monasteries in Sikhim.

Peshawar: A city in the northwest frontier province of India.

Piroschki: Pastry in Russia.

Polovtsi: A Tartar Tribe depicted in Borodin's opera, "Prince Igor," for which Roerich has painted the settings.

Potala: The Palace of the Dalai Lama in Lhasa.

Prjevalsky: Russian explorer, who explored Central Asia.

Puranas: Collection of cosmogonic writings supposed to have been composed by Vyasa, author of the Mahabharata.

Rahu: A demon who stole amrita from the gods.

Rajagriha, Vaisali, Patna: Seats of Buddhist councils.

Red Caps: Members of the sect founded by Padma Sambhava.

Ribhvas: Planetary spirits.

Rig-Veda: the first of the four Vedas or scriptures of the Hindus.

Rostoff, Suzdal, Yaroslavl: Russian cities.

Runes: The Runic language and characters are the mystery or sacerdotal tongue and alphabet of the ancient Scandinavians.

Rungit: A river in Sikhim, a tributary of Tista.

Saazes: Kashmiri stringed instruments.

"Sacre du Printemps": Sacred Rites of Spring, by Igor Stravinsky and Nicholas Roerich. Considered one of the greatest of modern compositions, composed by collaborated efforts of Stravinsky and Roerich who gave the libretto based on an ancient spring rite.

Sadhu: A saintly man.

Sadko: A leading character in Rimsky-Korsakoff's opera, "Sadko," of undersea life.

Sahib: Master, in Hindustani.

Sakya: A Kshatriya clan, which occupied a territory in the Nepal Terai, from which Buddha sprang.

Sanyasin: Hindu ascetic who has reached the highest mystic knowledge.

Sari: The shawl worn by all Hindu women.

Sarts: Tribes from eastern Russian Turkestan.

Sassar Sarai: A camping place beyond Sasser Pass.

Schaitans: Devils.

Sekmeth: The war goddess of Egypt.

Sengchen Lama: Incarnate Lama, high priest of Dong-ste monastery near Gyantse.

Senge: Literally, Lion, a title of Buddha. Here, apparently, the name given to the ceremonial dances.

Senusert: One of the Egyptian Pharaohs.

Serai: An encampment or inn.

Sergius of Radonega: Most beloved saint of Russia, lived in fifteen century.

Setara: Stringed instrument.

Shah Jehan: Son of Shah Jehangir.

Shamans: Tartar or Mongolian priest-magicians of the old Bön religion of Central Asia. They are found mostly in Siberia and the borderlands.

Shambatyon: A river mentioned in the Old Testament and said to have mystic significance.

Shambhala: The country believed by Asia to be the dwelling of the coming King of the World and his cohorts.

Shayok: A tributary of the Indus.

Sherpa: A Tibetan tribe of Nepal.

Sho: Copper coin in Tibet (ten sho make one ngusang).

Shuya and Kolomna: Ancient Russian cities.

Sir Aurel Stein: Eminent archaeologist.

Sir Charles Bell: British political officer for Sikhim and Bhutan. In 1921 conducted a diplomatic mission to Lhasa.

Sir Marshall: Sir John Marshall, Director General of Archaeology in India.

Soma: Moon.

Stelles: Prehistoric stone slab.

Stockzund: A small suburb near Stockholm.

Stupas: A monument, conical in shape erected over the relics of Buddha, of Arhats, or other great men.

Sutra: A sacred book.

Sven Hedin: A Swedish traveler in Asia.

Sweeper: One belonging to the Sudras, the untouchables, or lowest of the four castes.

T'ian Shan: Meaning Celestial mountains.

T'song-kha-pa: Founder of the Yellow Sect, the second great sect.

Taels: Chinese currency.

Takla Makan: The great desert covering central portion of Sinkiang where buried cities have been traced.

Tamasha: Entertainment, a spectacle show.

Tanguts: Branch of Mongol-Tartars spread in Central and Eastern Siberia.

Tantra: Books on mystical practices in medieval Hinduism.

Tao Te Ching: Indicating the Path; the "Book of the Perfectibility of Nature," written by the great Chinese philosopher Lao-Tze. Tao is the symbol of the Absolute, the Infinite.

Tao: The name of the philosophy of Lao Tze.

Taotai: Chinese official.

Tara: The principal feminine deity of Buddhism. Symbolizing the Goddess-Mother. The Merciful One, protector of mankind.

Tashi-Lama: Religious head of Tibet who made his home in the Tashi-lhunpo Monastery in Shigatse. For the first time in history he has fled Tibet thus fulfilling ancient prophecies.

Tchud: Derived from the word "wonder"—and attributed to a people.

Territ: A site on the Nubra River north of Leh.

"Throne of Solomon": Mountain in Kashmir.

Tokhar: A people spoken of by Fa-hsien and other pilgrims; once said to have inhabited the district around Kuchar, now vanished.

Torguts: A Mongol clan which settled in Russia, later emigrating into Sinkiang.

Trimurti: The Trinity. In modern conception Brahma, creator; Vishnu, preserver, and Shiva, destroyer. In ancient tradition, Indra, Agni and Surya, or Air, Fire and the Sun. A vast philosophy underlies this symbolism.

Tripitaka: The name of the Buddhist canon; composed of three divisions.

Troyka: Carriage with three horses.

Tsaidam: District in the north of Tibet.

Tseriks: Mobilized soldiers.

Tubeteika: Tartar skull cap.

Tun-huang: An oasis of western Kansu.

Turfan: A district in Chinese Turkestan.

Tzagan Khutukhta: Khutukhta is the highest rank of lama; Tzagan is white. This refers to a holy lama.

Uddaka Ramaputta: A Brahmin ascetic who was for some years the Guru of Gautama Buddha.

Uigurs: A Turki tribe conquering Turkestan and Dzungaria in 744 and maintaining an independent kingdom in valleys of T'ian Shan till 1000 A.D. when they migrated westward.

Ultus: Kalmuck villages.

Ulus: People, tribe.

Upanishads: Part of the Esoteric division of the Vedas.

Uræus: The snake, sacred symbol. Around the disk of Osiris and on the cap of Osiris and other deities.

Uruvela: A site near the forest in which Buddha spent six years of meditation.

Vaishas: The third of the Hindu castes.

Valhalla: Odin's hall. The final abode of fallen Norse heroes.

Vedanta: A mystic system of philosophy developing from the efforts of philosophers to interpret the Upanishads.

Vedas: The revelations or scriptures of the Hindus. The Vedic writings are divided into two great parts—the exoteric, namely, the "division of actions and works" and "divisions of knowledge." In the latter are included the Upanishads.

Vihara: A Buddhist monastery.

Vishnu: The Preserver, second personage of the Hindu Trimurti.

W. Filchner: The well-known German explorer of Tibet.

Wheel of Ezekiel: Mystic symbol used by the Prophet Ezekiel.

Wheel of Life: A symbol of the great cycle of life, the progress of the spirit or self through the lower nature.

White Burkhan: The name given to the Coming Buddha among the Altaian tribes of Siberia.

Yakhtan: A small leather-covered wooden box.

Yakub-Bek: Leader of a Mohammedan rebellion against the Chinese in 1865.

Yamen: Chinese public office.

Yarkandis: Natives of Yarkand.

Yermak: A robber chieftain who, outlawed by the Tzar Ivan the Terrible, went beyond the Ural and conquered a new territory. He was drowned shortly after, in 1584.

Yurtas: The native tents of the Mongols.

Zorawar: Leader of a Dogra force which invaded western Tibet from Kashmir and plundered the monasteries.

Printed in Great Britain
by Amazon